Failure in Palestine

British and United States Policy
after the Second World War

Failure in Palestine

British and United States Policy after the Second World War

Martin Jones

Mansell Publishing Limited
London and New York

First published 1986 by Mansell Publishing Limited
(A subsidiary of The H. W. Wilson Company)
6 All Saints Street, London N1 9RL, England
950 University Avenue, Bronx, New York 10452, U.S.A.

British Library Cataloguing in Publication Data
    Jones, Martin
        Failure in Palestine : British and United States
        policy after the Second World War.
        1. Palestine—History—1929–1948 2. Great
        Britain—Foreign relations—1945– 3. United
        States—Foreign relations—1945–1953
        I. Title
        956.94′04   DS126
        ISBN 0–7201–1797–6

Library of Congress Cataloging in Publication Data
    Jones, Martin (Martin Desmond)
        Failure in Palestine.
        Revision of thesis (Ph.D.)—University of London,
    1982.
        Bibliography: p.
        Includes index.
        1. Palestine—History—Partition, 1947. 2. Great
    Britain—Foreign relations—Great Britain. 4. Anglo-
    American Committee of Inquiry on Jewish Problems in Palestine and
    Europe. 5. United Nations. General
    Assembly. Special Committee on Palestine. I. Title.
    DS126.4.J66 1985   956.94′05   85–18758
    ISBN 0–7201–1797–6

Typeset by Activity Limited, Salisbury, Wiltshire.
Printed in Great Britain by Whitstable Litho Ltd., Whitstable, Kent.

For Jenny
and our parents

Contents

Foreword

The story which Martin Jones unfolds in this book is well epitomized by its title: it is a story of failure in imperial and foreign policy. Failure in the sense that the decision to terminate the Mandate in Palestine sparked off a conflict which has, as yet, found no resolution. But failure also in the sense that the British interests which the policy was supposed to protect suffered great damage. This was of course not the intention of the Foreign Secretary and the Foreign Office—who had become, after 1936, the prime movers in Palestine policy—when they tried to seek United States involvement and help, through the Anglo-American Committee on Palestine; then to reach a settlement through the London Conference of 1946 at which the Arab States, the Palestine Arabs and the Jewish Agency were represented; and when they decided that the problem should be handed over to the United Nations Organization. Dr Jones surveys these various strategies in succession, and registers their failure one after another.

Whence this cumulative failure? To account for it requires examining assumptions and intellectual commitments which became rooted a decade before the Labour administration of 1945 assumed responsibility for the problem and its settlement—assumptions and commitments which the new ministers seem to have, on the whole, uncritically accepted. Dr Jones refers to them in his Conclusion when he declares that Britain's failure was not so much a failure in her Palestine policy as in her Arab policy. What he means by Arab policy is the view that the Palestine problem could be solved only through the involvement of the Arab states. This view was tirelessly propounded in 1936–8 by George Rendel, the head of the Eastern Department at the Foreign Office, and it attained thereafter the status of an orthodoxy. But, as the story here recounted shows, an Arab policy in Rendel's sense itself made impracticable any conceivable Palestine policy.

Arab policy exacted a heavy price. This may be succinctly illustrated by a minute dating from the end of 1947 quoted by Dr Jones in his chapter on the end of the Mandate. It is addressed by Burrows, one of Rendel's successors, to Bevin. The minute declares that 'the essence of the question is that we should be able to complete our withdrawal from Palestine according to plan without becoming involved in repressive measures which will endanger our position through the Middle East'. By repressive measures Burrows meant action taken to suppress lawlessness in a territory for which the British government was still responsible. Another paper dating from March 1948, which Dr Jones thinks was probably written by H. Beeley, makes even clearer to what its own inexorable logic had reduced British policy and its executants. Beeley argues that 'it might be preferable to permit civil war to break out on the 15th May [1948] than to inaugurate a period of so-called truce'. A preference for war in Palestine leading to some kind of partition was now the ironic outcome of policies designed to avoid partition at all costs, since partition had been believed irretrievably to damage British interests throughout the Middle East.

The failure in Palestine, spectacular as it was, is only part of the larger failure which in a short space of time reduced the great ship of the British empire to a wreck. The onlooker, surveying this wreck will not help wondering about the—infinitely complex—antecedents and consequences of such a rare and awesome occurrence. He will be grateful to Dr Jones for elucidating, with exemplary care and precision, a small, but crucial and most instructive part of the story.

ELIE KEDOURIE

List of Maps

List of Abbreviations

AHC	Arab Higher Committee
AZEC	American Zionist Emergency Council
BLPES	British Library of Political and Economic Science
CAB	Cabinet Offices (documentary classes)
CIGS	Chief of the Imperial General Staff
CM	Cabinet Conclusions
Cmd	Command Paper
CO	Colonial Office
COS	Chiefs of Staff
CP	Cabinet Paper
CZA	Central Zionist Archives, Jeruslem
DEFE	Defence Ministry (documentary classes)
DO	Defence Committee of the Cabinet, meetings and papers
DP	Displaced Person
FO	Foreign Office
FRUS	*Foreign Relations of the United States*
GHQME	General Headquarters, Middle East
JA	Jewish Agency
JCS	Joint Chiefs of Staff
JIC	Joint Intelligence Committee of the Cabinet, meetings and papers
JPS	Joint Planning Staff of the COS
MEC	Middle East Centre, St Antony's College, Oxford
MFA	Minister of Foreign Affairs
NE	Division of Near Eastern Affairs at NEA
NEA	Office of Near Eastern and African Affairs, the State Department
NSC	National Security Council

OSS	Office of Strategic Services
PREM	Prime Minister's Office (documentary classes)
PUS	Permanent Undersecretary
PPS	Policy Planning Staff
RH	Rhodes House, Oxford
S/S	Secretary of State
TL	Truman Library, Independence, Missouri
UN arch	United Nations archives, New York
UNSCOP	United Nations Special Committee on Palestine
USNA	United States National Archives, Washington, D.C.
WM	War Cabinet Conclusions
WO	War Office
WP	War Cabinet Paper
ZOA	Zionist Organization of America

Acknowledgements

The first five chapters of this work were submitted and accepted by the London School of Economics, the University of London, for the degree of Ph.D. in 1982. They have not been changed substantially. During my research and writing I have incurred many debts of gratitude. My thanks are due first and foremost to Professor Elie Kedourie, my supervisor at the LSE, and to the Economic and Social Research Council (formerly the Social Science Research Council) for the financial support which made this study possible.

I am grateful to the British Library of Political and Economic Science, London, for permission to quote from the diaries and papers of Hugh Dalton, and for the permission of the Bodleian Library, Oxford, to quote from the Creech Jones papers deposited at Rhodes House. I am indebted to Lord Attlee for permission to quote from his father's papers deposited at the Bodleian and at Churchill College, Cambridge, and to the Fabian Society for their permission to quote extracts from the Fabian Colonial Bureau's papers at Rhodes House. I am grateful to the Executors of Sir Alexander Cadogan for permission to quote from the diary deposited at Churchill College, Cambridge. Quotations of Crown-copyright records in the Public Record Office appear by permission of the Controller of Her Majesty's Stationery Office. The Middle East Centre, St Antony's College, Oxford, gave their kind permission to quote from the papers of Richard Crossman. I am grateful to the US National Archives, Washington D.C., and to the Truman Library, Independence, Missouri, for their assistance. and also to the United Nations Organization for kindly allowing the use of the UN archives in New York and to quote from material there. The staff of all these institutions and archives have been unfailingly helpful. I am also grateful to the University of Southampton Library for allowing free use of the Parkes Collection.

The map showing the UN Partition Plan is based upon maps in M. Gilbert, *The Arab–Israeli Conflict* (1981), E. M. Wilson, *Decision on Palestine* and M. J. Cohen, *Palestine and the Great Powers*. All the other maps are based on those in the memorandum 'Palestine: A Study of Partition' submitted by the Colonial Office to the UN Special Committee on Palestine in 1947 and consulted at the UN archives (reference UNSCOP 1947 DAG-13/3.0.0. Box 15).

The completion of this study has depended heavily upon my wife, who typed the manuscript and put up with the hours, besides helping in many other ways, and also upon our parents for many kindnesses and encouragement.

Responsibility for the contents and conclusions of this study remains my own.

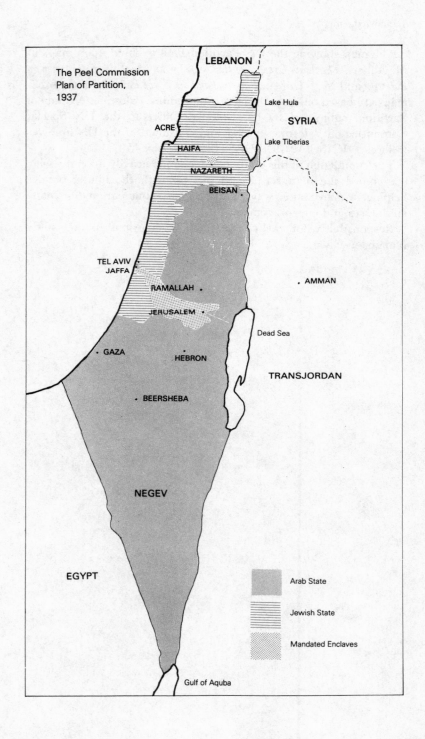

The Peel Commission
Plan of Partition,
1937

LEBANON

Lake Hula

SYRIA

ACRE

HAIFA

Lake Tiberias

NAZARETH

BEISAN

TEL AVIV
JAFFA

RAMALLAH

AMMAN

JERUSALEM

Dead Sea

GAZA

HEBRON

TRANSJORDAN

BEERSHEBA

NEGEV

EGYPT

Arab State

Jewish State

Mandated Enclaves

Gulf of Aquba

1

1945: The Legacy from the Past

On 9 December 1917, after a bloody battle, General Allenby's troops received the surrender of Jerusalem from the defending Turkish forces, and two days later Allenby himself entered the city by the Jaffa Gate. Just over thirty years later, early on the morning of 14 May 1948, His Majesty's last High Commissioner for Palestine, Sir Alan Cunningham, was escorted out of Jerusalem. The British consul pondered:

> A few bedraggled Arabs who happened to have gathered near the Damascus Gate, raised a feeble cheer. It is difficult to assess their motive, gratitude to the last representative of the British mandate or relief at his departure.[1]

The Suffolk Regiment followed hard on his heels, and long before Cunningham left the Holy Land from Haifa the ceasefire in Jerusalem, imposed on Arabs and Jews by British military power, had dissolved amidst gunfire and the reports of mortars. The failure in the twentieth century of what an earlier age had been pleased to call the *Pax Britannica* could scarcely have been more explicit.

How had this failure occurred? Why, in 1947, did the British Government take the decisions to refer the Palestine problem to the United Nations Organisation and to withdraw when just two years before that same government had envisaged such an outcome only as a most remote and unrealistic possibility? The aim here is to examine the objectives of British policy during the final years of the Mandate, and this will involve necessarily some analysis of US policy and pressure on Palestine. It will soon be apparent that in 1945 the Labour Government, despite the resolute stand taken by the Party in favour of a Jewish state in Palestine before coming to power, was not free to choose whatever course it fancied. More important than the golden promises of the past made to both Jews and Arabs were the

entrenched opinions and policies of Whitehall, notably those of the
Foreign Office. Of course the Palestine problem was also altered
drastically by the war with Germany and its consequences on
Zionism in the USA. The British Government had to face these
problems, made more acute by the passage of time, with diminished
resources and in the context of the gathering Cold War.

British policy before the Second World War

A selective examination of Britain's Palestine policy before the
Second World War is important for the understanding of the postwar
years. The Balfour Declaration, made in a letter to Lord Rothschild
on 2 November 1917 following the Cabinet decision of three days
before, embodied the famous formula that 'His Majesty's Government view with favour the establishment in Palestine of a national
home for the Jewish people, ... it being clearly understood that
nothing shall be done which may prejudice the civil and religious
rights. of existing non-Jewish communities in Palestine ...'. This
statement was issued for a variety of reasons. In 1906, Chaim
Weizmann had met A. J. Balfour, the foreign secretary who was than
a proponent of Uganda as a homeland for Jewry, and apparently
made an impression on him by explaining the spiritual quality of
Zionism and its messianic attraction to Palestine. During the First
World War Weizmann's work as a chemist was of sufficient value to
merit gratitude within the government, and in the War Cabinet Paper
of 17 October 1917 it was this eminent scientist who argued most
persuasively the Zionist case. But Weizmann's personal prestige
alone was not sufficient for the British Government to issue the
Balfour Declaration. His case was helped by the predilections of
statesmen like Balfour and Lloyd George who held the Holy Land in
great awe, and for whom the ending of the Jewish exile was of
considerable Biblical significance. However, the factor of commanding importance was the element of expediency and the British
Government's perceived self-interest. French interests in Palestine
were manifest before the war, and the Sykes–Picot agreement of 1916
established these further. M. Vereté (1970) has shown that the
concern of the British Government to counter French claims in an
area which was of strategic interest to the British Empire provided the
primary motivation behind the Balfour Declaration. The issue was
made more urgent when, by the beginning of 1917, the British Army
was poised to enter Ottoman-ruled Palestine, thereby threatening to
supplant the French claims to a dismembered Ottoman Empire. As a
result of the French claims, an interest in Zionism developed during
1916 in the British Government, where cultivating the Zionists

gradually came to be seen as a useful way of ousting the French from Palestine. Of course a gesture towards Zionism was not put forward diplomatically on these grounds, but proposed as a useful way of obtaining the support of world Jewry, especially in the United States and Russia, for the Allied cause. Nevertheless it is clear that, possessed by such a motive, it was the British Government which proceeded to turn to the Zionists, who quickly showed a preference for British rule over French dominion in Palestine. Backed by Zionist preferences and an army on Palestinian soil, and armed with a plausible Allied cause, the British Government proceeded with the Balfour Declaration not out of any altruistic or Zionist motives but rather from pure self-interest in excluding the French from Palestine.[2] In Cabinet the matter was discussed with less candour, and the desiderata of winning the support of world Jewry for the Allies was to the fore. With the USA in the war, it was argued that a gesture to win the support of American Jews would be useful, and following the March Revolution the same requirement was advanced for Russia. The Declaration provided useful propaganda against the Kaiser, and pamphlets advertising it were dropped by Britain over German and Austrian territory during the war.[3]

The importance of the Balfour Declaration was increased after the war through its inclusion in the terms of the Mandate for Palestine awarded to Britain by the League of Nations. The preamble employed the same formula as Balfour's letter, echoed in Article 6:

> The Administration of Palestine, while ensuring that the rights and position of other sections of the population are not prejudiced, shall facilitate Jewish immigration under suitable conditions and shall encourage ... close settlement by Jews on the land.

Article 25 excluded the Transjordan from these requirements. In view of subsequent events, Article 5 is interesting, charging the Mandatory with ensuring that no part of Palestine be 'placed under the control of' any other government.[4] The Mandate continued in spirit after the end of the League pending the issuing of a new trusteeship by the successor United Nations Organization. It is important to notice the element of expediency in the origins of the Mandate. Clearly also it belonged to a different world to Hitler's Nuremberg Laws and the holocaust, a world with which it was not designed to cope. As contractual obligations, both the Declaration and the Mandate looked decidedly dated by 1945.

It is not, however, in the origins of the Mandate but rather in the treatment of the Palestine question in the 1930s that we can perceive the fatal flaw which was to do such disservice to Britain's Palestine policy between 1945 and 1948. One component was the treatment of the correspondence between the British High Commissioner in Egypt, Sir Henry McMahon, and Husayn, Sharif of Mecca, in 1915. The British Government's intention at the time was to help the Gallipoli campaign by fomenting an Arab insurrection in the rear of the Ottoman Empire; Husayn's main interest was in furthering a dynastic struggle against the Ottoman authorities. McMahon's important letter of 24 October 1915 which excluded 'the portions of Syria lying to the West of Damascus, Homs, Hama and Aleppo' from the area of Arab independence because 'they cannot be said to be purely Arab' clearly went beyond the instructions issued to McMahon by the Foreign Secretary, Lord Grey. These instructions had been that the 'Arab districts of Aleppo, Damascus, Hama and Homs' be within the Arab boundaries. McMahon's letter was to be used later by the Arabs and the Foreign Office to argue that Palestine had not been excluded from the Arab domain, an inference which the Foreign Secretary's instructions avoided. By December 1915 the pressure for an Anglo-Arab contract had waned with the British withdrawal from the Dardanelles, and the negotiations lost their urgency. The Sykes–Picot agreement of May 1916 was fitted carefully into the McMahon correspondence, for the fourth letter sent to Husayn (dated 30 January 1916) reflected the need to preserve French interests in the Vilayet of Beirut. The Anglo-French agreement followed this while the Jerusalem area was to become an international enclave partly out of regard to the Zionist hopes for Palestine.[5]

So much for the correspondence. It did not constitute a contract but simply wartime negotiations, and it would be unreasonable to expect these to have any binding effect by 1945. But in 1939 the correspondence was officially published in a White Paper, and the background to this throws the most extraordinary light on the attitudes of the Foreign Office. The starting point was that Palestine constituted an embarrassment in the context of appeasing Germany, and a further offence to the Arabs at a time when Britain had been seen to be impotent over the Italian campaign in Ethiopia. There was a feeling that the Arab case had gone by default, reflected in an anecdote which Sir George Rendel repeats in his autobiography, *The Sword and Olive* (1957), in which Balfour, on visiting Jerusalem after the First World War, enquired 'who are all these people in long cloaks and white headdresses?'. On being told, Balfour replied: 'But if they are Arabs, what are they doing in this country?' Rendel in particular seems to have followed the advice given by a young army officer in Palestine in 1920 and recorded by Helen Bentwich: 'The

Jews are so clever, and the Arabs so stupid and childish that it seems
only sporting to be for the Arabs'. The aim of the Foreign Office was
to rid Britain of the embarrassment presented by the Palestine issue,
which was achieved through the elevation of the McMahon
correspondence to the status of a contract, so making Albion's
Government do penance for its previous perfidy in making promises
in the Balfour Declaration which contravened those already made.
This process involved a curious and inept piece of historical research
inside the Foreign Office which, according to E. Kedourie (1976 and
1980), in places 'amounted to falsification'. The postwar result of this
introspection 'did in the end demoralize British Middle-Eastern
policy, and imbue it with a corrosive feeling of embarrassment, if not
of guilt'. Consider for instance the reception in 1939 of a Foreign
Office memorandum by Mackenzie dealing with the 'Juridicial basis
of the Arab claim to Palestine', which explained, without reference to
Grey's instructions, what McMahon pledged to Husayn. Baxter,
Rendel's successor as head of the Eastern Department until 1947,
described the memorandum as an 'excellent piece of work'. Beckett,
the legal advisor to the Foreign Office until 1948, heartily endorsed
Mackenzie's analysis on 11 January 1939 without questioning the
legal status of the McMahon correspondence. The result was that the
memorandum went to the Cabinet in January 1939 prefaced by a
statement by the Foreign Secretary confessing that it 'emphasize[d]
once more ... the difficulty ... in attempting to explain the rival
promises made to Jews and Arabs ...'.[6] This apologia indicates the
climate of opinion in the Foreign Office during the 1930s, fostered also
by the publication in 1938 of Antonius' *The Arab Awakening* and in
1935 by T. E. Lawrence's tales of Britain's perfidy. Clearly this
climate touched officials who continued to be responsible for Britain's
Palestine policy after the war. One may detect it for example in the
vigorous representations made on behalf of the Arab states from 1945
onwards, representations towards which the whole system of
diplomacy was geared by tradition, habit and organization, and
which left Zionism outside, beyond the pale of diplomatic exchange.
No doubt, too, that McMahon's correspondence, like Banquo's
ghost, continued to walk the corridors of power, for in September
1945 a group of MPs, expressing the hope of setting up a Palestine
Committee of the House of Commons to watch affairs, circulated a
briefing paper of the received truth which Beeley, the Foreign Office
expert on Palestine, entered into the file without comment:

Had it been McMahon's intention to exclude Palestine he could easily have defined it as bounded on the East by the Jordan, Lake Tiberias and the Dead Sea, and on the West by the Mediterranean ... Palestine does not lie to the West of any of the districts mentioned.[7]

Lord Grey's original intention was of course omitted.

Inherited and engrained attitudes and sympathies were one thing; the other half of the walnut was the postwar result of the policies of the 1930s. The Arab rebellion began in 1936 as a result of the pressure of Jewish immigration into Palestine, which under Hitler's influence reached 61,000 souls in 1935. Purifying the Reich had the coincidental result of accentuating Britain's embarrassment over Palestine. Following the first disturbances in April 1936 the High Commissioner, Wauchope, failed to use decisive force. The trouble grew, and in June the crucial error was made in London when, following the Saudi Arabian Minister's expression of interest in events in Palastine to the Foreign Office, Parkinson of the Colonial Office wrote with Colonial Secretery Ormsby Gore's approval to Oliphant, the Deputy Undersecretary at the FO, saying, 'If King Ibn Saud can use his influence to persuade the Arabs to give up the campaign of violence he will be doing a service not only to H.M.G. but to the Arabs themselves.' With the thin end of the wedge now in position, the Saudi Arabian Minister returned to the Foreign Office a few days later and suggested that Ibn Saud joined with the King of Iraq and the Imam of the Yemen in making representations to the Palestine Arabs. July brought the extension of the scheme to embrace the Crown Prince of Egypt and Amir Abdullah of Transjordan; the fee was to be concessions by the British Government to the Arabs of Palestine which included the release of prisoners and the stopping of Jewish immigration. An expression of interest by the Saudi Arabian Minister had now blossomed into the offer of intervention by the leaders of five Arab states in territory mandated to the control of the British Government alone. The Cabinet found the price too high, and the Saudi Arabian Minister was informed that immigration was not to be halted, though Ibn Saud's moderating influence would be appreciated. If it was ever exerted this influence had no obvious effect. Following an attempt by Nuri al-Said, Iraqi Foreign Minister, to mediate between the Palestine Government and the Arab High Committee during a visit to Jerusalem in August, the Cabinet stuck to its decision and at a Ministerial meeting in September the idea, most strongly pressed by Vansittart, the Permanent Undersecretary at the FO, and Rendel, that a concession on immigration should be promised to follow the cessation of violence, was rejected. Reinforcements were sent to Palestine and under the threat of martial law the Arab Higher Committee called off the strike on 12 October. No significant price was paid by the AHC for months of civil disobedience. Furthermore on 10 October Saudi Arabia and Iraq issued an appeal to the Palestine Arabs which had been carefully negotiated with the Foreign Office in near defiance of the Cabinet's decision, and which embodied the phrase that the rulers relied 'upon the good intentions of His Majesty's Government to realize the legitimate claims of the Palestine Arabs'. The encouragement given throughout to the Arab rulers' mediation 'constituted a major shift in Mandatory policy' according to M. J. Cohen (1978), and this departure was proved to be 'irreversible' by the subsequent history of the Mandate. At the 1937 session of the League of Nations, the Permanent Mandates Commission justly rebuked the British Government for allowing foreign interference in the affairs of a Mandated territory. However, even with this behind them, the British Government's representatives at Geneva were reluctant to take issue in public with the Iraqi Government which had assumed a truculent attitude, for domestic consumption, both towards the Royal Commission's Report (recommending partition of Palestine) and also over the events of 1936; Baggallay of the FO warned the Colonial Office that otherwise the existing Iraqi regime may change to a 'violently Pan Arab' one.[8] So there was to be no way of reversing the mistake of 1936, and the involvement of the Arab states in the affairs of Britain's Mandate; to attempt to do so would jeopardize Britain's position in the Middle East even further.

The salient events which ensued show that this line of policy became well established. The Peel Commission was set up in November 1936 to investigate the disorders and its Report the following June proposed the partition of Palestine into Jewish and Arab states with the Mandatory continuing responsibility for Jerusalem, Jaffa, and the zone between. In December the Cabinet created another Commission to review the boundaries of partition. The Woodhead Commission was instructed, in a confidential letter from the Colonial Secretary, that if it was forced to the conclusion that partition itself was impracticable, it should say so. Through the Cabinet's decision, the Foreign Office had succeeded in turning the Commission's purpose from a technical investigation of the partition boundaries into one which could make a recommendation against partition itself, but this purpose was kept secret in order that the British Government would not appear in public to be preparing to disavow the Peel Commission's recent recommendations for partition. The Woodhead Commission's report of October 1938 found itself unable to recommend boundaries for the Arab and Jewish states on the basis of a strict interpretation of its terms of reference, but instead the four Commissioners between them put forward three alternative partition proposals. The plan which was supported by two Commissioners proposed a tiny Jewish state on the coastal plain, thereby ensuring strong Zionist condemnation of the report. The government, which had already decided that in the likely event of a war, partition and immigration alike would be suspended, seized the opportunity presented by the Woodhead Commission's uncertain conclusions to reject partition in a White Paper issued on 9 November 1938. A conference was now convened between the British Government, the Arabs and the Jews. So it was that in February 1939 St James's Palace, London, became the venue for the curious gathering of Arab delegations from Saudi Arabia, Egypt, Iraq, Yemen, Transjordan and Palestine, who met separately from the Jewish delegation and demanded that the British Government change her policy, in the territory mandated to her by the League of Nations, to one which halted all Jewish immigration and land purchase. The conference broke down in March, the McMahon correspondence was published, and on 10 May the White Paper appeared. There was to be no partition, no Jewish nor Arab state but the aim was to establish within ten years an independent state of Palestine. Jewish immigration meanwhile was to be up to 10,000 per year for five years if the economic absorptive capacity allowed, plus an immediate batch of 25,000 immigrants. After the 75,000 level no further Jewish immigration was to be permitted 'unless the Arabs of Palestine are prepared to acquiesce in it'. With Hitler's territorial aggrandisements extending Nazi dominion over more of Europe's Jews, and setting others to flight, the retreat by the British Government from the partition plan proposed by Peel was devastating to Zionist hopes. The capitulation to the Arab states seemed complete.[9]

It is not possible to explain this turn of events solely in terms of the appeasement of Germany and the imminence of war. Certainly this was the context, and appeasement of the Arabs was seen to be necessary because of their capacity to cause trouble near to Britain's communication route and oil resources. German propaganda also had to be neutralized. But there was more to the White Paper than *realpolitik*. The Foreign Office attitude has been considered over the McMahon correspondence and the 1936 disturbances, both representative examples. As E. Kedourie has shown, Rendel, the Head of the Eastern Department, successfully promoted the intervention of the Arab states in Palestine because in this he perceived 'the means by which the correct view of the Palestine problem would prevail in

London'. The working assumption was that Palestine was central to Britain's position and weakness in an Arab world which was regarded as a united entity. The orchestration of a united Arab view at the St James's Palace Conference, and of countenancing its intervention in Palestine in 1936, indicates this concept of an Arab world growing in unity and nationalism, a direction encouraged by Britain when the Arab League was created in 1945. In fact the Arab world was riven with jealousies and motivated by dynastic rivalry, most notably that between the Hashimites and the House of Saud, yet both before and after the war the Foreign Office failed to use these divisions in the policies it engendered. Convinced by his mistaken philosophy, Rendel energetically ensnared the path of the Peel Report. He tried to get the government to delay accepting partition in principle in July 1937, and when rebuffed here he succeeded in magnifying difficulties and raising complications while allowing Ibn Saud and other Arab rulers to acquire the impression that His Majesty's Government was not firmly in favour of partition. Arab objections to partition were solicited by the Foreign Office. By the time the Colonial Secretary brought partition before the Cabinet for a decision on 9 November 1937, Rendel had his suggestion for another Commission to re-examine partition ready. Eden proved a willing disciple and secured a victory for the Foreign Office on 8 December when the Cabinet decided that the Woodhead Commission should be able to judge the workability of partition itself. The Commission became the vehicle for the government to retreat from partition, and this it did. The conference and the 1939 White Paper was the crowning glory for the Foreign Office, securing not only the FO's case but also replacing the CO as the policymaking body for Palestine.[10]

Was the Foreign Office successful in closing with the question of partitioning Palestine all points of entry for German propaganda into the Middle East and securing Arab loyalty to Britain? Baxter seemed to think that it would be, since in August 1938 he minuted with Rendelian style on Weizmann's report of German agitation in Egypt that 'the original responsibility for these difficulties lies elsewhere', that is to say in Britain's Palestine policy. There was no questioning inside the Foreign Office of the assumptions upon which its outlook and policies were based. Yet it was not concessions on Palestine nor obeisance before Arab nationalism which forestalled Axis control of Iraq and Syria through Raschid Ali's attempted coup in Iraq in April 1941, but British tanks and soldiers who arrived with decisive speed. There was even less cause to fear Arab wartime restiveness after El Alamein when according to the US Government's Office of Strategic Services 'British prestige among the Arabs was restored'.[11] It would seem that in the Middle East, as with Hitler's Chancellery, concessions made or promises entered into without the sword do not endure.

Zionism and US wartime policy

The White Paper of 1939 was a devastating blow to the Zionist movement. Memories of partition were still fresh, and at the 20th Zionist Congess held in Zurich in August 1937 the Executive had been authorised by a vote of 299 to 160 to negotiate with the British Government on a Jewish state. Now Britain seemed to be cynically sacrificing the Jewish people to the gathering holocaust in furtherance of a policy of appeasement with Hitler which, by 1939, had clearly failed. Weizmann called the White Paper a death sentence, recording in his autobiography the horror and despair in his heart when he went to see Chamberlain in a final attempt to prevent the publication of the paper; the Prime Minister sat 'like a marble statue, his expressionless eyes were fixed on me, but he never said a word'. For years the advocate of working closely with the British Government, the blow fell especially hard upon Weizmann. The years of quiet, persuasive diplomacy, so evident in 1917, now seemed to have run away into nothing. Increasingly, Weizmann was to take a back seat in Zionist affairs, becoming the elder statesman, while more vigorous campaigners made the running. Ben Gurion was one. His background as a pioneer in Ottoman-ruled Palestine and as a labour leader inclined him to discount the value of personal influence in London to further the Zionist yearning for statehood. The events of 1939 confirmed his attitude and influence, his reaction being that, as his biographer records: 'He would fight the White Paper as if there was no war; but he would also fight the war as if there was no White Paper.' This became the motto of the Yishuv. But Zionism's links with Britain were not destroyed even in Ben Gurion's view as yet, and he wrote: 'Despite my bitter evaluation of the British attitude, ... obviously the fate of political Zionism is tied to England.'[12] Political Zionism was, however, to take a new road.

With Britain locked into war and the fate of most of European Jewry sealed, it became the turn of Zionism in the USA to gather its forces. The hope was that Britain would alter her policy during the war because of the influence of Zionist friends, notably Churchill, and as part of the process of utilising Jewish manpower in a Jewish Brigade. There was also some hope that British policy could be changed by the pressure of illegal immigration into Palestine and the non-cooperation of the Yishuv. But the Zionist aim of most interest to us here, from the aspect of 1945, was that by the exertion of organised Zionist pressure on the US Government, strengthened by humanitarian sympathies engendered by the holocaust, a change could be made to the British Mandatory policy.[13] This remained the guiding principle of American Zionism into the postwar period.

Initially there was an obvious ceiling on Zionist activity; American Zionism could not be too critical of Britain when she was the only nation fighting Nazism — not that gratitude was particularly important, but because to do otherwise would appear un-American and warmongering, and thereby ruin all standing in the USA. After Pearl Harbor Zionism was able to get moving. It had been present in the US since the 1930s, not merely as an humanitarian reaction against the Nazis but as a Zionist aspiration for a state, perhaps an expression of the Jewish émigrés' wish for a status comparable with that of other 'hyphenates' in the USA. In 1935 the membership of the Zionist Organization of America and the Hadassah (the women's organisation) totalled about 50,000. By 1939 it had doubled to 110,000 and by 1945 it had grown to number over 280,000. In 1948 there was a membership of half a million. There were other groups too which varied in their degree of support for Zionism. For example the American Jewish Congress was pro-Zionist and advocated mass pressure tactics to support Jewish rights, B'nai B'rith was a fraternal organisation which became strongly Zionist after the election of Monsky to its presidency, the Jewish Labour Committee was an umbrella organisation divided in its attitude to Zionism, and the American Jewish Committee was a small and influential group mainly concerned with fighting anti-Semitism but with Zionist sympathies. An early attempt was made to galvanise the American Jewish community into political action during October 1939 when Weizmann and the Zionist Executive created the American Emergency Committee for Zionist Affairs, with a membership drawn from the ZOA and Hadassah, Mizrachi and the Labour Zionists, and including the American members of the Jewish Agency. Rabbi Stephen Wise was Chairman until 1943. As was appropriate to the delicacy of the Zionist position in the USA before her entry into the war, Wise like Weizmann was a proponent of the value of quiet diplomacy and influence.[14]

Wise's style did not suit everyone, notably Jabotinsky and the New Zionist Organization, who held a militant outlook concerned in 1940 with the creation of a Jewish army. Jabotinsky died in August allowing the movement to split, the dissident element being headed by Hillel Kook (known as Peter Bergson in the US) and drawn from the Irgun. There were two elements in this group's campaign. A non-sectarian approach called the Yishuv (the Jewish community in Palestine) and European refugees 'Hebrews' but left 'American Jews' as simply 'Americans', thereby removing the stigma of dual loyalty and attracting support from non-Jewish Zionists, for instance in the American Christian Palestine Committee. Secondly, the battle was waged in militant style and with innovative publicity; for instance full page advertisements appeared in newspapers attacking Britain's policy, and plays like Ben Hecht's *A Flag is Born* were staged. In 1944 a Hebrew Embassy opened in Washington, D. C., symbolizing the level of Congressional support the campaign was aiming for. Ganin (1979) concludes that the development of the movement had its greatest importance in its effect on other Jewish leaders. The militancy of the group and its Congressional pressure 'forced the Zionist leadership to become more militant for fear of losing its appeal …'.[15] This militancy was accompanied by terrorism in Palestine, conducted by the Irgun and the Stern Gang, which grew rapidly after 1942. The Jewish Agency found it difficult and was unwilling to suppress this movement, which was directed against Britain's White Paper policy, and was fuelled by a particular grievance: the exclusion from Palestine of Jews fleeing from the holocaust.

The slightly hysterical and increasingly militant direction of Zionism in the US after the entry into war was reflected at the conference held at the Biltmore Hotel in New York. This meeting in May 1942 was the nearest thing to a World Zionist Congress permitted by the war. A resolution was adopted demanding free immigration into Palestine under Jewish Agency control, with the aim 'that Palestine be established as a Jewish Commonwealth'. Ben Gurion had drafted this resolution which drew upon an article Weizmann had written earlier for the quarterly *Foreign Affairs*, but he had made the resolution more sweeping and dramatic in deference to the growing militancy, with the hope of inspiring American opinion. Weizmann, though concerned to speak softly at a time when talks with the British Government on a Jewish army were going on, was compelled to follow the new line. And a new course it was; Zionism had at last framed a demand for sovereignty in Palestine, apparently to come when immigration procured a majority for the Yishuv. There was some dissent from the American Council for Judaism in the USA, from the President of the Hebrew University in Jerusalem, and also from the Stern Gang, but the Biltmore Programme 'became Jewish, not just Zionist, majority opinion' in P. J. Baram's analysis (1978). On 10 November 1942 the Executive of the Zionist Organization's General Council, meeting in Palestine, confirmed the Biltmore resolution by 21 votes to 4.[16]

The direction continued in 1943. In August the American Emergency Committee was reorganised and renamed the American Zionist Emergency Council, Wise becoming Co-Chairman with Rabbi Hillel Silver who, as chairman of its executive committee, was its effective leader. Silver epitomised the new Zionism; abrasive in style, without faith in quiet diplomacy, he was a brilliant orator with charismatic appeal. He made his mark at the American Jewish Conference (29 August–3 September) where many Jewish organisations met to consider the rescue of Jews from Europe and the postwar settlement. Breaking an agreement with Wise, Silver's emotive speech on the issue of Jewish sovereignty in Palestine secured the adoption by the Conference of the Biltmore Programme with only four dissenting votes. Having nailed its colours to the mast, American Jewry proceeded to lobby Congress and President to press for a change in Britain's policy, and work towards a postwar Jewish state.

It seems that under the impetus of the White Paper and the holocaust, Zionism underwent a metamorphosis. The centre of its activity moved from London to New York, and its style changed completely from the reserved diplomacy of the Weizmann era to that of a strident mass movement geared to publicity and advertisement, characterized by Silver's leadership. Above all its objective had altered as well; compromise settlements for Palestine, such as that approved by the Zionist Congress in 1937, as a basis for negotiation were now eschewed, and from 1942 onwards a Jewish sovereign state became the goal. The process was to be free immigration into Palestine, secured by lobbying the US Government to bring about a change in Britain's White Paper policy. This was in tune with the American governmental process which allowed the administration's foreign policy to be open to public pressure — in newspapers and the polling booth — and to Congressional scrutiny, and made a striking contrast with the comparatively silent world of British foreign policy.

During the war Zionism had two important successes. In July 1943 the State Department proposed an Anglo-American statement saying that the settlement of the Palestine question was not considered essential until the end of the war and urging the cessation of all agitation. The idea had first been raised in June 1942. Writing

in April 1945, Alling, the Deputy Director of the Office of Near
Eastern and African Affairs, recorded what happened in the July of
1943:

> a leak occurred and the Zionists learned in a general way of our plans.
> They immediately bombarded high Government officials with protests …
> Mr. Hull [Secretary of State] felt that the matter should be decided on a
> military basis. The Secretary of War concluded that the the military
> situation did not warrant the issuance of the statement and it was
> cancelled.

Despite further prodding by the Foreign Office during the First
Quebec Conference in August 1943, the Secretary of War was
unrelenting and the statement was never issued.[17] The following
summer Zionism won another victory by persuading both the
Republican and Democratic Party Conventions to adopt favourable
planks in the party platforms. Putting the Jewish vote up to the
highest bidder was typical of Silver's technique, and he used his
Republican connections to secure the adoption of a call for a 'free and
democratic Commonwealth' in Palestine, but Wise was able to get a
Democratic pledge for a 'free and democratic Jewish Commonwealth'. Notwithstanding these successes, Zionism in the US was by
1945 far from the pinnacle of its influence and in fact its record for
getting its way was not particularly good. Handicapped before the
US entry into the war, Zionist influence was discounted by the State
Department and the British Government, Ambassador Kennedy in
1939 reassuring the FO about agitation in the US. Baram's (1978)
conclusion is that 'the Department bested the A.Z.E.C. in close
combat, at least up to 1945'.[18] If the State Department was one reason
for Zionism's lack of success, Roosevelt was another. Typically he
jollied the Zionists along for good political reasons, giving an
impression of friendship and energy which had no concrete results in
policy. We shall see how the State Department's attitude, together
with the President's political skill in avoiding the conclusion of an
issue likely to be disruptive, resulted in the dissipation of American
Zionist pressure of which barely an echo reached Whitehall or
Westminster before Roosevelt's death.

The anti-Zionist credentials of the State Department were more
pristine than those of the Foreign Office. The private diplomacy
surrounding the Balfour Declaration in the US involved Wilson,
Weizmann, Brandeis and Colonel House but excluded Secretary of
State Lansing. To add insult to injury, the President's statement on
the Jewish New Year in 1918 was sympathetic to the Balfour
Declaration and had not been cleared with the Department. The

Anglo-American Convention on Palestine of December 1924, ratified
by Congress a year later, was designed to protect US interests in
Palestine as the Mandatory promised consultations with the
Americans before effecting any change in policy. Interestingly, the
Department managed to exclude any reference to the National Home
from the body of the Convention, and although the Balfour
Declaration was mentioned in the preamble the Department had
refused to agree to making Palestine a special case. This may have
been the source of some wry satisfaction to the Americans in the
second half of the 1930s as they observed their opposite numbers in
the FO retreating from the idea of a National Home with its risk of
statehood. By this stage the attitudes of the Foreign Office and
Department were similar. Baram remarks on the overt sympathy in
the Department for Arab independence which felt 'as the Arabs did
themselves, that because Britain and France had "betrayed" the
Arabs after World War I by reneging on promises of independence,
independence for the Arabs must not be indefinitely deferred'.[19] Here
is the stamp of American idealism found in Wilson's Fourteen Points.
During the Second World War the 'self-determination of peoples'
ethic was channelled into anti-imperialism and plans to substitute
UN trusteeships for colonial status. But beyond the idealism there
was self-interest in the Department's Arab bias; by the late 1930s it
was believed that the USA would automatically reap economic
benefits in the Middle East from the growth of Arab nationalism
which would cast out the old imperial powers and embrace the
American friend across the sea.

Naturally this aspiration was at variance with the Foreign Office's
but several parallels and common assumptions may be seen. Like the
FO, the Department had its diplomatic links with the Arab states and
these were always punctual in conveying protests and dire forecasts
whenever US policy, usually as expressed in Presidential statements,
seemed to be taking the Zionist path. Loy Henderson himself, the
Director of the Office of Near Eastern and African Affairs from April
1945 until after the creation of Israel, had been ambassador in
Baghdad since 1943 and was therefore well attuned to the diplomatic
system's bent. Zionism, by contrast, operated outside this system and
perhaps inevitably professional diplomats on both sides of the
Atlantic looked down their noses at it.

Another trans-Atlantic assumption was the perception of Arab
nationalism as a growing and united force. Independence was
undoubtedly an aspiration of most Arab areas under British and
French rule, but less for reasons of Arab nationalism so much as

dynastic ambition and particularism. In 1946 Ibn Saud's nationalism did not extend to wishing Abdullah, a Hashimite, well for his
reign over the newly independent Transjordan. The Arab League
itself was more to keep a safe distance between Arab nationalisms
than to unite them into some corporate entity, and the active
leadership of King Farouk derived not from his idealism but out of the
rivalries of Arab politics. Yet despite the reality this perception of the
Arab world affected the attitude taken by the Foreign Office and the
State Department to Palestine; both were anxious to avoid any
settlement there which was unacceptable to the Arab world, and so
the State Department regarded Zionist aspirations as likely, if
successful, to upset the whole applecart it expected the US to harvest
in the Middle East. When oil was involved, as in Saudi Arabia, the
Department's anxiety was redoubled. Finally the State Department
emulated Rendel's success in getting its views accepted as government policy. Indeed the parallel was very close. The influential Near
Eastern and African Division achieved wide currency for its views
without their being the subject of tough internal criticism, and most
serious of all 'there was a tendency to over-rely on those British Royal
Commission Reports of the 1930s which were least optimistic on the
Zionist enterprise and on partition', as Baram (1978) observes.[20]
Rendel's achievement in persuasion had large ramifications, and it
seems that the Foreign Office and the State Department had a
touchstone of faith in common in their views of Palestine.

With this common outlook, and also feeling that the USA would be
the residuary legatees once the imperial powers had been knocked
from their perches in the Middle East, the State Department's
attitude in the 1930s and war years was that Palestine was a British
concern, and US interests were safeguarded by the 1924 Convention.
This was the reply to the Zionists, but during the war the Department
formulated more detailed plans for the postwar Middle East. The
global principles were a return to the 1939 *status quo*, with state
boundaries drawn so that no state would be too large or small, and
thereby a neo-Wilsonian stability restored. Colonialism would be
replaced by the new trusteeship system to help new nations towards
independence. This meant that a Jewish state in Palestine was not
feasible in view of the existing Arab population and its economic
unviability, and the Department envisaged the resettlement of Jewish
Displaced Persons in Europe. The planners underestimated the
impact of the holocaust not only upon the survivors and Zionism, but
also on humanitarian opinion generally. By the end of the war the
Department looked forward to a bright economic future for the USA

in the Middle East as the influence of Britain, France and Zionism faded. Cynically hoping that Britain would wield the big stick in Palestine and the Middle East, the expectation was that the unblemished USA would be able to supplant her as the senior economic partner in the region. One instance of this was the aim expressed in an economic policy Report of May 1945 that the US should enter the gap between British and Soviet rivalries in the Middle East by seeking to remove all inequalities in trade and restrictive practices. In pursuance of this rivalry the Anglo-American Middle East Supply Centre was closed on 1 November 1945.[21]

Whatever plans the State Department had for future US economic advantage in the Middle East, short-term policy as a whole was supportive to Britain. The common assumptions of the Department and the Foreign Office helped. Furthermore the whole business of international trusteeship, the subject of much debate between the Department, which favoured rather idealistic international control, the Colonial Office, offended by such imputations on Britain's imperial honour, and the Foreign Office, hoping for compromise, affected Palestine very little and the problem there was not used as a stick with which to beat Britain. W. R. Louis (1977) concludes:

> Palestine, despite its status as a mandated territory, fell outside of the mainstream of trusteeship affairs during the war. It was *sui generis*.[22]

In fact the Foreign Office had a firm ally in the NEA Division of the Department, and in order to see the extent of this alliance during the war and appreciate its postwar potential we will look briefly at US policy on Palestine up to 1945. This will show Roosevelt's role and the impact of Truman's arrival.

A curious fact pervades Anglo-American policy on Palestine during the war. The Cabinet Committee set up in 1943 under Morrison made a recommendation for the partition of Palestine, but this whole matter was unknown to the US Government and the Zionists who continued to see a dogged British commitment to the White Paper policy. Together with the public attitude of the State Department that Palestine was a British concern, and Roosevelt's athletic avoidance of all commitments on Palestine, Anglo-American consideration of the problem was manifestly a 'dialogue of the deaf' as A. Ilan (1974) has commented. However it is clear that the State Department and the President succeeded in minimising the impact of Zionist pressure during the war, but at the cost of such twisting and turning that by 1945 Truman was faced with a double policy. The contradictions became clear in 1944, following the introduction in January of the Congressional Joint Resolution demanding the abolition of the White Paper and the creation of a Jewish state. Publicity followed the debate and the Zionists received another fillip when on 9 March Roosevelt authorised Wise and Silver to say that the government had never approved the White Paper. But with Roosevelt's approval the State and War Departments managed to get the resolution shelved, and the President sent assurances to the Arab states reaffirming the promise that no decision would be taken which altered the basic situation in Palestine without full consultation with Arabs and Jews. Further antics followed Roosevelt's endorsement of the Democratic Party pledge on a 'Jewish Commonwealth' in October, since the following month Senators Taft and Wagner re-introduced the Congressional resolution. The Senate Foreign Relations Committee was informed by the President and the State Department that this was an inopportune moment to be critical of an ally and also that it could disrupt US interests in the Middle East. Furthermore Roosevelt warned Wagner that rash action 'might precipitate a massacre of Jews in Palestine'. Obligingly, on 11 December the Committee voted by ten to eight against the resolution.[23] It is easy to see here the electoral concerns of Roosevelt and his party being brushed aside from the safety of office by the exigencies of war and the unbending advice of the State Department.

The Department continued with this line of advice in 1945, for example, in the preparations for Yalta. A memorandum prepared in the Near Eastern Division in January acknowledged that hitherto the aim had been to forestall any action in the near East which might upset the area, it now proposed as desirable 'a more positive policy'. Recommending that the British Government be asked to consider 'an interim policy of Jewish immigration, in view of the widespread humanitarian interest', the Department was now advocating the alteration of the White Paper provisions not out of a change of heart but rather as a device to separate the humanitarian element from the aspirations of political Zionism for a state. The memorandum went on to suggest that Britain be asked to implement her commitment to consult all those concerned with Palestine, 'including both Arabs and Jews', before deciding her policy. Noting indications that the Soviet Union did not favour a Jewish state in Palestine, the memorandum concluded that it would be inadvisable at present for the US to take a definite attitude about Palestine and furthermore

it would be inadvisable for the United States and Britain to undertake any

long range settlement for Palestine without the approval of the Soviet
Government. We should not give the Soviet Government an opportunity
to augment its influence in the Near East by championing the cause of the
Arabs.

Now it must have been clear to the State Department that the Foreign
Office needed no encouragement to consult the Arabs about
Palestine. The concern to bring in the Soviet Government was
predicated not upon her status as an ally nor her potential role in the
United Nations Organisation concerning trusteeship, but upon her
negative attitude to a Jewish state. This becomes clear when the
Department heard from Hoskins that Roosevelt had discussed
Palestine with Stalin at Yalta and the President had concluded that
'at least Stalin was not the Jew-hater that he had been charged in
some quarters with being' because he had claimed to be neither
pro- nor anti-Zionist. The revelation was of sufficient concern to the
Department for Merriam, the chief of the Near Eastern Division, to
write to Hoskins for further details on this 'matter of considerable
importance' because officially Palestine had not been discussed at
Yalta.[24] The intentions of the State Department, therefore, were not
benign toward the Zionist enterprise, as the ingenious suggestion
about interim immigration shows. Nor were the suggested consultations indicative of impatience to settle the Palestine question. The
purpose of both proposals was to kick up the dust of activity on the
issue for the benefit of Zionists at home while trying to ensure that
Zionism made little real progress.

Palestine was not discussed at Yalta officially and the State
Department's memorandum was not used. Similarly the issue was
avoided at the San Francisco Conference where Britain was fearful of
Soviet insistence on Arab self-determination in Palestine, which the
USA also feared would upset the Arab–Jewish balance; by popular
consent 'the *status quo* was frozen', as Louis (1977) observes. The
State Department's Yalta briefing paper must be seen in the context
of public promises to the Zionists and private assurances to the Arab
states, a pattern established in 1944 and continued in 1945.
Following the failure of the Joint Resolution, Zionist pressure turned
from Congress to the White House. On 22 January, Wise saw the
President and, though Arab and Soviet opposition was discussed, he
carried away the impression that 'President Roosevelt remains an
understanding and sympathetic friend of Zionism', as he declared
afterwards. But the State Department had been energetic in drawing
Roosevelt's attention to the Arab threat, Secretary of State Stettinius

warning on 9 January that

> Ibn Saud's statement that he regards himself as a champion of the Arabs
> of Palestine and would himself feel it an honor to die in battle in their
> cause is, of course, of the greatest significance.

On 17 January, Landis, the Director of Economic Operations in the
Middle East, wrote to the President warning that a Jewish state
would be unacceptable to the Arab nations and inconsistent with the
Atlantic Charter, while Eddy, the US Minister in Saudi Arabia,
followed this up with his own report. On his way back from Yalta
on 14 February, Roosevelt, the Zionists understanding and sympathetic friend, met with Ibn Saud and on his own admission learned
more about 'the Moslems — the Jewish problem — by talking to
Ibn Saud for five minutes than I could have learned in the exchange
of two or three dozen letters'.[25] On 1 March Roosevelt reported this
meeting to Congress, but his ambiguous phraseology disguises
whether he was won over by the force of King Ibn Saud's argument
or staggered by his fanaticism on the subject of the Jewish National
Home. Dismayed by the President's remarks, Wise saw him on 16
March and the *New York Times* the next day carried the Presidential
statement that Wise had been authorized to convey; Roosevelt had
not changed his attitude to Zionism as expressed in the previous
October and promised continued efforts to realise it. The State
Department was mortified. Mild reactions were reported from Iraq
and Syria, but the reaction of the Director of the NEA Divison was
anything but mild. Murray warned Acting Secretary of State Grew
that the repercussions would be 'serious', possibly leading to 'actual
bloodshed' and endangering the oil concession in Saudi Arabia.
Furthermore the Presidential statement 'may well result in throwing
the entire Arab world into the arms of Soviet Russia'. The upshot of
these lurid representations was that the President authorized
instructions for the *chargé d'affaires* in Iraq which underplayed the
importance of his statement, and soothing replies were sent to
representations made on 10 March by the Arab states, the most
important of which was the one sent on 5 April to Ibn Saud which
began 'Great and Good Friend'. Ibn Saud was informed that the
US attitude, in accordance with earlier promises, was that 'no
decision be taken with respect to the basic situation ... [in
Palestine] without full consultation with both Arabs and Jews'. For
good measure the message added that US policy remained
'unchanged'.[26]

Roosevelt died on 12 April 1945, the date of the soothing messages to Iraq and Syria, and there is no doubt that one of the burdens of the postwar world which death removed from his shoulders was the resolution of this double policy. The concern to retain the Jewish vote for the Democratic Party was Roosevelt's motive in making promises to the Zionists, and, according to Morgenthau, his anxiety to preserve his reputation as a sympathizer caused him to ask his Cabinet to 'let him hide behind their skirts' when the pressures became heavy. Roosevelt's real attitude, as Hoskins reported him saying informally, seems to have been that a Jewish state could be established only by force, and that therefore it would be best if Palestine became an international territory. Hence, he was happy for once to fall in with the State Department's efforts on this issue and smooth ruffled Arab feathers, thereby allowing the resolution of the Palestine problem to await a calmer postwar world. Isaiah Bowman, the influential Chairman of the State Department's Advisory Committee on Territorial Questions, in May 1943, had advised the President to adopt such a stance.[27]

Truman was catapulted into these problems, and quickly felt the whirlwind. Senator Wagner reminded the new President of his predecessor's endorsement of the Democratic Party plank, while Stettinius also wrote to the man from Independence, mentioning in rather elementary terms the complex nature of the Palestine problem and the need to consult before making statements. A memorandum from Assistant Secretary of State Grew followed, spelling out the 'dual' nature of Roosevelt's promises, and on 17 May Truman approved a letter to Abdullah, replying to his repesentation of 10 March, which made use of the same soothing formula as Roosevelt's replies had employed. For the Potsdam Conference the Department briefed Truman that Palestine would not require detailed discussion and that at the most he should do no more than request the British Government to keep him informed. But the tide was beginning to turn against the State Department, both over the exceptional hegemony it had exerted in the Middle East under Roosevelt, and also in its policy of keeping a low American profile on Palestine. Europe's war ended on 7 May, revealing the full horror of the holocaust and the extent of the DP problem. Zionists quickly harnessed the humanitarian concern and through the good offices of Morgenthau, Secretary of the Treasury, Truman approved a mission to be led by Earl Harrison to investigate the problem, particularly in relation to the Jews, on 22 June. Thus began, with Presidential approval, a chain of events destined to cause the State Department far more difficulty than ever Roosevelt's promises to the Zionists had done, due initially partly to the impact of the holocaust and partly to Truman's humanitarian concern to help Displaced Persons. The peculiar reconciling skills of Roosevelt, which had enabled him to gloss over contradictions in policy, were not Truman's forte at all. In the face of the new President's humanitarian concern, and later his growing support for Zionist aspirations, the State Department rapidly lost influence over Palestine policy. Upset at the turn of events and over the direction of a policy perceived to conflict with American interests, many of the NEA Division's officers and planning division staff had resigned or moved by the end of 1945 [28].

By the time the Labour Government took office in Britain on 25 July 1945, little had happened across the Atlantic to provoke undue haste over Palestine. During the war, Zionist organization had grown in scale and amplified its volume, but its successes had been extemely limited. Roosevelt had managed to sustain Zionist hopes but not make these policy, while the State Department acted from concerns which were so close to those of the Foreign Office as to render them allies. Both wanted a settlement in Palestine inoffensive to the Arab world, while the wartime debate on postwar trusteeship, even in 1945, skirted by the question of Palestine as one of too great delicacy for speedy resolution. Only Truman's arrival and interest in the refugee problem looked likely to make an impact on London, the force of which was yet to come.

British policy during the Second World War

Before examining the Labour Government's attempt to grapple with the Palestine problem, another aspect of the inheritance faced by the new government in 1945 must be considered: Britain's wartime policy on Palestine. A survey of the main events will reveal the great extent of the inheritance in 1945 of prewar policies and attitudes, and it will soon become apparent that Attlee's administration had no *tabula rasa* upon which to inscribe a policy plucked from the air, or even from Labour Party Conference resolutions.

The constitutional provisions of the 1939 White Paper, which required a representative body in Palestine to make constitutional recommendations in readiness for independence, were never put into effect. Arab agitation for their enactment was placated and diverted by land purchase legislation, which allowed Jews to buy land only in a small part of Palestine, and by the engagement of the Arab rulers' interest in schemes of Arab union.[29] The suppression of Raschid Ali's coup and the victory of El Alamein later enabled the British Government to resist Arab pressures more easily.

Churchill's attitude to the White Paper was that it represented a betrayal of pledges made to the League of Nations and to the Jewish people in their hour of need, and was shameful appeasement. His speech in the Commons debate on 23 May was amongst his finest. Churchill's motives were deeper than mere hatred of appeasement and the wish to make common cause with Roosevelt's pro-Zionist appearances; perhaps, like Balfour, his sense of Christian history fired an enthusiasm for the ending of the Jewish dispersion, while the plight of European Jewry deepened his compassion and understanding of the messianic quality of Zionism's quest for a homeland. His views were unchanged in office. But against the weight of Ministers who were directly responsible for Palestine and who were supported by the full force of departmental opinion and the advice of the diplomatic and colonial services, Churchill was powerless to overthrow the White Paper. In February 1940 his opposition to the implementation of the land transfer provisions of the White Paper was recorded in the Cabinet minutes, and it was not until September 1944 that Churchill's years of effort to obtain a Jewish Brigade bore fruit and the Zionists' wish to fight under their own colours was partially satisfied.[30]

The military turn of events rendered Britain's position in the Middle East more secure by early 1943, and if the only rationale behind the White Paper policy had been appeasement its days would have been numbered. But the Foreign Office's objective went beyond wartime appeasement, since in the FO's analysis any solution in Palestine which upset the Arab world would threaten Britain's commercial, imperial and strategic interests throughout the region and expose them to a reaction by Arab nationalism, and American and Russian encroachment. Hence the White Paper policy continued unchanged, but its opponents did achieve something. In April 1943 Churchill minuted angrily:

> I cannot agree that the White Paper is 'the firmly established policy' ... I have always regarded it as a gross breach of faith ... it runs until it is superseded.

In July the Cabinet set up a Committee to consider long-term policy and allowed Churchill to select its members. Morrison (the Home Secretary) became Chairman, the other members being Amery

(Secretary of State for India and a strong advocate of partition), the Colonial Secretary Stanley, Sinclair (Secretary of State for Air) and, after Eden's special appeal, R. K. Law (the Parliamentary Undersecretary) was allowed to represent the Foreign Office. Resisting Law's attempts to reduce the size of the Jewish state, the Committee reported in December, recommending a partition scheme with a Jewish state smaller than the Peel Commission had suggested, a Jerusalem enclave under Mandatory control, while the Arab areas of Palestine and Lebanon were to become part of a Greater Syria.[31]

The War Cabinet expressed grudging approval of the Report on 25 January 1944, saying it 'was probably as good as any that could be devised and was fair to all parties concerned'. In the face of the inevitable opposition the Cabinet felt that it should decide its policy and stick to it. The Foreign Office attitude was dusty, Eden reserved his position pending reports from Cairo and Baghdad, while Law went on record as believing the size of the Jewish state was 'unfair to the Arabs'. Churchill adroitly pushed aside the opposition of the Chiefs of Staff by explaining their view that partition would have to be forced upon an opposing Jewish community, then adding that he 'certainly did not contemplate' Britain enforcing partition against Arab and Jewish violent resistance. The Cabinet followed through the breach and agreed that the COS's views 'were not such as to necessitate a reconsideration' of the Report. But the opposition was granted a stay of execution, the Cabinet agreeing that there would be no announcement before Germany's defeat.[32] Now delay is one of the most important weapons in the bureaucratic arsenal, and we have seen how well the Foreign Office used the interval between the creation of the Peel Commission and the appearance of the Woodhead Commission's Report to wrest victory for its views from defeat. A sense of *déjà vu* may be felt as one surveys the eighteen months which followed the Cabinet decision of January 1944.

Before moving on it is noteworthy that one reason for delaying the announcement of any new policy advanced in Cabinet was 'the possible reaction ... in the United States and on the forthcoming Presidential elections', and it was considered potentially too embarrassing for Roosevelt for the President to be informed privately of the partition scheme. Apart from the Cabinet's delicate sense of tact, it is interesting to see the extent of immunity felt in London from the pressures of political Zionism in America which were perceived to be of greater moment for Roosevelt than for Britain's repute in the USA. This is an indicator of Zionism's lack of success in bringing pressure to bear on the British Government, and the episode is in strong

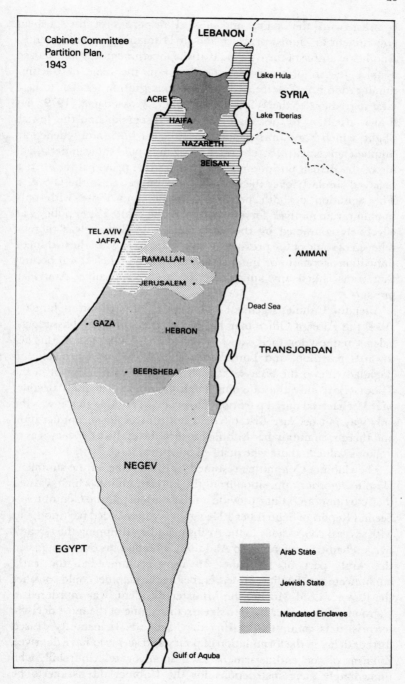

Cabinet Committee
Partition Plan,
1943

LEBANON

Lake Hula

SYRIA

ACRE

Lake Tiberias

HAIFA

NAZARETH

BEISAN

TEL AVIV
JAFFA

• AMMAN

RAMALLAH •

JERUSALEM •

Dead Sea

• GAZA

HEBRON •

TRANSJORDAN

• BEERSHEBA

NEGEV

EGYPT

Arab State

Jewish State

Mandated Enclaves

Gulf of Aquba

contrast with the angry and heated responses of the postwar
government to Zionist pressure and to Truman's pronouncements.
Another example of the way the British Government was immunized
against Jewish pressure may be found in the issue of wartime
immigration into Palestine. Restricted immigration was felt to be a
vital ingredient of the White Paper policy. Wasserstein (1979) has
drawn attention to the Anglo-American discussions on the Jewish
plight, which began in Bermuda on 19 April 1943, and reached an
'implicit agreement whereby the Americans would show understanding of the British position regarding Palestine, provided the British
behaved similarly over the question of immigration to the U.S.A.'.
The agitation of both political Zionists, and those with only
humanitarian motives, for a relaxation in the White Paper policy was
effectively contained by this agreement, and Britain was thereby
relieved of some of the pressure, which helps to explain the Cabinet's
punctilious concern for the niceties of Presidential electoral politics
that transcended any annoyance felt at 'irresponsible' American
pressure.[33]

After the Cabinet's general endorsement of partition in January
1944, the Foreign Office marshalled the views of its ambassadors.
Eden's request for their views reflected the dislike felt in the FO
towards partition, and Lord Killearn in Cairo and Cornwallis in
Baghdad rose to the occasion. Of all Britain's representatives in the
Middle East only the outgoing High Commissioner for Palestine,
MacMichael, favoured partition. However, in arguing that it was the
only way out because Britain could not control illegal immigration
and thereby maintain her Middle Eastern status, his advocacy was of
dubious value to those who disliked bowing to force.[34]

The Cabinet Committee resumed its discussions in the summer.
Despite vigorous opposition from the Foreign Office, which warned
that partition might not provide a final settlement, the Committee's
Second Report of September 1944 again recommended partition, but
with several concessions to the Arabs including dropping the Greater
Syria scheme in deference to Abdullah, who had his own designs on
the Arab part of Palestine. It also recommended the early
announcement of policy. However, before the Cabinet could consider
the Report, Lord Moyne, the Minister Resident, was murdered in
Cairo on 6 November by Jewish extremists, one of the most decisive
terrorist acts committed during the Mandate. It instantly caused
further delay in the formulation of policy and seems to have deprived
Zionism of the enthusiasm of its best advocate, Churchill, who
immediately gave instructions for the Cabinet discussion to be

postponed and spoke bitterly in the Commons. Before this murder Churchill had told Weizmann that a policy announcement would have to await Germany's defeat, and possibly a general election and US consultation, but now with discussions held up the tide began to flow inexorably in the favour of the Foreign Office and COS. The possibility of a policy announcement receded, and the waning of partition's chances is reflected by the uninterested and curt tone of Churchill's reply on 9 June 1945 to a letter from Weizmann. After acknowledging receipt, he added, 'There can I fear be no possibility of the [Palestine] question being effectively considered until the victorious Allies are definitely seated at the peace table.'[35]

Between the autumn of 1944 and the summer of 1945, the views of the Chiefs of Staff remained unchanged and provided not only support for Foreign Office thinking, but also a rationale for the delay of any announcement on policy. In January of 1944 the Chiefs of Staff Committee warned the Cabinet that partition would 'complicate military control' of Palestine, and enumerated Britain's strategic requirements in the Middle East as control of the Eastern exit of the Mediterranean, the security of oil sources and routes of supply, the safety of imperial air and sea communications and a base for the imperial strategic reserve. The attitude to partition survived the war; the assessment of Britain's strategic requirements proved even more enduring and continued to inspire the COS view of Palestine. In November 1944 the Joint Planning Staff of the COS reiterated the objections to partition in response to the Cabinet Committee's Second Report. Noting the Committee's expectation that disturbances would follow any announcement of partition, the JPS seized upon Eden's objections which went 'further than the Committee in prophesying trouble' in the Middle East. The planners, indeed, saw no end to the ramifications of partition which might add to latent problems in India and thereby affect the war against Japan. Conveniently neglecting to mention that the Secretary of State for India supported partition, the planners pointed out that the Viceroy had not been consulted. The COS Committee approved of this line, and in their Report the Cabinet was warned that reinforcements of three Infantry Divisions and one Tank Brigade would be needed in the Middle East to control the disorders consequent upon the announcement of a policy of partition. Crucially, the earliest foreseeable occasion for such reinforcements to be available 'without serious effects on operations elsewhere, would be some nine to twelve months after Germany's defeat'.[36]

In January 1945, following an examination of the Middle Eastern
Commanders in Chief's report on security, the COS reiterated their
recommendations. A policy declaration was the 'single factor most
likely to have a far reaching effect upon the internal security' of the
Middle East, which at present was in an 'uneasy equilibrium' and
threatened by the expiry of the Jewish immigration quota in the
autumn, and also by partition which it was 'generally agreed' would
'precipitate a crisis'. Finally Brooke, Portal and Cunningham (the
COS Committee) recommended to the Cabinet that, 'Except for
overriding political reasons, no aggravation of the present risks
should be allowed, at least until such time as the forces necessary to
maintain internal security can be provided without detriment to the
general war effort.' Portal himself had made this final paragraph
more forthright than in the draft.[37]

This view was held by the COS for some time to come, founded as it
was upon an appreciation of Britain's strategic needs in the Middle
East which, apart from the oil and air routes, Disraeli himself would
have recognized. But as a basis for planning the policy of a postwar
Britain which had lost both the will and means to govern a disparate
Empire, its tenets quickly became anachronisms. The Foreign Office
subscribed to the COS view as well, and when in March 1945 the Suez
Canal Committee questioned the Foreign Secretary's view that the
canal should remain Britain's responsibility 'in perpetuity', and
queried the assumption that Britain would continue to play a
'predominant part in the defence and political control of the Middle
East', Eden rose to the occasion manfully. Attlee, who chaired the
Committee, was answered by a resounding exposition from the
Foreign Office. The Middle East was 'one of the most important
strategic areas in the world' without control of which 'the Empire can
be cut in half', and to invite international control of the canal would
appear to the Arabs as an abdication by Britain, especially as the
'quality which the Middle Eastern peoples recognise above all others
is strength'.[38] Quite apart from the light this sheds on the
commonality of outlook between the Foreign Office and the COS, this
statement on the dangers of international interference in Britain's
sphere of influence and on the importance of strength in the Arab
world sounds strange indeed from the department of state originally
responsible for involving various Arab states in the affairs of Britain's
Mandate as early as 1936.

The views of the Chiefs of Staff are noteworthy for the reliance they
placed on the Foreign Office predictions of trouble in the Middle East
which would follow a policy of partition, and the support they gave to

the FO case against partition. In addition to arguing against partition itself, the COS supported the FO by talking of reinforcements and by counselling delay for any policy announcement, thereby helping to impose a moratorium on Palestine policy and allowing the Foreign Office to win its case.

In November 1944 the Foreign Office made ready to carry its battle against the partition plan into Cabinet. Butler, Superintending Undersecretary of the North American Department, gave the Cabinet Secretary (Sir Edward Bridges) early and private notice of the FO objections in two pages of 'comments'. Partition was criticized for being based on two questionable hypotheses that immigration could not be controlled and that partition was a final solution. Butler argued plausibly but mistakenly that immigration would be more controllable after the war as fewer Jews would want to go to Palestine. But he then warned, somewhat illogically, that under partition the Zionists would flood the Jewish state with immigrants and threaten the neighbouring Arab countries. This element of doublethink was to appear in the paper placed before the Cabinet in April 1945. Butler went on to say that partition 'would leave many of our most vital interests, oil, communications and strategic points surrounded by resentful populations inflamed by Nationalism'. All this was old hat, but a conciliatory note added: 'We could not recommend acceptance [of partition] until every other solution had been tried'. The theme of delay and caution was given a new twist: 'It may be necessary to work out with the Americans ... [a scheme] to which they as well as ourselves are committed'. Finally Butler seemed to hark back to the old introspection over the McMahon correspondence of the 1930s by saying that Britain's purpose should be 'to keep our word (as far as it is possible to reconcile mutually contradictory undertakings), and subject to that to maintain our position ...'.[39] This paper is important because it summarized the submission made to the Cabinet in the following April, it shows the continuity of the Foreign Office thinking since before the war, and it raises the question of US involvement — significantly in the context of postponing the partition scheme.

The Foreign Office was busy drafting its Cabinet paper in November 1944, and Bridges probably received these 'comments' to ensure that the Cabinet did not begin discussing partition, which Churchill was 'pressing for' urgently, before the FO had its case ready. On 9 November Butler minuted to Eden that Law had approved the draft paper and had said:

that the paper is not in the form which you and he discussed before you

went to Moscow. You then both had it in mind to state your objections to
Partition, but to say that as everyone was determined to have Partition,
you would not press them, provided that some of the more objectionable
features of the Committee's plan were removed.

This line, which Law had taken in the Cabinet Committee, was
dropped and the draft and final papers were uncompromising in their
opposition to partition. The Foreign Office was determined to make a
fight of it and was undeterred either by political pressures inside the
Cabinet which Eden and Law both felt, or by the absence of an
alternative policy. The attitude of the Chiefs of Staff, who on 7
November advised the need for a nine to twelve month reinforcement
period before any new policy on Palestine was announced, probably
encouraged the Foreign Office in its combative stance, and Butler
minuted optimistically to Sir Alexander Cadogan, his Permanent
Under-Secretary: 'The objections in this Report [of the COS],
together with the measures following Lord Moyne's assassination,
may lead to Cabinet consideration of the [partition] plan being
shelved.'[40] As we have seen, Cabinet discussion was postponed and
the delay proved invaluable to the Foreign Office to clarify its case.
The suggestion of involving the USA, the provision of an alternative
to the partition plan, and the wrangle between the Foreign and
Colonial Offices on these and other matters were the questions
tackled during the next few months.

Law recognized that postponement of the issue was not sufficient,
and he warned Cadogan that:

it will be necessary to find an answer to the large questionmark with which
the [draft Cabinet] paper ends. I don't think that the assassination of
L[or]d Moyne means that we can do without a policy.

In a minute on 'The Middle East' of 20 February 1945, Butler
gallantly attempted to clarify and to make more positive the FO's
position. Arguing that the application of the trusteeship system to
Palestine would help by establishing the international ramifications
of the problem, Butler also suggested an alternative
'Anglo-(Franco)-American arrangement to much the same effect',
adding that whichever course was chosen 'we should lose nothing by
consulting the Americans'. Gladwyn Jebb, who confessed to having
no direct knowledge of Palestine, minuted quite favourably and
suggested Anglo-American regulation of immigration. R. M. A.
Hankey, First Secretary of the Eastern Department, was however
appalled at this idea:

as immigration is what peace or war will depend on, we should keep it in our own hands. We cannot resign leadership of the M[iddle] E[ast] over this without losing our whole position there, because Jewish immigration is what the whole Arab world cares about most.

Hankey feared that Zionist pressure would cause the American government to exert power without responsibility, and he concluded that US involvement 'is attractive but seems almost impossible to apply without creating greater dangers than it avoids'. Butler had, however, been energetic in pressing his ideas for cooperating with the US, and on 10 March he sent a minute on 'Palestine' to Sir Ronald Campbell, who was about to take up his post as Ambassador in Cairo. Butler drew attention to the lameness of the FO proposals by comparison with the Cabinet Committee's 'laboriously worked out' scheme of partition, and noting the enthusiasm of the COS to get US involvement in the Middle East he suggested that American interest in Palestine could be secured by instilling suitable schemes privately into the State Department. Hankey was again highly critical:

We cannot maintain leadership if we have other peoples' plans foisted on to us, or if we pretend to. Palestine is *our* responsibility ... .

So it seems that while Butler was keen to involve the USA over Palestine, even to the point of some sort of partnership, the Eastern Department was much less keen on the idea and it featured only briefly as a suggestion in the paper circulated to the Cabinet on 10 April. In a draft of the previous November the suggestion of working out a solution with America had been the subject of the final paragraph, but this was deleted in favour of a promise that the Minister Resident in the Middle East (Grigg) would be making positive proposals. The Eastern Department was evidently pleased that US partnership was not pressed, Baxter closing the series of minutes which Butler's first paper had provoked with the exultant words, 'This has now been largely overtaken by the Grigg paper on Palestine.'[41]

This introspective debate is interesting and ironic in the context of events. Within months of the question of close US involvement being 'overtaken' to the Eastern Department's satisfaction, Ernest Bevin was himself to raise and initiate the search for a joint Anglo-American policy on Palestine and the Department's original distaste for anything which smacked of a leading American role must be kept in mind. So too should Hankey's extraordinary protestation that

'Palestine is *our* responsibility', for the Foreign Office had appeared singularly anxious to share this responsibility with the Arab States in 1939 at the St James's Conference, and was to repeat the venture in 1946.

We must now turn to the Grigg paper which Baxter apparently felt made all else obsolete. In a telegram dated 11 March 1945, Grigg made an ingenious suggestion to Eden and Stanley. Noting that the White Paper's immigration quota would expire in the summer, and describing the involved process of deciding upon a future policy such as supplying reinforcements and talking to the Americans and Arabs, Grigg concluded there was 'little chance of completing this process by July'. Instead he suggested approaching the Arab states immediately to get their agreement to continued interim immigration into Palestine pending the settlement of the whole problem at the Peace Conference. This was the genesis of what was actually to happen later in 1945. Policy would be split between the 'interim' and the 'long term', the Cabinet Committee's partition scheme would lose its urgency as the immediate problem of the immigration quota's exhaustion would be alleviated, and the search for a solution could continue indefinitely. This suggestion of Grigg's was very useful to the Foreign Office as it provided a way of postponing the battle against partition, to which the FO still had no alternative in the spring of 1945, until a later date when the plan could be defeated. Baxter felt the idea was 'sound' and added with revealing candour that 'the whole object of Sir E. Grigg's proposal is to gain time, in which to prepare a final solution'. Campbell was even more explicit:

> If, as we hope, a decision on the long term Palestine policy is postponed (as otherwise it would mean that the Palestine Committee's report in favour of partition would be adopted at the end of this month), there seems every advantage in securing as soon as possible some agreement on Jewish immigration pending final decisions.[42]

The immigration quota did not expire until later in the year and so the decision to divide the policy choices between the interim and long term was left to the Labour Government, but the attitude reflected in the Foreign Office minutes is revealing.

In March 1945 the Foreign Office was indeed getting very anxious that partition might go through. Baxter minuted that this would be 'disastrous' and drew attention to the absence of any alternative plan. Campbell wrote with dismay to Eden, explaining that the FO draft paper offered 'no constructive alternative' and that Grigg's proposals would not be ready in time if the Cabinet discussed the matter in March. Eden was not pleased: 'When shall we [be] ready? We don't want to seem to be merely causing delay.' But the Foreign Office was let out of its corner by a Colonial Office decision that Grigg's recommendations would have to be heard by the Palestine Committee prior to the Cabinet discussing them, and of the resulting delay Eden's Private Secretary noted: 'The position is thus, I think, safeguarded ... '.[43]

This is a convenient point at which to look at the several areas of contention between the Foreign Office and its unwitting benefactor on this occasion, the Colonial Office. Trusteeship and other ways of obtaining responsible US involvement in Palestine received consideration in the FO, but they held no charm for the Colonial Office. Resentful anyway of any international supervision of Britain's colonial rule, the CO was especially anxious to keep Palestine out of discussions on trusteeship with the USA. Boyd of the Palestine Department minuted in 1944 that 'The future of Palestine and Transjordan is an entirely separate problem', and referred to the partition scheme as the future for the country. This attitude persisted, and Hankey minuted in March 1945, following discussions between the CO, Baxter and Campbell, that the

> CO have no ideas on colonial trusteeship as applied to Palestine, nor on engaging American responsibility, nor on any plan except the Cabinet Committee's plan. Their attitude is that until the latter is rejected by the Cabinet, it should hold the field.

The Colonial Office inevitably regarded such ideas as red herrings proposed by an antagonistic Foreign Office to lure them away from the Cabinet Committee's partition plan. The CO reacted in a similar way to Grigg's idea for splitting policy between the interim and long-term questions, Baxter recording that:

> The Colonial Office are inclined to take an unfavourable view ... [Colonial Secretary] Stanley's first impressions seem to be that these proposals [for interim immigration] cannot possibly be considered in isolation, apart from the main question of the future of Palestine, and the Palestine Committee's revised Report.[44]

Baxter found the CO attitude 'disappointing', but he could scarcely have expected an enthusiastic reception for a scheme that postponed indefinitely the consideration of partition which the Colonial Office supported.

Following the referral of Grigg's paper to the Cabinet Committee in March the battle between the Foreign and Colonial Offices became heated. Eden was put out by the suggestion that he should attend the Committee, minuting

> I suppose I must? I hate this body. It consists of passionate Zionists and their influence on [the] War Cabinet as individuals is not great, so that I waste my time.

What may have stung the Foreign Secretary so badly was the paper Stanley circulated for the Committee. The Colonial Secretary annexed the views of the High Commissioner, Lord Gort, which urged caution over partition and warned that it was 'an artificial solution disregarding economics, history and geography'. Stanley felt his colleague may want to re-examine the matter as a result, and now reserved his final opinion. But his tone became increasingly bitter, 'The long delay in reaching a final decision on the Report of the Committee has been a grave disadvantage'. Unable to dissassociate a decision on immigration from one on partition, Stanley continued:

> The strongest argument for partition is that it represents the only policy in the field and my support of it will not be shaken until I see a better alternative.
>   [When Grigg's proposals are ready] I hope the Foreign Secretary will then be in a position to present some detailed plan.

Meanwhile Stanley thought it was unfair to ask the Cabinet to consider partition in the absence of an alternative scheme. Eden wrote on his copy: 'But C.O. refuses to produce any alternative and nobody else can!', and minuted on 8 April that 'Sir E. Bridges' attention should be drawn to the fantastic conclusion of Col[onel] Stanley's paper'.[45] However, the Colonial Office had no intention of putting up arguments against partition for which it still hoped to obtain Cabinet backing. But the balance of forces was now tilting against partition, no Middle Eastern representative favoured it and even the High Commissioner had come out against the scheme.

Grigg's proposals were at last circulated to the Cabinet on 4 April 1945. These suggested continued British responsibility for an undivided Palestine but on new trusteeship terms. The terms would provide for progress towards self-government and prevent Jewish Agency hegemony. Immigration was to be controlled by an international body which would balance the interest of Arabs and

Jews. Grigg's proposals were indeed to involve the USA, but not in the manner or to the degree Butler had been suggesting; instead the British Government was to retain leadership. This was to be the Foreign Office's positive offering, providing an alternative to the partition scheme for the Cabinet. On 3 April Grigg had convened a conference of the Middle Eastern representatives in Cairo and, although conference endorsed Grigg's opposition to partition and agreed on the need to carry the United States along with British policy, there was strong feeling that any departure from the White Paper required 'the greatest circumspection' and 'should be deferred as long as possible' to avoid trouble. Killearn also cabled to similar effect. Clearly, the more positive parts of Grigg's paper were his own only, while His Majesty's Representatives could agree merely upon their opposition to partition and preference for delay. Eden enquired whether Killearn's telegram should be circulated, and on Baxter's advice no action was taken.[46] After all, Grigg's proposal was the best the Foreign Office had.

Eden's Cabinet Paper of 10 April 1945 followed the draft of the preceding November, apart from the deletion of a final paragraph on US involvement mentioned earlier. The FO arguments against partition were rehearsed at length, obeisance made to past undertakings which were difficult to reconcile, and Britain's interests in the Middle East spelled out in terms of communications, oil, bases and the central need to retain 'Arab goodwill'. Growing Arab unity was detected and the forecast reaction to partition 'will be deep-rooted, permanent, and very severe'.[47] In 1945 the Foreign Office put precisely the same case against partition as it had advanced before the war. Despite the holocaust, despite the growing power of Zionism, despite the manifest failure of the White Paper policy to secure Arab allegiance during the war except in Saudi Arabia and Transjordan, and despite Britain's greatly diminished postwar displacement compared with the USA, despite all this and the passage of seven years, the Foreign Office seems to have learned nothing and forgotten nothing with regard to Middle Eastern policy.

The debate on policy continued in the spring, but the proponents of partition were now in retreat. Amery's parting shot was a plea that if partition had to be abandoned the alternative should allow equality of development between Arabs and Jews in Palestine. On 2 May the Joint Intelligence Committee of the Cabinet, no less, warned that the Arab reaction to a policy of partition or unrestricted Jewish immigration might snowball if the Arab states led it, and Wikeley of the FO's Eastern Department noted with satisfaction that it 'gives strong support to the FO view that Palestine can only be treated as part of the Middle East and not in a watertight compartment of its own'. The Colonial Secretary had not yet given up and on 7 May sent an advance copy of his Cabinet paper to the Foreign Office. Emphasizing the need for a speedy decision as the immigration quota was about to expire, Stanley argued that Grigg's proposals were no more promising than partition and he had 'no confidence' in them. The Cabinet could decide in principle between partition and Grigg's plan and, Stanley explained, it would be 'unfair' if the CO had to fill in the substance of Grigg's ideas. Accordingly the paper recommended that the Cabinet ask the Foreign Secretary to prepare a detailed plan from Grigg's proposals, but the CO began to concede the need for interim action on immigration 'if the War Cabinet feels that the possibility of a final decision upon policy before September is remote'. This remark clearly reflects how time worked in the Foreign Office's favour, for the CO was now anxiously contemplating the need to divide the policy issues between the interim and the indefinite. On the lines of Eden's previous minute that the Colonial Office should draw up an alternative scheme to partition, Law wrote a 'My dear Oliver' letter to the Colonial Secretary rebuffing his suggestion 'read with some dismay' that the Foreign Office should do the job which was, like Palestine itself, a Colonial Office responsibility. Law suggested that Grigg be called back to help. The Colonial Office paper was held up, and the minutes by Baxter and Campbell show their unbending efforts to keep the responsibility for writing an alternative plan firmly with the CO. Stanley's final paper, circulated to the Cabinet on 16 May, was much milder and instead of recommending that the Foreign Secretary prepare an alternative plan it meekly requested Grigg's return.[48]

But on 7 May Germany surrendered and, in deference to the wishes of the Labour Party for a general election, Churchill formed a caretaker Government from which the Labour Party members were absent. With an election fixed for 5 July and the immigration quota sufficient until September, there was no chance of any decision, interim or final, being made before. In the meantime the Foreign Office solicited the views of the Middle Eastern representatives on the various ideas. The verdict overall was heavily against partition, Grigg's scheme was not expected to prove acceptable, and the ramifications of either, as Sir Douglas Harris of the Colonial Office put it in his review of replies, meant that they 'could not possibly be undertaken in the comparatively short time still available' before the immigration quota expired, so the best course was an interim policy of continuing the quota with or if necessary without Arab consent.[49] These views crowned the Foreign Office's campaign against partition. Delay had permitted a leisurely harvest from the Middle Eastern posts, and the despatches were all ready to greet the incoming government.

Churchill's parting shot was a trenchant minute to the Colonial Secretary and the COS, written on the day after the election. He urged that the USA be asked to take the Mandate over, the gesture being a useful counter to anti-imperialist propaganda and also because:

> I am not aware of the slightest advantage which has ever accrued to Great Britain from this painful and thankless task. Somebody else should have their turn now. However, the Chiefs of Staff should examine the matter from the strategic point of view.

Harold Beeley, the expert on Palestine serving in the FO's Eastern Department, commented critically that the USA would be most unlikely to accept the Mandate, the USSR might demand a role, and the Arabs would conclude that Britain's power was 'on the wane' and her abdication in Palestine would be seen to be 'symptomatic of our abdication as a Great Power'. The Foreign Office, therefore, saw Churchill off by reiterating the argument for showing strength and upholding Britain's prestige in the Middle East, while avoiding having a policy for her mandated territory which might damage her standing with the Arab states. As for the COS, the Joint Planning Staff paper of 10 July provides an indication that the military pattern of thought had not altered at all since January 1944, for it explained that 'Palestine is the bottleneck of all land communications between Africa and Asia', and that military rights, founded upon Arab goodwill, could not be abrogated without damaging Britain's position. Thus the COS expounded Britain's strategic needs in the Middle East exactly as they had done for the Cabinet some eighteen months before in the midst of a world war.[50]

Here in microcosm in the summer of 1945 we see expressed for the education of incoming Ministers and despite the gallant efforts of some departing ones, notably Churchill, attitudes which had passed unscathed through the greatest war in history. The partition proposal had come and all but disappeared between 1943 and 1945, much as had happened between 1937 and 1939. A gap had been opened between the immediate policy requirements and the distant consideration of a long-term solution. Altogether this meant that the Labour

Government faced a policy inherited from 1939, and perhaps even more deeply entrenched behind years of Foreign Office experience and COS requirements. Furthermore the Foreign Office had now established its preponderent place in the making of Palestine policy above that of the Colonial Office. The pressures from the USA had yet to be felt properly, but an important new element in British policy discussions was an awareness of the need to involve America to some degree, although there was a distinct wariness in both the Foreign and Colonial Offices. A considerable legacy faced the new socialist government on the Palestine question, besides the many other problems of greater magnitude which were thrust upon it.

2

Labour in Power; the Creation of the Anglo-American Committee

Labour's victory at the polls and the formation of the new government inaugurated a curious period in the history of British policy on Palestine, a period in which fresh ideas and commitments were blended with old ones. The Labour Party had made its commitment to Zionism clear in the past, enthusiasm that had involved Bevin himself during the early part of the war.[1] Faced with the manifold responsibilities of office this enthusiasm, at least on the government front benches, waned. However, before the new Foreign Secretary became distracted from and demoralized by the seemingly intractable nature of the Palestine question he applied himself with great energy and vigour to securing some sort of US partnership in the matter. This step clearly surprised the Eastern Department of the Foreign Office which still showed antipathy to such co-operation and what it perceived to be the consequences. Yet, seeking a partnership with the US on Palestine was in complete accord with the direction of Bevin's policy in other areas. In time it was to elicit a powerful US commitment to Europe's security. But the seeds of failure in this Anglo-American venture on Palestine were clear from the start in the reservations of the Foreign Office and its perception that the US attitude would be manipulated by electoral concerns, a perception it felt was confirmed by the very terms of reference of the Anglo-American Committee of Enquiry. Consequent upon this belief was the underlying but ultimately dominant assertion by the Foreign Office that Britain's real and legitimate interests in Palestine were going by default, the victims of an unhelpful and irresponsible American component in the policymaking.

The Party's record on Palestine

When the Labour Party came to power in 1945 it had publicly placed on record its support for the Jewish National Home, a support that went back some years. In 1936 the Palestine Sub-Committee of the Party's Advisory Committee on Imperial Questions recommended that Party policy should accord with Article Two of the Mandate for Palestine, which called for the development of the National Home while safeguarding the rights of the existing population and progress towards self-government. The Sub-Committe, which comprised Dr Drummond Shiels, Norman Bentwich, G. T. Garrett and T. Reid, advised that the Mandate should continue 'until such time as Arabs and Jews can live together in tolerable harmony'. The Arab rebellion presented a challenge to this line of thought, but in April 1937 the Sub-Committee stalwartly declared that the 'policy of reconciliation is the correct one' and that the Arab demand for the total cessation of Jewish immigration could not be met: 'The pledge of the National Home must be honoured'. The partition of Palestine was not envisaged as an answer at this stage. Creech Jones, who was closely involved with the Labour Party's discussions on imperial and colonial questions, warned that partition 'may prove to be a big modification of the conception of the Balfour Declaration'. Of course there was a problem in determining what the conception of the Balfour Declaration actually was, and from the distance of later life Creech Jones reflected in the draft of a book on Palestine that the statesmen of 1917 had no thoughts of restricting Jewish immigration to Palestine but envisaged a Jewish state growing from the inflow into the National Home.[2] However, as things had developed by the 1930s, immigration was controlled and the 1939 White Paper made these controls firmer on the pretext that the pledge of a Jewish National Home had by then been fulfilled.

In December 1944 the Labour Party conference adopted a resolution framed by Dalton:

> But there is surely neither hope nor meaning in a 'Jewish National Home' unless we are prepared to let Jews, if they wish, enter this tiny land in such numbers as to become a majority ... Let the Arabs be encouraged to move out as the Jews move in.

That this scarcely sounded like the clarion call to reconciliation in Palestine which the party had discussed before the war may be attributed to the impact of the holocaust and the spectacle of the British Government, in furtherance of the White Paper policy, turning away from Jews desperately fleeing occupied Europe for Palestine. It was a Labour Party gesture and promise to make amends for the wartime hand-washing by reverting to a full-blooded interpretation of the Balfour Declaration. Dalton's intention seems to have been to reverse the pro-Arab direction of British policy, for he noted on the resolution that: 'We should lean much more than hitherto towards the dynamic Jews, less towards the static Arab'. This makes his intention sound racialist, not merely humanitarian or that of someone inspired by the Zionist ideal. In fact the resolution's wording about encouraging the Arabs to move out had occasioned some discussion between Dalton and Berl Locker of the Palestine Labour Political Committee in London who had been concerned 'that at the Conference the rapporteur should underline what is, in fact, clear from the text — that the object is a voluntary agreement, not any sort of compulsion'.[3] This wording, it was hoped, would avoid a blatant anti-Arab stance by the conference.

Dalton did quite well by the Zionists who, by the end of the war, were not at all inclined to appear in favour of partition. At the end of October 1944 Dalton persuaded Morrison to see Weizmann, who was most concerned about the rumour that partition was being discussed. In his letter to Morrison, Dalton noted with some glee that the Colonial Secretary, Stanley, 'paid me a special visit in order to deplore' the Labour Party Executive's statement on Palestine which the conference was to approve in December. Dalton continued cheerfully that with the Republican and Democratic parties in America favouring unlimited Jewish immigration into Palestine, with the Soviet Union now indifferent, 'the prospects of doing a good constructive job ... after the war, of doing the right thing by the Jews and of beginning a real economic revival of the whole stagnant Middle East seems pretty good'.[4]

So it was that when the Labour victory at the polls was announced on 26 July 1945, Zionist optimism was at its height and there was no disposition to compromise its maximalist demands. But this optimism overlooked or was ignorant of several factors already present in July which help to explain why the Labour Party in power proved less benign towards the Zionists than its conference resolutions suggested. First of all there was little public interest during the election in foreign and colonial matters, as Elizabeth Barker (1973) has commented; 'there was an urge to build a new life at home. Most people were uninterested in world roles or European roles'. The Labour Party's manifesto had barely mentioned colonial problems, and public interest was directed at reconstruction and the party's programme for building a better Britain. For most people in 1945 Palestine was a distant problem made more remote by the many difficulties nearer home. The destruction which had overtaken the Jews of Europe, having also engulfed its perpetrators, was seemingly a closed episode.[5]

The public, then, was uninterested in Zionist aspirations. Another blow for these was the way Ministerial offices were dealt out, for here too the Zionists had a very weak hand. Morrison became Lord President and Leader of the Commons and, although the Palestine Committee which he chaired continued to function in 1945, its existence soon became peripheral and Morrison was to have no direct bearing on Palestine policy. In any case his wartime labours on the problem had produced a scheme of partition, the very principle of which was unacceptable to the Zionists in 1945, as well as to the Foreign Office and Chiefs of Staff whose opposition had helped to halt it. Crucially, though, Dalton went to the Treasury and Bevin to the Foreign Office, and this decision meant that the proponent of free immigration into Palestine and a Jewish state there was immediately and indefinitely concerned with other problems, not least of which were Britain's external liabilities of £3.3 million (in June), nearly a sevenfold increase from their level in 1939, and the abrupt termination of US lend–lease supplies which followed in August. Attlee made the decision to appoint Bevin Foreign Secretary mainly because he felt that he would stand up to the Russians better than Dalton, and because he felt that Dalton may not possess the right temperament for the Foreign Office. Moreover the King had asked Attlee, upon kissing hands, to think carefully about the appointment and suggested Bevin for the post. Another consideration was that, as Attlee put it, Bevin at the Treasury 'would have been certain to have got into controversy with Morrison' who had Home Affairs responsibilities, whereas at the Foreign Office Bevin would work in a separate sphere.[6]

Bevin had distinguished himself amongst Labour leaders on foreign affairs long before entering the Foreign Office, and the character of his distinction boded very differently for Zionism than the somewhat maverick attention which Dalton had attracted. At the same party conference that endorsed the pro-Zionist resolution, Bevin incurred considerable criticism by his stalwart defence of British policy in Greece. In December 1944 this had involved the use of British troops against the Communist faction. Not yet accustomed to thinking of enemies on the political left, the conference perceived Bevin as defending a Churchillian vendetta against 'freedom fighters' in furtherance of the Greek monarchy's rule. This episode served to mark Bevin out from the ranks of his colleagues, and, together with his record as a member of the War Cabinet, indicated clearly that he would not champion a socialist foreign policy but strive towards a bipartisan one. During the war he had taken a special interest in foreign affairs and struck up friendships with Eden and also with the Chief of the Imperial General Staff, Brooke, providing yet another indication that Bevin was unlikely to champion Zionist aspirations for free immigration and a state if these contravened the united views of the FO and COS. In the first debate on foreign affairs in the new Parliament the extent of common ground between the preceding and new governments on foreign policy was exhibited, Eden agreeing with Bevin that there had been no serious differences of opinion between them.[7]

Altogether there was little in Bevin's past record to indicate that in 1945 he would champion a radical solution to the Palestine problem or enthusiastically implement the party conference resolution, nor were there many grounds in reality for the Zionists to sustain their high hopes at the Labour victory, for the electorate was uninterested and Dalton and Morrison firmly confined to the weighty domestic issues.

The pressures of office

Having seen the strength and longevity of the views held by the Foreign Office and Chiefs of Staff on Palestine, the sanguine expectation of their continued virility despite the new Labour Government was not to be disappointed. Bevin was to be an able advocate, the more so because he never became the cipher of Whitehall's views, as perhaps his predecessor was, but provided leadership and added the impetus of new ideas without repudiating existing analyses or disillusioning their adherents.[8] The salient features of the policy discussion on Palestine during the summer and autumn of 1945 were: delay of long-term decisions, born not from malice but out of caution; the growing urgency for an interim policy made necessary by the imminent expiry of the immigration quota laid down by the White Paper; and the growing pressure from Truman, which we shall consider first.

Notwithstanding the State Department's recommendations, mentioned before, that the President should keep a low profile on the Palestine question at Potsdam, Truman took the opportunity to raise the subject in quite pressing terms. In a memorandum to Churchill on 24 July Truman pointed out the interest of Americans in the matter and continued:

I venture to express to you the hope that the British Government may find

it possible without delay to take steps to lift the restrictions of the White
Paper on Jewish immigration into Palestine.

 ... I hope ... that you can arrange at your earliest convenience to let me
have your ideas on the settlement of the Palestine problem, so that we can
at a later but not too distant date discuss the problem in concrete terms.

Two days later the election result was known, Churchill resigned and
it fell to Attlee to reply with an acknowledgement and the promise to
'give early and careful consideration' to the matter. As far as the US
Government was concerned nothing more happened, and on 16
August Truman followed up his initiative by saying at a press
conference that he wanted as many Jews as possible to enter Palestine
as was consistent with peace, a diplomatic settlement involving
Britain and the Arabs, and not having to send American soldiers to
the country. Pressure on the issue of Jewish Displaced Persons and
immigration into Palestine continued to mount in August following
the Harrison Report, which had been highly critical of the way Jewish
survivors were being treated in Europe; a preliminary version of the
Report had forced Eisenhower to begin to set up separate camps for
the Jewish DPs in the US zone. On 31 August Truman sent Attlee a
copy of the Report and in his letter the President drew special
attention to Harrison's recommendation that 100,000 immigration
certificates be granted to allow refugees to go to Palestine, adding that
he believed 'no other single matter is so important for those who have
known the horrors of concentration camps for over a decade as is the
future of immigration possibilities to Palestine'. Attlee did not receive
Truman's letter until Byrnes handed it to him on 10 September, but
before he could reply the American press featured a story from the
Jewish Telegraphic Agency that Truman had told Senator Gillette of
his pressure on the Prime Minister to allow more Jews to enter
Palestine. The next day, 14 September, Bevin warned Byrnes that
Truman's projected statement on the Harrison Report would harm
Anglo-American relations, and Attlee wrote to Truman endorsing
this view. On 16 September Attlee replied to Truman's letter
concerning the Harrison Report, warning that if arrangements were
made in Germany to place 'the Jews in a special racial category at the
head of the queue' the result may be serious for them. Attlee felt that it
was better to treat all DPs alike. As for Palestine, he warned, 'we have
the Arabs to consider as well', and had promised to consult them,
while the Jews were not availing themselves of the existing
immigration quota in the hope of bringing about the collapse of the
White Paper and the entry of 100,000 Jews into Palestine. Moreover,

the Prime Minister pointed out, the Muslims of India had to be taken into account. Attlee concluded that the Harrison Report raised many complications for the long term policy, but stated that this policy would be referred to the UN as soon as possible. Meanwhile, he added, an interim policy on immigration was being formulated. Replying the next day, Truman promised to take no further action before Byrnes' return.[9]

What were Truman's motives for waging such a campaign? Certainly it made a dramatic contrast with Roosevelt's softly softly approach. It seems that Truman's first motive was a humanitarian one, in which he reflected the sympathies of many Americans for the victims and survivors of the holocaust. The revelations that accompanied the liberation of the concentration camps and the public realization of the scale of Hitler's genocide made a powerful impression — not least upon the new President who had been excluded by his predecessor from the confidences of office. The uninitiated were shocked at the Jewish tragedy, which is reflected in Truman's commissioning of the Harrison mission and subsequently in the emphasis placed in his messages to Churchill and Attlee upon the issue of Jewish immigration and the hopes of the survivors, rather than upon the Palestine question *per se*. Furthermore Truman's memoirs, written it is true some years later, reflect this humanitarian concern and sympathy, and note with disdain that the State Department officials 'didn't care enough about what happened to the thousands of displaced persons'. Truman was sustained in his campaign by public sympathy for the Jewish plight, sympathy which for instance led 59 per cent of respondents to an opinion poll to say that they favoured the establishment of a Jewish state in Palestine in May 1945. Additionally there was Zionist pressure on Truman as soon as he was in the White House, Wise leading an American Zionist Emergency Committee delegation to meet him there on 20 April. This pressure continued: for instance, on 2 July, fifty-four Senators and 250 Congressmen wrote to Truman urging free immigration into Palestine and the establishment there of a Jewish commonwealth. Truman also received encourage-ment from Samuel Rosenman, an adviser in the White House, who wrote to the President about his proposed statement in September:

> ... I do not think that opening the doors of Palestine is in any sense an act which is a 'move hostile to the Arab people'. Nor does it in my opinion contravene the conversation of President Roosevelt [with Ibn Saud?].[10]

The distinction Truman made between the humanitarian issue of Jewish DPs and the political issue of the future of Palestine was quite lost on the British Government who continued, as in the past, to see immigration as central to the Palestine problem. Truman felt, however, that the future of Palestine was a matter with which the United Nations Organization was designed to cope, but that the plight of the DPs and the immigration issue was a more immediate problem. Truman may have been encouraged to make this delicate distinction as a result of the Zionist drift towards extremism evidenced during the summer of 1945. He had never shown himself to be a champion of the aspirations of political Zionism, refusing to support the Congressional resolution in 1944 in deference to Roosevelt's wishes, but by giving support to the idea of the 100,000 immigrants, while leaving aside the question of Palestine's ultimate future, Truman was helping the moderate elements in the Zionist movement, epitomized by Weizmann and Wise and the broad humanitarian support they had, towards a modest goal. Truman was not giving support to the full-blooded and rather extreme demands that Silver and Ben Gurion had spear-headed at the London Zionist Conference in August, that demanded not only the Biltmore Program but also a Jewish state in an 'undivided and undiminished' Palestine. The US Ambassador in London reported to the Secretary of State on 8 July that Weizmann 'is tired and ill and completely discouraged because of the tragedies that have befallen his people but he is also aware that a more militant policy would undoubtedly follow his retirement'.[11] Truman's campaign for Jewish immigration was an attempt, therefore, to forestall the Zionist movement's fall into extremist hands.

It is important to notice that Truman was pursuing his own policy at this time, for since the President's initiative at Potsdam the State Department was left emitting a soft undercurrent of sound without discernible effect. Reactions from the Arab states to Truman's press comments in mid-August were reported by the Department, which did its best to play down their significance, even to the extent of instructing the Consul-General in Jerusalem and posts in Cairo, Baghdad, Jedda, Beirut and Damascus that to

any enquiries regarding this statement [by the President] you may ... state that the foregoing [summary] represents your understanding of the President's remarks. You should not unless otherwise instructed attempt to comment on these remarks or interpret them in any way.

On the same day that Truman wrote to Attlee endorsing Harrison's recommendation on the 100,000, Henderson (Director of the Office of

Near Eastern and African Affairs) sent Byrnes a memorandum by Merriam (Chief of the Division of Near Eastern Affairs) which summarized the Division's conclusions from a paper prepared by Yale that 'the United States should refrain from supporting a policy of large-scale immigration into Palestine' during the period before the UN revised the Mandate agreement. Merriam's Division knew nothing of Truman's communication to Attlee, as Merriam noted to Henderson later. Allen, Henderson's deputy, wrote to his chief in September:

> It seems apparent to me that the President (and perhaps Mr. Byrnes as well) have decided to have a go at Palestine negotiations without bringing NEA into the picture.
> ... on balance I'm inclined to recommend that we stand by for the moment ... we have already given Mr. Byrnes our fully considered recommendations on Palestine. I see nothing further we can appropriately do for the moment except carry on our current work, answering letters and telegrams ... as best we can, pending the time (which will come soon) when the whole thing will be dumped back in our laps.

The Division made vigorous representations through the usual channels, Henderson warning Acting Secretary of State Acheson on 1 October of his deep concern at the reports of Truman's pressure for 100,000 immigrants and the effect these were having on US standing with the Arabs. Acheson conveyed these views to the President with a reminder of past US pledges to the Arabs of consultations before a change in the basic situation. Acheson's memoirs record that Truman was personally in charge of Palestine policy in the autumn of 1945, and the President's sceptical views on those he called 'the "striped pants boys" in the State Department' ensured that the opinions of Henderson and his staff were taken very lightly by the new tenant of the White House.[12]

In pressing the new Labour Government in this way Truman had no reason to think that he was advocating anything different from the party's intentions, which had been expressed in opposition. But there was a strong element of continuity of attitudes and policies in London despite the change of government, and chief amongst the old retainers was the Foreign Office. Having solicited the views of the Middle Eastern representatives on the various options open to the government, a Foreign Office appreciation of the position was written by Baxter on 11 July, probably with an eye to the new administration. Of partition Baxter noted 'the existence of a Jewish State would provide a source of conflict which would inevitably continue to have a deplorable effect on Anglo-Arab relations', while Grigg's scheme may provoke less opposition, but the claims of the USA to assist in deciding the level of immigration may cause complications and be challenged by France and the USSR. The long-term settlement made necessary by the San Francisco Charter could not be rushed without provoking criticism, and for the interim Baxter showed some preference for continuing the present immigration quota following consultations with and the acquiescence of the Arab States. As with the State Department's analysis, Baxter saw the preservation of Britain's interests as being dependent on Arab goodwill, but he was painfully aware that the best way of keeping this was to adhere strictly to the White Paper and terminate immigration when the quota was full, a course which was 'most dangerous from the point of view of its possible effect on American opinion'. Beeley's minutes indicate the same concern for Arab goodwill, and he wrote at the end of August that the Arabs had to be convinced of the finality of any further immigration; the White Paper had promised a total of 75,000 immigrants, and another final 100,000 'would not be believed'. Truman's pressure on the subject served only to sharpen the anxiety felt in the FO about retaining Arab goodwill, Sir Walter Smart at the Cairo embassy reporting at the end of August that Truman's recent pronouncement had

> forced the pace here ... we should impress on the United States Government that, unless they are careful, they will start a fire here which we shall have to put out at considerable sacrifice to ourselves.[13]

There was nothing new in the way the Foreign Office perceived the Palestine problem, and had Truman been aware of these attitudes he would have felt the same way about them as he did about the State Department's analysis which seemed to him to disregard the holocaust, the European plight of the Jewish survivors, and to be obsessed with Palestine as the central issue in the Middle East.

Bevin was now responsible for this department, and there is no evidence that he challenged or repudiated the Foreign Office view of the Middle East. Dalton wryly records Bruce Lockhart's tale told some seven months after Bevin had taken up his post of how he had failed to live up to expectations that he would 'clear out all "the old gang"' at the Foreign Office. Cadogan and Sargent (the Permanent Undersecretary and his Deputy) had 'both thought they were out' but Bevin had not known by whom to replace them, and soon became 'devoted' and 'indoctrinated'. With the benefit of hindsight, this tale is wide of the mark. Generally, Bevin got on well with his officials, gaining their loyalty and respect, but he remained the leader of the department and not merely its mouthpiece, and he usually got his way in Cabinet. The Middle East provides an early example of the type of leadership Bevin gave to the Foreign Office. In August the Cabinet approved his suggestion of summoning His Majesty's representatives in the Middle East to a conference to discuss regional policy, and the result of this meeting was presented to the Cabinet in September and approved in October. Crucially Bevin's initiative and the Cabinet paper stressed the need for economic and social development in the Middle East to 'broaden the base on which British influence rests', promoting a partnership between Britain and the region on economic and defence matters. Bevin's suggestion to the conference also pointed out that: 'To reach the right solution of our Middle East problems it was necessary to consider the area as a single region'. This included the Palestine question, so Bevin's views were in harmony with the department's outlook here. Indeed there was little in Bevin's previous record to suggest that he might take issue with the Foreign Office or the Chiefs of Staff over Palestine and proceed forthwith to jettison the White Paper. Bevin in fact linked the importance of Middle Eastern oil to global power, which in turn, he perceived as the necessary accoutrements of a welfare state. His speech on foreign affairs at the party conference in May 1945 reflected this:

> You will have to form a government which is at the centre of a great Empire and Commonwealth ... and which will have to deal ... with every race ... Revolutions do not change geography, and revolutions do not change geographical need.

Bevin led the Labour Party's adoption of the strategic thesis of Whitehall, a path which was made easier by a reaction against Lansbury's prewar pacifism. Bevin's attitude and strength of mind made him very much the leader of the Foreign Office, bringing in new ideas but without overturning established views. His great achievement while in office of tying the USA to Europe, militarily and economically, and forcing her to take up world burdens which Britain could no longer carry, bear witness to the vigour and skill of the Labour Foreign Secretary. But of Zionist aspirations Bevin had no past experience and he tended, like Attlee, to regard the Jews as a religious group only, thereby underestimating the influence of the holocaust and the strength and messianic quality of the Zionist movement.[14]

The view taken by the Colonial and Foreign Offices of the European DP and immigration questions did not encourage Bevin to change his attitude towards Zionism. In January 1945, the Director of the Intergovernmental Committee on Refugees, H. W. Emerson, estimated that some 18,000 Jews were likely to want to leave Europe for Palestine after the war because 'first, … Palestine has never made a particularly strong appeal to Austrian and German Jews, and second, a large number of those to whom it did make a strong appeal have gone there since 1933'. Emerson suggested that Jewish DPs could be dealt with by repatriation, absorption into a new refuge or by individual emigration to various countries. There may be pressure to leave Poland, Rumania and Hungary, but the majority of Jews wanted 'to remain in those countries and to resume their former callings'. Eastwood, who superintended the issue of Jewish resettlement at the Colonial Office, was surprised at Emerson's estimates and commented, 'Personally, I feel sure that the Zionist urge will be a real and continuing one at least for some years'. However, Eastwood's feelings were not commonplace in Whitehall. Kirkbride (the British Resident in Amman) related that Shertok and Ben Gurion had shown some consternation about the view expressed by an American Jew that people in his place would not emigrate to Palestine, and Weizmann had reacted with 'Oh, we will get immigrants from somewhere to make up the numbers'. When Gort reported this, Wikeley of the FO's Eastern Department, who had responsibility for Palestine and Transjordan, failed to mention the possibility that large-scale emigration from Europe would supply the numbers. He minuted simply, 'There appears to be considerable doubt as to whether Jews will come forward for immigration in sufficient numbers to implement the Zionist plans'. In July 1945, the Cabinet discussion on a Report of the Committee on the Reception and Accommodation of Refugees merely reflected the feeling that a 'hard core' of refugees may prove to be non-repatriable. A few days later, when Truman wrote to Churchill about lifting the immigration restrictions into Palestine, Beeley minuted that there may be an advantage in temporizing; time may weaken the Zionists' argument that Palestine is 'their only hope of survival'. Generally, then, there seems to have been no idea of how intractable the problem of postwar Jewish DPs was to become, and there was a conspicuous failure to grasp the attraction of Zionism for the survivors of the holocaust and the prospect it afforded of realizing the old prayer, 'next year in

Jerusalem'. As a result there was nothing to challenge the conception held by Bevin and Attlee of the Jews as merely a religious group and of Zionism as something of a deception and mirage to the Labour Party. Accordingly, at the beginning of September the new Colonial Secretary, George Hall, presented his department's submission to the Cabinet Committee on Palestine which included an assessment of immigration that played down the size and difficulty of the problem. The Soviet Union, the paper argued, posed obstacles for emigrants, and the Histadruth (the Jewish Trade Union Confederation in Palestine) was already nervous about unemployment in Palestine during the postwar slump, aware that an 'excessive inflow of immigrants would ... enormously complicate the problems' and lower the living standards of its members. Events were to prove all these assessments wrong; the new Polish government and the Soviet Union were to encourage Jews to leave by issuing exit-only passports, and although in the autumn of 1945 the Jews comprised some 1 per cent of the total of 10,500,000 DPs, by 1947 the proportion had risen to 20 per cent as other refugee problems were solved.[15]

The most important factor in delaying progress on Palestine policy, certainly on long-term policy, during the summer and autumn of 1945 was not the hostility of the Foreign Office to the partition plan, which was by then practially defunct, nor the assessment of future immigration pressure. As had happened during the last year of the Coalition Government, it was the Chiefs of Staff who were the pacemakers of British policy for Palestine, and the pace they set was cautious and shot through with foreboding. We have seen how the COS viewed the Palestine problem earlier in 1945, warning the Cabinet in January that as the security forces would be below strength for between nine and twelve months after the end of the war, no destabilizing policy should be followed. Despite the conclusion of the Japanese war this view was repeated at the end of August in a paper submitted to the Colonial Office which examined the five policy options available. The COS felt that partition would cause serious trouble as far afield as India, that Grigg's scheme may provoke Arab and certainly extremist Jewish opposition, while the short-term option to end immigration when the White Paper quota expired would provoke the most intense Jewish reaction. The Chiefs of Staff argued that 'the most expedient' course was to permit continued Jewish immigration by extending the quota, preferably following consultations with or at lest notice to the Arab states. Whatever course was chosen reinforcements of between two and four divisions would be needed, and partition would impose the heaviest burden. By the end of 1945 the level of reinforcements would allow the lightest commitment to be met and internal security maintained when immigration was halted in accordance with the White Paper. By the spring of 1946 the military would be able to cope with anything, except partition. Brooke, Portal and Cunningham concluded that, 'From a military point of view, an announcement on Palestine at the present time would be most embarrassing, in view of our many occupational commitments.' Any announcement made before the end of September would be too early for reinforcements to arrive. The Commander in Chief of Middle Eastern Land Forces, General Paget, was even more explicit. He told the COS a few days later that the adoption of a interim immigration policy would make it 'desirable to put off a decision on the longer term policy almost indefinitely'.[16]

Something akin to a moratorium on Palestine policy resulted from this appreciation by the Chiefs of Staff, evident in a paper the Secretary of State for War had circulated to the Cabinet in April. Following the Prime Minister's efforts to redeploy Middle Eastern manpower, the War Secretary told the Cabinet that:

> After consultation with the Chiefs of Staff I informed the Prime Minister that I was prepared to accept these implications [that the level of forces would be well below that required for internal security in the Middle East] on the understanding that everything possible should be done to ensure that relations between His Majesty's Government and the local Governments ... remain friendly. In particular it is essential that: In Palestine our policy is not such as to lead to armed rebellion.[17]

The Prime Minister approved the proposal. The result of the COS's caution towards Palestine was to remain in evidence in September and October.

On 6 September the Cabinet Committee on Palestine met again in reconstituted form under Morrison's chairmanship, and the Labour Government's consideration of policy began in earnest. The submission by the Colonial Office was notable for its retreat from partition, and having observed that the Arabs and Jews were irreconcilable, Hall's paper now expounded an alternative to partition, a scheme of local autonomy for Arab and Jewish provinces with the overseeing Mandatory authority also controlling Jerusalem. The National Home could develop in a Jewish province containing 451,000 Jews and 301,000 Arabs. The Committee's meeting accepted without demur the division between interim and long-term policy which Grigg had mentioned in March and which the Colonial Office had once been anxious to prevent. But now Hall told the Committee:

> The immediate essential was to reach a decision on the short-term policy. Once that had been done the long-term policy could be examined at greater leisure.

The new Colonial Secretary was clear about the expiry of the White Paper's immigration quota in November, and he unequivocally recommended adhering to, or as Bevin put it 'extending', the present level of 1,500 per month beyond the total limit, pending the formulation of long-term policy. He hoped that the Jews would accept this recommendation for the time being, and that the Arabs would acquiesce, but he noted: 'The attitude of the Arab States was likely to be of decisive importance'. Hall did not explain that the Mandatory's policy was subject to the approval of the neighbouring states because their involvement during the 1930s had established the precedent; he was, however, following in that tradition.

Bevin echoed Hall's remarks about the more leisurely consideration of long-term policy and the involvement of the Arab states. Crucially the Foreign Secretary believed that time was on the side of the British Government and that immigration pressure would wane quickly, and the minutes record that he argued

> that in his judgment pressure on immigration was likely to decline as the months went by and the resettlement of Europe progressed. ... But this year was our saving grace. The important thing therefore was to find an interim solution.

Here we see not only Bevin's lack of understanding of the power and appeal of the Zionist movement, but also a reflection of the commonplace appreciation in the CO and FO that the immigration pressure on Palestine would soon dissipate. Bevin perceived that 'the solution to the Palestine problem was the key to many of the problems of the Middle East' and as a result of viewing the issue centrally in this way the involvement of the Arab states in the affairs of Palestine was allowed to proceed unchallenged. But Bevin's contribution to the Committee's discussion typically went beyond the established arguments by putting forward new ideas. As a rival to the Colonial Secretary's provincial autonomy scheme Bevin suggested that a federal solution should be examined; the plan comprised the three states of Transjordan, a Palestine Arab and a Jewish state, and it was hoped this package would find more favour in the USA as well as being more economically viable. But of greater significance for the future was Bevin's forthright view that, 'We must not overlook the crucial importance of the United States ... and, certainly so far as the long-term policy was concerned, it should be our aim definitely to associate the United States with it beyond any question.' Hall agreed with Bevin on this point, but was more in favour than Bevin of bringing in the United Nations on long-term policy as well.

Dalton made a brief and flamboyant contribution to the discussion, remarking that he felt it was hard that Jewish resettlement, after all their sufferings and achievement, 'should be held up merely by the intransigence of a backward local population'. However, he also recognized 'the need for taking account of Arab feerling and the importance of avoiding serious civil outbreaks'. It seems that Dalton was now well versed in the views of the Foreign Office, the Chiefs of Staff and the Middle East commanders on the likelihood of civil disturbances, and he had tempered his Zionist sympathies since joining the Labour Cabinet; certainly he did not press them on Bevin now. Morrison also sounded resigned, commenting wistfully on the earlier failure to forward the Coalition's policy of partition. Now he mentioned the 'need to give due weight to the advice of our diplomatic representatives in the Middle Eastern area' and to weigh 'very important Imperial strategical considerations', concerns which under his earlier chairmanship the Committee had worried about rather less.

Overall the meeting passed off with agreement that in the short term the current immigration quota should be continued, and in connection with this announcement Hall drew attention to the security situation in Palestine as the COS viewed it and 'trusted that every effort would be made to expedite the despatch of the troops necessary to meet this commitment'. For the long term, the attitude was much less rushed, and the Committee agreed that Bevin and Hall should consider and report on the question of involving the United Nations.[18]

On 8 September Morrison submitted the Committee's recommendations to the Cabinet, stressing the importance of consulting both the Palestine Arabs and the Arab states before making an announcement about continuing the immigration quota. The mechanism of the Arab League meeting would, it was argued, prevent the Palestine Arabs from voicing their views independently of the other states which were all represented at the League. Two days later Hall submitted a paper drawing attention to the rising tension in Palestine and the urgent need for reinforcements. The Cabinet met the next day and generally approved the Committee's recommendations, and Attlee suggested that before any final decision was made Morrison, Bevin, Hall and he should consider the timing of an announcement while the Chiefs of Staff again examined the security aspects. During the next few weeks the sense of urgency increased. Hall submitted a draft Cabinet paper to Bevin on short-term policy on 14 September, and his analysis made plain the importance of the COS appreciation of the situation; once the Arabs were consulted about extending the quota, Hall argued, 'the military commitment foreseen may mature at any moment. The forces necessary to meet it will not, however, be in the Middle East before about the end of October'. Furthermore the British representatives in the region urged that the consultations with the Arabs await the end of the Mecca pilgrimage and the dispersion of the faithful. But on the other hand parliamentary pressure and the growing threat to security in Palestine made an early announcement desirable, and accordingly Hall recommended speeding up the despatch of the reinforcements so that military arrangements could permit the go-ahead by mid-October. In marked contrast with the interdepartmental wrangling between Stanley and Eden, Bevin agreed with his colleague's paper. On 19 September Hall sent Attlee a memorandum informing him of the views agreed between himself, Morrison and Bevin, and now also with the Middle Eastern representatives, in favour of an early annoncement, the date of which 'will depend solely on the date by which the forces necessary to maintain order and to quell possible disturbances in Palestine can reach the Middle East.' Hall recommended the immediate acceleration of this deployment. As it was finally submitted to the Cabinet on 28 September Hall's paper made the same recommendations as the earlier draft but couched them in more urgent and pressing terms. Two days later the COS were able to inform the Cabinet that General Paget felt that 23 October was the earliest possible date for a policy announcement, although full reinforcements would not be deployed until the end of the month. The Cabinet considered the 23 October date on 4 October when Attlee informed his colleagues that once Parliament had reassembled the pressure for a statement would mean that an announcement could not be delayed beyond the week beginning 15 October. As it happened no announcement was made until 13 November when Bevin also informed the House of the creation of an Anglo-American Committee of Enquiry to examine long-term policy, while in the interim the Arabs would be consulted to try to arrange continued immigration of 1,500 per month. The delay had been necessitated by the protracted negotiations over the Committee's terms of reference, and it was found to be possible to delay the announcement on interim immigration as well because the existing White Paper quota lasted longer than was originally anticipated.[19]

The Foreign Office applied itself to obtaining Arab acquiescence to continued Jewish immigration. As early as 21 September, Grafftey-Smith in Jedda had been instructed to intimate to King Ibn Saud that as the British Government would be in touch about Palestine quite soon it would be inadvisable for the Arab states to issue any pre-emptive condemnation of Zionism, and the King took the hint. At the end of November indications that the Arab League meeting would reject the continuation of the quota were answered firmly through diplomatic channels in Cairo. The Arab League's eventual reply to the British Government was artfully phrased, alluding to Zionist pressure in Britain and America behind both continued immigration and the idea of the Committee of Enquiry: 'If it is so it is the more reason for refusal to consent to a new immigration than to accept it.' However, outright rejection of continued immigration was avoided, and Killearn reported that the Secretary General of the Arab League (Azzam Pasha) 'states that he was asked by the Council of the Arab League to explain orally in handing over the note ... that the Council does not consider this note to be an outright rejection of your proposal.'[20]

So it was that the party, that had resolved at its conference in December 1944 to let Jews enter Palestine in sufficient numbers to become a majority, achieved a year later and after five months in office the continuation of the quota permitted by the White Paper it despised. We have tried to suggest why the commonplace phenomenon of a party saying one thing in opposition and doing differently in office operated in this instance. After all, the main proponents of the Zionist case in the Labour Party were not involved in foreign policy, Dalton going to the Exchequer and Morrison being concerned with home affairs, while the Committee which Morrison chaired on Palestine existed under the Labour Government for two meetings only, in September and on 10 October, after which it faded away. Moreover, Bevin's own experience and outlook led him to feel that Zionism was something of a charade and that the Jews were merely a religious group, a point of view which the Prime Minister shared. In addition, Bevin was the last person likely to challenge head-on the views of the Foreign Office and COS on Palestine, for he shared their perception of the centrality of Palestine for Britain's Middle Eastern position, adding to the strategic interest in bases and oil the rationale of competing with the USA economically and supporting the welfare state at home. The powerful but mistaken views of the Foreign and Colonial Offices on the trend of postwar immigration to Palestine, the entrenched attitude of the FO and COS on the dire consequences of partition, and the COS inspired timescale of reinforcement require- ments needed prior to any policy announcement, together made for a powerful element of continuity in policy and served to confirm Bevin in his views of the Palestine question while not deterring him from adding fresh ideas. However the continued currency of the Foreign Office analysis was in time to prove overwhelming and decisive.

The genesis of an Anglo-American enquiry

Meanwhile there was another side to the coin: the Labour Govern- ment's initiative in setting up an Anglo-American Committee of Enquiry to consider the whole problem of Palestine and the DPs over the long term. We have seen the pressure that Truman brought to bear on the British Government during the summer and autumn of 1945 over the immigration issue, which provided one of the main reasons for trying to involve the USA in the formulation of policy and thereby ensuring that the US Government was tarred with the same brush as Britain. At the Cabinet Committee's meeting in early September, Bevin had forcefully suggested that the USA should be associated with the long-term policy, following it up in Cabinet on 4 October.

When Palestine was considered at the 4 October meeting, Attlee began by pointing out the 'marked increase' in US agitation. On 29 September the White House had made the Harrison Report public. Bevin now made his suggestion that he and the Colonial Secretary should submit new proposals to the Cabinet:

> The long-term problem should, of course, be referred to the United Nations Organisation, but His Majesty's Government must do more than suggest a reference to the United Nations Organisation if they were to avoid the criticism that they were evading the urgent issues. What he had in mind was a solution based on the immediate establishment of an Anglo-American Commission ... .

Bevin suggested that the terms of reference should be to examine ways of ameliorating the position of the Jews in Europe, and to examine 'the possibility of relieving the position in Europe by immigration into other countries, including the United States and the Dominions'. The process would be through consultations with Arabs and Jews, and a submission to the sponsoring governments with the aim of making recommendations to the UNO. The order of the terms of reference is significant: the Palestine issue was deliberately placed second to the European DP problem and made independent of the question of Jewish settlement in other countries as a riposte to the Harrison Report and Truman's pressure which, much to the annoyance of Bevin and the Foreign Office, connected the Jewish plight in Europe directly to the issue of letting 100,000 Jews enter Palestine. The Palestine Committee of the Cabinet met to consider Bevin's suggestion and reported to the Cabinet on 10 October. Its conclusions completely supported Bevin's wish to involve the USA in the problems of Jewish DPs and Palestine. The White Paper was not regarded as a permanent solution. The British Government would submit a new policy and trusteeship agreement to the UNO which

> will naturally depend largely on the recommendations of the [Anglo-American] Committee ... and the United States will thus be placed in the position of sharing the responsibility for the policy which she advocates. She will no longer be able to play the part of irresponsible critic.[21]

The Cabinet considered the matter the next day. The Committee had revised the terms of reference and avoided any reference to Palestine: the Anglo-American Enquiry was to examine the position of the Jews in Europe, estimate the number who were non-repatriable, examine the possibility of relief through immigration 'into other countries outside Europe including the United States', and consider ways of meeting the immediate situation. In discussion Bevin again stressed that 'it was essential to take steps to allay the agitation in the United States which was poisoning our relations'. His conception of immigration pressures and Zionism was also apparent: 'He did not accept the view that none of the Jews now in Europe could ever find a permanent home there'. Bevin also suggested that the USA could help by taking some emigrants herself. Attlee wrapped up the discussion in a business-like way, concluding that there was 'general support' for the proposed Enquiry. The Cabinet approved the Committee's report in principle and agreed that the US Government should be invited to join the Enquiry. Attlee felt that despite the pressures the public announcement of Britain's new policy could now be delayed until the week beginning 21 October. However, it proved harder to land the fish and the drawn out negotiations with the US Government delayed the announcement.[22]

Before considering these negotiations we must pause to assess the motives behind and the significance of Bevin's proposal for the Anglo-American Committee of Enquiry. It was very much Bevin's own brainchild to involve the US in this way, and it is clear from his comments and the attitude of the Prime Minister and the Colonial Secretary that the US Goverment's pressure was felt and keenly resented as being irresponsible. The mechanism of a joint enquiry was perceived to be a skilful, apt response. The proposal also fitted well into the broader context of Bevin's foreign policy as it emerged, since US involvement and close Anglo-American co-operation were the hallmarks of his tenure of office. It should be remembered that Bevin's proposal did not break entirely new ground, for Butler had put forward various schemes for involving the US on Palestine earlier in 1945, and Churchill had suggested offering the Mandate to her; the common motivation was the prospect of lowering the profile which Britain offered to her critics.

Bevin's remark in Cabinet on 11 October about America helping by taking more immigrants herself, and indeed the revised terms of reference approved by the Cabinet, betray considerable anger at the US Goverment not simply for her apparent hypocrisy in urging the Jewish DPs to go to Britain's mandated Palestine while refusing to accept more than a few herself, but because it was felt that Truman's pressure over the 100,000 contravened the accord reached between Britain and the United States at Bermuda. Truman appeared to be reneging on the understanding, mentioned before, that the US would not press Britain over the immigration quota for Palestine and Britain would not press the United States Government on her immigration policy. Accordingly, Truman's representations, when they came, were quite a shock and were answered by the British Government's prompt abandonment of its side of the deal as reflected in the proposed terms of reference for the enquiry. A partial result came in December when Truman announced arrangements to expedite the admission of all categories of Displaced Persons within the existing law, but deeper changes in US policy came very slowly and left the British and American governments in deadlock on the question of Jewish immigration.[23]

Bevin seems to have suggested the Committee of Enquiry for another reason; to postpone the submission of the problem to the United Nations. In the Cabinet Committee meeting on 6 September Hall had shown himself more eager to bring in the UN over long-term policy than Bevin, who saw this question as a difficult one. He would himself have been very ready to take the line [in public] that we proposed to extend the White Paper policy pending further examination of the issue as a whole, and to say nothing about the World Organisation.

The Cabinet meeting on 11 September showed in discussion and in Attlee's view that an announcement which showed the intention to submit the issue to the UN was well supported, and it was contended that the preparation of their respective cases would quieten Arab anger and divert the Jews from the bout of terrorism which had begun in October. On 28 September Hall circulated his paper, with Bevin's and Morrison's agreement, recommending the earliest possible announcement about continued immigration; on the subject of long-term policy he listed six current schemes and suggested that the Cabinet Committee make recommendations on them for submission to the UN 'with a view to a Trusteeship Agreement being approved'.[24] Now by suggesting and getting accepted the idea of an Anglo-American enquiry, Bevin not only cut out Morrison's Committee from the immediate deliberations on policy — no doubt he preferred the Americans to Morrison — but he postponed the involvement of the UN as well. His statement to the House of Commons on 13 November explained that the British Government would prepare a solution for submission to the UN after receiving the Anglo-American Committee's report.

Bevin's action cannot be explained solely in terms of his dislike for Morrison and distaste for the UN as a forum. Silencing US Government criticism was more important. There may have been another motive, which can be seen in the reception given to Bevin's scheme in the Air Ministry. The strategic thinking of the Chiefs of Staff on the importance of the Middle East in general and Palestine in particular had not altered since the statement to the Cabinet in January 1944, and it was to be reaffirmed in the Defence Committee in the spring of 1946 when Bevin lent it his support; in due course this attitude was to show itself in a reluctance to involve the UNO in Palestine because of the effect such involvement would have on the country's strategic value. Hence there was a strategic rationale for delaying the referral to the UN. But for the more immediate future also there was concern to delay the pace on Palestine, and in an Air Ministry brief prepared for the Secretary of State and the Chief of the Air Staff on the Cabinet paper which proposed an Anglo-American enquiry, this objective was made clear at the beginning:

The chief *military* consideration is that an outburst over Palestine should not occur until some of our other military commitments have been liquidated. The proposal for a full enquiry into the Jewish problem will make for delay, and is therefore satisfactory.

The brief suggested that the simultaneous announcement of interim immigration and the long-term enquiry should be made so that the Arabs could see from the terms of reference 'that both we and the U.S.A. regard the Jewish problem as quite separate from the Palestine problem'. Bevin's initiative, therefore, suited the military view for tactical reasons by imposing further delay, and also because the terms of reference provided a mechanism for calming Arab sensibilities and retaining Arab goodwill. There is nothing in the files to suggest that helping the COS was a positive consideration behind Bevin's initiative. However, although the evidence is inconclusive, in view of Bevin's sympathies for the Foreign Office view of the Arab world, his support for the COS's strategic aims and his remarks in the Cabinet Committee on the merits of allowing time to dissipate the pressure of immigration, it seems reasonable to assume that Bevin had an interest in delaying the formulation of long-term policy and its submission to the UN for reasons which overlapped with those expressed in the Air Ministry.[25]

The attitude of the Foreign Office to their chief's proposals is illuminating and shows that the Anglo-American enquiry was Bevin's own idea and came unprompted by his department, where it created some confusion. The day after Bevin made his suggestion in Cabinet and was invited to formulate a detailed scheme with Hall, a Note was prepared in the Eastern Department. The authorship of the incomplete typed copy in the file is not indicated, but Beeley's hand entitled it 'first draft' and noted that it was submitted to the Secretary of State on that day, while textual clarifications are made in what appears to be Baxter's writing. These marginalia suggest that Beeley and the Head of the Eastern Department were responsible for the Note's curious argument and its criticism of the Anglo-American enquiry notion:

> This proposal does not provide a substitute for the short-term policy which the Cabinet has previously decided to put into effect. Nor could it take the place of the trusteeship agreement for Palestine which will eventually have to be concluded.

The procedure for negotiating a trusteeship agreement involved well precedented talks with the 'states directly concerned', followed by a submission to the UN General Assembly. The argument continued disparagingly, 'The findings of an Anglo-American commission, while they might be fitted into his process and might play a part in determining the character of the trusteeship agreement, would not eliminate either of these stages.' At this point the writings of Baxter's superior, the superintending Undersecretary, Howe, remarks 'of course not' and goes on to mark the next passage which concedes that it would be possible for Bevin's proposal 'to be fitted into the process ... by being inserted between the adoption of the short-term policy and the negotiation of a trusteeship agreement'. However, the author considered that the proposal was open to 'insuperable' objections, such as giving the Arabs the impression of Britain yielding to US pressure, a construction which both Baxter and Beeley had previously warned against allowing. Furthermore the United States would not be made responsible for the policy recommended by the Committee. After a missing page the Note concluded with the sour suggestion, 'we do not feel that there is any alternative but to continue with the policy proposed by the Palestine Committee', which was for the continuation of the immigration quota while a submission was prepared for the UN. This response from the Eastern Department followed closely the opposition it had shown to Butler's suggestions, made earlier in the year, for involving the USA, and Beeley's response to Churchill's scheme for committing America to the Mandate, which had been put forward on 6 July. It was of no help to Bevin's aim of silencing US criticism while postponing the issue of long-term policy.[26]

Howe and the Permanent Secretary, Sir Orme Sargent, now rose to the occasion and the next day submitted an utterly different note 'on the next step to be taken in view of the Cabinet Conclusion of October 4th'. They argued for a 'fresh approach ... with the object of ensuring that the United States, who now criticize us irresponsibly, should assume a share of the responsibility for the settlement ... .' A graceful gloss was put upon the reasons for delaying the submission to the United Nations; 'we cannot afford to mark time while waiting for the United Nations Organization to come into operation'. In an accompanying minute Sargent wrote to Bevin that this note, prepared by Howe and himself, could be used 'if you think fit' in talks with Hall. It is significant that this briefing for the Secretary of State in support of his idea originated at this level in the Foreign Office, and that the Eastern Department maintained its record of wariness towards US involvement. There was an epilogue to the exchange. Bevin replied to Sargent with the suggestion of holding a conference with Arab and Jewish representatives concurrently with the Anglo-American Enquiry, and it was Sargent himself and not the Eastern Department who advised strongly against doing so because Britain may have problems over the selection of delegates and be blamed for the conference's collapse.[27] Perhaps the Permanent Undersecretary foresaw the future value of such a conference for bringing any American-inspired British policy back into line with Foreign Office thinking by orchestrating the Arab case, once his Secretary of State's initiative had run its course, and perhaps Sargent recalled how useful the St James's Conference had been early in 1939.

The idea of involving the USA in Palestine policy had been mooted in the Foreign Office, but the Eastern Department continued to regard it unfavourably, and the initiative for the Anglo-American Committee of Enquiry was Bevin's own. The British Government had been stung by Truman's pressure for the entry of the 100,000, especially since it followed Roosevelt's quiet approach and seemed to overturn the Bermuda accord, so the primary motivation for proposing the joint enquiry was to silence American criticism. The hope of separating the issue of the European DPs from the Palestine question was reflected in the terms of reference. The delay of long-term policy was also an important consideration for Bevin and those who felt that immigration pressures would abate, and for reasons of military strategy and tactics which preferred the indefinite postponement of UN involvement and the arrival of reinforcements prior to any trouble arising in Palestine. At the level of departmental and personal politics, Bevin's proposal effectively gathered to the Foreign Office the primary responsibility for Palestine because not only was Morrison's Committee placed in limbo but also the issue of Palestine was elevated to the sphere of Anglo-American diplomacy, thereby confining the Colonial Office to a merely supervisory and consultative role in the day-to-day administration of Palestine.

Wrangling over the terms of reference

When the Cabinet approved inviting the US Government to join the enquiry on 11 October, Attlee seemed to be contemplating their acceptance and an announcement being possible in about two weeks' time. The Americans proved to be considerably harder to persuade than the Cabinet expected, and the negotiations over the Committee's terms of reference reveal not only the respective concerns of the two governments and what each wanted from the enquiry, but also Britain's relatively weak bargaining position.

The United States had early warning of the possibility of her
involvement by Britain in Palestine, Hoskins reporting a conversation with Clayton (Assistant to the Minister Resident in the Middle
East) in Cairo at the end of July. Clayton felt that the adoption of an
Anglo-American policy on Palestine was the only basis for a final
solution, and that meanwhile Britain would be seeking US Government approval for a continuation of the immigration quota. Byrnes
sent Clayton's views to various diplomatic posts for their information, concluding that there was 'some likelihood' of a British
overture.[28]

On 12 October Halifax, the British ambassador in Washington,
was sent a long telegram which Bevin had apparently drafted
himself. Bevin spoke of the problems of the Middle East, and
became very bitter over Palestine:

> I feel that the United States have been thoroughly dishonest in handling
> this problem. To play on racial feelings for the purpose of winning an
> election is to make a farce of their insistence on free elections in other
> countries.

Bevin told Halifax that he refused to accept the notion that the Jews
of Europe had to emigrate and could never be repatriated, and that
the Harrison Report seemed to be 'a device to put pressure on
England'. Bevin warned that the promises to the Arabs could not be
ignored, while he feared that bringing in the United States might
allow the propaganda of New York to poison the matter further.[29]

Armed with this explicit background, Halifax submitted the
proposal for a joint enquiry to the US Government on 19 October.
The terms of reference proposed were those the Cabinet had
accepted from the Morrison Committee, avoiding any reference to
Palestine by name while focusing primarily upon the problem of the
Jewish DPs. The reference to considering immigration into the
United States was tactfully dropped. In the text of the invitation it
was disarmingly explained that, 'The question of Jewish immigration into Palestine, among other countries, would fall to be
considered by the Committee of Enquiry under the third of their
terms of reference.' The British Government felt that the Committee's recommendations 'would be of immense help' in formulating a
policy and a trusteeship agreement for submission to the UN.
Meanwhile it was hoped that both the enquiry and the interim
immigration policy could be announced in the Commons on 25
October.[30]

In presenting this proposal to Byrnes at the State Department, Halifax also outlined Bevin's thoughts on the whole matter in diplomatic language. Byrnes' response was cool, and his major concern at this stage seemed to be the proposed timing of the announcement: 'Quite frankly, I am thinking of the New York City election ... when this is submitted to the President he has to think about that.' Halifax reported back to the Foreign Office, warning that Truman would have to decide whether the announcement may help the Democratic against the Republican (and Jewish) Mayoral candidate or may appear 'dilatory' and do harm. After a subsequent interview with the President, Halifax felt that a delay in the announcement might be requested. The election was not due until 6 November.[31]

Halifax saw Byrnes again on 22 October when the Secretary of State conveyed the sense of pressure he was under from the New York election and Zionist interests. But he also felt that Truman's agreement would come more easily to the joint enquiry if the terms of reference mentioned Palestine, and Byrnes rightly guessed that the Harrison Report was behind the artful and bland reference to 'immigration into other countries outside Europe'. Byrnes wanted the Committee to be charged with investigating the Palestine problem rather than the issue of world Jewry. Halifax duly reported the difficulties to London. Two days later Byrnes sent Halifax new terms of reference. The Committee which the US was prepared to join was:

1. to examine the political, economic and social conditions in Palestine as they bear upon the problem of Jewish immigration and settlement therein and the well-being of the peoples now living therein.
2. to examine the position of the Jews in those countries in Europe where they have been the victims of Nazi and Fascist persecution ... and to make estimates of those who wish, or will be impelled by their conditions, to migrate to Palestine or other countries outside Europe.

Item 3 required the Committee to hear witnesses and to make recommendations on interim and permanent policies, and item 4 charged the Committee to make suggestions for remedial action inside Europe and about settlement outside Europe arising from their investigation under item 2. Plainly the intention of Truman's administration in joining an enquiry was very different from Bevin's, for the new terms not only began by focusing upon Palestine's capacity to fulfil modest Zionist ambitions but proceeded to link the European DP problem with the issue of immigration to Palestine, both of which the British Government had sought to avoid. Byrnes' memorandum rubbed in this point by finishing with the statement that Truman still adhered to the views he had expressed on 'the migration of Jews from Europe to Palestine'.[32]

Byrnes' reference to the President's position is probably indicative of the source of the American terms of reference, for there is no evidence in the State Department files to suggest the NEA Division's involvement in their drafting. The day before Byrnes sent his terms of reference to Halifax, Truman had received some categorical advice from Rosenman about the British proposal for a Committee of Enquiry:

> I think it is a complete run-out on the mandate, as on the Democratic platform. I certainly do not think that you ought to agree to it ... . Apart from any politics, the whole scheme ... is merely one of temporizing ... .

Rosenman added that the information which the enquiry was supposed to gather was available already, and he was highly critical of Britain's apparent indication 'that if one additional person is to get into Palestine that would effect the "basic situation" '.[33] This advice was not followed to the extent of repudiating the British overture, but it seems reasonable to suppose that it stiffened Truman's resolve and Byrnes' hand in making sure that the terms of reference addressed themselves directly to the Palestine question and avoided any suggestion that the US Goverment was becoming a party to a British stalling device. If Britain wanted US participation in an enquiry, it was to be on terms that the White House found politically acceptable, an attitude reflected not only in the terms Byrnes proposed to Halifax but also in the time limit which was later placed upon the enquiry's duration.

With Byrnes' counter-proposal of 24 October, Bevin's prospect of making an early announcement to the House had receded, and the hope was that an agreement with the US Government would allow a statement to be made early in November. On 25 October Halifax replied to Byrnes and began the process of haggling over the terms of reference. Gracefully accepting the US agreement (in principle) to participate in the enquiry, Halifax mentioned how important it was to approach the Arabs in the right way and he reminded Byrnes of the Presidential promises of consultations. Accordingly, Halifax proposed changing the order of Byrnes' terms of reference, transposing numbers two and one. Bevin's instructions to Halifax, a copy of which was given to Byrnes, show he was anxious to retain the words 'or other countries outside Europe' in the new item 1 because 'Palestine cannot deal with the whole emigration problem'. In this way Bevin was trying to salvage something from his intention to direct the enquiry at the DP issue and separate this from Palestine.[34]

Possibly it was a mistake for Bevin's concern about the phrase to be paraded in this way, for Byrnes told Halifax that it would be extremely difficult to keep the wording if the order of the terms of reference was changed as the Foreign Office wanted. Forced to choose, on 27 October Bevin authorized Halifax to revert to the original order that Byrnes had proposed but to keep the phrase 'to which I attach very great importance'. Halifax later reported that, despite this concession, American agreement was still unlikely at the moment, Byrnes' remarks indicating 'that nothing stood between an agreement ... excepting the date of the New York elections. His demeanour was one of shamefaced embarrassment'. This was grist to the mill as far as the British conception of US policy was concerned, and through his inevitable anger at American vote-catching Bevin was ever less likely to perceive any sincerity in Truman's humanitarian concern. Byrnes' formal response, in a memorandum to Halifax on 28 October, was even more severe. It pointed out that the consideration by the enquiry of conditions in other countries besides Palestine may delay further the resolution of the Jewish problem, and Byrnes concluded that it was not possible to reach an agreement at present: 'It is therefore desired that it be clearly understood that the counter-proposals of this Government have been withdrawn.' Byrnes suggested that Attlee's visit to the USA during November might facilitate agreement.[35]

Exasperated and puzzled, Bevin and Halifax realized the weakness of their position. Halifax telegraphed to the Foreign Office that in view of the certainty of a Democratic victory in New York 'the attack of cold feet on the part of the President seems all the more pusillanimous', but he warned that if any unilateral announcement was made in London, Truman might go further and reaffirm his demand for the entry of 100,000 Jews into Palestine. Bevin replied that he was 'frankly puzzled' by the American attitude. The mistake in the transmission of Halifax's telegram of 30 October was apt: 'I told Byrnes this morning that you were prepared to wait till November 6th in a spirit of restrained hopelessness.' The last word was deleted, and an ink insertion made of 'hopefulness'.[36]

On 6 November Halifax discussed the matter again with Byrnes, and the terms of reference the Foreign Office preferred were sent on to the President with the crucial phrase included and Byrnes' order transposed. Truman rejected these on the grounds that he was 'fearful that [the] changes ... will be construed as turning the focus of attention away from Palestine', but the memorandum containing the President's views, which Byrnes sent to Halifax, helpfully pointed out that the US terms still included the crucial phrase and if Bevin wanted 'he can act upon our proposal as a firm commitment'. Polling day had been the day before and, with Britain's weak bargaining position clear, the US Goverment was ready to clinch the deal. On 9 November Halifax informed Byrnes of Bevin's acceptance of the US terms. Four days later Bevin was able to tell the Commons of US agreement to the joint enquiry, and Truman announced US participation over the radio. Later in the month a final concession was extracted from Bevin with the imposition of a time limit of 120 days within which the Committee had to report. Byrnes was concerned to counter criticism in the Senate that the enquiry was merely a delaying device, and to forestall another Congressional resolution reaffirming the US position on Palestine. Bevin's wish to permit an automatic extension of this period was rebuffed by Byrnes who would agree only to extending the time limit for 'good and sufficient reasons', and Bevin accepted this meagre proviso on 27 November.[37]

In the eyes of the Foreign Office this entire episode reflected the total preoccupation of the US Goverment with domestic politics, and the consequent connection of the Jewish DP problem with Zionism and Palestine. In fact the distinction, discussed earlier, which Truman intended between the immediate and humanitarian gesture on immigration and the longer-term appraisal of Palestine policy which had nothing to do with extreme Zionist demands, was preserved. It was evidenced at a conference between the President and the Chiefs of Mission in the Near East, held on 10 November just as the wrangle with Britain was going on. Here Truman

> pointed out that if Palestine could only take some refugees from Europe to relieve the pressure, it would alleviate for the time being the situation in Europe, and it might satisfy some of the demands of the 'humanitartian' Zionists and give us an opportunity to turn our attention to a permanent solutiuon of the political problem.[38]

The failure of the Foreign Office and the British Government to perceive Truman's distinction, and to forgive his party political concerns, was reflected in and made more serious by the bitter wrangle over the terms of reference. In time this failure and the bitterness were both to become more acute, and the gap between the two governments on this issue was to widen.

In conclusion, these negotiations show the concerns and interests of the British and US governments on Palestine. They also reveal the weak bargaining position Britain now found herself in as a result of having no policy on Palestine herself and simultaneously being highly sensitive to American pressure. Consequently His Majesty's Government was prepared to pay a high price to secure not only US participation in a joint enquiry but also various other benefits that it was hoped the resulting delay would bring.

3

The Collapse of the Anglo-American Initiative

Several factors contributed to the speedy collapse of the Anglo-American initiative. Among these were the politically unsympathetic policy recommendations of the joint enquiry, the pressures of terrorism in Palestine and the impatient nature of the military response to these, and the public pronouncement of President Truman. But we have seen how the demise of the Anglo-American initiative was foreshadowed in its very origins. The Eastern Department of the Foreign Office was against the idea and, although its views were mostly held in abeyance while the Anglo-American Enquiry was at work, they rapidly reasserted themselves afterwards. Furthermore Bevin found it increasingly difficult to sustain a partnership with the Americans in the face of the growing disillusionment of other members of the Cabinet. It was these factors which above all account for the expiry of Bevin's attempt to find a joint policy. Thus it was to be that the ancient Whitehall view of the Palestine question again emerged to overwhelm the so-called 'expert' discussions between British and American delegations after the Committee of Enquiry had reported, and thus any prospect of arriving at a truly joint Anglo-American policy on Palestine was to be rendered null and void. The Foreign Office was then back in charge.

The Enquiry and the Report

The names of the twelve-man Anglo-American Committee of Enquiry were released on 10 December 1945. Bevin had stressed to Byrnes the necessity of finding 'impartial people who have not been connected publicly or officially with either the Jewish or the Arab cause', and just ten days later the list of British members was ready and delivered to the US Secretary of State. Sir John Singleton, a High Court judge, chaired the British delegation which comprised Lord

Morrison; Sir Frederick Leggett, formerly the Deputy Secretary of the Ministry of Labour; Wilfred Crick, the Economic Adviser to the Midland Bank; Manningham-Buller, a Conservative MP; and Richard Crossman, a Labour MP. The US administration had done nothing yet to select its delegation, pending the resolution of the problem of fixing a time limit for the Committee to report, and when the choice was made it had to be confined to judicial, professional and academic walks of life since no Congressman was willing to risk being associated with a committee which might report against Zionist wishes. The names of the American delegates were given to the British Embassy on 6 December. Joseph Hutcheson, a judge at the Houston Circuit Court, chaired the group, which consisted of Aydelotte, the Director of the Institute of Advanced Study at Princeton; Buxton, the editor of the *Boston Herald*; James McDonald, a former High Commissioner of Refugees; and Phillips, a former Undersecretary of State and Ambassador to Italy. The sixth member, Gardner, was replaced a week after the list was published by Bartley Crum, a lawyer from San Francisco. The American delegation was less obviously objective than the British group. Crum, though ostensibly neutral when he joined the Committee, was soon to become a vocal proponent of Zionism. It is noteworthy that he had been recommended by David Niles, Truman's White House assistant on minority group affairs, which included Jews. Niles was himself a moderate Zionist, a retiring and elusive operator who had the President's ear on the Palestine issue, and a good friend of the Zionist leader Wise and of McDonald, as well as of Crum, from whom he received intelligence of the Committee's proceedings. McDonald had had considerable experience of the Jewish refugee problem and soon became a champion of the Jewish Displaced Persons' cause in the Committee, a role that made him increasingly isolated in its discussions. Felix Frankfurter, Associate Justice of the Supreme Court and a Zionist, had recommended Buxton's candidature to his friend Byrnes and, out of gratitude to his sponsor, the editor of the *Boston Herald* wrote frequently to Frankfurter, who in turn informed Byrnes of the Committee's progress. Against these mildly Zionist overtones to the US delegation as it stood in December, the State Department had its man, Phillips; however he proved a bad informant and the Department was to be left in the dark about the enquiry's deliberations.[1]

The initial Zionist reaction to the announcement of the Anglo-American Enquiry was that Bevin had secured a coup to the detriment of the movement by involving the US in a mission which threatened to disconnect the European DP issue from Zionism, and to establish Palestine's inability to solve the refugee problem. The American Zionist Emergency Committee, meeting in New York on 14 November, was treated to a militant exposition from Silver on the need to boycott the enquiry. The statement issued accused Britain of a 'betrayal of pledges' and having 'now succeeded in enlisting the inadvertant support of the President ... [the] U.S. Government has fallen into a carefully prepared trap'. At the meeting of the Inner Zionist Council in Jerusalem in December calmer councils prevailed. Shertok, the head of the Jewish Agency's political department, argued successfully against Silver's wish to boycott the enquiry and for the moderate policy of participation. This policy was favoured by Weizmann, Wise and Goldmann, and was approved thereby clearing the way for the Agency to give evidence before the Committee.[2]

On 14 December the US delegation assembled in Washington and met Truman, who apparently gave no inkling of his interests in the Palestine question but merely urged the Committee to report as promptly as possible. Truman had in fact dusted down his neutrality on the subject some days before at a press conference when he stated that he no longer favoured a Congressional resolution calling for unrestricted immigration into Palestine and the creation of a state. This manoeuvre was an attempt to head off a joint resolution, sponsored by Wagner and Taft, being backed by the Zionists during November against considerable opposition from Truman and Byrnes. The Secretary of State had insisted on the 120-day limit for the enquiry in order to defuse Congressionl pressure for this resolution, embarrassing to the US Government at a time when it was participating in a supposedly objective investigation of the Palestine problem. The administration's efforts were to no avail, for on 17 December the Senate adopted a composite resolution calling upon the US Government to use its good offices to open Palestine to free Jewish immigration up to its economic absorptive capacity, and towards

> the upbuilding of Palestine as the Jewish National Home, and, in association with all elements of the population, establish Palestine as a democratic commonwealth in which all men, regardless of race or creed, shall have equal rights.

The House of Representatives concurred in this resolution two days later, completing the Capitol's snub of the President. The resolution differed from its predecessors in dropping the phrase 'Jewish commonwealth'; however the use of the definite article in calling for 'the Jewish National Home' was a departure from the wording of the Balfour Declaration and the Mandate, and helped to ensure Zionist satisfaction and governmental embarrassment.[3]

The Arab states reacted with predictable bitterness to the resolution, but there is no evidence to suggest that the American members of the Committee of Enquiry were influenced by it. Hutcheson, commenting to a member of the British embassy's staff in Washington with all the asperity of a judge exerting his independence from Congress, reportedly said

> American members of the Committee would not (repeat not) be influenced by Zionist agitation in Congress. They hoped on [the] British side it would be appreciated that [the] Senate resolution was merely an expression of opinion which had no operative force.[4]

The British delegates joined their American colleagues in Washington after Christmas, and hearings began there on 7 January. Representatives were heard from various shades of American Zionist and non-Zionist opinion, together with a rather weak presentation of the Arab case. In the middle of the month the Committee crossed the Atlantic in rather unpleasant conditions aboard the *Queen Elizabeth*. During the journey the record of the conversations between Roosevelt and Ibn Saud was seen by the Committee, together with the late President's public assurances to the Zionists. According to Crossman, Hutcheson reacted to these relevations with the phrase 'a duplicitious son-of-a-bitch', but Crossman believed that all of the Americans except Crum knew of the records previously. Apparently the relevation of the double policy made an impression upon Crum, who was horrified, according to his autobiographical account, and the experience may well have inclined him against the pro-Arab bent of the State Department which seemed to have subverted Roosevelt's public purpose.[5]

The Committee's visit to London was important because it established a significant consideration in the minds of the members. Bevin promised the assembled members of the Committee that if a unanimous report was made he would 'do everything in his power to put it into effect'. In November Bevin made another determined comment in the House of Commons when the joint enquiry was announced: 'I will stake my political future on solving this problem', and, taken together with his undertaking to the Committee, these remarks seem to imply a complete faith on the part of the Foreign Secretary that the enquiry would vindicate his contention that the

Jewish DP issue and the Palestine question were completely separate matters, thereby endorsing the wisdom of British policy. It is most improbable that Bevin relayed his genuine conviction to the Committee merely to allay any suspicion that the enquiry was just a delaying device. These suspicions were not a problem at this stage. Furthermore, there is no evidence to suggest that Bevin entertained any doubts about the wisdom and accuracy of Britain's policy on Palestine, or that he harboured serious misgivings about the involvement of the USA, so naturally he assumed that an objective investigation would concur. Naïve this outlook might seem, but it is borne out by Bevin's misconceptions about Zionism and about the emigration pressures in Europe, as well as by Crossman. Crossman records talking at this time to Dalton, who 'knew practically nothing of the issues involved' in Palestine, to Creech Jones, the only 'genuine Zionist' in the government, and to Bevin, who 'in a three minute conversation confined himself to asking me whether I had been circumsized'; Crossman concluded 'that the Labour Party's Zionism was about as half-baked and ill thought out as policy as I could conceive'. Self-confidence, derived from lack of understanding, Bevin's own ideas and the unchallenged sway of the Foreign Office view, were the roots of the Foreign Secretary's rash promise.[6]

Whitehall showed rather less faith in the Committee's ability to arrive at the right solution. Martin, Assistant Undersecretary at the Colonial Office, suggested to Howe (who superintended the Eastern Department at the FO) that the Committee should be informed of the British Government's views while it was in London so as to forestall any recommendations that might diminish the government's freedom of action. He feared that partition might be recommended 'without fully realizing the repercussions elsewhere' and without taking account of the views of the Chiefs of Staff and the Viceroy. Bevin's federal scheme requred the co-operation between Arabs and Jews, which was absent; Martin suggested therefore that a provincial autonomy scheme would pave the way for future co-operation. Baxter felt it would be wrong to recommend a favourite scheme to the Committee, and Howe agreed in case the enquiry 'pronounced against it', but it was decided that the Colonial Office could prepare a 'factual' paper on the advantages and disadvantages of various policies. Harris, the Palestine adviser at the Colonial Office, recorded the ensuing argument at a meeting between Baxter and Sir Kinahan Cornwallis (former Ambassador to Iraq, then Chairman of the FO Middle Eastern Committee) of the Foreign Office and Martin, Trafford Smith and himself for the CO:

neither Sir Kinahan nor Mr. Baxter were greatly interested in the
provincial autonomy scheme except in so far as its presentation might
afford an opportunity for getting the White Paper policy (to which they are
both firm adherants) into the picture again.

The old inter-office disputes were raising their heads, and as a result
Harris recommended that the efforts to sponsor the provincial
autonomy scheme as a government favourite before the Committee of
Enquiry should now be dropped. However, at Martin's suggestion,
the scheme for provincial autonomy which Harris had originally
drawn up was submitted, perhaps one should say slipped, to the
Committee unofficially before it left London with the approval of
Hall, Creech Jones (the Parliamentary Undersecretary at the CO)
and Gater (the Permanent Undersecretary) following the favourable
impression Amery had made in arguing for partition. Neither
partition nor provincial autonomy was to find favour with the
Committee, but the episode shows a clear apprehensiveness about
what recommendations might emerge.[7]

After sampling London's postwar austerity the Committee split
into several groups to visit Europe and see the Displaced Persons'
camps. These visits made a tremendous impression on the members
of the Committee. Even Crossman, whose wartime work on
anti-German propaganda might have prepared him for the worst,
was horrified by the scale and institutions of genocide. For years the
Jews of Europe had been persecuted and murdered because they were
Jews; Hitler's research into the birth and marriage records had
wrested his victims from the oblivion of mixed marriages and Aryan
nationality. Now the Anglo-American Committee saw there was no
desire amongst the survivors of the holocaust to try to return to an old
and integrated existence; as Jews they had suffered and seen their
relatives die, and as Jews the remnant wished to live. But the Zionists,
never likely to leave anything to chance, nearly overplayed their
hand. Cunningham, the High Commissioner of Palestine, had
warned the Colonial Secretary in December of 'reliable secret
information' that the Jewish Agency intended to wage a propaganda
campaign in the European camps in order to coach the Jewish DPs on
how to give evidence before the Committee. Zionist bodies were set up
in every European country to be visited by the Committee, and it has
been suggested that Jews who it was suspecterd might give unhelpful
testimony about their emigration wishes were spirited away. The
Committee members saw through this orchestrated demand for
emigration to Palestine, but discounted it rather than reacted against

it, as evidenced by the report of the sub-Committee which visited Poland:

> The Jews are motivated by a mass hysteria natural to a persecuted people in a hostile country, as well as by sound reasons. ...
>
> About 90% of them publicly express a desire to go to Palestine, but privately many of them admit that they would prefer the United States if it were open to them. This contradiction is accounted for by the influence on the Jews of organizations which favor a Jewish State or which have chosen Palestine as the destination on which to concentrate ....

The report also noted that many survivors had relatives in Palestine. It would appear that the conditions in Europe and the plight of the Jewish survivors provided sufficient testimony for the Anglo-American Committee; the vigorous propaganda campaign arranged by the Zionists bordered on the superfluous, and the Committee could perceive the nature of Palestine's strong but not exclusive attraction without prompting.[8]

At the end of February the Committee reassembled in Cairo. There the Arab case was heard and given its most eloquent expression by Azzam Pasha. His statement has been widely quoted. In part he explained:

> Our Brother has gone to Europe and the West and come back something else. He has come back a Russified Jew, a Polish Jew, a German Jew, an English Jew. He has come back with a totally different conception of things, Western and not Eastern. ... the Jew, our old cousin, coming back with imperialistic ideas, ... with reactionary or revolutionary ideas and trying to implement them first by British pressure and then by American pressure, and then by terrorism ... we do not extend to him a very good welcome.

It is interesting that this explanation of the Arab view was supplied to the Committee not by a representative of the Arabs of Palestine, but by the Secretary General of the Arab League.[9]

In Cairo the Committee heard another important and influential point of view; that of the British Commanders in Chief, Middle East. The Chiefs of Staff in London had already supplied the Committee, via the Foreign Office, with an analysis of the 'Military Implications of the Maintenance of Law and Order in Palestine', prepared by the Joint Planning Staff to a specification that ensured the leakage of any part of the document would not be serious. It concluded that either the Jews or the Arabs were capable of causing serious trouble in Palestine, and that their present quiescence was contrived in order to impress the

Anglo-American Committee. It continued that a solution which was acceptable to the Arabs but not to the Jews would cause a serious situation that would be confined to Palestine, while a solution acceptable to the Jews but not to the Arabs would cause trouble in Palestine and in other Muslim countries. Finally the paper pointed out:

> A compromise solution which gained the support of a majority of both Jews and Arabs would be the only one that could result in a reduced military commitment. A compromise, however, which failed to satisfy either Jews or Arabs might well result in a heavier and more protracted military commitment than any other solution.

Now the Committee of Enquiry really did not need to be told that an acceptable compromise was the best solution to the Palestine problem, and the bland turn of phrase in this submission led to some sharp questioning in Cairo when the military commanders appeared before the Committee in camera:

> Manningham-Buller: ... Under the heading of compromise solutions do you include partition?
> Air Marshall Medhurst (C. in C. Air, Mediterranean and Middle East): I do not think that is a military question.
> Manningham-Buller: I was wondering whether you put that under the heading of compromise.
> Medhurst: Partition presumably would be a compromise solution.
> Manningham-Buller: That is what I thought. ... In the event of there being partition ... would it be necessary in the interests of preserving the peace of the world that some part of Palestine should not be handed over either to Jew or Arab?
> Medhurst: I think that depends entirely upon what the partition solution is.

Medhurst, Vice-Admiral Tennant and Major-General Oliver would not be drawn on this tricky point, which involved the importance of Haifa as the pipeline terminus and port; by expressing the view that partition was a possible compromise they had gone beyond the brief issued to them by the COS which required that in giving evidence they be guided by the paper, quoted above, that had been submitted to the Committee. The Anglo-American Committee had been posed a riddle; the military men thought that an acceptable compromise was best, but were reluctant to argue about the form of the compromise, especially if it involved partition. The evidence heard on this occasion gave the riddle a further twist because Medhurst and Oliver warned that civil war would ensue in Palestine if the British forces withdrew, Medhurst arguing that the Jews would

> get what they wanted to begin with, but if Azzim [sic] Pasha's views ever came to anything and the Arabs got together there would be only one result.
> Aydelotte: In the long run they would exterminate the Jew?
> Medhurst: Yes. It might take a long time … .[10]

If all this pointed to a military liking for a compromise that satisfied the Arabs, permitted a continued British presence in Palestine, and relegated satisfying the Jews to third place, when the Committee went to Jerusalem yet another facet was added by the General Officer Commanding Palestine, Lieutenant-General D'Arcy. As the man who would have to deal with a dissatisfied Yishuv, he was able to give the Committee some unequivocal advice. Responding to Manning-ham-Buller's question about the Hagana, D'Arcy said:

> The actual disarming of [the] country would be a most difficult operation. The arms in the settlements are extremely well-hidden in underground caches, and even if we could occupy a settlement for two weeks or more by troops we might not find all the arms. [I] think the disarming of the country can never be guaranteed 100 per cent.

D'Arcy added that if the Hagana came out in the open fully armed it could be fought and disarmed, and that any disarmament would have to be accompanied by the removal of the leaders of the organization. Clearly, the threat presented by the Hagana was more apparent to the military authorities in Palestine, and D'Arcy's emphasis on the consequences of not satisfying the Jews was understandably different from that of his military colleagues and superiors in Cairo and London. His testimony on the difficulties of disarming the Yishuv was of importance in the light of the Committee's eventual recommenda-tions and the reaction of the British Government.[11]

After the Committee had heard evidence from Jews and Arabs in Jerusalem, it split up to visit the neighbouring Arab capitals and to pursue further enquiries in Palestine. At the end of March the delegates retreated to Lausanne to write their report. To begin with, Crossman, McDonald and Crum favoured a solution based on partition, but when it became clear that the others would not support this idea it was withdrawn 'in the interests of unanimity'. This group then joined Hutcheson, who with three compatriots had favoured making recommendations that Palestine should be neither a Jewish nor an Arab state, that 100,000 immigration certificates should be issued immediately and that the terms of the Mandate should be reaffirmed stressing the obligation to facilitate Jewish immigration. While the British chairman and some of his compatriots agreed that Palestine should be neither a Jewish nor an Arab state, Singleton was adamant that the entry of the 100,000 should be conditional upon the disarming and disbandment of the Hagana and the removal of the Jewish Agency's authority to issue immigration certificates.[12]

From the cacophony of the increasingly heated debate a unanimous report was to emerge. The reasons were several. The personalities of the members were an important unifying influence, and both Nachmani (1980) and Wilson (1979) comment on Hutcheson's strong leadership, Nachmani remarking that the 'Hutcheson Committee' would be a safe description. Leggett and Crossman were expert conciliators, and Crossman was acutely aware of the need to avoid making 'conflicting reports'. Singleton, legal and precise, was to become increasingly isolated in sticking to his disarmament condition, and eventually he lost all suasion with his colleagues. The Committee was mindful, arguably too mindful, of D'Arcy's evidence about the problem of enforcing any disarmament of the Yishuv, and the question of whether or not to make disarmament a condition precedent for the entry of the 100,000 became central to the discussions, as Crossman told the Prime Minister afterwards:

> we very nearly broke on this issue, because a clear majority of us, both British and American, were convinced that to demand that the Jews surrender their arms before the immigrants are admitted would precipitate a terrible conflict between the British Army and the Jews of Palestine, not dissimilar from the Irish affair after the last war.

Crossman noted for McNeil's benefit that a division on this issue could have ranged all American opinion against a minority British recommendation. What was required, he noted, was a gesture to defuse the crisis,

> to remove the conditions under which the illegal army had grown up and the excuses for terrorism. It would not be our duty to recommend what was virtually a declaration of war against the Jews in Palestine.

The force of this argument and the problems of disarming the Hagana were not alone sufficient to convince Singleton and his group. What forced the change was the pressure to make a unanimous report. According to Wilson (1979), the Committee members 'constantly had in mind Bevin's remarks about a unanimous report', and two sharp reminders of it were delivered. Crossman, convinced on the need for unanimity, took advantage of the presence in Lausanne on other business of the Minister of State at the Foreign Office, and he prompted Noel-Baker to press Singleton in this direction and remind the British chairman of Bevin's promise. More direct pressure came from Washington. On 5 April, Goldmann, who was in Geneva and probably in contact with Crum and McDonald, reported by telephone to Weisgal (the Secretary-General of the Jewish Agency in the USA) who in turn sent a note of the conversation to Niles; the note said that Hutcheson

> is continuing to maintain a friendly attitude; that it is extremely essential that the boss in Washington should cable him, encouraging him in his stand ... there seems to be more or less general agreement among the American members....
>
> The British, on the other hand, are in a terrible stew and trying to drag the thing out unreasonably.

With deadlock persisting in Lausanne, on 16 April, Niles gave Truman a draft telegram for him to send to Hutcheson. This was despatched within the next two days and read in part:

> I have followed reports of your inquiry and deliberations with great interest. The world expectantly awaits a report from the entire Commission which will be the basis of an affirmative program to relieve untold suffering and misery. In the deliberations now going on ... it is my deep and sincere wish that the American delegation shall stand firm ....

Hutcheson was suitably galvanized by this into a burst of activity, and, led by Manningham-Buller, the five British members were persuaded to trade their wish to make the entry of the 100,000 conditional upon the disarmament of the Yishuv in exchange for the unconditional entry of these immigrants, together with a strong statement in the body of the report about the illegal army.[13]

The Report was completed and signed on Good Friday, 20 April, and Hutcheson left Switzerland immediately afterwards to deliver a copy to Truman. It was published late on 30 April. Acknowledging that Palestine alone could not help all the Jewish victims who would need the assistance of other countries, the Report recommended that only Palestine could give substantial help on the Displaced Person issue and should admit 100,000 Jewish DPs immediately. The analysis behind this unconditional recommendation followed Truman's own reasoning closely; Palestine alone offered hope to the survivors, weary of camp life which had gone on for so long since the 'liberation', and Palestine alone could take such a number. 100,000 was still a meaningful number at this stage since it represented the bulk of the Jewish DPs in Europe, but by the summer it had lost its significance as their numbers were swollen to 250,000 by the exodus of Jews from Eastern Europe. However, in recommending the entry of the 100,000, the Committee, like Truman, saw a way of satisfying the demands of humanitarian opinion and meeting some hopes of moderate Zionism, while by making the immigration unconditional Jewish terrorists and extremists were dealt a calculated slight and their influence ignored. Politically such a recommendation would be a bitter pill for the Mandatory government to swallow; arguably this consideration should have weighed more heavily with the Committee of Enquiry. The Report continued in a rather general way, laying down guidelines that Palestine was to be neither a Jewish nor an Arab state, and Christian, Muslim and Jewish faiths were to have equal rights in the Holy Land. The Report recommended that the Mandate should be continued until it was replaced by a UN trusteeship agreement, which should run until Arab and Jewish hostility had disappeared. Until trusteeship came into being the Mandatory was to continue to facilitate Jewish immigration without prejudicing the rights of the existing population, and the free exchange of land was to be allowed. The tenth recommendation of the Committee advised strongly that the threats or the use of violence or the employment of illegal armies to prevent the implementation of other recommendations should be suppressed, and that the Jewish Agency should resume co-operation with the Mandatory authority.[14]

His Majesty's Government's reaction

While the Committee investigated and deliberated, the problem of Palestine was not forgotten within the corridors of power in London. In order to understand the British Government's reaction to the Anglo-American Committee's Report it is necessary to return to the autumn of 1945 and follow the policy debate since then.

Near the end of September 1945, the Zionists learned that the British Government was moving towards the rejection of Truman's request that 100,000 immigration certificates be issued, and towards a continuation of the White Paper policy. The Jewish Agency reached a decision that Ben Gurion communicated on 1 October by telegram to Moshe Sneh, the head of the Hagana in Palestine:

> Sabotage and retaliation actions should be undertaken; but no personal terror, yet a retaliation for each one murdered by the White Paper authorities. Every action should be substantive and impressive.

In July 1946, the British Government published several intercepted telegrams between London and Jerusalem which dated from September 1945, and which implicated the Jewish Agency with the illegal organizations and terrorism. The consequence of the Zionists' growing desperation and extremism was felt in Palestine on the night of 31 October. The railway system was cut in fifty-one places, three small naval craft were sunk, Lydda station was attacked by the Irgun and Haifa oil refinery by the Stern Gang.[15]

As a direct result of these incidents the Defence Committee considered the situation in Palestine on 5 November. The Colonial Secretary reported that organized Jewish forces in Palestine numbered about 70,000, that the illegal army 'was dangerously strong and well organised, and it was significant that the Hagana and Stern organisations now appeared to be cooperating, under the control of the Jewish Agency.' Military counter-measures 'to bring about the surrender of illegal arms' were considered, and the Committee decided to ask the COS to consider requesting the views of the C[ommanders in Chief, Middle East, about the required action. The Chief of the Imperial General Staff, Brooke, was not present at the meeting and his place was taken by the Vice-Chief, Lieutenant-General Nye, who confessed two days later at a meeting of the Chiefs of Staff Committee that, 'Before deciding whether or not to consult the C[ommander]s-in-C[hief] M[iddle] E[ast], he would like time to give the matter careful consideration.' Nye's fear was that 'any action taken to achieve the surrender of illegal weapons ... would undoubtedly precipitate an outbreak of hostilities.' This view, as it turned out, was more farsighted than the views expressed by most of his military colleagues and subordinates. Interestingly it was also much the same line which Lieutenant-General D'Arcy, General Officer Commanding Palestine, was to take in his evidence before the Anglo-American Committee. Having thought about it, on 9 November Nye recommended that the views of the Middle East Commanders should be sought, although he felt that there were 'still very strong arguments against initiating a search for arms'. At the consequent invitation, the Commanders in Chief, Middle East, began their reply in this robust spirit:

Sooner or later it will be necessary to disarm the whole population Arab and Jew in Palestine. This applies especially to the Jewish illegal organisation and cannot be effected through consultation with Jewish leaders.

Sensibly feeling that the immediate seizure of arms would provoke a crisis and torpedo the Anglo-American Enquiry, the Commanders in Chief, Middle East, recommended that the right psychological moment for action should be awaited, such as would follow a terrorist outburst. Bloodshed would be likely, but troops were now sufficient for resolute action. Understandably, Nye's reservations were not dissipated by this reply, and a week later he warned the COS Committee that

it did not cover the point that even after action had been taken to disarm the populace, the operation would only succeed in obtaining a certain percentage of illegal arms, since the possibilities of concealment and evasion open to the population were boundless.

Nye suggested that the views of the Commanders in Chief be referred to the Defence Committee with a warning by the COS that any operation 'could not achieve all that was desired', and that the Commanders in Chief should be reminded of the limitations of such a scheme. This was agreed, the COS submission to the Defence Committee particularly endorsing the Commanders in Chief's warning that immediate action might lay the British Government open to the criticism of torpedoing the Anglo-American Enquiry. The matter paused here for a while, helped by the view of the Commanders in Chief that no 'large scale anti-British action would take place until after the Anglo-American Commission [sic] had declared its findings'. Accordingly on 1 January 1946 the Cabinet decided there would be no wholesale arms searches, nor any action against the Jewish Agency, as the disadvantages were too great; the Colonial Secretary's instructions to the High Commissioner to this effect were approved.[16]

The incidents, however, continued. On 17 January a ship was intercepted with 911 illegal immigrants on board, all young and healthy. Two days later terrorists attacked the Central Prison in Jerusalem, killing an Army officer and a policeman. The catalogue continued with attacks on British military installations, the most serious of which occurred on 25 February when three RAF airfields were attacked. Within the next two months two more ships, carrying a total of 973 illegal immigrants, were arrested to the accompaniment of further terrorist activity.[17]

Against this background the notion of disarming the populace of Palestine underwent an important development during the early months of 1946. The Commanders in Chief, Middle East, set the ball rolling in a telegram to the COS on 1 January. Acknowledging that with such an operation 'the degree of success attained would be problematical', they now extended the concept and argued that the

> Plan likely to achieve greatest success is to combine search for arms with seizure of leaders of Hagana and Palmach. ... it is considered that seizure of leaders in order to break up the illegal organisation is of primary importance and seizure of arms is secondary to this.

This line of reasoning was given powerful support by the High Commissioner himself, who added a note of urgency. In an important telegram to Hall on 19 February, Cunningham warned that relations with the Jewish Agency were growing 'more intolerable', that the Agency was being carried along by the momentum of its own propaganda amongst the Yishuv, that the Agency had links with the terrorists and had been quite uninfluenced by the decision to continue the immigration quota beyond the total laid down by the White Paper. Hall sympathized with the position but reaffirmed his earlier instructions to take no action at present as this was 'the only policy which will enable the inquiry of the Anglo-American Committee to be satisfactorily completed'. In his reply Cunningham drew attention to the change in the Commander in Chief's view that in the event of action being necessary 'against the Jews', as well as disarming them,

> it would be necessary at the same time to seize the leaders of the Hagana insofar as they are known and the executive of the Agency. I am in agreement ... that searches for arms would be ineffective without also taking action against the leaders.

It would appear that the idea to disarm both the Arabs and Jewish populations of Palestine, which started life the previous autumn in response to an outburst of terrorism, had now changed into a scheme to disarm the Jewish organizations and seize the leaders of the Jewish Agency as well. This change had been wrought under the continuous terrorist activity in Palestine and by the non-cooperation of the Jewish Agency with the Mandatory Government. It is more important to notice that despite the normal military appetite to get on with the job and 'win', there was an awareness that disarming the

Yishuv might prove virtually impossible, which D'Arcy's evidence to the Anglo-American Committee reflected. Of greater significance was the continuous sensitiveness, shown by the Commanders in Chief, Middle East, the Chiefs of Staff, the Government of Palestine and in the Cabinet, to avoid damaging the Anglo-American Committee's chance of success by taking any action.[18]

By the beginning of April 1946, projected action against the Jewish organizations became mixed up with expectations about what the Anglo-American Committee would recommend. Lord Morrison, one of the members of the Committee, called on Bevin to request permission for the Committee to use in its Report some evidence taken in camera from military witnesses in Cairo and Jerusalem. The request and the reasons Lord Morrison gave for it were conveyed by the Foreign Office to the COS:

> It appears that the Committee, and in particular the American members, were both surprised and deeply shocked by the state of armed preparedness and the readiness to go to extremes of violence that the military evidence and their own investigations revealed as existing among the Jews in Palestine. The Jewish Agency's abuse of the authority delegated to them made a similar impression ...

Accordingly, the FO explained, the Committee's preliminary recommendations were that there should be no Jewish state, Jewish para-military organizations should be disarmed and the Agency 'abolished or radically reconstituted'. It would help the Committee's recommendations to carry weight, especially in the USA, if all the relevant evidence could be used. Clearly the impression Lord Morrison had managed to convey was that the view of the British Committee members such as Singleton was commonplace throughout the whole Committee of Enquiry; as we have seen, such was not the case. However, the Chiefs of Staff were not to know this at the beginning of April 1946, and the Joint Planning Staff enthusiastically recommended that the Committee should be allowed to use any military evidence to support these recommendations, subject only to the obvious security precautions. More importantly the JPS paper went on:

> The only military implication of this appears to us to be that we shall reveal to the Jews the extent of our knowledge of their military plans ... However, any gain the Jewish organizations might obtain ... [from this] might be countered by action before the report was published.

In this way a connection was drawn between the COS hobby-horse of military action against the Jewish organizations and the expectations of what the Committee of Enquiry was about to recommend.[19]

Inevitably the COS could scarcely contain themselves, Tedder's briefing paper beginning:

> These Papers disclose a most satisfactory state of affairs in the deliberations of the Palestine Commission [sic]. The crux of the whole thing is whether they will be able to carry with them world opinion and particularly American opinion ....

Accordingly, Tedder argued in the COS Committee meeting on 8 April for the release of the military evidence for use in the report of the joint enquiry. Lord Alanbrooke (CIGS) went further, explaining that the JPS report 'had considerable military implications', and these were to be the subject of further recommendations from the JPS 'concerning the action which would have to be taken' if the Anglo-American Committee recommended the disarming of the Jewish organizations. Now that the COS Committee had established this connection, it turned to the extensive ramifications such as the timetabling of Cabinet approval for military action in Palestine, the publication of the Committee of Enquiry's Report and the action itself. On 15 April the COS Committee considered the delicate problem of the timing of the Report's publication and what were coyly referred to as subsequent governmental decisions; Vice-Admiral McGrigor (representing the First Sea Lord and the Chief of the Naval Staff) warned that if these decisions followed too closely upon the heels of the Report the government might be accused of having influenced its recommendations; on balance, however, he felt that the advantages of taking speedy decisions outweighed this drawback. The meeting concurred, and the Foreign and Colonial Offices were informed. Two days later Tedder's briefing paper entitled 'Anglo-American Committee of Enquiry. Military Implications' commented:

> There are already signs that we will have political pressure to delay military action against the Jews ... [However] It can be argued that the report of the Commission [sic] will produce evidence to the world of a state of affairs in Palestine that may well necessitate drastic military action if we are to retain control of the situation in that country.

The brief stressed the military importance of retaining the freedom 'to act quickly', and warned that if 'we are to hold our hand while the

Jews complete their preparations, we may find that they have taken such precautions as to make our contemplated action extremely difficulty [sic] ....' At the COS Committee meeting later in the day, Tedder followed this line and proposed sending a short telegram to the Commanders in Chief, Middle East, warning them of possible political pressure to delay action, and requesting their views on the result of 'an arbitrarily imposed delay between the publication of the report and the disarmament and suppression of the Jewish military organisations'. The eventualities to be considered were a delay of one week, or of two weeks or more. The COS Committee approved Tedder's draft, which was sent.[20]

In requesting the views of the Commanders in Chief, Middle East, on the consequences of a political decision which had yet to be taken, the Chiefs of Staff were manoeuvring to establish a conclusive case for taking speedy military action following the completion of the Anglo-American Committee's Report. This case would then be ready f4r the discussions in the Defence Committee and Cabinet. The concern for safeguarding the success of any recommendations the Committee might make now appears to have diminished. Earlier it had been an important concern to avoid torpedoing the Enquiry, but now the primary objective was that the military action contemplated should be effective. Perhaps the COS were no longer optimistic about what the Report would say, or perhaps the commonplace military fascination for action and a clear-cut settlement had, under the pressure of terrorism and illegal immigration, reasserted itself. By the time the Report was ready on 20 April the Chiefs of Staff had built up a considerable momentum behind the plan to disarm the illegal Jewish organizations and to arrest the Jewish leaders; although the Report did not in fact recommend such action, the force of the COS view was to have an important bearing upon the reaction of the British Government to the Anglo-American Committee's Report.

The first problem was the matter of continuing the immigration quota beyond the total laid down by the White Paper. In December 1945 the Arab League had replied warily on the subject, neither rejecting nor accepting the continued quota. On 1 January 1946 the Cabinet invited Bevin to secure the Arab states' acquiescence to a continuation of the 1,500 a month quota, and noted 'that in the meanwhile immigration at the existing rate should not in fact be stopped'. Howe was quick to point out the problem. In a minute to his Secretary of State on 3 January he referred to the guidance which had been given to the Middle East posts about the British Government 'adhering to the White Paper policy', and warned that 'it seems most undesirable that we should go back on our word'. Howe added that military dispositions had been made on the assumption that Arab wishes would not be overruled. Grafftey-Smith, the Minister in Jedda, soon added his voice to the appeal, warning that Ibn Saud wanted an assurance about the ending of the quota. The mininster pointed out unctuously, 'It may not be realised that the Arabs take His Majesty's Government's departure from this [White Paper] policy much more seriously than His Majesty's Government do themselves'. The Colonial Office had stayed its hand and delayed implementing the Cabinet decision to continue the quota, and the Jewish Agency had not been told, because of the problem which Howe mentioned. The matter was referred to the Prime Minister for him to adjudicate. Hall's minute to Attlee, sent with Bevin's approval, mentioned that the Cabinet's decision 'ran to some extent counter to the instructions' the Foreign Office had sent to the Middle East representatives. The problem was still unresolved over a week later, and Creech Jones (the Parliamentary Undersecretary at the CO) described to Bevin the growing problem in Palestine. In the absence of an immigration quota, the detention camp at Athlit was filling up, and adverse propaganda at this breach of the terms of the Mandate to facilitate immigration was being fuelled in the United States. He recommended that the Cabinet's decision of 1 January to continue with the quota should now be implemented. Attlee was sent a copy of this minute, and he told the Foreign Secretary simply: 'I think we should continue the present quota'. Bevin agreed, and on 28 January the Middle East posts were informed that the quota of 1,500 a month would be continued. He instructed the posts to approach the Arab governments informally to avoid provoking formal and possibly negative replies. Grafftey-Smith reported that Ibn Saud spoke 'with unusual bitterness' on Palestine, and Baxter noted despondently that 'increasing bitterness ... is certainly a cause for anxiety'.[21]

There was another problem which not only heightened Foreign Office fears about Arab reactions but also brought out clearly the conflicting concerns of the Foreign and Colonial Offices — the problem was Transjordan. At a meeting on 3 January between official representatives of these two departments it was decided to make a recommendation to the Cabinet for the independence of Transjordan, together with a treaty arrangement to allow British military rights there. The negotiations and the framing of a treaty, which was signed on 22 March, need not concern us here. The result is, however, important. Ibn Saud's reaction to the increased stature and independent status of his Hashimite rival, King Abdullah of

Transjordan, was predictable and vigorously represented to the
Foreign Office by Grafftey-Smith. On 16 March he reported Ibn
Saud's request that the British Government should guarantee
Abdullah's future behaviour, and his claim to Akaba and Maan. A
soothing reply was sent by the Foreign Office through Grafftey-
Smith. It proved useless, however, and the next day the British
Minister conveyed Ibn Saud's anger with feeling, warning that Ibn
Saud believed we 'have been clever at his expense' in ignoring his
claims to Akaba and Maan, and in suggesting that the United
Nations Organization should settle the frontier dispute. Grafftey-
Smith continued ominously:

> I fear that we have here yet another factor likely to embitter Ibn Saud's
> reception of anything short of full Arab expectations from [the] Palestine
> mission of enquiry. Any development which diminishes his belief in our
> good faith is much to be regretted.

The Foreign Office received this coolly, but the apprehension of the
officials can be detected through their minutes. Wikeley wrote:

> It is a measure of Ibn Saud's greatness that he can inspire the
> representative of a foreign power with such devotion to his cause as Mr.
> Grafftey-Smith evidently has. It is a little unfortunate however that our
> own Minister should so frequently take Ibn Saud's side against us.

Baxter added his dislike of the tone of the telegram, and Howe
minuted cautiously: 'This may or may not be the forecast of Ibn
Saud's reaction'. The Eastern Department bore the warning from
Jedda in mind, and took it seriously enough to convey a watered-
down edition to Bevin over two weeks later. This warning did not
deter the Foreign Office from endorsing the suggestion of Killearn
(the British Ambassador to Egypt) that Ibn Saud should send a
message of congratulations to Abdullah. Though Grafftey-Smith
thought the expectation 'idle' that this would in fact be done, Ibn
Saud did eventually send a cordial message, probably not from a
change of heart but in the hope of getting Britain to mediate on the
matter of Akaba and Maan.[22]
  A further dimension to the Transjordan settlement arose from
Abdullah's desire to secede, with Iraq, from the Arab League. It was
brought to Abdullah's attention that such action, if it followed
Transjordan's independence too closely, would appear to have been
inspired by Britain and may therefore do harm to Britain's standing
with other Arab states, and instructions in this sense were sent to the

British ambassador in Baghdad for use in the event of the matter being raised. Although this came to nothing, the Foreign Office was very sensitive about the repercussions that might ensue because, in the Foreign Office view, they threatened not only Britain's retention of Arab goodwill but also that incarnation of the concept of a united Arab world, the Arab League. This raised a bone of contention with the Colonial Office, as Trafford Smith (Assistant Secretary in the CO dealing with Palestine) recorded bitterly after a meeting with the representatives of the Foreign Office on 22 March:

> Mr. Baxter rather evaded my question as to action taken by H.M.G. to guide the activities of the Arab League 'into sensible and constructive channels'. ... But it is essentially the policy of the Foreign Office that the outward appearance of the independence of the League shall be maintained ....
> ... a feeling emerged from the meeting that, provided that the Arab League can be maintained in a reasonably pro-British frame of mind, its continuance is a good thing and outweighs any disadvantages which may or may not follow from interferance by the League as a whole e.g. in Palestine affairs. In this connection it was considered that secession of Iraq and Transjordan would not really provide us with an Arab ally in any Palestine settlement ... .

Bennett (Assistant Secretary in the International Relations department of the CO) put his finger on the problem:

> The virtual lack of any effective comprehension of regional issues in Middle East policy was only too apparent in the attitude of the F.O. representatives ....[23]

As had happened over the question of continuing the immigration quota, the Colonial and Foreign Offices found themselves preoccupied with different concerns. The Foreign Office had eyes only for the Arab world, and Palestine was a subordinate issue to be fitted into the requirements of Arab diplomacy, while the Colonial Office, as the department with the responsiblity for administering the Mandate, was predominantly concerned with the considerable problems of Palestine *per se*. The events which took place between the Anglo-American Committee's creation and the writing of its report, such as the continuation of the immigration quota and the independence of Transjordan, served only to raise Foreign Office anxieties and its awareness of the Arab dimension, and to compound the difficulties the Colonial Office perceived and experienced in dealing with Palestine. It was not an auspicious background against which the Anglo-American Committee issued its report.

These difficulties were made more acute by the expectations entertained in the Foreign and Colonial Offices as to what the enquiry would recommend; expectations which were to be disappointed. The Colonial Office's expert on Palestine was Harris, and his report on 21 March expressed the feeling that on the subject of immigration: 'Provided that the recommendation is not too bizarre ... it will almost certainly be best to accept it as it stands and to urge the United States to do the same'. He added, however, that it was 'unlikely' that the Committee would repeat Truman's 'sweeping' proposal for the entry of the 100,000. A meeting held at the Foreign Office on 6 April, attended by representatives from the Colonial Office, the Cabinet Office and the War Office, discussed the Committee's likely recommendations and agreed that they would require lengthy discussion. However, certain short-term recommendations, like the suppression of the Hagana, would require forewarning and implementation at the same time as the Report appeared. There is no evidence that these forecasts were discussed much within the Foreign and Colonial Offices, but these expectations are interesting. Together with the other problems which concerned the Foreign and Colonial Offices between December 1945 and April 1946, which we have considered before, the circumstances suggest that the Anglo-American Committee's recommendations came as rather a shock to these departments of state.[24]

There was another important factor which had a bearing on the reception accorded to the Committee's report in London. This was the strategic debate which focused on the Middle East; it began during the second half of 1945 and reached a crescendo in the Defence Committee in 1946. It is a large subject involving Britain's global position, but it must be considered here briefly because it revealed not only the Chiefs of Staff's strategic concerns in the Middle East and Palestine, but also Bevin's growing misgivings over the Soviet Union's conduct. These led Bevin to support the COS position generally, but his acute awareness of the need to secure an American commitment against the Soviet Union transcended other concerns, including the Chiefs of Staff's wishes for Palestine.

Immediately the war against Japan ended, Attlee requested a report on planned Middle East forces and pointed out that he wanted the 'maximum possible reductions consistent with our commitments'. It took a full two months for Lawson, the Secretary

of State for War, to reply, and the Prime Minister answered
waspishly:

> This will not do at all. ... unless I can get a satisfactory account ... I shall
> be obliged to order a drastic percentage cut as the only effective way of
> reducing these swollen establishments.

The matter was not resolved, but dragged on, Lawson reminding
Attlee on 15 January 1946 'of some of the considerations which make
more far-reaching reductions impracticable', such considerations as
security problems in the Middle East and the safety of Imperial
communications. Attlee now took the fight to the Defence Committee
where on 15 February he asked that the assumption that there would
be no 'major emergency' in the next two to three years be accepted,
and that the size of Britain's armed forces reflect this. He also thought
that

> the strategic assumption that it was vital to us to keep open the
> Mediterranean, and that in fact we could, should be re-examined. He did
> not see how we could possibly do it under modern conditions.

This was bringing into question the most sacred cow of British
imperial strategy, venerated for more than a century. Bevin deflected
the blow at this meeting by asking that the forces should not be
reduced appreciably during the next three months but lowered in the
second half of 1946. A submission was made to the Cabinet on these
lines by the Prime Minister, and a reduction in the defence estimates
was accepted by the Cabinet.[25]

On this occasion Bevin had told the Defence Committee of his
concern with such problems as the negotiations with the Egyptian
Government over the revised treaty, and the Greek elections. This, he
said, made him anxious that the forces should be maintained for three
months to support Britain's foreign policy. The Foreign Secretary's
underlying concern was over the direction of Soviet policy. At the
beginning of January he had reported to the Cabinet that at the recent
Foreign Ministers' conference in Moscow, Stalin had pressed
informally for the withdrawal of British troops from Greece, and
Molotov had broken off discussions on Bevin's proposal for
facilitating the withdrawal of Soviet troops from Persia. All of Bevin's
concerns seem to have revolved around Soviet policy. The revision of
the 1936 Treaty with Egypt became more urgent in the light of Soviet
intentions in Turkey, Persia, the Italian colonies in North Africa and
Greece. Bevin told the Cabinet that these intentions

all pointed to a [Soviet] desire to reduce British influence in the Mediterranean. This made it more than ever important that we should proceed without delay with the revision of the Egyptian Treaty; for a satisfactory Treaty with Egypt was the clue to continued British influence with the Arab States ... .

Persia provided the most significant lesson for Bevin and for the USA, and was to elicit the first clear American move to contain communism. On 4 March, Bevin told the Cabinet that the USSR had announced its intention of retaining troops in Persia on some pretext and in contravention of the Anglo-Soviet Treaty of 1942. The Soviet move was designed to procure oil concessions. Within a few days Byrnes threatened to bring the matter before the UN Security Council, and the Cabinet agreed to support this move. The pressure was effective, and on the very eve of the Security Council meeting the Soviet Union broadcast an announcement that its troops had begun to withdraw from Persia. The lesson had been learned by Bevin and Byrnes, and all pretence at harmony between the erstwhile Big Three now vanished. After this incident the US Government moved steadily towards a policy of containment, and Bevin was confirmed in his distrust of Soviet intentions and in his belief in the need for strength and co-operation with the United States in order to counter them.[26]

Against the background of these events Attlee pressed forward with his attack on Middle East forces and Mediterranean strategy. In a paper of 2 March for the Defence Committee entitled 'Future of the Italian Colonies', Attlee began by questioning the 'strategy formulated in the past' that the route through the Mediterranean and Red Sea was vital to the British Commonwealth. He argued that this strategy depended upon Britain's past monopoly of sea power, and that now air power was decisive. The cost of keeping air superiority over the Mediterranean was simply too expensive, and the route around the Cape was more sensible. Attlee also questioned the underlying rationale of British strategy: 'Presumably, the strategic communications which it is suggested we must preserve are those with India, but the position of India is changing.' Furthermore, Britain was unable to defend Iraqi and Persian oilfields against attack from the north. Accordingly, Attlee called for a complete rethinking of Britain's strategic concepts. Bevin supplied the counter-blast in a paper for the Defence Committee which echoed the sentiments on the iron curtain Churchill had expressed at Fulton, Missouri, on 5 March. Bevin argued with Churchillian phraseology that Britain's position in the Mediterranean went beyond the military purpose and was 'vital to our position as a Great Power'. Without being able to influence 'the soft underbelly' of Europe, the Mediterranean states 'would fall, like Eastern Europe, under the totalitarian yoke'. 'If we move out of the Mediterranean', Bevin warned, 'Russia will move in'. Furthermore Britain would carry no conviction of purpose in the negotiations with Egypt if the Mediterranean was abandoned. It was an extraordinary and impassioned paper, made more odd because it did not follow through the argument and endorse wholeheartedly a British military presence in Palestine, Egypt or Cyprus but expressed instead a strong interest in the idea of setting up the main British base in Mombasa, which, as British territory, had a more certain future. Bevin's imagination had been stimulated, no doubt, by the Persian crisis, which was at its height at this time, and Dalton records that Bevin was 'in a great state' about it all. Although the COS did not like the idea of having the main British base as far south as Mombasa, they were, however, overjoyed at Bevin's gladiatorial performance in the defence of the Mediterranean's importance, and the Chiefs of Staff followed this up in their own paper for the Defence Committee. Alanbrooke, Cunningham and Tedder fully agreed with the Foreign Secretary and informed the Defence Committee that their strategic requirements were

> the establishment and maintenance of our position in:-
>   Western Europe, including Scandinavia.
>   The Iberian Peninsula and North-West Africa.
>   The Middle East, particularly Egypt and Palestine.
>   India and South-East Asia.[27]

Although this was the position when the Anglo-American Committee's Report was ready, it is useful to follow through the debate now. The COS's position was to be eroded, but very slowly. The first damage was done when the Defence Committee decided, on 24 April, to authorize the British delegation in Egypt to negotiate for the new treaty on the basis of the complete evacuation of British forces from Egypt. Unabashed by this setback, the COS submitted a paper to the Defence Committee a month later on 'Strategic Requirements in the Middle East' which concluded that, 'In war, the security of Egypt and Palestine is vital to the defence of the Middle East.' Accordingly, in peace time the COS required a treaty with Egypt which would ensure that bases were available for Britain's use in an emergency; the requirements in peace-time Palestine were:

Full military rights. We must be in a position to locate in Palestine any forces which we consider necessary, and we must have complete control of the organisation of the defence of the area. ...

Unless we obtain these minimum requirements, no effective defence of the Middle East is possible with all that this implies.

Prior to submitting this paper, various small amendments were discussed at a meeting of the COS Committee, and it is noteworthy that although the Anglo-American Committee's Report has been out for some time, no changes were discussed about the references to Palestine in the paper for the Defence Committee; evidently Palestine's importance was established beyond debate and irrespective of the labour of the enquiry. Two days after the paper was circulated, the Prime Minister gave the COS a mauling in the Defence Committee. Pressed to show why the Headquarters base had to be as far forward as Palestine or the Canal Zone, the Chiefs of Staff gave a most unconvincing reply to the Prime Minister and referred to the lessons of the last pre-atomic war and the difficulty of locating the Record Office, which housed details of the personnel stationed in the Middle East, further away than Cairo. Significantly, Bevin did not support the COS's position on Palestine and he was very critical of the damaging effect the size of the British force in Egypt had on the treaty negotiations. The Prime Minister summed up with general agreement that the COS's report on 'Strategic Requirements in the Middle East' could not be endorsed, and that the COS were invited to re-examine their requirements. Quite undeflected, the COS submitted a remarkably similar paper on 18 June, repeating the Middle East requirements even to the extent of wording their needs in Palestine in a similar way. Perhaps significantly the Defence Committee did not consider this paper for a month, and when it did the minutes suggest that it was Attlee who set the pace. He adroitly argued against making any definite conclusion yet until 'other general factors governing the overall strategy of the British Commonwealth' were settled, and at his prompting the Defence Committee merely took note of the COS recommendations. The matter was left like this until the end of the year.[28]

In this affair it is important to note where the Foreign Secretary and the COS parted company. Bevin was quite prepared to take issue with the Prime Minister on the question of the Mediterranean's importance, but not to support COS designs on Palestine and Egypt. The events in Persia helped to establish Bevin's awareness of the need to work with the United States in countering the Soviet Union, and in this lies the great significance and achievement of his time in office. Bevin was ahead of his colleagues in his eagerness to tie the US to Britain, and this was evidenced in a small way in the spring of 1946 by his wish that the Pacific island of Tarawa should be ceded to the USA as a base and memorial to the Marines. When the Cabinet rejected this, Bevin, although he was attending a Foreign Ministers' meeting in Paris at the time, urged his colleagues to reconsider the matter, but to no avail. Bevin's concern was not simply to smooth the path of Anglo-American relations, but a response to Byrnes' suggestion that the secession of Tarawa would help the passage of Britain's loan through Congress.[29] In a curious way this small affair mirrored the discussion of the Anglo-American Committee's Report in London, for with this likewise Bevin, from the distance of the Foreign Ministers' conference, showed himself more eager than his colleagues and officials to fall in with the Americans and implement the recommendations. The underlying thesis was undoubtedly Bevin's Anglo-American policy, but there was probably an awareness also of Britain's desperate need for the US loan.

Bearing in mind all these factors such as Bevin's concern at Soviet intentions, the strategic debate in the Defence Committee on the Mediterranean, the respective concerns of the Foreign Office in the Middle East and the Colonial Office in Palestine, and the COS's eagerness to mount a military operation in Palestine to disarm the Jews, it is apparent that the Anglo-American Committee's Report of 20 April was launched onto a veritable sea of troubles. During the ensuing weeks all of these factors may be seen at work.

At Bevin's decision the Report was considered by the Defence Committee first. Wikeley of the Eastern Department prepared a brief for his Secretary of State, commenting that in the Report the Arabs 'lose nearly all along the line' although no Jewish state was to be created. Wikeley advised that it was 'essential' to ensure the cooperation of the US Government, and he recommended that the Jews should be required to surrender their arms. When the illegal forces had been disbanded, the Report should be submitted to the United Nations Organization. This brief foreshadowed subsequent Foreign Office representations, but Bevin did not follow it in the Defence Committee on 24 April to the extent of lamenting the Arab losses or suggesting a referral to the UN. Attlee chaired this important meeting, which was attended by Bevin, Hall, Addison (Secretary of State for Dominion Affairs), Lawson, the Parliamentary Undersecretaries for the Admiralty and Air Ministry as well as Alanbrooke, Tedder, McGrigor, Ismay, an official from the treasury, and Howe.

Bevin began by mentioning his apprehension at the effect the entry of the 100,000 and the ending of the restrictions on land transfer would have, but:

> Nevertheless, he felt that it would be difficult to avoid acceptance of the broad outline of the report. It was a unanimous document and, as such, he hoped that it was an augury of co-operation by the United States Government in solving the problems of Palestine.

Bevin went on to say that the first step was to obtain the surrender of illegal arms, and until this was done 'we could hardly agree to accept new immigrants who might swell the ranks of the illegal organisations'. Bevin hoped to obtain US military assistance. Attlee, however, 'took a less rosy view of the report' as Palestine was to bear the brunt of the Jewish DP resettlement, and because there was little in the Report to promise US co-operation in Palestine. Attlee felt that 'the report proposed a policy which would set both the Arabs and the Jews against us and that we should implement it alone.' Hall remarked on the absence of any recommendation on the disarming of the Jewish illegal organizations, and he felt, much as Cunningham did, that unless the US would share the responsibility for implementing the Report 'he greatly doubted the wisdom of so doing'. A note of exasperation entered the discussion, portending things to come, when

> Ministers emphasised the heavy burden that was laid upon us by our responsibility in Palestine. Could we not relieve ourselves of these responsibilities?

Hall suggested this could be done by submitting a trusteeship agreement to the United Nations giving another country or countries the task but, predictably, Alanbrooke said

> that from a strategic point of view he considered it would be most unwise to give up our position in Palestine ... [which] might well be our last foothold in the eastern end of the Mediterranean.

There was 'general agreement' with this view. This meeting exhibited well all the various preoccupations of the departments and personalities; Bevin's to secure US co-operation, Attlee's to lighten Britain's burden, Hall's concern, which he shared with others, about the likelihood of trouble in Palestine and the consequent need to disarm the illegal organizations, and the COS preoccupation with Palestine as a base. As the next step the Committee managed to agree only to refer the whole matter to an Official Committee of 'the interested Departments' for it to submit recommendations to the Cabinet.[30]

Bevin suggested to Attlee on 24 April that Sir Norman Brook, the Cabinet Secretary, would be an acceptable chairman for the Official Committee as he himself was busy and because 'Palestine has been in the past rather a bone of contention between the Foreign Office and the Colonial Office'. Having given this advice, Bevin departed the next day to begin a long spell in Paris at the Foreign Ministers' conference, and in his absence the officials had free rein.[31]

The Chiefs of Staff's submission to the Committee was important, and Tedder's brief on this subject is illuminating. Tedder was advised that the Anglo-American Committee's Report fell into the category of a compromise unacceptable to either Arabs or Jews, that the military consequence of allowing 100,000 immigrants into Palestine 'is not acceptable', and warned that 'whatever the Government do with the Commission's [sic] report, we are in for trouble in Palestine'. It was recommended that 'disarming of the Jews must be a cardinal part of our policy'. When the COS Committee met on 26 April to decide upon its submission to the Official Committee, Tedder clearly used his brief and advocated, amidst general agreement, the vital necessity of disarming the Jews 'as the primary requirement'. The COS decided to advise the Official Committee that 'disarmament was the first step before allowing immigration to begin', to be effected either through persuasion, involving the USA, or through force. The implementation of the Report as it stood 'would ultimately result in a situation necessitating the provision of reinforcements beyond our capacity to effect'. As for opting out, the COS argued, 'An appeal to U.N.O. would be fraught with very grave military consequences.' This would be the case because assistance would not be forthcoming immediately, while the situation would deteriorate in Palestine following the referral to the UN, and furthermore the loss of the British foothold would leave the Middle East open to Soviet encroachment. These views of the Chiefs of Staff followed directly from the well-established plan to disarm the illegal Jewish organizations and from the strategic concept of the Middle East, both of which had been very clearly in evidence even as the Anglo-American Committee got on with its task. The Report had elicited nothing new from the military.[32]

The Foreign Office speedily received evidence from the Middle East posts of Arab hostility to the Anglo-American Committee's Report, in particular to the abolition of the White Paper and the entry of the 100,000. Reviewing the telegrams, Wikeley minuted laconically: 'They are all unfavourable' and distributed them to the Cabinet. Brook's Committee's Report, fifteen pages long, was prepared very quickly and was ready on 27 April, the day after the COS had made their submission. Knowing the attitudes of its constituent parties, the Committee's recommendations for the Cabinet were utterly predictable and delivered with the full *gravitas* of Whitehall. The reactions of the Palestine Arabs to the Anglo-American Committee's Report would be 'grave' because their national aspirations were denied, and these were unassuaged by the mere absence of a Jewish state. The Committee drew attention to the Presidential promises of consultations with the Arabs before any change was made in the basic situation. If the Report was implemented, the catalogue of woe would be enormous. There would probably be 'a general Arab rising in Palestine', the Arab states would lose their 'good faith' in Britain and may become 'accessible to Russian propaganda' as they would regard the implementation of the Report as a betrayal of American and British promises to consult them. Furthermore the negotiations with Egypt would be hampered and problems would arise with the Muslim population in India. Even the Yishuv would not remain satisfied with the entry of the 100,000, and the extremists would soon capitalize on the rising expectations this gain would engender. However, the Committee felt that the acceptance of the 100,000 and the Report might split US Zionism by satisfying its humanitarian supporters but not the extreme political demands. Curiously, the Official Committee's report did not pursue the logic of this analysis and perceive, as the Anglo-American Committee had done, the potential gain to the strength of moderate Zionism and the benefit this might have on the situation in Palestine if the 100,000 were accepted unconditionally. Instead, Brook's report concluded that acceptance of the Anglo-American Committee's Report politically

> would have disastrous effects on our position in the Middle East and might have unfortunate repercussions in India. It would not silence Zionist clamour in the United States ... .

The Chiefs of Staff's analysis was given great prominence in the Official Committee's report, and accordingly the need to disarm the Jewish illegal organizations was stressed, as was the belief that the implementation of the Anglo-American recommendations would cause a widespread Arab reaction which militarily could not be faced single-handed. On this basis Brook's report then proceeded to weigh the options. One was to obtain US help, which the COS wanted but which the Official Committee felt would damage Britain's prestige in the Middle East, and which would in fact be unlikely to materialize. Alternatively the Anglo-American Committee's Report and the situation in Palestine could be referred to the UN Security Council. Judging by the weight of arguments in favour of the latter option, Brook's report seemed to prefer it, although it meant the loss of Palestine as a Middle East base and ran the risk of trouble flaring up in the country and of Soviet interference in the UN. The rationale advanced for this option was that the problem was likely to come before the UN sooner or later as a threat to the peace, and the time gained by a referral might allow for a compromise in Palestine or for US help to materialize. Furthermore, the British Government had already promised to submit a new Palestine settlement to the UN. These then were the options presented to the Cabinet by the official representatives of the Foreign and Colonial Offices, the Treasury and the India Office. Brook's report finished by emphasizing once again the Chiefs of Staff's view on disarming the Jewish illegal organizations, by persuasion or by force, and ended with the unequivocal recommendation that

> if the policy advocated in the [Anglo-American Committee's] report is adopted, the disarming and disbandment of the Jewish illegal organisations and an assurance of the co-operation of the Jewish Agency should be conditions precedent to any extension of Jewish immigration.[33]

As this official submission to the Cabinet indicates, there was little enthusiasm to pursue Bevin's Anglo-American initiative and to treat it in reality as a 'fresh approach' to the problem of Palestine, as Howe and Sargent had called it in October 1945. All the established attitudes were paraded in Brook's report; the COS's eagerness to disarm the Jews, a policy which was endorsed by the Foreign and Colonial Offices, the FO's concern at the reaction of the Arab world, and the preference for taking the whole problem to the United Nations which we have noticed in the Eastern Department before. On 26 April, Butler, the Superintending Undersecretary of the North American Department of the Foreign Office, wrote an interesting minute to Howe, his opposite number at the Eastern Department, in which he argued ingeniously for a return to the pristine position. Rejection of the Anglo-American Committee's Report, Sir Nevile Butler argued, would not upset the United States too much if 'we play our hand well' because the enquiry was not regarded 'as an American "show" '; Truman's view, however, 'is less calculable', which was to say different. Rejection of the 100,000 could be made on the grounds of Britain's 'inability' to accept these immigrants without the support of the United Nations, and Butler felt that British firmness on the subject would also secure her standing with the Arab world. As we have seen, the previous year Butler had been an advocate of a policy of involving the United States in the Palestine question, to the distaste of the Eastern Department, and his position, plainly, had shifted. However, he had not abandoned altogether the preference for an American role and he now argued that it was axiomatic that US assistance came most readily beneath the umbrella of the UN. Butler's views now accorded with those well established in the Eastern Department, and Beeley minuted that this was: 'A most useful paper. Keep it available for use during [the] S[ecretary] of S[tate]'s discussions in Paris'. Evidently the attitude of the Eastern Department to the whole Anglo-American enterprise had not altered at all.[34]

While the officials and Chiefs of Staff were polishing up their arguments in London, Bevin sought to continue the Anglo-American initiative through his talks with Byrnes in Paris. He told Byrnes of his worry at the existence of the Jewish illegal organizations and their potential for causing trouble, and he hinted broadly that: 'We were seriously considering whether we would not throw the whole matter up'. However, Bevin indicated his preparedness to accept the entry of the 100,000 if the Jews were first disarmed and if the immigrants were *bona fide* DPs and not merely young and healthy reinforcements for the Hagana. Bevin expressed the hope that the US would give military help with the disarmament.[35]

On 29 April, the day before the Anglo-American Committee's Report was published, Bevin returned to London to attend the Cabinet meeting which was to decide British policy. The Foreign Secretary gave a powerful performance and argued that

> if the situation were skilfully handled in consultation with the United States Government, it might be possible to bring about a reasonable settlement on the basis of the [Anglo-American] Committee's recommendations. He was not in favour of an immediate reference to the [United Nations] Security Council. He thought that this would be regarded as a confession of failure and would have unfortunate effects on other aspects of our foreign policy. The essence of our policy should be to retain the interest and participation of the United States Government in this problem.

The contrast with Brook's report was made even more acute by Bevin's assertion that 'we should not be unduly alarmed by some initial clamour from the Arab States'. Hall agreed that policy should be decided in concert with the United States, and in the discussion the anxiety to obtain American assistance was clearly in evidence because: 'It would be very difficult for His Majesty's Government to carry out alone the Committee's recommendations'. There was general agreement also on the necessity of disarming the Jewish illegal organizations before adopting the recommendations of the Committee of Enquiry. The Cabinet minutes record that 'some Ministers' wanted the United Nations to be notified of the Anglo-American discussions simultaneously with these talks proceeding, but Bevin overruled this. Bevin said that he would try to get Byrnes' agreement to a meeting between a body of experts from the Foreign Office and State Department to consider in detail US assistance and that meanwhile no official statement should be made on the British Government's attitude to the Report. Bevin secured the agreement of the Cabinet to this policy and then returned to Paris.[36]

At this most delicate juncture for the survival of Bevin's Anglo-American policy, a statement by President Truman caused the Foreign Secretary acute embarrassment. On 30 April, coincidentally with the publication of the Anglo-American Committee's Report, Truman issued the following comment:

> I am very happy that the request which I made for the immediate admission of 100,000 Jews into Palestine has been unanimously endorsed.
>
> I am also pleased that the Committee recommends in effect the abrogation of the White Paper ... .
>
> In addition to these immediate objectives the report deals with many other questions of long range political policies ... which require careful study and which I will take under advisement.

The result of Truman's apparent intention to take the recommendation on the 100,000 out of the context of the rest of the Report and endorse it with much the same fervour as he had following Harrison's report was acutely reminiscent in London of past US irresponsibility which Bevin's policy had sought to end, and it weakened Bevin's case for standing by the Anglo-American initiative. Francis Williams (1952) records that this statement, issued without consultation with the British Government, 'threw Bevin into one of the blackest rages I ever saw him in'. As the Prime Minister's public relations adviser, Williams was instructed on this occasion to brief overseas correspondents that strong protests came 'directly from a Downing Street spokesman'. Bevin sent a telegram from Paris to the Prime Minister, asking him to make it clear in the Commons that

we cannot be anything in this matter [of the 100,000] unless the Jewish
agency and others disarm. This is vital.
I consider that the United States must be put right up against it.

The insistence on disarmament as a prerequisite had been made more
emphatic not simply by Truman's statement but because, on 25
April, seven soldiers had been murdered in Tel Aviv by Jewish
terrorists, and when the Colonial Secretary reported this in the
Commons on 30 April there was obvious pressure there for the
disarmament of the illegal organizations. Bevin sent a stiff letter to
Byrnes on 1 May reminding him of British casualties in Palestine and
the public pressure for the disarmament of the illegal forces, from
which it followed that the 'private armies must be dealt with' before
the 100,000 could enter Palestine. On the same day Attlee told the
House of Commons that the Report as a whole was being studied by
the British and US Governments 'to ascertain to what extent the
Government of the United States would be prepared to share' the
burden of implementation and that the immigration of the 100,000
was not possible until the illegal armies had been disbanded.[37]
    What had provoked Truman's untimely statement? The record
shows that it was partly a suspicion of the British Government's
prevarication, but mainly the result of Zionist pressure. When
Halifax relayed Bevin's request, made to Byrnes, that no action
should be taken by the US Government on the Anglo-American
Committee's Report 'without prior consultation with me', and that
the Report should not be published immediately, Truman noted
suspiciously: 'Approved — but it [might] just give the British a
chance to pull their usual stunt'. Even as Bevin sought to continue
with an Anglo-American policy by negotiating with Byrnes for
further talks between officials to work out the details, Zionist pressure
mounted. Silver, who, in common with other militant Zionists, was
highly critical of the Anglo-American Enquiry's Report, was
persuaded by McDonald and Crum to hold his tongue. Silver then
suggested that the best step would be to capitalize on what the Report
did offer the Zionists by getting Truman to issue a statement
welcoming the recommendations on the 100,000 and for the ending of
the White Paper. A draft was prepared by Silver and Neumann which
Crum took to Niles at the White House. Truman was apparently
eager to respond positively to the Report at an earlier stage than the
cumbersome Anglo-American talks would allow, and he accepted the
draft which Niles brought him with the addition of two items about
safeguarding the Holy Places and the Palestine Arabs. The result was

to place a feather in the cap of the American Zionists, but the statement they had persuaded Truman to issue served principally to antagonize Bevin and make his case for pursuing Anglo-American co-operation seem weaker to its critics in the Cabinet and Whitehall.[38]

It is appropriate to place the initial reaction of the British Government to the Committee's Report in perspective at this stage. If the reception accorded to the Report appears rather as a postscript to the policy concerns which were in evidence in London during the Committee's investigations, this is accurate. Under the influence of terrorism, illegal immigration and the uncooperative attitude of the Jewish Agency, the Chiefs of Staff had developed a plan to disarm the illegal Jewish organizations and to arrest the Jewish leadership on the next available pretext, be that a terrorist incident or an Anglo-American Committee recommendation. The operation was held up by a consideration for the enquiry's success, and then frozen by the absence of a recommendation in its Report, but against this background the suggestion that 100,000 immigrants should be allowed to enter Palestine was viewed with something approaching apoplexy. Furthermore, it was a natural emotion, shown in Parliament and in the Cabinet discussions, to regard such a 'concession' very unfavourably while illegal terrorist organizations were murdering British soldiers. While the Anglo-American Committee probably failed to consider the strength of these feelings, there is a conspicuous absence of any consideration in London of the Enquiry Committee's rationale in suggesting the unconditional entry of the 100,000. There is no evidence to suggest that the immigration of this number was ever properly considered as a useful means whereby the situation in Palestine could be defused and the hands of the moderate Zionists strengthened. The explanation for this is the entrenched recommendation of the COS for disarmament, the engrained apprehension of the Foreign Office at the reaction of the Arab world, and the understandable human distaste for ignoring murderous terrorist activities. The consequence was the unequivocal demand that the Jewish illegal organizations should be disarmed before the recommendation on the 100,000 was implemented, and this position of the British Government focused Zionist opposition once again upon Britain's policy and spared Zionism from dividing in its own reaction to the Report.

There was a deeper failure in London, exhibited most conspicuously in the submission the Official Committee made to the Cabinet, in that there was no disposition to treat the Anglo-American

Committee's Report as a new factor and a fresh basis on which to proceed in future. The continuity of the Foreign Office thinking, before, during and after the Enquiry had laboured, is manifest. So too is the attitude of the Chiefs of Staff both on disarmament and also on Palestine's strategic role. Bevin, with little encouragement from his Cabinet colleagues or anyone else, sought to preserve the Anglo-American initiative and turn the Enquiry's recommendations into a policy which was acceptable within the British Government, and during May 1946 he continued with his labours.

The experts' discussions

There is no record of activity in the State Department during the Anglo-American Committee's enquiry which paralleled that of the Foreign Office, and it would appear that the subject of Palestine was left alone. Once the Report became available, however, the State Department re-engaged its attention and began to organize the next step. Its progress was undoubtedly ruffled by Truman's statement of 30 April, Henderson (Director of the Office of Near Eastern and African Affairs) telling a member of the British embassy staff that he and the Department had

> made every effort to head off the unilateral statement ... but forces had been at work in the White House, which the State Department had been quite unable to control.

Halifax reported to the Foreign Office that 'Henderson deeply regretted the occurrence'. The wish to persevere with an Anglo-American approach to the Palestine problem was clear following a memorandum by Hilldring which was sent to Acheson on 3 May. Hilldring was Assistant Secretary of State for Occupied Areas and a Zionist sympathiser, and he argued: 'As anticipated, the British are stalling on the Anglo-American Committee's recommendation for authorization of 100,000 immigration visas', and Hilldring proposed 'an aggressive public policy of needling the British' in order to force their acceptance of the Report and thereby relieve the extent of the DP problem in the parts of Germany and Austria occupied by US forces. Merriam, Chief of the Division of Near Eastern Affairs, replied in a way that would have done justice to the Foreign Office itself. He pointed out that Hilldring considered the matter from the European view only and ignored the other recommendations in the Report, its purely advisory status, and American relations with the Arab world including her educational links which 'constituted a sheet anchor in the Middle East'. The Anglo-American initiative precluded any unilateral policy, Merriam argued, and he warned against courting British resentment and betraying the promises to consult the Arab states.[39]

This was indeed the spirit in which the State Department proceeded. On 3 May, Henderson sent Acheson, who was Acting Secretary of State, a draft memorandum for the President in which he bravely assumed 'that the [Anglo-American Committee's] report constitutes a valid basis for determining this Government's policy toward Palestine'. Accordingly he proposed holding talks with the British Government and consultations with the Arabs and Jews, and that this procedure be followed by an Anglo-American decision on the policy to be adopted towards the Report. The subsequent announcement of this policy 'would include references to the placing of Palestine under United Nations trusteeship'. Henderson added, in a marginal note for Acheson; 'We are of course playing with dynamite'. Acheson sent the memorandum to the President above his own signature on 6 May, together with a draft telegram for Attlee. Truman approved the draft telegram, which was sent on 8 May, proposing that the views of the Arabs and Jews be obtained by the US and British Governments separately first, and that then an Anglo-American policy should be formulated. Truman expressed the hope that the consultations would proceed quickly 'in view of the urgency surrounding the question' of the 100,000. In Paris the next day Bevin warned Byrnes that to consult the Arab States just now 'would prejudice the Egyptian negotiations and might set the Middle East in an uproar', and he asked that the approach should wait until 20 May. Bevin proposed that talks between experts from the British and US Governments should take place before the approach to the Arabs and Jews, and to substantiate the need for this expert discussion Bevin gave Byrnes a memorandum outlining the military and financial costs of implementing the Anglo-American Committee's Report. This memorandum also stressed the need for the illegal Jewish forces to be disarmed, and Britain's requirement for US military and financial help. At Bevin's suggestion, Attlee asked Truman to consider Bevin's proposal for talks between experts. Bevin's objective in pressing for this discussion between experts was not to find a pretext for delay, but to nail down the US Government on the precise degree and nature of their support for Britain in implementing a policy based on the Anglo-American Committee's recommendations. In this Bevin was pursuing the objectives set out and agreed in the Cabinet discussion of 29 April.[40]

The process of organizing the experts' conference and the consultations with the Arabs and Jews was a little protracted and untidy, but throughout the British Goverment's concern, inspired by Bevin, to follow up the Anglo-American initiative is clear. Clear also was Truman's pristine anxiety about the urgency of the Jewish DP problem, and the State Department's concern to act honourably before the Arab world by discharging the US promise that consultations would precede any change in the basic situation in Palestine.

On 13 May the Cabinet approved the line which had been agreed at a meeting at Chequers, attended by Bevin, on the previous day. As a result Attlee sent Truman a message setting out his government's position; it was hoped that consultations with the Arabs and Jews could wait until 20 May because of the Egyptian negotiations, and thereafter one month should be allowed for the Arabs and Jews to give their views on the Anglo-American Committee's Report. Preferably the talks between the expert delegations would precede this, but Attlee showed a willingness to concede to American wishes if these preferred the talks to be simultaneous with or after the consultations. As a final stage Attlee suggested a conference between Arabs, Jews, and the British and US governments 'to consider the whole question on the basis of the Committee's report and the results of the preliminary consultations both between [the] Arabs and Jews and between our own experts'. Truman accepted the date and period for consulting the Arabs and Jews, but urged that no more than preliminary talks between experts should begin before the process of consultation was complete, and he left open the matter of the conference as something 'to have in mind' in future. The Prime Minister concurred, and later in May he followed up Truman's request with a comprehensive list of 'the various matters on which decisions would be required before the report could be implemented' for the experts to consider. This agenda for the officials' discussion clearly reflected the British Government's concern at the burden the Committee's Report placed upon them, and their quest for US assistance in bearing it. The problems associated with the entry of the 100,000 were listed, including transport, housing and employment. The difficulty perceived by the British Government in translating the recommendation that neither Arabs nor Jews should dominate Palestine into 'a workable constitution' and into a trusteeship agreement for submission to the UN was also conveyed.[41]

On 5 June Truman in reply came up with an agenda of his own. He informed Attlee that he was sending experts to begin preliminary discussions on 'the urgent physical problems arising out of the transfer to Palestine of the 100,000 Jews'. Truman promised that the United

States would transport the immigrants and help with their housing in Palestine. Now while there was momentum in London behind the experts' discussions, the implication in Truman's telegram that the matter of the 100,000 could be settled first was reminiscent of his earlier statement on the Committee's Report and aroused considerable misgivings in London. Truman's motivation seems to have been unchanged throughout; to assist with the humanitarian cause of resettling the remnant of the holocaust. The White House was being pressed by American Zionists to work for the entry of the 100,000, and following the American Zionist Emergency Committee's decision on 9 May a campaign to bombard the President with telegrams and letters got under way. Truman may have been given a more specific stimulus, however. A short while before sending this to Attlee, Truman had received a letter from Myron Taylor, representative to the Vatican, in which the perils of upsetting the Muslim world were expounded and the benefits of resettling the Jews by 'a broad dispersion' throughout the world were advocated. Truman requested Niles' opinion on this letter, and this elicited an emotional memorandum which may have prompted Truman's offer to help with the transfer of the 100,000. Niles' memorandum read in part:

> May I again respectfully point out that you are concerning yourself now only with the transference of 100,000 Jews. The other parts of the [Anglo-American Committee's] report you, yourself have publicly said that you would take under consideration for future study.

Rebutting Taylor's suggestion that the entry of the 100,000 into Palestine would drive the Arabs into a Soviet embrace, Niles concluded fervently, 'If the transference of 100,000 Jews were responsible for a future war the world is certainly in bad shape.' There is no direct evidence to connect Niles' advice to Truman with the President's offer to Attlee, but it is clear that Truman was in sympathy with the views Niles expressed. Not only did they accord with Truman's earlier pronouncements, but also they were reflected in the reply the President sent to Taylor on 27 May in which he defended the need for speedy action on the question of the 100,000 in view of their current plight and argued that 'we dare not wait on ... [the] consideration by a large number of individual countries' for coping with the emergency; Palestine alone could do this. It would seem, therefore, that Niles' advice encouraged Truman in his policy, and in passing it is interesting to note, alongside Niles' ardent Zionism, the depth of his ignorance about the concerns which so haunted the Foreign Office and Chiefs of Staff: 'The danger of unifying the Moslem world can be dismissed', he advised the President 'because a good part of the Moslem world follows Ghandi and his philosophy of non-resistance'.[42]

The new British Ambassador in Washington, Lord Inverchapel, reported Henderson as saying informally that Truman's despatching of the expert delegation did not mean that the question of the 100,000 was going to be considered apart from the rest of the enquiry's recommendations. However, Inverchapel added, 'I should not ... be at all surprised if the President does ... nourish hopes that it will prove possible to push on with the transfer of the 100,000 before deciding upon long-term policy.' Wary of just such an intention, Attlee told Truman that the British Government 'will not feel able to determine their policy on any one of the [Anglo-American] Committee's recommendations until they have examined the results of the official consultations on the Report as a whole.' Attlee was as able as Truman to stick to his position, and he went on to 'doubt whether any useful purpose would be served by the sending of an advance party'. Henderson tried to reassure Inverchapel that the preliminary talks would in fact become merged with the general discussions between the officials, and that the White House was pressing in this way 'to deflect American criticism of inaction' and to endeavour to meet Attlee's request that the talks commenced on about 13 June. The potential impasse was avoided by the diminution of the importance of these preliminary talks, and by leaving their real objective vague.[43]

On 11 June, Truman announced the creation of a Cabinet Committee on Palestine consisting of the Secretary of State and the Secretaries for War and for the Treasury to undertake the negotiations with the British Government in the wake of the preliminary talks. Byrnes announced that his alternate would be Grady. This announcement helped to diminish the significance of the preliminary talks. Furthermore, this Cabinet Committee effectively replaced the State Department's monitoring of the Palestine question, Henderson minuting with Acheson's approval that the Department ought 'not to take any action regarding ... [Palestine] except at the Committee's direction or with its concurrence'.[44]

Harriman, the US Ambassador in London, had been instructed on 10 June to commence discussions 'of a purely exploratory nature' with the British on the physical problems of transferring the 100,000. Truman turned aside Attlee's doubts by arguing:

I consider that our two Governments should without delay endeavor to make detailed plans for the transfer of the 100,000 ... These plans would thus be ready for use when definite decisions were made. I feel moreover that considerable time would be saved … .

Attlee satisfied himself by reiterating the British Government's position while pointing out that the American advance party would be contacted immediately by the delegation of British officials 'with a view to preparing the ground for their discussions with the Representatives of your Cabinet Committee'. Clearly the exact purpose of the preliminary talks was left vague so that it could satisfy the mutual imperative for both governments to begin discussions, without these early meetings being required to settle anything. It was an inauspicious prelude to Grady's mission, and there is clear evidence of continued British misgivings about American intentions as well. Inverchapel warned the Foreign Office on 13 June that from a talk with Byrnes 'it was quite apparent that despite all we have said, he takes for granted admission of the 100,000 as an immediate step.' Byrnes apparently felt that the sole purpose of the Cabinet Committee itself 'was to implement the findings of the Anglo-American Committee'. Sargent, the Permanent Undersecretary at the Foreign Office, drew these ominous signs to Attlee's attention, noting that 'the two Governments still have different ideas as to the purpose of the talks … [which] should be to provide data which will help the Governments to determine their policy on the [Anglo-American Committee's] report … as a whole.'[45]

These preliminary talks were a low-key affair, the resulting memorandum which was ready by the end of June conceding that the discussions 'have been limited to the physical and economic problems involved' in the transfer of the 100,000; 'No account has been taken of political and military repercussions'. The Cabinet had decided that this report 'should be made in the form, not of a report to the two Governments, but of a memorandum for the use of the main conference of officials', again indicating the British Government's anxiety that the whole of the Anglo-American Committee's Report would be considered. Even while the preliminary talks were in progress, Attlee urged Truman that the main conference should begin early in July. On 4 July he sent the President an anxious request that, in view of the parliamentary pressure for a debate on Palestine policy, the departure of the American delegation be expedited. As a result Grady and his Committee left the United States on 10 July and were ready to begin discussions on 12 July.[46]

Throughout these events the British Government's anxiety to avoid the singling out of the recommendation on the 100,000 from the rest of the enquiry's Report is manifest. It was evidenced again in an interesting exchange which followed from a telegram Bevin sent from Paris on 20 June to the Cabinet. Bevin suggested publicity should stress that, 'His Majesty's Government accept [the] entry of 100,000 Jews as part of a comprehensive plan to solve [the] two problems of Palestine and Jews in Europe, but will not tolerate having their hand forced by terroristic methods.' Beeley minuted that this 'go[es] beyond anything to which His Majesty's Government have yet committed themselves', and Attlee replied sharply to the Foreign Secretary that he did not understand his point: 'His Majesty's Government have not (repeat not) accepted this proposal' for the entry of the 100,000. Bevin's telegram may have been in part an aberration, but it also reflected that he was more willing to accept the Anglo-American Committee's Report and to press on in the cause of Anglo-American co-operation than his colleagues.[47]

The Middle East posts, as we have seen, were quick to warn the British Government of the unfavourable repercussions that would follow the enquiry's recommendations—this providing grist to the Foreign Office mill. Once the Report was published, the Arab reaction was speedily reported back both to the Foreign Office and State Department. On 3 May the US Minister in Cairo, Tuck, reported Azzam Pasha's anger at Truman's statement welcoming the recommendation for the entry of the 100,000 and his critical view of the Report which 'gave [the] Zionists two things that would lead to a Jewish state: Immigration and [the] right to purchase unlimited land'. This reaction was typical, and it encouraged the movement in both London and Washington for holding formal consultations with the Arab states before reaching any policy decision on Palestine, thereby discharging the undertakings given to the Arabs when the enquiry was announced. Stonehewer-Bird, the British Ambassador in Baghdad, reminded the Foreign Office on 27 April about this promise, and Beeley minuted that: 'We are certainly pledged to consultation'. Henderson's draft memorandum which Acheson submitted to the President on 6 May included the holding of consultations with both Arabs and Jews in the proposed steps to be taken, a proposal that seems to have been taken seriously by Truman who told Niles in an undated note about this time that:

> The late President made a commitment to the King of Arabia in a famous letter, which I later confirmed. We have to consult both sides. I doubt if the 1,000,000 [sic] necessarily means a change of policy — but the whole report does.

On 10 May Acting Secretary of State Acheson received the Ministers of Egypt, Iraq, Lebanon, Saudi Arabia and Syria, and reassured them that their governments would be consulted before a policy decision was made and that such consultations were provided for in the exchanges between the President and the Prime Minister about the timetable for proceeding. Accordingly, US posts were instructed to deliver requests to the Arab governments on 20 May for their views on the Anglo-American Committee's Report. The approach, which was made to the Arab League, the Arab Higher Committee, and the Jewish Agency as well, was to be co-ordinated with a similar British overture. The Arab Higher Committee replied that they 'reject[ed] it completely', and called for the termination of Jewish immigration and land purchase, and the creation of an Arab government in Palestine. In London 'this warning' that the Arab Higher Committee was preparing to fight was circulated to the Cabinet. Eddy, the US Minister in Saudi Arabia, reported an angry reaction to American involvement and her request for speedy Arab comments on the Report 'which renders the pretense at prior consultation a mockery'. Dire warnings were reported by the US Minister in Beirut, who tersely summarized part of the reply to the American request for views:

> If Zionist threat of force continues Arabs cannot stand supine. It is unlikely a clash could be localized. Mandatory power's inability to disband Zionist army is already apparent. ... American support of Zionism is poisoning Arab thought ...

This response from the Arab governments and bodies was predictable and served to confirm the thinking of the Foreign Office and State Department.[48]

Three important points about the Arab reaction may be noted. First was the resentment at US involvement and the suspicion at American suasion over Britain. Shone, the British Minister in Beirut, reported on 27 May the local American suspicion that the British were encouraging these views in Arab circles; in denying the American suspicion, Shone observed:

> There is no doubt that Arab public opinion lays a large measure of responsibility for the [enquiry's] recommendations on the Americans; ... but the press is little, if any, less bitter against us, not least for having brought the United States into the question.

This view was used to reply to enquiries by the State Department about the allegations made by US diplomatic posts, and Inverchapel reported that Henderson 'seemed well satisfied at the rebuttal' but added, 'with a smile "it is in fact no less true that we Americans must be held largely responsible for the Committee's recommendations".' The Arab states could not fail to be aware of Britain's dependence on the United States, exemplified by her efforts to secure the American loan at this time, and it was an obvious connection to make between this relationship and the Report of the Anglo-American Enquiry; Clayton reportedly felt that this impression was 'almost universally held' in the Middle East.[49]

The second feature of the Arab reaction emerged from an extraordinary meeting of the Arab League at Bludan between 8 and 12 June. Publicly, the result was the creation of a Palestine Committee of the League and a special Palestine fund. In secret, decisions were made that if the enquiry's Report was implemented, British and American interests would be boycotted and the situation would be brought up in the United Nations. This direct threat fulfilled the worst fears of the State Department and the Foreign Office by striking at American and British economic and military interests in the Middle East, and by involving the Soviet Union via the machinery of the UN.[50]

In the Arab response there was a persistent indication that the cursory convassing of views by Britain and the US during May did not discharge properly the undertaking to consult, exemplified in a Note Verbale the Minister of Foreign Affairs in Baghdad sent to the US Legation on 19 June, long after the views of the Iraqi Government had been solicited. The note which referred to Roosevelt's promises and requested their fulfilment, considered together with, say, the Saudi Arabian reaction to the American invitation for comments on the enquiry's recommendations, would suggest there was still some mileage left in the process of consulting the Arabs.[51]

We have seen already how the Anglo-American Committee's Report threatened to divide the Zionists. In Silver's case, for instance, the initial hostility to the Report was overcome by more moderate counsels who seized upon and exploited what was offered—the entry of the 100,000. The US consul in Jerusalem, Pinkerton, reported the reaction of a member of the Jewish Agency's Political Department to the Report: 'Zionist political aims have been sacrificed to philanthropy'. This comment put the Zionist dilemma in a nutshell, but for the present all pressure was directed towards the implementation of the positive recommendation for the entry of the 100,000. To this end representations were made to Truman, and Crum made capital in the press out of Bevin's promise to the Committee of Enquiry that he would do everything in his power to get a unanimous Report implemented. The formal response by the Jewish Agency to the US Government's overture showed that the Zionist objective at present was to obtain the entry into Palestine of the 100,000, for while the reply began by pointing out that the reasons for a Jewish state 'remain valid and unaltered', the primary concern was shown to be with these immigrants. The delay in their arrival in Palestine, the Agency urged, was causing misgivings, and their entry remained the prerequisite for the consideration of the other parts of the Anglo-American Committee's Report. Zionist pressure to secure this objective provoked Bevin into making an observation to the Party Conference on 12 June that the American Jews were so keen for the 100,000 to go to Palestine 'because they don't want them in New York'. Inverchapel reported the resulting storm of protest from a meeting of Zionists in Madison Square Garden, and he commented ruefully: 'Your criticism of New York has, of course, not only hit the nail on the head but driven it woundingly deep'. Bearing in mind the sensibilities of Americans, Jewish and non-Jewish, and the breach of the Bermuda accords on the immigration levels for the United States and Palestine by the US Government, Bevin's remark contained some truth but great tactlessness.[52]

It was particularly ill-timed because the American Zionists were in the process of deciding their policy on the US loan for Britain. Wise was consistently in favour of the loan going ahead, writing his views in *Opinion* in April, and telling Niles on 18 June:

> We should proceed to counteract the Silver mischief. I am not prepared to hurt the interests of the American and British people, alike involved in this loan to spite a man [Bevin] however nasty his speech ... .

Silver, of course, saw the loan as another means whereby pressure could be brought to bear upon the British Government, and on 21 June he secured a partial victory in the American Zionist Emergency Council's decision to work for a delay of the loan in Congress, but not to oppose it completely. However, on 9 July, Wise published his support for the loan again, and many other such prominent Zionists as Proskauer and Morgenthau followed; on 13 July, two months after going through the Senate, the loan passed the House by 219 votes to 155. The British Cabinet's reaction to this pressure was cool, and when Bevin relayed from Paris Byrnes' suggestion that a statement sympathetic to the Report should be issued beccause Congress was debating the loan, the Cabinet decided that such a move would be a mistake. This attitude repeated that taken over Tarawa island. There is no evidence to suggest that Britain's Palestine policy, or the Anglo-American Committee members, were in fact influenced by considerations of the US loan. It seems fair, however, to regard this episode as an example of Britain's growing dependence upon the United States, which Bevin perceived acutely, and to conclude that the matter of the loan was subsumed into this general consideration.[53]

The most dramatic events to take place in the period between the publication of the enquiry's Report in the spring and the conference with Grady's team in the summer were connected with terrorism and illegal immigration into Palestine. They reflect also a partial victory for the Chiefs of Staff in London. We have seen the evolution of the plans to move against the Agency and to disarm the Yishuv, how these were held in readiness for use on a suitable occasion, and how they helped to condition and shape the British Government's attitude that the recommendation for the entry of the 100,000 required first of all the disarmament of the Jewish illegal organizations. Once the Report had been published, the COS resumed their campaign. Although a small Staff Conference, attended only by the Chiefs, Hall, Addison and Sargent, concluded on 30 April 'that it was important to avoid anything which would alienate the Americans' by delegating powers to the High Commissioner to take action against the Jewish Agency on a large scale, just eight days later the COS Committee agreed to Tedder's suggestion to refer the question to the Prime Minister. Attlee replied firmly:

> wider considerations must be borne in mind. To put into operation the full plans against the Jewish Agency and the Hagana on account of an outrage for which they cannot be proved to be responsible would have widespread repercussions at a time when it is hoped to deal with the Palestine problem through Anglo-American cooperation. We, therefore, cannot give authority for large scale action in advance.
>
> In the event of an outrage, action must be local ... .

Attlee's statement reflected Bevin's continued influence in Cabinet for pursuing the Anglo-American initiative, and his ban on taking action was a continuation of the instructions issued in January out of regard for the policy of co-operation with the United States.[54]

The prohibition on taking action was to be eroded by the situation in Palestine. A continuous problem was illegal immigration. On 13 May, a ship carrying 1,600 illegal immigrants was intercepted and the Commander in Chief, Middle East, warned the War Office that 'a whole series of other boats' might follow while the Jewish Agency, aware that whether or not the illegal immigrants reached Palestine they would be counted against the quota, were playing up the situation. The number of illegal immigrants apprehended in March had been just under 1,000, with only ninety-four in April, but in May, June and July the figures were 1,663, 1,758 and 1,100 respectively. There was considerable apprehension that these numbers would become uncontrollable, or that disorders would occur and break-outs be engineered in the detention camps, and the Chiefs of Staff began to consider diverting the ships to Cyprus in order to detain the illegal immigrants there. There was some evidence to suggest 'Russian complicity in illegal immigration traffic from Roumanian ports' as a War Office report put it, and such suspicions were compounded by the departure of the *Smyrna,* carrying 1,600 illegal immigrants, in May. Representations made in Moscow gave little satisfaction, and a few weeks later the British Vice-Consul in Stettin added to the evidence of Soviet complicity, pointing out that:

> The system adopted by the Russians in selecting candidates for repatriation, would appear to have been so lax, that it is more than possible that any Jew desirous of leaving Russia could do so with little difficulty.

More serious still was terrorism in Palestine. On 15 May the Chiefs of Staff were told by the recently retired General Officer Commanding Palestine, D'Arcy, possibly for that reason,

> that if we forcibly implemented the disarming of the Palestine population and broke up the illegal armed organizations, no other action would have such a beneficial effect towards influencing the Arabs to accept a compromise and to accept a certain measure of further immigration. They would then see that our intentions were firm … .

Not only was this line completely different from that which D'Arcy had taken in his evidence before the Anglo-American Enquiry, when he had appeared more concerned at the difficulties of disarming the Yishuv than the benefits of such action, it was also precisely the opposite line of reasoning the Anglo-American Committee had followed in thinking that the situation in Palestine could be defused and a compromise reached most easily if the entry of the 100,000 was allowed without any such military action.[55]

The pressure of events in Palestine continued to be remorseless and crucial. On 10 June trains were damaged by Jewish terrorists, on the night of 16–17 June eight road and railway bridges were badly damaged and numerous casualties inflicted upon both sides, and on 18 June six British officers were kidnapped. Two officers were released a few days later, but this kidnapping seems to have been the last straw for the military. Colonel Meinertzhagen, a Zionist supporter formerly with the British Army, recorded in his diary that this 'is hitting below the belt apart from doing their cause great harm'. The tone of the COS Committee meeting on 19 June reflected this feeling. The Commander in Chief, Middle East, General Paget, reported in his telegram that he felt 'the time had come' for the High Commissioner and himself to be given authority to take action. The COS agreed, arguing in discussion that the 'restrictions were tying the hands of the military authorities in dealing adequately with the present outrages'. The Colonial Secretary reported the position to the Cabinet, adding that Cunningham also wanted the talks with the American advanced party on the entry of the 100,000 halted. Hall advised the Cabinet against taking this latter step, and the Cabinet agreed. At the Cabinet meeting Attlee read Bevin's telegram from Paris in which he urged, like Hall, the need for strong action. The Cabinet agreed to an operation to break up the illegal organizations which, in view of the Jewish Agency's involvement, meant also raiding the Agency's premises. Instructions were to be sent to the High Commissioner for this action to be carried out; there was to be no general disarmament of Palestine at present, nor was the Jewish Agency to be closed.[56]

The operation in Palestine was delayed because the list of those to be detained was leaked and found, as Cunningham graphically reported, 'plastered all over the walls of Tel Aviv'. However, on 29 June the operation went ahead; over 2,600 Jewish suspects were detained, including four members of the Agency's Executive, and the Jewish Agency's premises were occupied. Truman was informed immediately before the action, and on 2 July, following a meeting with Wise, Goldmann, Silver and Lipsky, the President issued a statement regretting the developments in Palestine. He hoped that the Jewish leaders would be released soon, and expressed 'his determination that these most recent events should mean no delay in pushing forward with a policy of transferring 100,000 Jewish immigrants to Palestine'. It seems that the operation was thus a partial victory all round, for the Chiefs of Staff, the Commander in Chief, Middle East and the Government of Palestine in carrying out in part an operation to which they attached so much importance, and for Truman in seizing the opportunity to parade his resolve over the

100,000. It did not affect the progress of the Anglo-American consultations, which continued to bump along despite these events. As for the success of the operation itself, it cannot be rated very highly. The Jewish Agency building was released on 10 July, but the process of screening and releasing the detainees continued. On 24 July a White Paper was published to display the evidence of the Jewish Agency's control over the Hagana and Palmach; two days before, however, the Irgun had destroyed a wing of the King David Hotel in Jerusalem, containing the Secretariat of the Mandatory Government, at the cost of eighty-eight lives. Far more than the military operation, this Irgun action strengthened for the time being the hands of the moderate Zionist leaders against the extremists. In conclusion, the events in Palestine did not affect the consideration of Anglo-American policy significantly. They did, however, contribute to the sense of urgency felt in Cabinet to press the Anglo-American initiative to a concrete conclusion, for the troubles in Palestine made it clear that the problem could not be ignored.[57]

It was the Cabinet's anxiety over exactly what this concrete conclusion might be that initiated the chain of events which ended in the failure of the Anglo-American initiative. Basically the Cabinet was, as we have seen before, unconvinced that Bevin's policy of trying to secure US responsibility in Palestine would work. On 4 July, with Bevin in Paris, the Cabinet seems to have lost its nerve. Attlee told the meeting that, as Grady's delegation was not proposing to arrive before 15 July, the Cabinet should consider meanwhile when the parliamentary debate on Palestine could be held before the Recess. He warned:

> If, as a result of this delay in the official consultations, no agreement had been reached between the Governments of the United Kingdom and the United States, it might become necessary for His Majesty's Government to indicate that they were prepared to adopt a given line of policy in Palestine if they were assured of the support and co-operation of the United States Government.

It was agreed that the Colonial Office should prepare memoranda which 'should summarise the recommendations of the Anglo-American Committee ... and the difficulties which the responsible Departments of His Majesty's Government saw in giving effect to those recommendations'. These instructions merely invited a repetition of the recommendations Brook's Official Committee had made to the Cabinet in April. However, the Cabinet added the crucial new element, for it instructed that the memoranda should also outline alternative policies which might be adopted.

These alternative policies were to be ready within the week. The Anglo-American Committee had laboured for over three months to produce its recommendations which in their turn were the subject of Anglo-American conversations to transform them into concrete policies, but now incredibly the Cabinet was calling for an alternative to be ready within the week. There is nothing in the anodyne official minutes to indicate that the Cabinet was aware of the significance of what it had collectively accomplished, nor is there any suggestion of a lengthy or acrimonious debate. The matter seems to have been treated as a routine precaution.[58]

Just four days after the Cabinet's decision, the Colonial Secretary circulated two memoranda. The first was a critique of the Anglo-American Committee's Report, and this followed closely the submission of the Official Committee in April. Hall told the Cabinet that the Report had dealt with the resettlement of the Jewish Displaced Persons 'in an entirely inadequate manner'. He referred to the preliminary talks with the American delegation on the 100,000 and stressed the British delegation's contention that large-scale capital expenditure would be required to cope with this influx, the meeting of which would be beyond the Jewish Agency's professed capacity. While the Report had recommended that Palestine should be neither a Jewish nor an Arab state, Hall pointed out, 'The Committee have, however, made no attempt to face up to the difficulties of framing a type of constitution which will secure these ends.' The large-scale economic development projects which the Committee had advocated would, Hall argued, be thwarted because the Palestine Arabs would have no interest in them, regarding them 'as devices to enable further Jewish immigrants to enter Palestine', and because they would be open to sabotage. The Colonial Secretary warned of the difficulties of implementing the Report's recommendations on future immigration, the resentment this would face from the Arabs and the opposition from the Jews. Having found nothing to praise and nothing that was useful in the Report, the Colonial Secretary concluded his wholly negative paper with several heavy warnings. The hardening of Arab feelings meant that the acceptance of the Report 'may be expected to lead to an Arab rising in Palestine'. The Jewish Agency's attitude remained that 'the only just and lasting solution ... was the establishment of Palestine as a Jewish State'. The unanimous view of the representatives in the Middle East, Hall noted, was that the adoption of the policy recommended in the Report 'would have disastrous effects on Great Britain's position in the Middle East and might have unfortunate repercussions in India'. To implement the Report the COS would require reinforcements of two divisions, an armoured brigade, three infantry battalions and more naval and air power, and it would not be possible to find these except by 'withdrawing from other commitments from which, in fact, withdrawal is not possible'. Hall rounded off the paper with this utter rejection of the Report:

> the implementation of the Commitee's recommendations ... seems likely, by estranging the Arab States, to imperil our position ... at the same time to involve us in military and financial commitments beyond our capacity ... implementation would provide no solution of the Palestine problem since no long-term policy is suggested and no proposals are offered for the final determination of the major issues of immigration and land sales.
>
> As I consider that the recommendations of the ... Committee, taken as a whole, are unworkable, I have in a separate paper put forward ... an alternative proposal ... .[59]

There was nothing that was new in Hall's paper, which in attitude to the Anglo-American Committee's Report followed Brook's submission closely. If anything, the Colonial Secretary's view of the Report came across as even more damning because his paper was more concise, and because his stated objective was to cast the recommedations aside and to supply his own alternative. Hall circulated the Colonial Office alternative in a Cabinet paper of the same date. As the four days which had elapsed since the Cabinet had instructed the preparation of an alternative scheme scarcely allowed time for much original thought, let alone the careful elaboration of detail, it should come as no surprise to find that the CO merely dusted down its old standby, the scheme for provincial autonomy in Palestine. This long-term policy proposal had been made by Hall to Morrison's Cabinet Committee the previous September, when consideration of it had been forestalled by Bevin's initiative in creating the Anglo-American Enquiry. The Colonial Office had then pressed this scheme for provincial autonomy, the Harris plan, on to the Committee of Enquiry while it was in London, but it had vanished without trace and had not featured in the Committee's final recommendations. Undeterred by the past, Hall now vigorously recommended the scheme to the Cabinet nearly a year after he had first espoused it. Hall's paper argued that a continued trusteeship of Palestine, as the Report had recommended, must surely be dismissed as impracticable. We are at present holding the position ... by force of arms and can hardly contemplate continuing so to hold it for all time ... .

The argument continued disarmingly:

It is, of course, too early to forecast the results of the forthcoming official conversations [with Grady], but it is at least possible that the verdict will be that it is impracticable to implement the Committee's recommendations as a whole.

Accordingly 'we should have concrete proposals to advance in place of them'. The scheme of county-council style self-government for Palestine was dismissed as being 'not nearly far reaching enough to form the basis for a new start'. A bi-national state was rendered impossible by non-cooperation between Arabs and Jews. The only possibilities, Hall argued, lay in partition or provincial autonomy. Partition was felt to be far too difficult; the Arabs and Jews would not agree on the boundary, the United Nations would be involved in the settlement and thereby further complicate the problem by adding another international dimension, while Britain would continue to carry the burden of Palestine:

The best hope may thus well lie in the adoption of the alternative ... of semi-autonomous areas under a central Trustee Government.

This arrangement had an important advantage; it could be implemented unilaterally, without departing from the provisions of the Mandate and thereby necessitating a reference to the UN. Britain's strategic position would also be unaffected in Palestine. The 100,000 could enter the Jewish province and thereby US support of the scheme may be forthcoming. The Arab states would be reassured that the Palestine Arabs would be free from the threat of Jewish domination, and in future years the scheme could develop into federation, with the Arabs and Jews as partners, or into partition. Hall annexed the details of this miraculously endowed scheme, which the Committee of Enquiry had spurned. Given the force of the arguments advanced in this paper and the preceding one many of Hall's Cabinet colleagues must have read the cheerful ending with some relief after traversing the apparently exhaustive and negative examination of all the other possibilities. However, the Colonial Office had not in fact advanced the matter at all despite the passage of nearly a year and the labours of the Committee of Enquiry, and their submission to the Cabinet placed no emphasis upon persevering with an Anglo-American initiative.[60]

At this time the Chiefs of Staff were in the thick of their battle in the Defence Committee over strategic requirements in the Middle East, and Hall's damning indictment of the Anglo-American Committee's Report was quickly pressed into the fray. In a paper for the Cabinet, Tedder, Cunningham and Simpson (Vice-Chief of the Imperial General Staff) 'emphatically endorse[d]' Hall's assessment of the strategic damage which would be caused by the implementation of the Report. The COS spelt out the ramifications clearly:

> All our defence requirements in the Middle East, ... oil supplies and communications, demand that an essential feature of our policy should be to retain the co-operation of the Arab States ... .
> ... without the facilities in Egypt, and without any permanent or assured control of Cyrenaica we should find it difficult to ... protect our vital interests in the Middle East unless we have full control of Palestine.

To those ministers and officials who were privy to the Defence Committee's discussions, the Chiefs of Staff's comments would have had a familiar ring about them.[61]

The Colonial Secretary's provincial autonomy proposals, however, met with rather less favour from the COS, and the first sign of their reservations came in a minute Ismay sent to the Prime Minister on 10 July pointing out that the COS Committee 'assume ... that there will be no question of the Cabinet reaching a final decision on the matter [of provincial autonomy] at tomorrow's meeting,' because their urgent consideration of the scheme would not be ready by then. This had little effect for the next day the Cabinet approved the provincial autonomy scheme for use in the talks with Grady. The COS Committee met on 12 July. Tedder, agreeing that the adoption of the Anglo-American Committee's Report 'would be disastrous', went on to say that the 'question was whether this alternative scheme was as bad or better'. Cunningham and Montgomery had similar reservations and Montgomery 'challenged the estimate of probable Jewish and Arab reactions [in Hall's paper and] ... He felt that the picture painted ... was much too optimistic and felt certain that the adoption of the scheme would mean a considerable reinforcement of our forces in the Middle East.' The Chiefs of Staff decided to inform Brook, who was leading the British delegation in its talks with Grady, that they felt 'it would be dangerous' to give copies of the provincial autonomy scheme to the Americans, and that they 'would much prefer that he should refrain from discussing the scheme at all with the Americans'. If this proved impossible Brook should 'confine discussion of it to general terms'. The Chiefs of Staff's representations, which were tantamount to a repudiation of the Cabinet decision, had no effect on the progress of the talks with Grady. On 15 July the COS Committee again considered the matter, the Joint Planning Staff and the Commanders in Chief, Middle East, having now expressed their views. The COS Committee now 'agreed that the military risks involved in adopting ... [provincial autonomy] would certainly be less than those which would be involved ...' in implementing the Report of the Anglo-American Enquiry. Montgomery suggested that the COS, in commenting upon Hall's scheme,

> should confine themselves to the two main essentials of any scheme that might be adopted for Palestine. First, it must give us the power to control and co-ordinate the defence of the country and maintain forces and military facilities in it as and when we require; and secondly, it must not alienate the Arab States against us.

The COS Committee agreed that a minute on these lines should be submitted to the Prime Minister. Ismay submitted the minute to Attlee, pointing out also that provincial autonomy was unlikely to fulfil the second condition mentioned by the COS Committee.[62]

It is quite clear that the Chiefs of Staff's attitude on provincial autonomy must be seen in the context of their concurrent representations to the Defence Committee about Britain's strategic requirements in the Middle East. As we have seen, the COS resolutely maintained their position in the Defence Committee that full military rights were needed in Palestine and that Arab goodwill was the *sine qua non* for British power in the Middle East. Feeling that provincial autonomy may be unacceptable to Arab opinion, the COS regarded it unfavourable because it was perceived as threatening Britain's Middle East requirements and ultimately Palestine's value as a base. Ismay's note was coldly received at Number 10; an unsigned 'Note for P.M.'s own use' of 15 July, which by its trenchant tone might have been written by Rowan (Attlee's Principal Private Secretary) pointed out:

> The views set out herein are really opposed to *any* scheme which would in any way offend the Arabs. This is politically an impossible attitude. Allowing for this devotion to the impossible the opinion given is more favourable to this than to any other scheme yet suggested.

The Chiefs of Staff's representations on provincial autonomy had no effect, and on 19 July their main campaign over the strategic requirements in the Middle East met with defeat in the Defence Committee when Attlee prompted the meeting merely to take note of the reiterated views of the COS. With their underlying philosophy thus for the time being neutralized, the Chiefs of Staff's reservations about provincial autonomy lost their import [63].

In contrast to the opposition the Foreign Office had shown towards the provincial autonomy scheme in January when its submission to the Committee of Enquiry had been discussed, in July the Foreign Office seemed uninterested in, but not opposed to Hall's scheme. One reason was the Foreign Office's utter dislike of the Report the enquiry had produced in the meantime, and this dislike had been manifest in the Official Committee's report to the Cabinet in April. As a result, any alternative, even provincial autonomy, became palatable. In July Clayton sent the Foreign Office his views on the provincial autonomy scheme. He felt that the Jews, excepting the extremists, would accept it, but that the Arabs might fear that 'measures designed in their favour (may be) upset by pro-Zionist influences' and therefore they would give the scheme 'a very poor reception'. Clayton believed that partition would be more acceptable to the Arabs because it offered an element of finality. Beeley's minute on this report is interesting and it suggests, by its persuasive and amenable tone, that Foreign Office objectives could still be fulfilled through provincial autonomy:

> Brigadier Clayton is probably right in thinking that at first sight the Arabs will find the scheme of provincial autonomy less attractive than partition. But there are arguments that can be used against this view. So long as Partition is avoided, no part of Palestine is irrevocably lost to the Arabs. If ... events show that the Jews will never overtake the Arabs in numbers, a time may come when some sort of federation will be advantageous .... If ... their fears are justified ... they will be able to work for partition at a later stage.

This suggestion that the Eastern Department regarded provincial autonomy as a useful intermediate arrangement, harmless to an eventual settlement acceptable to the Arabs, was furthered by Bevin's own reaction. Brook went over to Paris especially to gather the Foreign Secretary's views for the Cabinet and he reported on 10 July that Bevin

was ready to explore the scheme for provincial autonomy ... and agreed that it should be discussed with the American officials. But he doubted whether this plan would be satisfactory as a definite settlement.

Bevin went on to say that he was considering a partition proposal allowing a Jewish state and for one part of the Arab province to be attached to Transjordan and the other part to Lebanon. Jerusalem would be under UN auspices. 'This settlement', Bevin said of his scheme, 'should not be put forward at the present stage, but the immediate proposals should leave the way open for its eventual adoption.' Hence Bevin led the Foreign Office in acquiescing in the scheme for provincial autonomy provided that it was an intermediate device. As for Bevin's own proposal, it was merely a derivative of the federal scheme which he had suggested to the Morrison Committee the previous September as a rival to the provincial autonomy plan then; however, his support of partition was momentary only, and its significance should not be exaggerated.[64]

It should not be concluded that Bevin had now abandoned all hope of finding an Anglo-American policy. The most important part of Brook's note on his conversation with the Foreign Secretary was concerned with maintaining the joint initiative. Bevin had said that he would press Byrnes to consider making an announcement that the United States would take a substantial number of Jewish refugees in order to render the entry of the 100,000 more palatable to the Arabs. He did not add that it would help to redeem the American breech of the Bermuda accords. Bevin added:

he did not feel able to oppose the admission of the one hundred thousand ... so long as there was proper consultation with the Jews and the Arabs. Every effort should be made to convene a Conference in London ....

In turn this would mean that the final settlement could not be hurried. Now, while Bevin's attitude to the plan for provincial autonomy accorded well with that of the Eastern Department, the Foreign Secretary's position on the entry of the 100,000, which derived from his eagerness to find an Anglo-American policy, was regarded without favour there. On 13 July Stonehewer-Bird reported from Baghdad that the admission of a large number of immigrants into Palestine, followed by a complete stoppage, would cause a strong but tolerable reaction. He warned, however, that the absence of any finality to the immigration flow would cause political instability and damage British and American interests to the benefit of the Soviet Union. Baxter, the Head of the Eastern Department, needed no further prompting and he speedily took the lesson to heart. He noted the danger in the entry of large numbers of immigrants into Palestine, and, although the comments were not directed at the provincial autonomy plan which was then in the forefront of affairs, Baxter dubbed it 'an important telegram'. Presumably it received this accolade because it accorded with the departmental thinking about the continued immigration which the Anglo-American Committee had recommended [65].

On 11 July the Cabinet held an important meeting to discuss Hall's provincial autonomy scheme. Brook presented Bevin's views to the Cabinet, stressing the Foreign Secretary's wish to avoid having to refuse the entry of the 100,000. Bevin was said to be 'favourably disposed' towards provincial autonomy, but doubted whether it 'would provide a lasting solution'. He was also eager, Brook informed the Cabinet, for the United States to be ready to give financial and military help in support of any new policy in order to persuade the US Government of the need for trying to secure Jewish and Arab concurrence. In discussion 'there was general agreement' that the Anglo-American Committee's Report

> offered no practical prospect of progress towards a solution of the constitutional problem in Palestine, and discussion turned on the alternative policy.

Hence with Bevin going along with the scheme vigorously propounded by the Colonial Office, the Cabinet was able to continue in its alternative direction. Significantly, the Foreign Secretary's absence allowed this trend away from the Anglo-American initiative to proceed unchecked. The Cabinet was much impressed by the ease with which provincial autonomy could be implemented by comparison with partition, and concluded with some gullability that

> it would be inexpedient to put forward at this stage proposals for the partition of Palestine ... The intermediate solution [of provincial autonomy] ... was, however, a constructive and imaginative plan which ... should be commended to the favourable consideration of the Jews and the Arabs if United States support for it could be secured.

US support was of course the remaining hurdle facing what had now become the British Government's alternative to the Anglo-American Committee's Report, and in the official talks the Cabinet directed that the British delegation 'must seek the appropriate moment for bringing forward this alternative' when the limitations of the enquiry's recommendations had been established.[66]

The reason the Foreign Office had so much confidence in the usefulness of provincial autonomy as an alternative to be going on with was not simply because the scheme looked as though it could be an intermediate one, but more importantly because parallel arrangements were being made which would guarantee its temporary nature should the Arab states oppose it. The mechanism for this was the proposed conference with Arab and Jewish representatives, which had been foreshadowed in the exchanges between Attlee and Truman as early as May.

In June the British Minister in Beirut, Shone, sent the Foreign Office a message from Azzam Pasha. It had been recommended that all states members of the Arab League should send such a message, contending that the Mandate was a variance from the UN Charter and as 'a State having direct relations with Palestine', calling upon the British Government 'to negotiate for the conclusion of an agreement to put an end to the present situation'. Bevin minuted on this telegram: 'We must deal with this', and on 5 July Howe submitted to Sargent a draft Cabinet paper prepared, presumably in the Eastern Department, in consultation with the Colonial Office. The draft paper referred to the Arab League's meeting at Bludan and the subsequent identical representations which had been made to the British Government by the Arab States, and it noted that the word trusteeship had been avoided, presumably because 'the Arab Governments are unwilling to commit themselves to anything less than the full and immediate independence claimed by ... the Palestinian Arabs'. Nevertheless the Arab case was based on Article 79 of the UN Charter which read in part, 'The terms of trusteeship for each territory to be placed under the trusteeship system ... shall be agreed upon by the states directly concerned.' Here of course the Foreign Office was on traditional ground, as the draft Cabinet paper acknowledged; the Arab states' claim to be directly concerned

is supported by geographical proximity, by ethnic and cultural similarity, by the undeniable strength of Arab feeling ... and by the precedent of the St. James's Palace conference of 1939 ... The notes of May 20th, 1946, [from the US and British Governments to the Arab states] constitute a more recent admission of the direct concern of the Arab states with Palestine.

With the status of the Arab states thus established, the argument presented in the draft continued by pointing out that as Article 79 also

required Mandated territories to be placed under trusteeship
agreements which had been negotiated with the states directly
concerned, the members of the Arab League would inevitably be
involved if the British Government decided to place Palestine under
trusteeship. The draft paper continued with a reference to another
form of negotiations concerning Palestine which had been mooted to
the US Government: the Conference. Although Truman had been
non-committal, the draft argued that it was evident that the Arab
States would have to be consulted about any solution, whether or not
this involved trusteeship, in order to try to secure their 'consent or
acquiescence' to it. Accordingly the draft paper proposed sending a
reply to the notes from the Arab states promising further consultations and recognizing their direct concern in any trusteeship
agreement.[67]

Bevin did not like this paper because it placed so much stress on his
old bugbear, the involvement of the United Nations which the
making of trusteeship arrangements for Palestine would necessitate.
His reaction was entirely consistent with his earlier attitude. He
expressed doubts 'as to whether our strategic requirements as laid
down by the Chiefs of Staff could be met if Palestine were to be placed
under the Trusteeship system', and accordingly, the draft was held up
pending the COS views. Although Howe minuted that the consultations proposed did not effect the strategic position at all, and merely
promised to talk further with the Arab states before making a final
decision, Sargent had the last word and directed 'that this question
should be held up while we see how the Anglo-US conversations
progress'. As we shall see, these conversations went very well from the
British point of view. Furthermore, the representations of the Chiefs
of Staff on the strategic position were effectively neutralized. On 21
July Bevin gave his approval to the draft paper, but it was not now
circulated to the Cabinet but merely submitted to the Prime Minister.
In a covering note Bevin pointed out that the Colonial Office agreed
to a generally worded invitation being sent to the Arab states for them
to attend a London Conference. The next day the Cabinet approved
the issuing of these invitations and agreed that the United States
might wish to send observers to the Conference. Brook invited
Grady's comments on the invitation, pointing out that as the US was
not a state directly concerned with Palestine for trusteeship purposes
the British Government had better run the Conference, although
American observers would be welcome. Byrnes informed Grady, in
response to his request, that 'We consider US commitment [to]
consult Arabs and Jews was discharged by our invitation [of] May 20

for their views.' The communication was sent to the Arab states on 24 July, and the British Government was ready to pursue its lonely and pristine policy of consultations.[68]

By comparison with the complicated and involved preparations in London which lay behind the Anglo-American official conversations, the American preparation was brief and straightforward. The thorniest problem arose from the question of the US provision of military forces to assist Britain in implementing the Anglo-American Report, which Bevin had mentioned in his conversation with Byrnes in Paris on 27 April and repeated in a memorandum to the US Secretary of State on 9 May. The previous August Truman had told a press conference that he was eager for the maximum possible immigration into Palestine as was consistent with peace, and added that he had no desire to send half a million American soldiers to Palestine to keep the peace. Truman had not departed from this position, and on 3 May the aide to the Secretary of the Army noted on White House paper for the Joint Chiefs of Staff: 'Admiral Leahy believes the J.C.S. should study the possibility of providing troops or Marines to help in Palestine, with the understanding that the President does not intend to order such employment of US troops.' This move by the JCS was made considerably ahead of instructions, and not until 7 June were their opinions requested through the mchinery of the State-War-Navy Co-ordinating Committee with the Anglo-American official conversations in mind. The response was unequivocal:

> We urge that no US armed forces be involved in carrying out the [Anglo-American] Committee's recommendations. We recommend that in implementing the report, the guiding principle be that no action should be taken which will cause repercussions in Palestine which are beyond the capabilities of British troops to control.

The JCS report argued that the very limited forces which could be spared under the present military estimates may help inside Palestine, but their presence would risk provoking 'serious disturbances' throughout the Middle East, thereby invalidating the current estimates. Furthermore, in common with the Chiefs of Staff, the JCS pointed out

> that implementation of the report by force would prejudice British and US interests in much of the Middle East ... The USSR might replace the United States and Britain ....

At Byrnes specific instructions, this report was brought to Truman's attention. Byrnes showed himself particularly anxious to avoid giving any sign of US military involvement, and on 23 June he rebuffed the British suggestion that representatives from the JCS should meet their opposite numbers from the COS to discuss Palestine. Accordingly, in a 'Memorandum of instructions to the Committee', Grady's delegation was told firmly that the US Government would not be prepared to employ military forces. Grady's team was aware of the difficulty this placed them in, and in an undated memorandum on 'matters to be discussed' in London the Cabinet alternates argued:

> It must be recognized, however, that ... [this] definitely weakens our negotiating position ... and the *finality* in the eyes of the Jews and Arabs of any joint position we may be able to arrive at with Great Britain ... U.S. military forces would, of course, be available as a part of United Nations forces acting pursuant to the United Nations Charter.

This perception of holding a weak hand was something of a handicap for the American delegation in facing the well-practised operators from Whitehall.[69]

The rest of the briefing for Grady's team does not seem to have been especially significant. A memorandum entitled 'Considerations bearing upon [the] handling of the Palestine Question' was prepared in the State Department, apparently during June, and its tone and general approach suggests that it was written as a briefing paper. It reviewed British and US interests in the Middle East and noted Britain's awareness of popular aspirations there. The paper drew attention to US standing in the region and the damage which would ensue if Arab goodwill was lost. In this context Roosevelt's promise to Ibn Saud about consultations was mentioned. The second half of the paper was concerned with the issue of the 100,000 and it recommended that their transfer to Palestine 'should be carried out if at all possible'. Truman's position on the use of American troops was mentioned, as were Arab sensibilities, and the paper concluded

> we should do our best to prevail upon the British, in a friendly and understanding way, to agree to ... [the 100,000's] immediate admission. We should not, however, exert pressure to force the British against their will to adopt a policy with regard to the 100,000 Jews alone, without reference to the remainder of the report, since such a course might well result in a complete failure in our joint efforts to find a solution of the Palestine problem.

This memorandum was rather more cautious in its tone than the instructions given to Grady's team, which emphasized more the degree of support the President was prepared to lend to the movement of the 100,000 through loans and with economic development schemes, and by helping the British Government's position through a request to Congress to admit about 50,000 Displaced Persons into the USA. However, most significantly for the British point of view was the instruction that the United States was willing to support the Anglo-American Committee's Report 'as a whole', a position distinctly different from merely supporting the recommendation on the 100,000 by itself. The Board of Alternates was aware of the delicacy of the issue of the 100,000, and in their note on matters to be discussed in London they remarked that their instructions could not be acted upon 'without involving a risk under the broad expressions of the JCS report'. However, the Alternates submitted that: 'There is some opinion that the dangers have been exaggerated' and, although there was a 'calculated risk' in espousing the entry of the 100,000, 'it seems to the Board of Alternates that our relationship to the Palestinian situation and the commitments of the President are such that we should take this course.' It is clear, however, that some misgivings were felt by Grady's team in following this approach, misgivings fuelled by the JCS and the State Department's views, and as a result the delegation's support for the 100,000 entry was less wholehearted than Truman's public position.[70]

The London conversations themselves were an anti-climax. Grady, the Secretary of State's alternate, was accompanied by Dorr, the Secretary for War's alternate, and Gaston, the alternate for the Secretary to the Treasury, as well as by a number of other officials, including Rood, who had been the secretary to the US delegation on the Anglo-American Committee. Brook led the British team of officials which included Harris, Mason (the Head of the North American Department at the FO) and Beeley. The meetings considered the enquiry's Report in detail, Brook ably pointing out the deficiencies in the recommendations in accordance with the instructions the Cabinet had given him on 11 July. Sub-Committees were set up to consider various aspects of the Report. According to the official record, the US delegation sprang the trap on 13 July when Gaston commented that the Report's third recommendation (on the form of government) was merely a statement of the principle of non-domination by either Arabs or Jews, and that the practical means for effecting this non-domination may be either to allow a degree of regional autonomy under a federal authority or by means of the development of co-operation between the two communities in local government. Brook seized his chance. The British delegation, he said, had been thinking along the former lines 'and had worked out a tentative plan for regional autonomy'. Harris followed this up with a fairly detailed description of his provincial autonomy scheme. A fifteen-page memorandum dated 13 July and entitled 'A Scheme of Provincial Autonomy for Palestine' was submitted by the British delegation as a basis of discussion on Brook's 'tentative plan'.[71]

This British proposal, it would seem, carried all before it, and on 19 July Grady informed Byrnes that, having explored 'numerous possible solutions', he now believed:

> This plan seems to offer the only means now apparent of moving the 100,000 into Palestine in the near future. It is strongly backed by the British Gov[ernmen]t.

Grady reported that the financial plans were well within the targets, that Britain had indicated 'no desire for our military aid', and that the British Government planned to convene a conference of Arab and Jewish representatives in London as soon as the policy was accepted by both the British and US Governments. Grady reported that Britain proposed to implement the plan at that point, pending the reference to the United Nations; if, however, Arab and Jewish agreement was not secured, the whole problem might be referred to the UN first. Although Grady admitted that the provincial autonomy plan was the same as had been submitted to the Committee of Enquiry, the State Department was none the wiser as the documents still awaited customs' clearance, and accordingly Grady was asked for a summary. Byrnes also showed unease about the condition attached to the movement of the 100,000 'lest transfer of these Jews be almost indefinitely delayed', and he wanted to know, 'Have Brit[ish] definitely refused [to] agree to adopt plan along lines recommended in principle by Anglo-American Committee ...?' Notwithstanding these adverse signs from Washington, Brook was able to tell the Cabinet on 20 July that the US delegation found the provincial autonomy scheme acceptable for giving effect to the third recommendation of the enquiry, and Brook sought guidance on the position of the provincial boundary. He suggested that the line proposed in the Colonial Secretary's paper, which the American delegation supported, should be agreed to 'in the last resort' only, and that a boundary more favourable to the Arabs should be advocated first. The Cabinet decided against over-using the British success in the talks, and instructed on 22 July that the US delegation should be asked to agree to the original boundary subject only to any modifications which may be discussed subsequently with the Arabs and Jews. This move enabled the final hurdle in the discussions to be overcome, and on 24 July Grady cabled to Byrnes the 'complete text of [the] agreement on joint recommendations'. Grady replied roundly to Byrnes' inquisition:

> Joint committee [is] unanimous in conviction [that] plan agreed to is only realistic solution at this time particularly if any extensive Jewish immigration is to be realized.[72]

The plan agreed was to be known as the Morrison–Grady plan because the Lord President made the announcement of it in the House of Commons. It recommended making efforts to resettle Jewish DPs through the machinery of the UN and by allowing their entry into the USA and the British Dominions, and that these steps be announced in order to minimize the Arab reaction against the entry of the 100,000 into Palestine. The plan approved of their transfer and recommended that it should be 'initiated immediately it is decided to put the constitutional proposals into effect' with the aim of completing the movement within a year of commencing it. Thereafter immigration would be controlled ultimately by the central authority on the basis of economic absorptive capacity. The plan for provincial autonomy was the mechanism for giving effect to the Anglo-American Committee's constitutional recommendations, and it followed the Colonial Secretary's scheme exactly. While the Arab province contained 815,000 Arabs and 15,000 Jews, the Jewish province proposed would have 451,000 Jews and 301,000 Arabs. Provincial autonomy would leave the future path open to co-operation and federalism, or to partition. It was also recommended that armed organizations which were not prepared to submit themselves to the central government should be dissolved. Various economic schemes were outlined, and the 'Morrison–Grady' report closed with the recommendation that once the policy had been adopted by the British and US Governments it should be submitted to Arab and Jewish representatives 'as a basis for negotiations' in an 'effort to obtain at least a measure of acquiescence'. Thereafter it should be embodied in a trusteeship agreement and submitted to the United Nations.[73]

Why had Brook's team been able to persuade the American delegation to accept all that the British asked for? The most important reason seems to have been the superiority of the British preparations for the conference. Not only was there a consistent and unanimous resolve on the British side not to allow the 100,000 to be transferred except as part of an overall scheme, but as a result of the Cabinet's decision to call for an alternative to the Anglo-American Committee's Report the British delegation was in possession of a fully-fledged and Cabinet-approved substitute. As the Report had been unspecific in its constitutional recommendations, and arguably inadequate in other respects, the British experts had an easy time in persuading their relatively inexperienced American counterparts that provincial autonomy represented a suitable vehicle for implementing a version of the enquiry's recommendations. The other reason for the British victory was the experience and professionalism of its delegation, which was led by Brook, the formidable Secretary to the Cabinet, whereas the American team was led by alternates who had no prior experience of Palestine and whose credentials were comparatively meagre. Apart from being better prepared for the negotiations, the British delegation out-gunned the Americans as well.

Grady's conduct in accepting the British position engendered resentment among members of the US delegation's staff, some member of which leaked the provincial autonomy scheme to the *New York Herald Tribune* where it was published on 16 July. Further reports of dissatisfaction among the members of Grady's staff were published in the *New York Times* on 4 August. Objections were felt about Grady's acceptance of the British wish to make the entry of the 100,000 conditional upon US acceptance of the whole plan, and in consequence some staff members felt that Grady was more interested in reaching an agreement with the British Government than in the substance of the agreement. These reactions were to have their effect in Washington.[74]

Truman's rejection of the Morrison–Grady plan

The Cabinet in London was understandably eager to get the United States Government's approval of the officials' report in order that a joint policy could be announced in the Commons at the end of the month. On 25 July the Cabinet approved the report of the British and American delegations as a basis for the conference with the Arabs and Jews, and agreed that if there was a sufficient degree of acceptance the British Government would implement the scheme and inform the United Nations in September. Meanwhile a trusteeship agreement would be prepared. Bevin, with some support, expressed his doubts about reporting the matter to the United Nations General Assembly lest 'other Governments might seize this opportunity of raising difficulties', and consequently this proposal was held up. The Foreign Secretary's old reluctance to allow the United Nations to become involved was again manifest. Following this Cabinet meeting, the Foreign Office informed Inverchapel of the need for a speedy US decision in view of the forthcoming parliamentary debate, and Attlee sent a message to Truman asking him 'to give urgent attention to the agreed recommendations'. In fact the Cabinet's anxiety to press on seems to have been an important contributory factor in the decision, taken on 25 July also, not to react too strongly to the destruction of the King David Hotel. The Yishuv was not to be fined in general, nor was immigration to be halted, and the extensive arms search which was allowed as a consequence categorically excluded the old military hobby-horse by banning any search 'throughout the whole Jewish community'. The expressed aim was to avoid any action that 'might prejudice the chances of this new policy being accepted'.[75]

There were many other factors which were to prejudice these chances. Byrnes had already indicated to Grady on 22 July his anxiety that the conditions attached to the transfer of the 100,000 would cause delay, and on 24 July he warned:

> It would place this Gov[ernmen]t in [an] almost impossible position if it would agree arrangement whereby transfer would not begin until after full agreement had been reached with Arab and Jews or, in absence of such agreement, until action had been taken by United Nations.

Grady spoke to Brook and tried to reassure his Secretary of State, reporting 'there is not the slightest doubt that the British Government will give the green light on the 100,000 at the earliest possible moment', but that it was felt some measure of Arab and Jewish acquiescence was the prerequisite. Byrnes' feelings were unassuaged, and he replied:

> We can appreciate British position. Nevertheless after the stand that the President has taken we do not see how we can enter into any arrangement ... [conflicting with] the position that the 100,000 should move without awaiting for [the] agreement ... of Arabs and Jews.

Forrestal recorded in his diary the dilemma felt in the State Department and by the US Cabinet at this time: 'The problem is complicated by the fact that the President went out on a limb in endorsing the ... [Anglo-American Committee's] report saying that a hundred thousand Jews should be permitted entry'. With the President's colours nailed firmly to the mast, it would be difficult indeed for the Brook–Grady report to change them.[76]

In fact, Truman's real position at this stage is rather hard to explain. Nachmani (1980) argues that Truman was in daily contact with Grady's delegation and that it therefore followed his wishes. There is certainly other evidence to suggest that Truman was momentarily ready to accept the Morrison–Grady plan. On 27 July Senators Wagner and Mead (of New York), and McDonald (of the Anglo-American Committee) were granted an interview with the President which, according to McDonald's account, was a stormy one. Truman was stung by McDonald's criticism of Grady's lack of experience and his capitulation to the British position, and although the President asserted that he would 'strive for the 100,000', he was quite defensive about the officials' recommendations. McDonald felt that Truman 'had been convinced that this was the solution. He would get his 100,000 and he would have no obligation about these other things.' Another piece of evidence to suggest Truman's preparedness to accept the plan is the proposed press release which Byrnes sent to him from Paris on 29 July. Truman's position was sufficiently favourable, or at least irresolute, even five days after the Brook–Grady report had been available to encourage Byrnes to send this lengthy statement of acceptance which had been seen and approved by Attlee, who was also in Paris. It would appear, therefore, that Truman's response to the Morrison–Grady plan was not a spontaneous one, and that to begin with he was disposed to accept it. His change of position and the final rejection of the plan occupied a few days.[77]

It seem that Zionist pressure was the principle cause of Truman's ultimate rejection of the plan. Due to the leakage in London of the provincial autonomy scheme by disaffected members of Grady's staff and its subsequent appearance in the press, the Zionists in the United States had ample time to mobilize their campaign against the plan. On 25 July, Silver described the plan in a public statement as creating a Jewish ghetto in Palestine, and he warned that the Jews 'will not submit to this evil decree'. On the same day Grady telegraphed to Byrnes the text of a letter that Goldmann of the Jewish Agency had delivered to him, warning that the urgency of the question of the 100,000 meant that, if their entry was to be conditional upon further consultations, it would be impossible for the Jewish Agency to participate in such talks. The Zionists reacted against the plan not only because it fell well short of sovereignty, but because it threatened also to make the entry of the 100,000 conditional upon Arab agreement and left subsequent immigration where was currently, in the hands of the Mandatory authorities. A great campaign was organized by the American Zionist Emergency Council with advertisements condemning the scheme appearing in the press, letters being sent to the White House, and Taft and Wagner speaking out against it in the Senate. On 30 July, Celler and eight other New York Congressmen went to see Truman to protest at the absence of progress with the movement of the 100,000; the President showed himself at this meeting to be irritated by all the lobbying, and he abruptly ended the interview. However, as Forrestal's diary entry reflected, Truman was in an awkward position in view of his previous commitment to the cause of the 100,000.[78]

Niles' influence was probably of importance as well. On 28 July Oscar Gass, a Washington economist and an expert on Palestine, reported from London to Epstein, who was the Jewish Agency's representative in the USA, on the subject of the Brook–Grady discussions:

> The Americans were going about quietly to accept everything the British suggested …. To say that Grady was acting as a British 'stooge' is a gross understatement. He was actually publicly reprimanding his staff for venturing to differ with the British even over secondary matters ….
>
> It is impossible for you to go too far in emphasizing to our friends and to the press the complete abandonment of the President's declared program by Grady.

Evidently this report found its way to Niles. It would be difficult to conceive a more diplomatic and effective way of bringing the inadequacy of the Brook–Grady report to Truman's attention than that which Niles suggested at the end of July. He recommended to the President that he should not commit himself over the report until a meeting had been arranged between Grady's team and the American members of the Committee of Enquiry 'with a view to reconciling the differences' as its sanguine aim.[79]

But already by this time there were clear indications that Truman would not support the provincial autonomy scheme and the rest of the Brook–Grady report. On 30 July, Acting Secretary of State Acheson called upon Inverchapel. He seems to have been acting on instructions. He told the British Ambassador that Truman was not able to make the statement which Byrnes had drafted and Attlee had seen in Paris. Acheson's report of the conversation described the reason given: 'In view of the extreme intensity of feeling in centers of Jewish population in this country neither political party would support this program.' Grady's team was being recalled for consultations. Inverchapel reported to the Foreign Office that Acheson had said Truman was thinking of getting the whole matter reconsidered by the Grady team and the American members of the Committee of Enquiry, and this would suggest either that Niles had made his proposal to this effect already, or that by now it was current in the Cabinet's thinking and had been encouraged, perhaps, by McDonald's stormy meeting with Truman on 27 July. Inverchapel's report was entered in the Foreign Office files without comment. The Ambassador also reported the statement which Acheson had informed him the President would be making the next day. This was a clear indication of the impending repudiation of the Morrison–Grady plan, stating that 'in view of the complexity of the matter' Grady was being recalled for further discussions. Also on 30 July, Grady was informed that:

> Following discussion with full Cabinet today [the] President has regretfully decided he is unable to accept recommended plan ... He hopes further study might produce plan which would be likely of public acceptance in this country.[80]

The gratuitous reference in this message to a Cabinet discussion suggests that there was more behind Truman's rejection than Zionist pressure and lobbying. Two years afterwards Bromley of the British embassy in Washington wrote to Burrows, who was then Head of the Eastern Department of the FO, reporting a tale told to the BBC correspondent, Miall, by Acheson. Acheson said that the Cabinet sub-committee on Palestine, consisting of himself, Snyder (Secretary of the Treasury) and Patterson (Secretary of War), had recommended to the President that the Morrison–Grady plan was a viable one, and that with two years to go before the Presidential elections the Zionist outcry could be countenanced. Truman allegedly acquiesced in this view, but then a telegram arrived from Byrnes in Paris which warned of the domestic repercussions if the Brook–Grady report was accepted. Byrnes also disavowed earlier telegrams which had been sent over his signature. Despite this, the sub-committee's views were still apparently accepted by the President, and when a meeting of the full Cabinet convened later in the day approval for the Morrison–Grady plan was forthcoming, until Byrnes' telegram was read out. Acheson said that this caused an attack of 'cold feet'. At the vote

Acheson was alone in supporting the plan, even Forrestal having sided with the opponents, one may presume due to his awareness of Truman having 'gone out on a limb' earlier by his support for the 100,000. Bevin scrawled furiously on this letter: 'This shows Byrnes a double crosser [;] he took the other view with me'. Even when due account is taken of the interval of two years on Acheson's memory, as well as the second-hand nature of the story and the absence of dates, some significance may still be attributed to it. On 30 July, the same day that Acheson had warned Inverchapel of Truman's position and, the same day as Grady had been recalled, Byrnes cabled Truman saying, 'I hope you will consider [Brook–Grady] proposal entirely independent of any view I may have expressed because I do not know [the] views [of] people at home.' The next day Byrnes elaborated further, explaining that the purpose of his earlier message 'was to let you know that if you declined to agree to the [Brook–Grady] proposals it would not embarrass me'. This was something of a retreat from the position taken in the draft statement of acceptance for Truman which Byrnes had sent on 29 July, and it is understandable that the Cabinet members may have felt uneasy now that Byrnes was shifting the responsibility for domestic considerations onto them and adopting a disinterested attitude towards Grady's achievement. It is entirely possible that the Secretary of State was being strictly honest and candid, and that the Cabinet read more into his messages than they were entitled to. Some support for this idea can be evidenced from Forrestal's diary entry of 3 December 1947 when, at a lunch with Byrnes, the former Secretary of State recalled that he had disassociated himself from the rejection of the Brook–Grady proposals, and that he blamed Niles and Rosenman for the decision because they had warned Truman that the Republican candidate was about to come out with a statement in favour of the Zionist claims to Palestine. Altogether the evidence is not irreconcilable, but there is some mystery surrounding Byrnes' position and it seems fair to conclude that the ambiguity of his conduct towards the Brook-Grady recommendations contributed to the Cabinet's advice to Truman and thus to the President's decision, taken apparently on 30 July, against accepting the plan.[81]

On the very eve of the adjournment debate in the House of Commons, the British Cabinet's hopes of being about to announce a joint Anglo-American policy were shattered. Matters were very difficult, for Bevin had fallen ill in Paris and the Prime Minister had had to replace him at the conference at the last minute, so it fell to the Lord President, Morrison, in consultation with other senior members of Cabinet, to decide what to do when Truman's position became known. Inverchapel contributed some advice. He observed that Truman's rejection was 'acutely embarrassing' and reported Henderson's view that it was due entirely to the condemnation of the proposals by American Zionism, and to the rivalry between Wise the Democrat and Silver the Republican which had prevented either from being conciliatory. Inverchapel advised that the Commons should be told that the matter was still *sub judice*, and that for Britain to press on alone would create an 'extremely unfortunate impression' in the United States. This line was impossible because of the mounting parliamentary pressure, from the opposition and government back benches, for a debate on Palestine; this had been held off by the continued Anglo-American conversations but could not be left until after the summer Recess. Morrison, in discussion with Dalton, Hall, Addison, Cripps and the Lord Chancellor, decided to take the line that the British Government would be ready to go ahead with the conference of Arabs and Jews, as the Brook–Grady report proposed, with US assistance. Without this assistance, it was agreed, the Government would have to reconsider its position, especially over the 100,000 whose transfer to Palestine and settlement there required American financial support. Morrison initiated the debate on the afternoon of 31 July, describing in detail the provincial autonomy plan and accompanying proposals, and then declaring Truman's position. He concluded:

> The full implementation of the experts' plan as a whole depends on United States co-operation. I hope that that will be forthcoming. If not, we shall have to reconsider the position.

The debate continued into the next day, and throughout the weakness of the government's position was brought out. Stanley argued critically:

> this policy still awaits the agreement of America. Until that is received, he [Morrison] can make no definite statement

On 1 August Churchill made a powerful speech, arguing that:

> almost any solution in which the United States will join us could be made to work.
>   ... If this Anglo-American co-operation fails, as it seems so far to have failed, then I must say that the record of the Administration ...

in the handling of Palestinian affairs will stand forth as a monument of incapacity.[82]

Churchill was certainly correct that the policy of Anglo-American co-operation had failed. The finishing touches were applied in Washington between 7 and 9 August when Grady and his team met the American delegates to the Committee of Enquiry. Acheson was in the chair. It was a furious confrontation, Hutcheson accusing Grady of having violated his mission. As the Committee of Enquiry had rejected the provincial autonomy scheme which Grady had subsequently adopted, and had laboured longer and harder in the cause of Palestine than had Grady's experts, the Committee members' anger was understandable. On 8 August Truman told Attlee that:

> Mr. Byrnes and Mr. Harriman have, I believe, discussed the matter with you and have explained that I do not feel myself able in present circumstances to accept the plan proposed as a joint Anglo-American plan.

The matter was, however, still under discussion. Attlee's reply conveyed the British Govenment's disappointment and pointed out that the plan offered the only way of getting a substantial number of immigrants into Palestine peacefully. It was no use, and on 12 August Truman confirmed the decision not to support the plan, mentioning that public opposition was too intense. Truman expressed the hope that the forthcoming Conference in London might produce a policy 'for which we can obtain necessary support in this country and in the Congress so that we can give effective financial help and moral support.' Attlee was unimpressed by this prospect, and his reply tolled the end of Anglo-American co-operation on the problem and the two countries' joint efforts to find a common policy:

> We earnestly hope that, as a result of the conference, some solution will emerge which ... may be possible of implementation without too greatly endangering the peace of Palestine or of the Middle East as a whole. But you will appreciate that any such solution must, as matters stand, be one which we can put into effect with our resources alone.[83]

The Anglo-American initiative was at an end. Was Churchill right that the government's conduct was a monument of incapacity? With due allowance for a fine parliamentary turn of phrase, the answer is yes. The Anglo-American Committee of Enquiry had been Bevin's creation, and the Eastern Department of the Foreign Office was never happy about it nor with the initiative it represented. Furthermore, Bevin's enthusiasm for Anglo-American collaboration proceeded in advance of his Cabinet colleagues', and the strain soon told. No significant attempt was made by the British Government to influence the Committee of Enquiry, and it was Bevin's own promise that he would try to implement any unanimous report, made out of his faith in British policy and his confidence in the Anglo-American initiative, which provided the most important stimulant from London. While the Committee laboured, the Foreign Office was confirmed in its pristine outlook by reports from representatives in the Arab states. Terrorism and illegal immigration impressed the Colonial Office with the mounting problems of administering Palestine, and the Chiefs of Staff developed with vigour their plans for taking military action to counteract terrorism. As a result of these concurrent concerns, when the Anglo-American Committee reported there was no official or military disposition to take the new recommendations seriously or as a fresh opportunity. Of equal importance was the reaction—public, parliamentary and in Cabinet—to insist on making the entry of the 100,000 into Palestine conditional upon Jewish disarmament. This view was supported by Whitehall and the Chiefs of Staff, and had been conditioned by terrorism. Notwithstanding all this, Bevin succeeded in persuading the Cabinet to persist with the Anglo-American effort by proceeding to secure US involvement through holding the official conversations. As the strategic debate on the Middle East and other events reflected, the Foreign Secretary's motivation was faith in Anglo-American collaboration and a suspicion of Soviet policy, but during the spring and early summer of 1946 his enthusiasm for finding an Anglo-American policy on Palestine outstripped that of his colleagues. The Cabinet decision to prepare an alternative policy to that proposed by the Committee of Enquiry was the crucial indicator of the loss of faith in Bevin's Palestine initiative. But the death blow was dealt by the British official delegation in the experts' discussions, the same official representatives of the British Government who had been so bitterly critical of the Anglo-American Committee's Report in their submission to the Cabinet in April, and whose recommendations on that occasion Bevin had managed to deflect. In the talks with Grady's delegation, Brook's team heavily over-employed their advantage and got their own way entirely, but at the cost of writing a report which not only supported the provincial autonomy plan the Committee of Enquiry had rejected, but also one which Truman was unable to accept as a result of past Presidential promises and present Zionist pressure. The disease had been cured, but the patient of the Anglo-American joint policy was now a corpse. There was no sinister intention behind this, no evidence of a purpose to subvert the aim of the Foreign Secretary, but merely the exercise and triumph of the Foreign and Colonial Office conceptions of the Palestine problem and the Middle East. For Bevin, ill in Paris, the failure was cushioned somewhat by the apparently unhelpful interventions of Truman and the President's ultimate rejection of the Morrison–Grady plan for what were perceived to be reasons of party politics. Furthermore, the question of referring Palestine to the United Nations, a course of which Bevin disapproved, was to be delayed by the conference with Arab and Jewish representatives, which also softened the blow of the failure of his Anglo-American initiative on Palestine.

4

The London Conference and Truman's Yom Kippur Statement

By the late summer of 1946 the British Government's Palestine policy was sliding apparently unstoppably towards its nadir. Never again would it be able to muster the semblance of a fresh initiative which the new circumstances and personalities of the previous year had allowed. Now close co-operation with the US government had been written off due to a collection of pressures and circumstances in Washington, Palestine and London. The upshot had been the formation of a Foreign Office approved policy substitute for the Anglo-American Committee's recommendations which, remarkably, the US expert delegation under Grady had accepted but which, utterly predictably, Truman felt unable to support. The business of resolving the Palestine question was now back squarely with the British Government and the initiative, although it scarcely merits this description, lay with the Foreign Office. However the Foreign Office had nothing new to propose, merely the rehearsal of old and discredited diplomacy which allowed the small opportunities still available for carrying forward a fresh approach to slip by. The pathetic slide towards the year's end and the impotence of the Mandatory government was relieved only by the comic spectacle of the London Conference at which British officials sought to negotiate and compromise with an assemblage of delegates from most of the Arab states on the subject of Britain's Palestine policy. The auction-like atmosphere inevitably drove up the demands while the sweet reasonableness displayed by the British delegation appeared ludicrous alongside.

The FO view and the conference of 1946

With the Anglo-American initiative dead, the British Government was free to embark upon its chosen path: the conference with Arab and Jewish representatives, mentioned as early as May 1946 in the exchanges between Attlee and Truman, and subsequently made the subject of the Foreign Office's policy proposal in July. The FO's submission, sent eventually to the Prime Minister, argued the case forcefully for consulting the Arab states before implementing any new policy. The rationale was not simply to discharge promises of consultations and to minimize Arab opposition to the new policy, but was based, the Foreign Office argued, upon 'the precedent of the St. James's Palace conference of 1939'. By the Foreign Office's own admission, the idea for the conference rested on the policy the FO had advocated before the Second World War—surely a most unhappy pedigree. A further parallel existed: just as the Foreign Office had manoeuvred to defeat the Report of the Peel Commission in the 1930s, employing the St James's Palace conference, so in the summer of 1946 the erstwhile opposition of the FO to the Colonial Office's provincial autonomy scheme was quietened with the Morrison–Grady plan. The Foreign Office produced the proposal to consult the Arab states about the new plan, thereby ensuring that Britain's Palestine policy remained the subject of a debate between most of the Arab states in the Middle East and the British Government. As the events in the late summer and autumn of 1946 show, the pre-eminent consideration of the Foreign Office remained as always to avoid jeopardizing 'Arab goodwill' towards Britain, and to eschew any policy which threatened the delicate façade of Arab unity presented by the Arab League.[1]

The United States Government's non-involvement in the proposed conference seems to have been desired on both sides of the Atlantic. The US was not a 'state directly concerned' for the purpose of negotiating a trusteeship agreement for Palestine, and therefore the US Government could be excluded from any discussions in furtherance of Article 79 of the United Nations Charter. However the primary purpose of the conference with the Arab and Jewish representatives was to discuss the Morrison–Grady plan, and there is no reason to doubt that the US Government could have been involved in the conference had this been felt desirable in Washington and London. On 22 July the Cabinet, while agreeing that invitations should be sent to the Arab states to attend the conference, concluded without demur that the US Government should not become jointly involved, but might send observers. Brook conveyed this attitude diplomatically to Grady who understood that US involvement might provoke demands from other countries to take part as well. Byrnes, as we have seen, was against US participation on the grounds that the Arabs had been consulted already by the US Government. Once Truman had rejected the Morrison–Grady plan it became impossible

for the United States to participate in a conference that had as the first
item on its agenda the plan itself. This distancing of the US
Government from involvement in the conference passed unlamented
in the Eastern Department of the Foreign Office. The disdain felt
towards a US role is evident from the response to remarks Truman
made at a press conference on 5 September, when he said that both
the Morrison–Grady plan and the $300,000,000 loan which formed
part of it were 'still under consideration'. Beeley of the Eastern
Department was utterly unimpressed by the prospect of such colossal
US assistance with economic development in Palestine and the
Middle East, and he minuted sourly that Truman, 'No doubt hopes
that this half-promise will enable him still to exercise indirectly some
of the influence which he is no longer bringing to bear directly.' Later
he noted for Sargent that Truman was holding out the prospect of
financial support if the British Government's policy was palatable to
the Americans. Beeley continued:

> This promise is so vague, depending as it does upon the mood of Congress
> and on the almost incalculable reaction of American public opinion to
> whatever we decide, that it would probably be unwise to take seriously
> into account the prospect of financial help from the United States in the
> framing of our Palestine policy.

However, privately provided dollars flowed to the aid of the Yishuv
before and after the creation of Israel. An official dimension was given
to this funding before 1948, as a result of the tax-exempt status of
contributions of a 'charitable' nature which, in the case of the Zionist
fund-raising organizations, the Treasury Department proved slow in
challenging despite pressure from the State Depatment. After the
setting up of Israel, official financial aid from the United States came
in the form of a $100,000,000 loan, authorization for which was
announced by the White House on 19 January 1949. Bearing this
financial involvement in mind, Beeley's attitude towards an American financial role is dismissive to the point of contempt. Taking into
account the process by which the US partnership in a policy for
Palestine had ultimately been prevented, that is, through the official
discussions between Brook's team and Grady's delegation, and the
complete absence from the Foreign Office files of anything approaching self-criticism or an expression of regret at the demise of the
Anglo-American initiative, it must be concluded that the Foreign
Office now steered Britain's Palestine policy towards the traditional
device of a conference with complete indifference towards the

widening gap that separated the British and US governments on the whole issue.[2]

Following the Cabinet's decision on 22 July, invitations were despatched to the Arab states for delegations to attend the conference in London. A few days later the Colonial Secretary circulated a paper to the Cabinet proposing that representatives of the Arab Higher Executive should be invited, with the exception of the Mufti who was in Egypt, and also that delegates from the Jewish Agency should be called. The Jewish delegation was to exclude those members who were detained following the recent military operations in Palestine, as well as Ben Gurion who had escaped the net through his absence in Paris. It was to include other Jewish representatives selected in consultation with Bevin, Weizmann and the Chairman of the Board of Deputies of British Jews. The Cabinet generally agreed to Hall's proposals, but concluded that while the nomination of the Mufti and Ben Gurion should be discouraged 'it would in the last resort be necessary to accept such nominations if they were made'. This attitude towards the Jewish Agency was in sharp contrast with the thoughts Beeley had minuted in the preceding few days. On 23 July Beeley had observed that the Arab governments would want to know who else was being invited to the conference, which was a tricky point since the Jewish Agency could not be invited at present. Two days later he referred to the White Paper of 24 July, which set out evidence implicating the Jewish Agency with the Hagana and terrorist activities, noting that it 'makes negotiation with them [the Jewish Agency] even more difficult'. A concurring minute, apparently by Baxter, observed that it was clearly going to be difficult to find a Jewish team to negotiate with. However, despite these perceptions in the Eastern Department, no doubt was cast upon the feasibility of holding the conference, ostensibly to consult both the Arabs and the Jews, but which seems to have had as its principal purpose, in Foreign Office thinking, the airing of Arab views.[3]

The conference itself was entertaining enough in a predictable way. Of greater significance for illuminating British policy was the change in the Zionist position and the various reactions of the Arab states to this change and to the conference, all of which were in evidence during the late summer and autumn of 1946.

The Zionist negotiating position

Goldmann was the moving force behind the new Zionist position. As a follower of Wise and his more gentle style of lobbying, Goldmann found himself at odds with Silver's more combative leadership

technique. The friction between the two had increased since
Goldmann had opened a branch office of the Jewish Agency in
Washington in 1943, giving him a platform for his independent
activities. Before the National Board of Hadassah in July 1946
Goldmann expounded his argument in favour of jettisoning the
Biltmore Programme and instead embracing partition as the Zionist
proposal for Palestine. This course strongly appealed to Goldmann:

> Partition would mean today that you take out 600,000 Arabs from
> Palestine, in the central plateau, and you tie them up with Transjordan.
> That gives the Jews a slight majority right away, or certainly when the
> hundred thousand are in.

This proposal attracted the strong opposition of Silver and his
followers, and the battle was taken to the meeting of the available
members of the Jewish Agency Executive in Paris which began on 2
August. Goldmann himself attended and explained his case for
pressing upon Truman an adaptation of the Morrison–Grady plan.
Goldmann argued that the plan should be taken to the logical
conclusion of partition. The alternative was to reject the Morrison–
Grady plan in favour of pristine Zionist objectives, which Goldmann
believed would merely allow the continuation of British rule and the
White Paper policy. The matter was put to the vote on 5 August.
Goldmann proposed explaining to Truman that the Jewish Agency
Executive regarded the Morrison–Grady plan as an unacceptable
basis for discussion, but that it was prepared 'to discuss a proposal for
the establishment of a viable Jewish State in an adequate area of
Palestine' together with the immediate entry of the 100,000.
Goldmann's proposal and was adopted by the Agency Executive, and
the next day Goldmann arrived in New York to take forward this new
and important policy.[4]

On 7 August, Goldmann saw Assistant Secretary of State Acheson,
laid before him the Executive's proposal and apparently convinced
him that it represented a realistic course. Ganin (1979) quotes
an interview with Goldmann in which the crucial reasoning was
attributed to an appeal to American interests, for Goldmann argued
that if compromise failed the moderate Zionists would succumb
entirely to a more militant leadership and thereby present the US
Government with an agonising choice between supporting a Zionism
which was employing violent means, and supporting Britain. On 12
August, Acheson sent details of Goldmann's plan to US Ambassador
Harriman, in London, concluding with remarks that were praise
indeed, coming from the State Department:

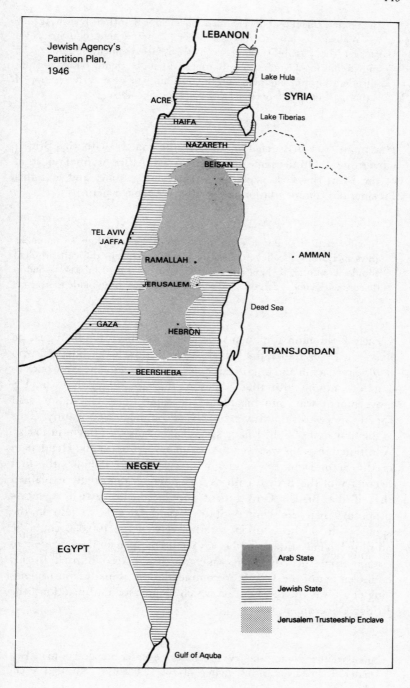

Jewish Agency's
Partition Plan,
1946

LEBANON

Lake Hula

SYRIA

ACRE

Lake Tiberias

HAIFA

NAZARETH

BEISAN

TEL AVIV
JAFFA

RAMALLAH

• AMMAN

JERUSALEM

Dead Sea

• GAZA

HEBRON

TRANSJORDAN

• BEERSHEBA

NEGEV

EGYPT

Arab State

Jewish State

Jerusalem Trusteeship Enclave

Gulf of Aquba

In our view this recent development offers hope that [the] Jewish Agency will realistically join in [the] search for [a] practicable solution. ... we suggest [the] possibility that [the] Brit[ish] G[overnmen]t might let it be known that [the] coming consultations will not be rigidly bound to [the] consideration [of] one plan and the possibility of [the] early creation of viable state of Jewish portion [will] not [be] precluded.

Harriman was instructed to discuss the matter with the British Government. On the same day Truman sent Attlee his final rejection of the Morrison–Grady plan, not yet made public, and lent this Presidential commendation to the Jewish Agency's plan:

In view critical situation Palestine and of desperate plight of homeless Jews in Europe I believe search for a solution to this difficult problem should continue. I have therefore instructed our Embassy London discuss with you ... certain suggestions which have been made to us.

Clearly Goldmann's mission was having an effect. On 9 August he had seen Inverchapel, the British Ambassador in Washington, who had relayed a full and uncritical report of Goldmann's scheme back to London, noting also that Acheson 'did not deny' that the US Government was thinking along the same lines. Goldmann said shortly afterwards that Inverchapel had commented buoyantly: 'This is the first sign of light I have seen. Take it up with Bevin in Paris.' Additional impetus ws given to the Agency's proposal by Henderson of the State Department in an interview with Balfour, the first Secretary of the British embassy. Henderson reportedly explained that if the British Government supported the Jewish Agency's proposal, then the United States would be able to join in the sponsorship of the solution; alternatively, if the 100,000 could be admitted to Palestine then 'the way would be open for the President to escape from the corner in which he has placed himself by his endorsement of the 100,000 recommendation'. Finally, most menacing of all was the third option which Henderson outlined, for if the British Government was

unable either to meet the Jewish Agency's counter proposal or to make a material advance in the mater of the 100,000 ... In that event

Henderson, while unable exactly to predict the attitude of the Administration, foresaw that Mr. Truman might feel constrained publicly to re-affirm his attitude in regard to the 100,000.[5]

Despite these signs, Goldmann's mission and the new Jewish proposals he carried were to have little effect on the course of British policy. There is nothing to suggest that Henderson's last warning, to be borne out by Truman's statement in October, made any impression in the Foreign Office which continued to busy itself with conference concerns and failed to make use of the new Zionist position. There were several factors which helped the Foreign Office to proceed unconcerned. In response to Goldmann's efforts, Truman issued a singularly bland statement on 16 August, that merely expressed the hope that the consultations with the Arabs and Jews would be approached 'in a spirit of conciliation' and would produce a 'fair solution', and that 'immediate steps can be taken to alleviate the situation of the displaced Jews in Europe'. This statement was unlikely to impress itself forcefully on the British Government, and in this regard it is interesting to see the account Bevin sent to the Prime Minister of his meeting with Goldmann in Paris on 14 August. Bevin reported that Truman had conveyed to Goldmann that, having pressed the issue of the 100,000 in the past, Truman felt unable to do any more, was preparing to extricate the US Government from the entire business, and to mend his bridges with the British Government. The burden of Goldmann's representations spelling out the Jewish Agency Executive's proposals apparently made a much smaller impression on Bevin who seems to have got the idea that Goldmann agreed that the provincial autonomy plan should still be treated 'as a kind of Agenda' in the forthcoming talks during which the Arabs would be free also to put forward their own plans. In London, Hall had seen Weizmann, Goldmann and Wise and gathered a clearer impression of where the Jewish Agency stood; the Colonial Secretary had rejected the condition for the Agency's participation that its proposal should be made the basis for the conference discussion, but, he told Harriman on 15 August, he remained optimistic that the Jews would participate in the conference. Accordingly it would seem that, despite the success Goldmann achieved in peddling the new Jewish Agency proposals in Washington, this success was not communicated to London. US pressure was gentle and there was a sense of optimism that the Agency would participate in the conference anyway, and as a result, on 19 August,

Attlee returned a stout reply to Truman on the subject of the Jewish partition plan:

> it is, as I have said, our intention to place the outlines of the provincial autonomy plan before the conference. … While we are adopting the plan as the initial basis for discussion, we do not propose to take up an immovable position.

It would be up to the Arab and Jewish delegations to submit counter proposals.[6]

The ultimate collapse of Goldmann's initiative followed. Furious at Goldmann's secretive diplomacy, Silver resigned from the Executive of the Agency on 14 August in protest at Goldmann's undermining of Zionist pressure on the US Government. Recriminations were hurled during the meetings of the Executive in Paris, Lipsky commenting perspicaciously:

> The whole purpose of our maneuvres in Paris was to produce in the British Government a change of position … The President has informed the British Government of his support, which has in no way indicated that this decision had any effect on its policy. It has not even indicated that it is aware of this American decision.

Evidently the Zionist movement, having made its concession without discernible benefit, now felt discouraged. There was no further room for movement internally, and the proposal conveyed to Bevin and Hall in Paris was that the conference should be delayed while informal talks proceeded between the Agency and the British Government in order to 'prepare the ground'. The British ministers rejected this request as a transparent attempt to predetermine the area of discussion at the conference and to lure the Arab states into talking about partition. Crucially, Bevin and Hall felt unable to compromise in the way the Agency wanted, having already invited the Arab states to the conference in order to discuss in the first place the Morrison–Grady plan. Any signs of a disposition to fix things with the Jewish Agency beforehand might encourage the Arab states to think that the British Government was negotiating behind their backs. Later in August Goldmann saw Bevin in Paris and told him of the split in the Zionist leadership, describing the need for the moderates to obtain some success in the talks with the British Government. Goldmann asked, much as before, that the conference be held in two stages, beginning with the Arabs, the Agency coming in as soon as the Arab representatives were ready to talk about partition,

since the Jewish delegation would be unable to talk about anything
less. Bevin, reporting the interview to the Prime Minister and the
Colonial Secretary, gave no sign of changing his earlier response in
answer to Goldmann's frank admission of the divisions in the Zionist
leadership, nor did he suggest that the government's attitude should
now be altered in any way. Attlee and Hall quickly reiterated their
position and supported Bevin's line. It would appear that the British
Government's preoccupation with the forthcoming conference ruled
out the possibility of a different attitude being adopted on this matter,
as well as on other points.[7]

The Executive of the Jewish Agency had not altered its position by
the time the first plenary session of the conference convened in
London on 10 September, without any Jewish representatives
present. Another hindrance to Jewish participation was the situation
in Palestine. Illegal immigration harassed the government considerably, and on 29 July, the Chiefs of Staff had circulated a paper to the
Cabinet recommending direct diplomatic action to stop the flow of
immigrants at its source, together with a policy of transshipping the
illegal immigrants from the ships which did get through. The
unhappy passengers would then be ferried to detention camps in
Cyprus. The next day the Cabinet accorded a favourable reception to
the COS's proposals, and showed an awareness that the Arab
reaction to continued immigrtion might be severe. The Colonial
Secretary gave further expression to these apprehensions in a Cabinet
paper on 5 August. He argued that there was a military necessity of
avoiding a two-front war, taking on both the Yishuv and the Arabs
simultaneously, and he pointed to transshipment and the detention of
illegal immigrants in Cyprus as the correct course. Accordingly, on 12
August, the Government announced its transshipment policy and
enforced it on the same day by deporting nearly 1,300 illegal
immigrants from two ships to Cyprus. At the same time a vigorous
diplomatic campaign was waged throughout Europe in an attempt to
halt the traffic of illegal immigration. Poland, still steeped in popular
anti-semitism, was the major source of illegal immigration to
Palestine and the exodus of its Jews had been intensified by the Kielce
pogrom on 4 July when forty-two were murdered. Despite British
efforts which heavily engaged the diplomatic service, the Royal Navy
and the Cabinet's attention, the ships continued to arrive in
Palestinian waters. On 15 August a vessel carrying nearly eight
hundred illegal immigrants was intercepted, on 3 September another
containing nearly one thousand, and on 22 September one carrying
six hundred. This illegal immigration undoubtedly coloured the

feelings of those in London, Ministers and officials alike, who had to grapple with the Palestine problem, yet it cast only part of the shadow, the rest being cast by terrorism. On 22 August, one of the British ships being used to ferry the immigrants to Cyprus was sabotaged, and in September the tempo increased with the murder of various British service personnel on the ninth and attacks on banks in Tel Aviv and Jaffa on the thirteenth. Cunningham reported some exasperation among the Jewish Agency and Hagana 'High Command' at the activities of the Irgun and Stern Gang coming at a time when restraint would have best served the Jewish cause, but the High Commisioner noted that there was no Jewish move to collaborate with the British authorities to counter the extremes of terrorism as there had been after the murder of Lord Moyne. Undoubtedly the events in Palestine, together with the Agency's delicate position about participating in the conference, contributed towards raising the temperature of the whole matter. Bevin evidently became increasingly irritated at the Jewish Agency's response to the government's invitation to attend the conference, telling the Prime Minister and the Colonial Secretary of 5 September that in his draft letter to Weizmann

I have tried to place the blame for refusing to attend the Conference squarely on the shoulders of the Jewish Agency ... the Jewish Agency Leaders are sacrificing the prospects of peace in Palestine for the sake of their own ambitions.

Clearly there was no sign of any awareness on the part of the Foreign Secretary that the adoption of partition by the Executive of the Jewish Agency represented a move towards compromise.[8]

The atmosphere engendered by the events in Palestine had a direct bearing upon the Jewish Agency's refusal to participate in the conference, as reflected in the correspondence between Weizmann and the Colonial Secretary, which was published in London on 6 September. Not only did the Jewish Agency refuse to participate in any discussion of the Morrison–Grady plan, but it demanded the right to nominate all the Jewish representatives at the conference. These delegates would include, if the Agency wished, members who were still detained or liable to detention following the British military action on 29 June. Naturally this condition stuck in the throats of the British authorities who were still contending with Jewish terrorism and illegal immigration, just as earlier in the year the Anglo-American Committee's recommendation for the entry of the 100,000 had proved unacceptable to the British Government without the disarmament of the Yishuv. On 16 September, Weizmann himself wrote to Martin, the Assistant Undersecretary at the Colonial Office, pleading the case for the release of the detained members of the Jewish Agency Executive:

> I do not need to tell you that I have myself all along been in favour of coming into the Conference ... my position is made almost intolerably difficult by the fact that members of our Executive are still detained in Latrun, among them most loyal supporters of the British cause, who have always been towers of strength both to the British Government and to me ... Their presence would greatly strengthen my hands, would help to maintain the unity of the Movement ... I feel that the Government should understand this, and doing so, should help to create an appropriate atmosphere.

Notwithstanding a statement issued by the Inner Zionist Council in Jerusalem on 25 September refusing Jewish Agency participation in the conference, Weizmann made some progress. On 26 September, partially blind and recuperating from an operation, he received a visit from the Colonial Secretary and the Permanent Undersecretary, Gater, at the Dorchester Hotel. Weizmann frankly explained that he felt 'like a squeezed lemon' between the demands of co-operating with the British Government and attending the conference on the one hand, and not allowing himself to become isolated from an increasingly militant Jewish Agency on the other. He warned that he might resign, a move that Hall was quick to deplore. Weizmann's request for travel facilities for five Jewish representatives was granted, and the Government of Palestine was instructed to assist with the departure for London of Rabbi Fishman, Kaplin, Meyerson, Horowitz and Rawikowich. The subsequent meeting, held at the Foreign Office on 1 October between Bevin, Hall and Creech Jones, accompanied by Brook, Gater, Harris, Howe and Baxter, with Weizmann and Goldmann, accompanied by Fishman, Locker, Brodetsky, Kaplan and Linton, represented the British Government's final effort to get Jewish participation in the current session of the London Conference which was about to adjourn. Weizmann urged the release of the detained leaders of the Jewish Agency, and Locker recommended that as a gesture the detainees in Cyprus should be released. Bevin rebuffed this last as not being a matter for the conference, although he felt that it could follow an agreement on law and order. Bevin's attitude reflected the governments's inability to make any concession, even for the benefit of the moderate Zionists, in the face of violence. Common ground was discovered between the

Arab and Jewish positions in the mutual recognition of the need for a transitional period, and the meeting expired with Weizmann's agreement to discuss this further with the Colonial Secretary. However, there were signs of progress towards the release of the Jewish Agency leaders, for on 25 September, Hall had informed Cunningham that consideration was being given to their release 'In connection with current negotiations'. The Colonial Secretary felt it necessary to add:

> I should of course make it clear that there is no question of release of these leaders as [the] price of Jewish participation in [the] Conference.

Hall was referring to the stigma attached to apparently bowing to violence, but his qualification had an ironic meaning; the detained leaders were not released until 5 November, long after the conference had adjourned. The irony was indeed acute, for during the week before their release terrorist incidents claimed the lives of two soldiers and a policeman in Palestine, inflicted severe damage on the railway station in Jerusalem, and a ship carrying 1,300 illegal immigrants was brought into Haifa. What had rendered the release of the Agency leaders acceptable was the statement by the Inner Zionist Council, issued on 29 October, which included *inter alia* a sentence denouncing bloodshed caused by 'terrorists who defy national discipline'. The new Colonial Secretary, Creech Jones, confessed to the Cabinet that this condemnation was not as strong as had been hoped, but nevertheless he felt that the time was ripe to make the release.[9]

Why had it taken so long for the British Government to make this concession? It could have been made at the beginning of October in the face of terrorism almost as easily as a month later. Part of the reason seems to have been the High Commissioner's advice, given on 27 September, to the then Colonial Secretary Hall, that the releases should be part of a general settlement on law and order, clearly implying some action to curb the terrorists. On this occasion Cunningham had reminded Hall of earlier Arab criticism of British leniency. Ominously he urged also that Ben Gurion and Sneh would have to be detained if they returned to Palestine because of the potential harm they could cause; 'Their exclusion until a settlement is reached seems to me essential'. On 12 October Cunningham amplified his warning about Arab reactions, arguing that 'temporary expedients in the absence of an imposed solution are, I am afraid [,] only apt to lead us deeper into the mire.' Montgomery, the Chief of the Imperial General Staff, undoubtedly felt the same way and recalled in his autobiography his exasperation at the release of the detained leaders. The powerful advice from such quarters, together with engrained ministerial attitudes, meant that it was left until November and to the new man, Creech Jones, to make the move on the flimsy pretext of the Zionist statement condemning violence.[10]

Therefore, there seem to have been two reasons behind the Jewish Agency's absence from the London Conference. One was the ultimate failure of Goldmann's mission to make an impression on British policy, and the other was the situation in Palestine and the detention of the Agency leaders there. Goldmann's espousal of partition was without doubt a significant turning point for Zionism, overturning as it did the inflexible Biltmore Programme, and Goldmann achieved notable success in pressing his proposal upon the US Government. However, this Zionist move towards compromise came late in the day. US support for it was tacked onto the US Government's rejection of the Morrison–Grady plan, and therefore it came at a time when US influence upon Britain's Palestine policy was waning. Furthermore, Goldmann's proposals were made long after the Arab states had been invited to the conference to discuss, as the first item on the agenda, the Morrison–Grady plan; the Jewish Agency's position that it could participate only to discuss its own proposals was made known too late for the British Government to feel able to make overt signs of accommodating them. But in fact the government in London made no sign that it was impressed by Goldmann's proposals for partition, or by US backing for them. The significance of the Jewish Agency's decision really seems to have passed the British Government by. No gesture of recognition or optimism was made in public or in private by the British Government, and the moderates in the Agency Executive were thrown onto the defensive. The business of releasing the detained leaders of the Jewish Agency followed a similar pattern. Weizmann clearly attached much importance to their release not only as a sensible concession on the part of the British Government towards the Yishuv, facilitating Jewish participation in the conference, but also as a means whereby moderate counsels amongst the Zionists could be dealt a fillip. But in London the matter was always regarded from the opposite end of the telescope, and the pervading attitude was that while terrorism and illegal immigration continued on such an aggressive scale, no concession was possible which could be construed as condoning it, accepting it or bowing to it. Undoubtedly a cardinal consideration of British policy was what the Arab states would think. This consideration governed the reaction of Bevin and Hall to Goldmann's proposal to hold informal talks before the conference got under way. This sensitivity to the Arab dimension may be seen in the important reasons which Wikeley of the Eastern Department and his Superintending Undersecretary Howe found to advance to Bevin for deporting the illegal immigrants to Cyprus. In the absence of this policy of transshipment, the Foreign Secretary was advised, an Arab explosion was to be feared, while to take this action against illegal immigration would provide a gesture of faith on the part of Britain to encourage Arab acquiescence at the conference in the Morrison–Grady plan. As usual, consideration for the Jewish Agency's participation in the conference was not in evidence in this tortuous piece of reasoning. In fact the preocupation with getting the representatives of the Arab states to London to discuss, in the first place, the Morrison–Grady plan, not only rendered the Foreign Office unperceptive of the position of the Jewish Agency and its requirements for participating, but also blinded the Foreign Office to the opportunity which did present itself for bringing to bear pressure on the individual members of the Arab League to accept the partition of Palestine.[11]

Anglo-Arab diplomacy

Superficially the Arab response to the invitation to the conference was not promising. The British Ambassador in Beirut reported the Syrian President speaking angrily of 'the iniquities of the Jews' and lashing out against Truman's responsibilities for the impasse. Young was evidently taken aback by the performance and cabled the Foreign Office hoping that he had correctly interpreted the invitation by saying that 'there was not ... any question of their [the Arabs] having to get together' around the table with the Jews. The Foreign Office replied sympathetically, but added for the future that:

> Sooner or later there will have to be some kind of understanding between Arabs and Jews regarding Palestine, and if they could only get together and discuss matters with each other in a dispassionate and constructive way, this departure from their present negative attitude would mark a great step forward.

It is worth bearing in mind this expression of interest by the Foreign Office in dispassionate and constructive talks between the Arabs and Jews, for this earnest of the FO's interest is belied by events. The Syrian President did not in fact refuse to send a delegation to the conference, but contented himself merely by expressing the view that there was not really much point in the discussion as the White Paper was the only acceptable solution. This type of Arab response was repeated throughout the Middle East. The British Ambassador in Baghdad reported the strong criticism of the Iraqi Minister of Foreign Affairs at the USA's involvement, adding that he was 'violently anti-Jewish in his actions and utterances'. Azzam Pasha, the Secretary General of the Arab League, asserted the opposition of the Arab States to the Morrison–Grady plan and to partition in conversation with an attaché at the US embassy in Cairo at the beginning of August. However, despite these drum-beatings and protestations, all the Arab states decided to accept the invitation to the London Conference when the Arab Foreign Ministers met in Alexandria in mid-August. The Arab Higher Committee, representing the Arabs of Palestine, themselves decided to refuse the invitation, which caused some of the Arab states a certain amount of embarrassment. Notwithstanding this refusal, representatives of Egypt, Iraq, the Lebanon, Saudi Arabia, Syria, Transjordan and Yemen, together with the Secretary General of the Arab League, turned up in London on 9 September, prepared to discuss with the British Government her policy on Palestine in the absence not only of representatives of the Palestine Arabs but also of the Jewish Agency.[12]

Yet this was but half of the nonsense involved. The first sign that the Arab states' position was something of a façade and might offer points of leverage to British diplomacy came on 5 August in a report from the British Ambassador in Beirut following a meeting with the Lebanese President. To Young's surprise, the President thought the British proposals for discussion at the conference were entirely reasonable. Young believed that this attitude 'does not represent the President's real position, and is chiefly due to his erroneous, but (group indecipherable) conviction that we are grooming Emile as a successor', for he asked whether the Foreign Secretary had entertained Emile Edde recently. Young requested guidance on the degree of pressure to be used on both Syria and the Lebanon 'in favour of acceptance of [the] Palestine proposals'. He continued:

> There is quite a lot of heat which we could if necessary turn on both in Syria and in the Lebanon; as regard the former there is Greater Syria and as regards the latter there is Emile Edde. But these are trump cards which I do not feel justified in playing without specific instructions.

Beith, who was responsible for Syria and Lebanon in the Eastern Department of the Foreign Office, explained that in Syria, Young was referring to the intrigues between leading personalities with the aim of establishing a royalist regime under Abdullah, thereby forming a union between much of Syria and Transjordan. Beith noted that: 'The Syrian Government are disproportionately sensitive about all this'. Concerning the Lebanon, Beith explained, Edde was a former President who was exiled in Paris and whom the present head of state feared might be negotiating his return with the British. These 'trump cards' were not to be played, however, and Young never received the specific instructions he referred to. Instead he was told brusquely that it was at present undesirable to apply pressure and that the London Conference remained open to all suggestions, since the British plan was only a basis for discussion. For the future, if it was decided to implement the Morrison–Grady plan against the wishes of the Arabs, 'we shall at that stage consider whether we can take any steps to secure the *de facto* acquiescence of the Arab Governments.' Manifestly this eventuality was unlikely to arise given the attitude and preoccupation of the Foreign Office and the domination of the conference by the Arab states. Hence an opportunity to apply 'a lot of heat' before the Arab states' position because unified and intractable, and orchestrated at the Alexandria meeting and in the conference in London, was allowed to pass by the Foreign Office in the misguided belief that the conference would prove to be a better negotiating forum than its forebear at St James's Palace had been.[13]

There is other evidence to suggest a positive aversion in the Foreign Office towards anything which might fragment a unified Arab position or facilitate a compromise deal on Palestine outside the London Conference. Reflecting upon the likely outcome of the meeting at Alexandria of the Arab Foreign Ministers, Baker of the Eastern Department minuted that Abdullah and his Prime Minister were in favour of partition as a solution for Palestine but would not dare to speak out. On 16 August, Kirkbride reported a further development from Amman. Abdullah had just had a meeting with Sasson of the Jewish Agency, himself fresh from a meeting with the Egyptian Prime Minister. Sasson conveyed the Egyptian position that partition of Palestine would be accepted if the British Government requested it and if another Arab state would support it. Abdullah indicated his interest to Sasson, but pointed to illegal immigration as the stumbling block. There was certainly an awareness in the Foreign Office that the Arab states were motivated by rivalries. Wikeley minuted that, 'King Abdullah has I think always been inclined to favour partition, as he hopes to absorb the Arab part of Palestine!' A member of the Egyptian Department added:

In general ... [the Egyptian Government's] attitude will probably be a compromise between their fundamental lack of interest in the whole business of Palestine and the necessity of taking an extremist line in order to maintain their hegemony over the Arab League.

Clearly the Foreign Office could see that the process of the Arab states meeting together to decide a policy inevitably, through a kind of bidding mechanism, led to the adoption of a more extreme attitude than quiet and individual diplomacy might have secured. It came as no surprise when Sir Ronald Campbell reported from Cairo that Azzam Pasha had told him that the Arab Foreign Ministers had rejected partition as 'The adoption of any other policy would have caused upheaval in [the] Arab League'. Howe's minute, written on 17 August, was indeed a *cri de cœur*: 'I believe most of the Arab States would accept partition if they only had the guts to do so.'[14]

The prospective deal with Egypt which Sasson of the Jewish Agency had brought to Abdullah's attention offered a point of departure for British diplomacy had there been a disposition to take it. Locker, who represented the Agency in London, wrote to Bevin on 26 August, drawing attention to the Egyptian Government's readiness 'to open informal and confidential discussions with us ... on the basis of partition'. However, the prompting of the British Government was required, and Bevin dismissively replied that he had not heard of this readiness from the British Ambassador in Cairo. Of course, Kirkbride had made his report from Amman some ten days before. On 31 August, the British Ambassador in Cairo, Sir Ronald Campbell, relayed a summary of the report that Brigadier Clayton had received from a 'police source', which recounted a meeting betwen the source, Sasson and Sidky Pasha, the Egyptian Prime Minister, on 26 August. They discussed the Morrison–Grady plan and variations upon it including partition, the Jewish Agency's preference, and Sasson argued that the Agency might be able to assist Egypt by mobilizing its contacts with the British Labour Party and 'approach His Majesty's Government pointing out the value of a situation in Palestine to offset any concessions His Majesty's Government might make over [the] Anglo-Egyptian Treaty.' Such a deal evidently appeared interesting to the Egyptian politicians, but Sidky said finally that he would not make any move until the British Government approached him. Azzam Pasha, who was apparently at the meeting as well, seemed ready to countenance partition as part of a deal which also allowed Libya to be independent or under Egyptian trusteeship. Clayton reportedly commented that Azzam's attitude

was plausible. In a separate telegram Campbell gave his comments
which, coming from such an authoritative source, constitute a serious
indictment of the course the British Government was to pursue.
Campbell argued:

> There is a tendency among Egyptians to exercise moderating influence
> upon the Arabs, partly because of being really out of the Arab work they
> do not feel so strongly as the Arabs about Palestine, and partly because
> they would like to conciliate us over Palestine in the hope that we will
> respond by being conciliatory about [the] Anglo-Egyptian treaty ...
> Azzam particularly has shown unexpected moderation recently but he is
> afraid of starting the ball rolling in ... [making] concessions. If,
> however, initiative were taken by representative of any other Arab State
> he would probably play up. Sanhouri, head of the Egyptian delegation
> [to London Conference], has useful contacts with Iraqi and Syrian
> politicians ... which are the two countries most likely to be troublesome.
> Both he and Azzam might be nobbled if tackled judiciously. Azzam has
> recently been almost pathetic in his persistence in asking us for
> guidance. ...

Campbell went on to say that the Egyptian attitude would depend
upon the state of play in the Anglo-Egyptian negotiations, and that
any proposed solution to the Palestine problem had to offer the
element of finality in order to win Arab acceptance. Campbell closed
with a warning to which the Foreign Office seemed blind:

> As already reported Azzam himself views this London meeting with great
> apprehension as he sees no chance of it being successful and fears it may
> lead to a head on conflict which he is anxious to avoid.

The suggestion Campbell made for 'nobbling' the Egyptian delegation and the Secretary General of the Arab League to assist the British
Government in working out a compromise could of course be linked
with Young's suggestion, made earlier in the month, for bringing
pressure to bear upon the Syrian and Lebanese governments.
Sasson's mission on behalf of the Jewish Agency provided the outline
of a deal, but it was clear, most significantly to Azzam himself, that
the London Conference would not be a suitable arena to negotiate a
sensible compromise.[15]

These proposals were to meet with no more success than those
advanced by the British Ambassador in Beirut for splitting the Arab
front. Initially, though, the signs were auspicious. Beeley minuted
uncritically on Campbell's comments: 'This is an important tele-

gram' and it was given Cabinet distribution. On 2 September
Campbell reported that Sasson had seen Clayton three days before
and said that Sidky was awaiting a move from the British
Government. Sasson also felt that the Arab governments 'would
refrain from opposing partition' if Britain came out in support of such
a plan forcefully, and he urged that the conference should be delayed
to give the Egyptian Government more time. The death blow to all
this seems to have been dealt by Bevin himself from Paris where he
was attending a conference, but he did not advance as his reason that
the fiction of Arab unity should be preserved. Instead he instructed
Sargent to sent on to Campbell this message:

> I cannot help thinking that Sidky Pasha may be thinking of striking a
> bargain with the Jews by which, in return for supporting partition, he
> will get the Jews to promise to provide a British base in the Jewish State,
> thereby relieving the Egyptians of pressure from His Majesty's
> Government with regard to the latter's Middle East security require-
> ments.
>
> ... You can leave him in no doubt that the interests of His Majesty's
> Government are not, and never will be, the counters in a bargain of this
> kind.

Clearly the prospect of a deal over Palestine involving the Anglo-Egyptian treaty negotiations and above all Britain's strategic requirements in the Middle East had touched a raw nerve in Bevin, and the
whole matter was effectively killed. Beeley's attitude also followed his
Secretary of State's, and he became highly critical of the whole
business, interestingly rationalizing it with the usual hobby-horse of
avoiding the disruption of Arab unity. On 5 September he minuted:

> The object of the Zionists in these hole-and-corner talks seems to be to
> persuade the Arabs to permit them to extract concessions from us in
> return for Zionist support of Arab demands upon us.
>
> ... If we were to enter into a bargain of this kind we should quickly find
> ourselves in an embarrasing position. The other Arab Stats would not
> see the matter in the same light as Transjordan and Egypt—the two
> beneficiaries on the Arab side of the deal.[16]

Thereafter the question subsided. On 8 September Campbell
reported with less optimism than before, saying that Sasson rather
than Sidky had made the running in the discussions. The Egyptian
Prime Minister had said definitely he was in favour of partition but,

Campbell felt, he was merely toying with the idea of a deal. On the same day Campbell reported an Egyptian newspaper quoting Azzam as stating that the first principle agreed by the delegates of the Arab states was 'that they refuse any idea of partition of Palestine'. There was an interesting postscript to the whole affair. Brigadier Clayton, whom Bullock remarks was 'one of the shrewdest observers of the Middle East scene', had sent a reflective memorandum to Sir Walter Smart at the Cairo embassy on 31 August. His paper argued the case for partition, and in his covering letter Clayton wrote with feeling:

> In some ways, for me, it is a council [sic] of despair since I have been uncompromisingly against Partition ever since it was first mooted but there seems no chance of anything like the White Paper (the only reasonable solution) going through and to go on as we are is going to put us deeper and deeper in the mire ....

> If anything is done I think it ought to be done before the delegations have committed themselves irretrievably in London. We could undoubtedly exercise a good deal of pressure either on Syria or on Trans-Jordan if we had made up our mind what our policy was to be.

Unfortunately news of Clayton's change of heart travelled rather slowly, and it did not reach London until later in September. Brook, who was Chairman of the Advisory Committee to the British delegation at the London Conference, noted dismissively that in view of Clayton's last paragraph 'it was not much use to get this in the 3rd week of the Conference'. Brook's remark was singularly inappropriate for there had been abundant indications that the Arab position would become more unified as time passed and once the conference opened. Furthermore, Clayton was not the first British representative on the spot who perceived the potential for some British diplomatic pressure in the Middle East. Indeed, when the High Commissioner eventually saw Clayton's memorandum, he told the Colonial Secretary that it was probably correct in its forecast of the Arab reaction to imposed partition, and he exhibited a disposition to agree with the paper.[17]

It must be recognized, of course, that a bargain on the basis of the Jewish Agency's proposals, with or without a degree of British diplomatic pressure, would have been very difficult to arrange. As Beeley noticed, a partition scheme acceptable to the Agency, and therefore demonstrably final and binding, might prove wholly unpalatable to even pressurized or tempted Arab governments.[18] However, the fact remains that the British Government made no attempt to bargain. Negotiations in anything resembling a 'hole-

and-corner', together with the notion of bringing pressure to bear upon individual Arab governments, were eschewed. One reason was evidently Bevin's aversion to bringing Britain's strategic requirements into the already over-complicated problem of Palestine, but in the Foreign Office there was still that ancient preference for dealing with 'the Arab world' as a whole which meant pursuing joint and collective discussions and avoiding individual arrangements with the Arab states. This preference, in the autumn of 1946, was well established as the policy of the British Government, and the conference which convened for its first plenary session on 10 September represented the summit of the Foreign Office's Arab policy.

The Conference in session

On that day Attlee addressed the assembled representatives of the seven Arab states and the Secretary General of the Arab League. He mentioned that the conference had a similar purpose to the one which had met in 1939, and he followed this unfortunate recollection by regretting the absence of any representative of the Palestine Arabs. However, Attlee continued, 'knowing how near this question of Palestine is to the neighbouring Arab countries, I feel fully satisfied that ... the Arab point of view is adequately and effectively represented by the present gathering.' He did not explain how this Arab point of view could be represented sensibly by the veritable spectrum of interests and attitudes which had sent delegations to sit around the same table, nor how the rivalries of Saudi Arabia and Hashimite Transjordan could be set aside, nor how the Egyptian concern to maintain her hegemony in the Arab League could operate to represent the interests of the Arabs of Palestine in a way compatible with, say, Syria's preoccupation with Abdullah's ambitions.[19]

Bevin spoke after Attlee, explaining again that the British Government's proposal, the Morrison–Grady plan, would be the first item on the agenda. Even at this stage there were reservations about this amongst the Arab delegations, and in the discussion it was agreed merely that the Morrison–Grady plan 'might serve as a point of departure'. Clearly no Arab representative present was keen to appear over-accommodating towards the British Government's provincial autonomy scheme in front of his brothers. Over the next few days the various Arab delegations embarked upon a recitation of their opposition not only to provincial autonomy and the Jewish position in Palestine, but to the British Government's record and US involvement as well. Replying on 11 September to Attlee's speech, the

Syrian delegate, el Khouri, argued bluntly that, 'The impossible has been asked of Palestine, for she alone has been required to be an instrument in the realisation of the dreams and ambitions of political Zionism.' Attlee and the press then departed, and Bevin tried to call the attention of the meeting to the realities of the current situation in Palestine: 'Whatever policy is decided on after these discussions, the decision will be taken with the intention of finding the shortest route to independence for the Arab and Jewish inhabitants of Palestine.' Azzam answered that Britain had created the problem through the Balfour Declaration, and Hall then managed to introduce the Morrison–Grady plan. El Khouri said that it 'could not be taken as a working basis because it did not contain principles which would be acceptable'; it divided Palestine and gave the Jews a bridgehead which could be consolidated and expanded. Azzam, no doubt foreseeing a premature end to his stay in London, closed the day with the more gentle remark that: 'He could not see much in favour of the proposals ..., but that did not prevent them from being considered'.[20]

Whatever hopes Sir Ronald Campbell may have had in the Egyptian delegation's moderating influence, on 12 September in the conference hall Sanhouri evidently felt it more useful to take a powerful Arab stance instead. He bitterly criticized the Morrison–Grady plan as paving the way not only to partition but to 'a Jewish state [which] will be a grave menace to the neighbouring Arab countries, and will be a jumping off stone that may enable the Jews to overrun the whole Arab World in the East.' Carried along by momentum and his own exuberance, Sanhouri warned that partition might secure 'peace for a few years' but that soon 'a cry for *lebensraum*' would go up; Judaic thinking, with notions of being a 'Chosen People' with their 'Promised Land' were unfavourably compared with Nazi ideology. Now this speech set quite a standard for the other delegates to rival, and generally it must be said that none did so that day, although all who spoke were elaborately opposed to the Morrison–Grady plan. Partition was, of course, utterly unthinkable, at least in the conference hall. Beeley had lunch with Jamili, the Iraqi Minister of Foreign Affairs and delegate to the conference, between the two sessions on 12 September and concluded that there was no chance of the Morrison–Grady plan being accepted, though Beeley felt that the Arab delegations 'may be willing to consider [an] intermediate position between that and the White Paper'. Bevin wisely excused himself from the afternoon's session of posturing, and it was left to the Colonial Secretary to thank the delegates for their full and frank views.[21]

The following week Bevin attempted to bring the conference around to more sensible negotiations, and in a strong speech on 16 September he drew attention to the five 'essential elements' in the problem which any solution had to take into account. There were already 600,000 Jews in Palestine who insisted on their political rights and, Bevin argued, although Palestine could not solve the whole problem of the Jewish Displaced Persons there had to be further Jewish immigration. Palestine had to progress towards independence, and to this end institutions had to be set up and the intolerable tensions ended. The conference then broke up to allow the Arab delegations to formulate their own proposals. From this point onwards there was a distinct lack of urgency in the pace and frequency of the meetings, and it is increasingly obvious that deadlock and failure were being postponed in the idle hope that Jewish participation or a miraculous breakthrough might be forthcoming.[22]

The Arab delegates proposed a scheme for ending the Mandate and creating an independent, unitary state with a democratic government. The Jews were recognized 'as a religious community' only, and they were to be able to exercise political rights 'in accordance with their numerical proportion as legally registered citizens of Palestine'. Immigration was to end. Bevin criticized this rejection of any further immigration and he quickly proposed that a Committee of the Conference should try to bridge the gap between the British and Arab proposals. This Committee, naturally, took minutes and sat for days, spinning out the conference without useful effect. The Secretary to the Cabinet, Norman Brook, chaired the committee's five meetings that convened between 21 September and 1 October. His avowed intention was 'to apply the test of practicability' to the Arab proposals, and he immediately enquired whether the Jews would be free to purchase land. Azzam replied that the land transfer regulations would remain, which Brook duly noted was a qualification to Jews' status as full and equal citizens. Brook's immense experience of draftsmanship allowed him to subject the Arab position to an exhaustive and time-consuming inquisition. On 23 September the depths of Arab intransigence were plumbed when Brook explained that currently Palestine Jewish citizens numbered some 200,000 and that the law allowed naturalization after two years' residence. Brook enquired what arrangements the Arab delegations proposed to ensure that the balance of 400,000 Jews was not disenfranchised. Jamali argued that only those Jews who were already citizens should be enfranchised, and that no further time should be granted for naturalization. Azzam suggested a ten-year period of qualifying residence. Howe thereupon pointed out that the period for the United Kingdom was only five years; unabashed Azzam replied that 'any or no period would be safe in the United Kingdom, but that in Palestine the Jews were a disturbing factor'. Eventually the Arab delegations' proposals were slightly amended and technically refined so as to include, for example, the ten-year residence requirement for citizenship. Having laboured to produce this much, Brook devoted his efforts in a final meeting of the committee to making a forceful representation to the assembled delegates on the need for further immigration into Palestine on grounds of justice, world opinion and practicability. It was of no use, and the meeting ended in outright disagreement, Azzam reiterating that, 'Palestine was an Arab land and the Jew was an alien in it.'[23]

On 2 October the full conference convened for a brief meeting. Bevin assured the delegates that the British Government would consider their proposals but could not discuss them now. He said that the Jews must be given a final opportunity to state their case and suggested, in view of the demands of the forthcoming UN session upon the time of the delegates, that the conference should be suspended. In discussion afterwards with Brook, 16 December was felt to be the earliest possible date for reconvening. A communiqué was agreed, drawing a graceful gloss over the utter and complete failure of the conference to make any progress towards compromise or to embark on any useful negotiation.[24] It was indeed a sorry affair, fully justifying the warnings that had been conveyed to London from the Middle East. The conference, originally called to discuss the Morrison–Grady plan and then to hear the Jewish and Arab proposals for Palestine, had simply disappeared into the sands of Araby with the participants vying with each other for the champion's laurels. Representatives of the chief claimants, the Palestine Arabs and the Jewish Agency, were of course absent.

As the conference was such an unmitigated waste of time, it seems relevant to consider whether Britain had an ulterior motive in calling the conference. In the autumn of 1945, after all, the Chiefs of Staff had shown an interest in the Anglo-American Committee precisely because it was likely to delay the formulation of a policy for Palestine. However there is no evidence that the military appetite for delay provided the rationale for proceeding with the conference in the late summer and autumn of 1946. In fact, the COS seem to have been very quiet about the whole thing. At the end of August the embassy in Washington sent the Foreign Office a request for information on 'the strategic importance of Palestine to His Majesty's Government', asking that any relevant COS or Cabinet papers should be sent as background information in order for the embassy to keep those 'sections of the Administration (e.g. in the State and War Departments), who understand our dilemma in Palestine' fully abreast of British thinking. The response was significant, for in reply the Foreign Office pointed out that 'the principal' COS paper was DO(46)80, originally submitted to the Defence Committee on 18 June. Attlee had later asked the Defence Committee to take note of, but not to approve, this paper in revised but substantially unaltered form. Hence Britain's strategic requirements in the region were unresolved and the Chiefs of Staff's views on the subject were effectively placed on ice where they remained while the London Conference took place. In the minutes of the 19 September Defence Committee meeting, Attlee is recorded as saying that it was 'a little premature' to decide the permanent location of forces while Palestine's future was still under discussion. The Prime Minister would only go so far as to express his preparedness to agree to the COS wish to locate the forces being evacuated from Egypt in the Aden–Port Sudan area temporarily, and to allow only the planning of accommodation in Palestine. Clearly, then, the Chiefs of Staff were still without suasion on the subject of Palestine. In fact it may be suggested that the uncertainty surrounding Palestine's future was now becoming a greater planning inconvenience to the military than the effective but inconclusive defeat which their strategic plans for the region had met with in the summer.[25]

All the evidence points to the Foreign Office as the supplier of the rationale for holding the London Conference. It was a Foreign Office proposal in the first place, advanced with the precedent of the St James's Palace Conference specifically in mind. The plan had been put forward in the summer in parallel with the Colonial Office's provincial autonomy scheme, and one avowed purpose of the conference was to consult the Arab states about this British proposal for Palestine. This process subjected the provincial autonomy scheme to an orchestrated barrage of criticism which was the inevitable consequence of summoning all of the Arab states together to go on record, in front of each other, on any scheme which fell short of the White Paper of 1939. The single-minded intent of the Foreign Office to press ahead with the London Conference allowed a considerable shift of position by the Jewish Agency in adopting partition to pass practically unacknowledged, and very little significance seems to have been attached to the temporary ascendency of the moderates in Zionist counsels. Similarly the Eastern Department of the Foreign

Office showed no disposition to bring pressure to bear upon
individual Arab states, despite cogent advice from various representatives in the Middle East about the feasibility of so doing and the
consequences for the conference of not so doing. And the prospects
of a bargain between the Jewish Agency and some Arab governments had no chance—not only would it have required an acute
awareness in London of the Jewish Agency's position and a
preparedness to pressurize the Arab governments concerned, but it
also was quite unpalatable to the Foreign Secretary himself since it
threated to draw into the debate Britain's strategic requirements in
the Middle East, itself an area of contention. The Foreign Office
seems to have had no master plan of its own to put forward when the
conference ground to a halt, taking with it the provincial autonomy
scheme. The underlying purpose of the Foreign Office in embracing
the device of a conference was not to cause delay or further its own
scheme for Palestine. Rather, the motivation was, as always, the
concern to be seen to be doing the right thing by the Arab world,
thereby safeguarding that strategic and commercial essential in the
Middle East, Arab goodwill. The forceful reassertion of another and
more real dimension to the Palestine question, that of the US
President's views, appears to have been completely outside the
range of the Foreign Office calculations.

Truman's statement of 4 October and Anglo-
American relations

While the hour of the Foreign Office was at hand and while the
conference was under way, the US Government had shrunk from all
involvement. The information supplied secretly by the Secretary of
the British delegation to the US embassy was kept for the record but
evoked no response. However, this quiet was to end with dramatic
suddenness. After the conference adjourned on 2 October and the
official communiqué issued by the British Government and the
Arab delegations referred to 16 December as the earliest date for the
resumption of the conference, Attlee explained in a message to
Truman that the British Government was not prepared to give its
views on the Arab delegations' proposals before the views of the
Jewish Agency had been heard. The Prime Minister referred to
on-going talks with Weizmann and his colleagues and expressed the
hope that some arrangement could be reached so that the detained
Jewish Agency leaders could be released which would, in turn,
facilitate Jewish participation when the conference resumed.[26]

Truman responded on 3 October, informing the Prime Minister that he deeply regretted the adjournment and hoped it would prove possible 'in the interim' to begin transferring the 100,000. He said that in view of the deep sympathy felt in the US for these DPs and the widespread interest in finding 'a fair and workable solution' to the Palestine problem, 'I find it necessary to make a further statement at once'. The text of the statement, planned for release the next day on the eve of Yom Kippur, was given in the message to Attlee. It reviewed the US administration's record on Palestine since the Harrison Report, the early support for the entry of the 100,000 into Palestine, and the participation by the United States in the joint enquiry whose report had endorsed the government's suggestion on the 100,000. Truman in his statement referred to the Morrison--Grady plan and now confessed publicly that he could not support this plan. The President repeated his wish that the 100,000 should be admitted to Palestine, and then referred to the Jewish Agency's proposals for the partition of Palestine and the creation of a viable Jewish state. He continued crucially,

> it is my belief that a solution along these lines would command the support of public opinion in the United States. I cannot believe that the gap between the proposals which have been put forward is too great to be bridged by men of reason and goodwill. To such a solution our Government could give its support.

On the same day Acheson saw Inverchapel and gave him a copy of this message to the Prime Minister. Inverchapel reported that Acheson had explained the President's motivations in terms of electoral and party pressures that had been rendered acute by the forthcoming Congressional elections. The Ambassador concluded portentously, 'I fear that we must be prepared for something like a whirlwind here.'[27]

The British attempt to delay the statement

All the evidence suggests that the British Government and the Foreign Office were anything but prepared, even though there had been ample warning. On 14 August Inverchapel had conveyed Henderson's views, expressed to Balfour, that if the British Government failed either to meet the Jewish Agency's proposals or to make progress with the 100,000, Truman might feel constrained to reaffirm publicly his commitment on the latter. Since then there had been rumblings: Inverchapel also reported that at a press conference on 5

September Truman had reaffirmed his interest in securing the admittance of the 100,000 to Palestine. Despite these omens of trouble, Truman's statement seems to have fallen like a bolt from the blue so far as the British Government was concerned, and the Foreign office utterly failed to anticipate it.[28]

The consequence was something akin to panic in London. Attlee drafted a reply in his own hand to Truman at once, pointing out that Bevin was in Paris and hence, 'I would ... earnestly request you to postpone making your statement at least for the time necessary for me to communicate with Mr. Bevin.' Attlee himself handed this message to Gallman, the *chargé d'affaires* at the US embassy, at 1A.M. on 4 October, for immediate transmission to the President. It was a busy night for Attlee: at 4A.M. a telegram was despatched to Bevin, in Paris, proposing that several points should be put to Truman to make clear the unfortunate effect his statement might have on the progress of the talks, although the Prime Minister doubted that Truman could be dissuaded from going ahead. Attlee proposed that Truman should be told that the delay in the conference was inevitable in view of the timetabling of other international meetings, and was made necessary in the first place by the Jewish Agency's refusal to participate. However, Attlee argued, the signs were promising for future Jewish participation. Truman's statement might provoke an angry Arab reaction, while his position on the 100,000 overlooked the fact that 'Jewish immigration is the crux of the Palestine Problem' and hence the admission of that number would cause disorder in the country. A copy of Truman's message was sent to Bevin, who concurred on these points, stressing the progress made in talks about the Jewish Agency's participation in the resumed conference. He agreed that 'a strong effort' should be made to get Truman to postpone his statement and added that he would see Byrnes, who was in Paris too, and 'make it plain to him that if the result of the President's statement is to provoke further discords in Palestine there is a real risk of His Majesty's Government throwing their hand in.' Evidently Bevin made some impression upon Byrnes who said that the President would try to hold up the statement until the next day. Bevin advised the Prime Minister that if there was a delay then amendments to the statement should be suggested proposing, for example, that 100,000 should be admitted to the US and to Britain while Palestine's monthly quota was increased.[29]

It was all to no avail. Inverchapel reported Acheson as saying it would be difficult for Truman to postpone the statement because he felt 'threatened by immediate dangers' presented by the forthcoming

elections. In due course Truman's statement was issued, and after
8P.M., London time, a forlorn telegram was received by the British
embassy in Washington requesting background information. The
Foreign Office had hoped to send the text of Attlee's full reply to
Truman before the statement was issued. The text followed the line
Attlee had proposed earlier to Bevin, and pressed Truman strongly to
avoid promising his support to the Jewish Agency's plan before this
plan had been considered by the London Conference. Perhaps if the
answer Attlee framed for Bevin's approval had been sent at once to
the White House, instead of the short request for delaying the
Presidential statement, Truman could have complied. However,
Attlee's conduct on this occasion was typical of his non-involvement
in the Foreign Secretary's sphere, and indicative of the authority
Bevin carried.[30]

Truman's motives

What caused Truman to make the statement? He had recently shown
some public reticence, and his statement on 16 August appeared very
gentle. Acting Secretary of State Clayton wrote an important
memorandum to the President on 12 September which indicates the
reasons for Truman's silence during the autumn. Referring to the
Zionist pressure for his endorsement of partition for Palestine,
Clayton warned Truman that the State Department was against the
idea. The matter was the subject of delicate negotiations in London,
and both Byrnes and Harriman had warned against further US
intervention. Furthermore, Clayton warned that to yield to Zionist
pressure now would open the flood gates, for 'we do not believe that,
without sacrificing the public interests, we shall be able to go far and
fast enough in rendering them support to keep them satisfied very
long.' Instead it would be preferable to draw the line early. Finally
Clayton forcefully reminded the President that the Anglo-American
Committee of Enquiry had advised against partition, and that the
Joint Chiefs of Staff 'have urged that we take no action with regard to
Palestine which might orient the peoples of the entire area away from
the interests of the Western Powers', which the adoption of partition
would do. Clayton attached a draft statement for Truman to make in
case he still felt some compelling reason for saying something, and the
draft in fact said very little beyond expressing the wish that the Jewish
Agency should participate in the London Conference and promising
US support for any solution acceptable to the various parties.
Truman told Clayton in reply that he had been 'very hesitant about
saying anything on this subject' and hoped that it would not become

necessary. The statement was not used, and it would seem that Clayton's advice was heeded in the White House for a few weeks, until the London Conference adjourned.[31]

When the conference adjourned, however, the pressures on Truman to say something became irresistible. The Zionists cashed in on the campaign for the impending Congressional elections, and on 30 September an advertisement appeared in the *New York Herald Tribune*, reviewing the past pledges of the Democratic Party, the platform on which Truman had been elected, and drawing attention to their non-fulfilment:

> We do not seek new promises or new planks. The old ones are good enough. What we ask is that our Administration fulfill those old promises now.

Most ominously of all, the advertisement was signed by a Greater New York Actions Committee that boasted Bernard Rosenblatt as its chairman; Judge Rosenblatt was vice-President of the Zionist Organisation of America. Similar advertisements appeared in other New York newspapers, and on 1 October, Rosenblatt announced to the American Zionist Emergency Council the creation of the Actions Committee to bring pressure on the administration in furtherance of Silver's wish to effect a programme of political action. This tactic was not to the taste of Wise, who earlier in September had been bitterly critical of Rosenblatt's efforts to pillory the Democratic administration for its record on Palestine. Now, clearly, Wise's counsel of moderation were eschewed, and Silver's tactics proved more efficacious in obtaining a strong Presidential statement in October than Goldmann's diplomatic efforts had been in August. But this success must not be attributed solely to Zionist tactics, for the interval of time had brought other factors into play.[32]

In some contrast to this aggressive public campaign, pressure mounted from within the Democratic Party and the White House for Truman to make a statement for electoral reasons. Inevitably, Niles played a prominent part, and when news reached the White House that the Republican Governor Dewey was due to make a speech to the United Palestine Appeal on 6 October in which he would call for free immigration into Palestine, Niles urged that Truman should make an effort to pre-empt Dewey and secure the Jewish vote in New York for the Democratic Party. Wise and former Governor Lehman concurred in their appeal to Truman. Following Truman's statement, Dewey was left to call optimistically for the entry into Palestine of several hundred thousand Jews. Significant pressure had come from the national chairman of the Democratic Party, Hannegan, who became convinced of the need for Truman to make a statement that would secure the Jewish vote, especially in New York. According to Epstein, the Jewish Agency's representative in Washington, who wrote to Goldmann on 9 October, it was Bartley Crum who was primarily responsible for obtaining Hannegan's support. Epstein forwarded to Goldmann a copy of the letter Crum had sent to Hannegan which was, Epstein said, 'inspired by our friend and even written in his office'. The 'friend' was evidently Niles, unnamed no doubt in deference to Niles' own predilections, although all the other actors in the drama are mentioned by name. Epstein continued:

> credit for the statement must go again primarily to our friend who at this time, as in the past, has shown determination and great courage in attempting to overcome all kinds of intangible difficulties in order to accomplish the matter at hand. He consulted me frequently during the critical days preceeding the statement.

It would seem that Niles was the chief in-house proponent of Truman's statement, and in his task he was ably assisted by Epstein and Crum.[33]

Together with the failure of British policy to make any progress towards a settlement of the Palestine problem, party political and electoral considerations were evidently the predominant motives behind Truman's Yom Kippur statement. Yet underlying it was Truman's genuine and well established humanitarian concern for the Jewish DPs. Another clue to his attitude is provided by his daughter, who mentions that 'Dad continued to press his 100,000-refugee compromise'. To the British Government it scarcely appeared to be a compromise, but for Truman that was precisely what it was. The actual entry of the 100,000 into Palestine would allow Truman to escape from the political corner in which his early support of the Harrison Report had placed him, and it would leave the rest of the Palestine problem to the UN. The major theme on 26 September of a discussion on Palestine between Truman and Wadsworth, the US Minister to Syria and the Lebanon, was 'that, as an international problem, it could appropriately be dealt with on the international plane at the forthcoming United Nations General Assembly.' Meanwhile, Wadsworth gathered, the issue of the European DPs should be 'kept in the forefront of our thinking'. Truman's Yom Kippur statement must be viewed in this context. As such it was a reassertion of his position on the 100,000 coupled with an expression of support for partition along the lines of the Jewish Agency's proposals for Palestine. Support for the Agency's call for a viable Jewish state was noticeably qualified by the sentence, 'I cannot believe that the gap between the proposals which have been put forward is too great to be bridged by men of reason and goodwill.' It would seem, therefore, that although Truman had taken a significant step in showing in public his qualified support for the Jewish Agency's plan, his position remained consistent with his previous attitude on the whole problem, and thus the underlying rationale for the Yom Kippur statement was not new. The novelty derived from the occasion, the conjunction of the Congressional elections with the collapse of the London Conference.[34]

It is pertinent to note in passing the attitude of the British Ambassador in Washington to the affair. In contrast to the strenuous efforts made in London and Paris to delay or alter Truman's statement, Inverchapel's representations, to say the least, lacked vigour. When he reported to the Foreign Office his interview with Acheson on 3 October, warning of the forthcoming statement, he seemed to be at greater pains to describe Acheson's explanation of electoral pressures than to render an account of his own representations. In the circumstances his position was not at all surprising, for Acheson's account of the interview, written on the same day, indicates that Inverchapel reacted in a wonderfully magnanimous way on being informed of the statement's contents:

> The Ambassador stated as his private opinion and quite confidentially to me that, while the statement would probably make London very angry, he believed that in the long run it might be beneficial to the solution of the whole question.
>
> The Ambassador asked me whether I could give him any information which he might use to ameliorate the feelings of London by indicating the difficulties of the President.

Thus an opportunity to make a spontaneous and uninstructed *démarche* at the action proposed by the US administration was instead used by Inverchapel to enquire solicitously of the Acting Secretary of State whether he could be given something with which to mollify his own government. If news of this had reached the Foreign Office it would probably not have occasioned much surprise there. Inverchapel was well connected in Zionist circles, his appointments diary indicating frequent meetings with prominent Zionists such as

Goldmann, Frankfurter, Silver and Epstein. On 20 June he had written personally to 'My dear Foreign Secretary', reporting on a conversation with Goldmann and urging Bevin to see Weizmann. His friendliness to the Zionists had not passed unremarked in the Eastern Department where as early as 26 June Beeley had felt it appropriate to minute:

> I think the time has come to ask the Embassy to justify their general policy of appeasing the Zionists. Its results are not up to now encouraging.

Evidently the resultant rebuke did not have a lasting effect. On his visit to Washington, Dalton recorded in his diary for 5 October a note about Inverchapel's trenchant views. Apparently he told the Chancellor of the Exchequer that he

> thinks that Palestine is being badly mishandled by H.M.G. We must, he thinks, choose between friendship of world and all Arab States. He is quite clear that we should prefer the former ...

The Ambassador made his sympathies known to a wider audience than one senior Cabinet minister. Epstein, in his letter to Goldmann of 9 October, recorded his meeting with an exceptionally cordial Lord Inverchapel, apparently on the very day of Truman's statement. The Ambassador indicated his support for partition and his belief that the Arabs would yield to a determined British position, and Epstein drew from this the inevitable conclusion:

> Whether he is fully sincere or not, Lord Inverchapel likes to indicate his sympathy toward our cause. ... The fact that a pro-Zionist sympathy is considered by the Ambassador to be, in Washington, an asset and not a liability is in itself an interesting point for us to exploit.

The consequences of the British Government's flawed diplomatic representation in Washington must, in the absence of evidence of its effect, be left to conjecture. It would seem to be a valid hypothesis that Inverchapel's strongly held and publicly displayed beliefs on this question diminished the pressure which the British Government sought to direct on the US administration in the twenty-four hours before Truman issued his statement.[35]

The results of the statement

The Truman statement failed to win the support it set out to capture, and many Zionists received it dismissively. There was indeed a widespread impression that the statement had been issued purely with the Congressional elections in mind, as Reston's article in the *New York Times* argued. Epstein, in his letter to Goldmann of 9 October, seemed disappointed at the statement's mention of bridging the gap between the various proposals, while Silver adopted a still more critical view, calling it 'harmful' at the American Zionist Emergency Council's meeting on 14 October because of its apparent confession that Truman was in fact unable to shift Britain on this issue. By contrast, Wise applauded the statement and he grew increasingly angry at the continuation of the programme of political action. Eventually, with election day approaching, Wise cast off the mantle of party political neutrality which AZEC's programme had enjoined upon the Zionist leaders, and endorsed the Democratic candidates Mead and Lehman in New York. Neither this action, which brought much criticism upon Wise, nor the President's statement secured the return of the Democratic candidates in November. Mead was defeated by Dewey with a majority of 650,000 and Ives replaced Lehman by a margin of nearly one-quarter million votes, while in Democratic New York State Republican candidates now secured a majority for the first time since 1928. The Republican Party won a landslide victory throughout the country, returning with a majority of fifty-one to forty-five in the Senate, and 245 against 188 Democrats and one Laborite in the House. Any ground which Truman's Yom Kippur statement might have held was inundated and lost without trace in the returning tide.[36]

However, Truman's statement bode fair to secure a more lasting effect upon Anglo-American relations. Truman had turned down Attlee's request that the statement should be postponed for what he called 'imperative' reasons. Attlee's response must surely be one of the most scalding communications a British Prime Minister has ever sent to a President of the United States. It was drafted in his own hand, and continued with rising anger:

> I have received with great regret your letter refusing even a few hours grace to the Prime Minister of the country which has the actual responsibility for the government of Palestine in order that he might acquaint you with the actual situation and the probable results of your action. These may well include the frustration of the patient efforts to achieve a settlement and the loss of still more lives in Palestine.
>
> I am astonished that you did not wait to acquaint yourself with the reasons for the suspension of the conference with the Arabs. You do not seem to have been informed that so far from negotiations having being broken off, conversations with leading Zionists with a view to their

entering the conference were proceeding with good prospects of success.

I shall await with interest to learn what were the imperative reasons which compelled this precipitancy.

Arguably the positively menacing tone of this amazing message more than compensated for Inverchapel's mildness. However, in both cases it is hard to discover any major consequence, and the potential antagonism subsided. It was the State Department's unenviable task to draft a reply to Attlee which was approved by Truman. The embarrassment caused was 'very much' regretted, and Truman's message gently emphasized the need for action on the 100,000 before winter again closed upon the DP camps of Europe. The message also referred to Jewish feeling of frustration on the eve of Yom Kippur. The US Government expressed its determination to stand by its promises of help with the transfer of the refugees. No reply was made by the British Government and, as Wilson correctly surmises in his account (1979), certainly not because the Prime Minister accepted the US explanation. The British reticence was more of the nature of a withering silence. A reply was in fact drafted, evidently in the Foreign Office, and Creech Jones, the Colonial Secretary, approved it during Bevin's absence in Paris. Attlee, however, was having none of it, minuting on 22 October,

I do not care for this draft. It appears to accept the President's reasons for his hasty action as valid.

Bevin fully concurred, and his Private Secretary, Dixon, informed Howe that the Foreign Secretary agreed with Attlee that no reply should be sent. Wisely for the future health of Anglo-American relations, replies were not bandied about any more and the matter was allowed to drop from the realm of summit exchanges.[37]

However, Truman's statement continued to rankle in private, Bevin informing the Cabinet on 25 October that he had hoped to make more progress in the talks with the Jewish Agency, 'but the prospects of persuading them to adopt a more reasonable attitude had been impaired by the public statement issued by President Truman.' Attlee's angry message to Truman had contained a similar charge, but there is little evidence to suggest that it was justified. It may be that far too much weight was read into a report the Colonial Secretary sent to Cunningham on 10 October about a meeting with Weizmann, Goldmann, Fishman, Locker and other members of the Jewish

Agency. A copy of this appears in the Prime Minister's files, with
certain passages marked. In one of these Weizmann 'considerd that
now the U.S. had indicated their willingness to accept full responsibility for the policy they advocated, there was no longer any obstacle
to at least a partial solution of the problem of immigration.' Similarly,
Goldmann 'welcomed President Truman's intervention' and acceptance of responsibility. Rowan, Attlee's Principal Private Secretary,
minuted that, 'An important telegram—the evil effects of the
President's incursions are seen clearly.' Attlee added : 'Yes'. Clearly
at this particular meeting the Jewish Agency representatives were
trying to make as much capital from Truman's statement as possible,
but no more than that should be read into their comments. The
implications in Rowan's minute and Bevin's accusations cannot be
evidenced clearly in the subsequent negotiations between the Jewish
Agency and the British Government about participation in the
London Conference. Terrorism and the continued detention of the
Agency leaders in Palestine were the most serious stumbling blocks to
this participation during October. Indeed some powerful elements in
the Zionist movement were acutely aware of the limitations of what
Truman had said, and it seems most improbable, give these
reservations and the qualifications in Truman's actual statement,
that the Jewish Agency altered its negotiating position with the
British Government as a result of what the President had said. The
impression within the British Government at the time, however, was
different. Attlee and Bevin had shown in the past a disposition to
attribute to Truman only the basest motives of electoral politics in his
every action on Palestine, so the President's statement on the eve of
Yom Kippur and the Congressional elections merely confirmed this
perception of the suasion wielded by the Jewish vote. That this was
the received truth in Whitehall as well was instanced by Butler, the
Superintending Undersecretary of the North American Department
at the FO, who wrote to Howe on 7 October raising and replying to
the grounds for possible US criticism of British policy 'insofar as their
criticism is not dictated entirely by considerations of internal
policies'. Both arrogance and misunderstanding were responsible for
this outlook: arrogance in believing that British policy was substantially above criticism, and a misunderstanding of Truman's motives
which may have had its origin in Bevin's angry and embarrassed
reaction to the President's hasty endorsement of the recommendation
on the 100,000 contained in the Anglo-American Committee of
Enquiry's Report.[38]

US pressure and the perceived strength of American Zionism

contributed in the longer term to the British Government's growing desire to cast down the burden of the Mandate. Truman's Yom Kippur statement contributed to this pressure, but it is not possible to identify it as the single or the most decisive American contribution. Of importance also was the record of the United States in getting the problem of Palestine referred to the United Nations. Truman had consistently maintained that, apart from short-term action on immigration to alleviate the problem of the Jewish DPs, the question of the future of the Mandate was a job for the UN. The State Department was also gently lobbying in this direction, Byrnes advising Bevin when they met in Paris on 26 September that, failing an agreement with the Arabs and the Jews, Britain should refer the matter to the United Nations Organization. Bevin of course foresaw strategic problems in such a move, and he told Byrnes so. Nevertheless, a month later Henderson, the Director of the Office of Near Eastern and African Affairs at the State Department, sent a memorandum to Under Secretary of State Acheson outlining the various courses of action which could be followed in the UN General Assembly 'in the light of the President's statement'. These ranged from keeping silent to supporting the Jewish Agency's proposal for partition, or taking some intermediate position. The urgency which Henderson attached to the selection of the appropriate course is indicative of the State Department's thinking that Palestine would shortly appear on the General Assembly's agenda. For the purposes of determining the precise role played by Truman's statement in the subsequent policy decision of the British Government, the interest of the President and of the State Department in a decision by the United Nations serves only to confuse the analysis. The impact of the Yom Kippur statement alone becomes subsumed into an American interest in employing the UN to solve the problem of Palestine, as well as into the widespread American criticism of British policy.[39]

Other more tangible consequences followed from Truman's statement. Ibn Saud sent a highly critical but politely worded message to Truman, referring to previous conversations with Roosevelt and mentioning his astonishment and incredulity at Truman's recent statement which went against the earlier assurances of the US Government that it was itself proposing no new solution but had faith in the London Conference. The King continued in fine oratorical style to berate Zionist aggression. Truman's reply, drafted in the Near Eastern Division, was unrepentant. It referred to the European DP problem and the hopes of the refugees in 'the further development of the Jewish National Home', and acknowledged the

United States' interest and responsibility in its establishment
although it did not refer specifically to the creation of a Jewish state.
Truman's message roundly rejected the Arab charge about Zionist
aggression as well as the contention that his original statement
contradicted a previous promise or was an act hostile to the Arabs.
Ibn Saud was clearly unimpressed, and there were other signs of Arab
resentment. The US *chargé d'affaires* in Damascus reported that:

> Despite assurances ... that questions of Palestine and our negotiations
> concerning oil and aviation would be treated as separate subjects, Syrians
> friendly to America believe public demand for 'action' may soon force
> Gov[ernmen]t to take measures indicative of its displeasure.

There are *already signs of non-cooperation on routine matters*.[40]

Traditionally it was the State Department which showed itself more
aware of an Arab dimension to and a Middle Eastern context of the
Palestine problem than the White House, and there is an important
piece of evidence to suggest its alarm and disaffection at Truman's
statement. Merriam, Chief of the Division of Near Eastern Affairs,
sent his superior, Henderson, a most significant memorandum on 15
October. Merriam set out to consider 'what we can and should do'
following Truman's statement, feeling that while the entry of the
100,000 may be urged on humanitarian grounds, it was unlikely to
achieve success in the absence of a world scheme to settle the DPs and
because Arab resentment towards partition, which the US had
endorsed, precluded Arab acceptance of further immigration. Hence,
Merriam felt that continued urging of the 100,000 would create bad
feeling but 'can be done without too much risk of serious long-term
damage' to US relations with Britain and the Arab world. Of
partition, Merriam believed categorically that it could be justified
only on the basis of Arab and Jewish consent: 'Otherwise we should
violate the principle of self-determination ... a principle which is
deeply embedded in our foreign policy.' Even if the UN adopted
partition, consent of the Arabs and Jews would still be required.
Merriam then analysed Truman's wording closely, drawing attention
to the President's use of the phrase 'a solution along these lines' when
referring to Goldmann's proposals for which Truman had expressed
support. Merriam went on:

> The key word seems to be 'solution', not 'partition'. That is, if partition is
> a solution, we can support it. If it is not, we are not bound to do so. The fact
> is, however, that the partition of Palestine cannot be a solution unless it is

an *agreed solution*. If it is not an agreed solution, it will result in bloodshed and chaos.

Hence Merriam argued that Truman's statement did not require abandoning America's traditional principles of foreign policy. If these were abandoned, Merriam went on to outline a scenario involving:

1. A serious break with the British. ... it would cause the British to become unreliable as a working partner. ...
2. A serious break with the Arabs. ...
3. The resulting disillusionment and cynicism with respect to the U.S. will cause the Near East to turn increasingly toward the U.S.S.R. ...
4. Risk of losing a part of the world which we are endeavouring to preserve for western influence by a strong attitude in Greece, Turkey and Iran. There is no use in strengthening the arch if we are going to kick out the pillars.

Merriam concluded this powerful memorandum by stating that US policy should be either to support partition once the parties had agreed to it, or at the most to support it with the proviso that it required agreement. Finally Merriam closed by quoting from the Anglo-American Committee's Report the passage which dismissed partition on the grounds that the Arabs and Jews would not accept it. That such a paper should have been submitted at all is indicative of the feelings within the State Department, feelings which helped to impose a ceiling upon the pressure brought to bear by the United States on Britain and which also helped to compartmentalize the Palestine problem and insulate it against affecting Anglo-American co-operation generally as well as US strategic interests. The fate of Merriam's paper serves only to confirm its significance. Henderson showed it to Acheson who, according to Wilson of the Near Eastern Department, 'thought it so explosive that he directed that it [should] not be placed in the Department's files and that all copies be destroyed—except for the original which he said the author might keep'.[41]

In the wider context of Anglo-American relations there can be no doubt that the arguments about Palestine had no discernible effect. Co-operation between the two countries proceeded in measured steps in the face of the Soviet challenge, first apparent over Iran in March 1946, and manifest again during the summer when the Soviet Union demanded from Turkey transit rights through the Dardanelles. In early 1947 Britain was to announce that she could no longer support Turkey and Greece, not because Britain was becoming what

Merriam called an unreliable working partner, but as a result of financial exhaustion. A phased British withdrawal followed, and far from allowing the arch to collapse the US responded with the so-called Truman Doctrine, a programme of support for the Near East, supplemented later in the year by the Marshall Plan itself which rescued an ailing Western Europe. There was in the US Government no evident disposition to make Anglo-American co-operation conditional upon Britain following an approved policy in Palestine; to have done so would have been to get matters wildly out of proportion, as Merriam perceived. Hence, on Palestine and on Palestine only, Britain and the United States settled into an acrimonious stalemate. The US Government manifestly had no clear policy; Truman's statement had been vague on all but the issue of short-term immigration, and the State Department was left to cobble something together in case the matter came up before the UN General Assembly. Truman's Yom Kippur statement derived from his well-established views on Palestine, but was occasioned by electoral pressures and by the evident bankruptcy of British policy. Yet there was little disposition in London to perceive anything other than the electoral motive, and it is clear that with the adjournment of the London Conference in October 1946, British policy on Palestine was at its nadir. Not only had the prospects of American partnership been overturned some months earlier, but by the autumn the ingrained attitude of the Foreign Office had contrived to repeat the débâcle of 1939. It had contrived that a scheme inspired by the Colonial Office for dealing with the British Mandate should be held up before representatives of various Arab states as a target for their orchestrated criticism. The remonstrance which Truman directed at Britain's policy on 4 October was undoubtedly most richly deserved.

Decision Time: the Winter of 1946–7

The winter of 1946–7 was a turning point for Britain's Palestine policy. The government at last faced up to the fact that, over the previous eighteen months, it had run through all the options without a palatable policy emerging. An attempt was made within the government to go 'back to basics', to define the options clearly and to reassess them, but this process was brought to a grinding halt by the resumption of Foreign Office diplomacy in the London Conference of January 1947. The deliberations of this session made the original performance of the previous autumn look like an exercise in moderation. Thus the British Government had to admit that it had no policy for Palestine and that the Foreign Office had been unable to fill the gap left by the collapse of the Anglo-American initiative. It is in this context that the referral, without recommendations, of the whole question to the United Nations must be seen. Clearly it was not merely the next stage in the apparatus of protraction and delay, as Churchill suggested, to allow a continued and indefinite British presence in Palestine. Rather it was the final resort of a government with no policy, wearied and harried by the burden of the Mandate, stepping out of its predicament with almost petulant resolution; for it is obvious the Cabinet perceived the referral of the Palestine question to the UN as the precursor of British withdrawal.

His Majesty's Government debate policy

Late in 1946 the policymaking institutions of Whitehall embarked upon a protracted debate about Palestine. During the adjournment of the London Conference, not destined to reconvene until January 1947, the full spectrum of the various departmental views were paraded and their protagonists eventually engaged one another in the Cabinet and the Defence Committee. Many of the arguments and attitudes were old and familiar, but outside influences impinged as well: terrorism in Palestine, the Zionist Congress which convened in Basle during December, and the attitude adopted by the United States Government. Of greater significance, however, was the new feeling that the British Government was running out of options on Palestine, that it was nearing the end of its tether.

No great sense of urgency was evidenced by the Foreign Office as the Arab delegations to the London Conference departed. On 3 October, Howe, the Superintending Undersecretary of the Eastern Department, minuted reflectively that the hypothetical possibility should be considered that the government might wish to refer to the United Nations a solution involving the termination of the Mandate and the granting of independence to Palestine without concluding a trusteeship agreement first. There was nothing new in the Eastern Department entertaining thoughts of involving the UN, despite Bevin's previous dislike of the idea, but the suggestion of terminating the Mandate was new. However, the hypothesis merely went to the Foreign Office Legal Adviser, Beckett, who considered that there was no legal obligation to place a mandated territory under trusteeship.[1]

When, on 12 October, Inverchapel reported suggestions in the US press that the UN should take over the Palestine problem, a move that Truman might favour, Beeley minuted caustically that the US Government would be relieved of domestic pressure initially but eventually 'they would have to take some definite line, and they might find this embarrassing'. Beeley noted that the Eastern Department favoured obtained the General Assembly's approval for British policy, 'But we do not think it would be wise to go to the Assembly except upon the basis of a clearly defined policy.' But with no clearly defined policy in the offing, referral to the UN was a distant prospect. No sense of urgency can be detected in these casual minutes, nor is there evidence to suggest that the Eastern Department had any concrete proposals with which to fill the policy vacuum consequent upon the adjournment of the London Conference. Bevin's attitude reflected this indecision, for when he returned from Paris later in October he decided against saying anything about Palestine in the House of Commons. On 25 October, Bevin outlined to the Cabinet the three choices with which they would be faced if there was no prospect of resuming negotiations with the Arabs and the Jewish Agency. To impose a solution acceptable to one of the two communities in Palestine, to surrender the Mandate and withdraw, or to 'propose a scheme of Partition'. Bevin, however, urged the Cabinet against considering these options at this stage, for he hoped he might have useful talks with the US Government and the Jews when he was in New York at the forthcoming meeting of Foreign Ministers. For the time being, therefore, the Foreign Office seemed content to mark time on Palestine and to toy gently with a few ideas.[2]

Not so the Colonial Office. Not for the first time had the Colonial Office witnessed the destruction of its favoured scheme for Palestine at the hands of the Foreign Office whose accomplices were, on this occasion, the Arab states' delegations to the London Conference. The consequence was a vigorous reassessment in the Colonial Office and the reappearance, on traditional lines, of the old arguments with the Foreign Office. Creech Jones, the new Colonial Secretary, gave an early indication of these developments in a letter to the Foreign Secretary on 18 October, and gently drew Bevin's attention to a despatch from Cunningham, the High Commissioner in Palestine, which argued that 'partition would appear to give the only hope of peace in this country'. Cunningham's despatch was dated 20 September and referred to Brigadier Clayton's paper of 31 August, which set out the apostate's case for backing partition now. Cunningham commented that the Jewish Agency would accept partition, assuming that the term 'means a Jewish State in part of Palestine of a size which the Jews would regard as viable'. Beeley commented in the margin: 'This is not what Clayton means'. Cunningham continued, arguing that the Palestinian Arab leadership was 'vested in men who have repeated the same parrot cry for so long that they are completely incapable of seeing any other point of view'. Finally, the High Commissioner concluded, 'I believe that unless assistance in money, men and arms were provided by the Arab States, and unless the Mufti were allowed to intervene, the resistance of the Arabs in this country to a scheme of partition would be confined to rioting in the towns.' Beeley minuted simply : 'Both would happen'.[3]

As Beeley's notes indicate, this despatch and the Colonial Secretary's covering letter looked all set to reopen an old debate. The Foreign Office rose to the challenge and, with Sargent's approval, Howe administered the antidote to his Secretary of State on 23 October. Howe quickly seized upon the conditions in Cunningham's conclusion, warning that the Mufti may well intervene:

> I do not think we would be justified in hoping for non-intervention from the neighbouring Arab countries.

Coming from the department which was in a position to know the flaws in Arab unity and which was fresh from the organization of another incursion by the Arab states into the affairs of Palestine, this sober reflection by Howe was ironical to say the least. Clayton was in London at this time, and Howe wrote that he had recanted from his support of partition on the grounds that 'during the last two months Arab opinion had hardened' against it; probably the spectacle of Arab opposition provided by the London Conference had impressed the Brigadier. Howe ably rehearsed the usual objections to partition; boundaries which the Arabs might be persuaded to concede would be rejected by the Jews, while the Arab states' recent objections to provincial autonomy had been founded principally on their fear that it might bring partition nearer. Howe concluded with the dire warning that the imposition of partition would provoke

> a violent outburst of anti-British feeling in all the Arab countries. ... The adoption of this policy by His Majesty's Government, therefore, might gravely weaken our position in the Middle East as a whole.

Clearly, then, the Foreign Office had not altered its fundamental position following the adjournment of the London Conference and it seemed to have nothing new to say.[4]

By contrast, within the Colonial Office, a scheme of partition was in the ascendant. Provincial autonomy, of course, had been shot to pieces at the conference, but Sir Douglas Harris rose to the defence of his brainchild. In a memorandum of 28 October he argued that it might yet prove acceptable to the Jews as a stepping stone to partition, while the Arabs had yet to be confronted with the bankruptcy of their own plan. Accordingly Harris urged that provincial autonomy should be laid before the conference, when it reconvened, as a compromise, and that if it became clear that it would cause serious disturbances in Palestine, the government should then present provincial autonomy to the United Nations as the best scheme in the hope that it would then be accepted. This proposal must have had a hollow ring about it following the attitude taken by the Arab delegations, and it failed to impress Assistant Undersecretary J. M. Martin. In a minute to the Permanent Undersecretary, Sir George Gater, he argued that Harris' memorandum

> does not do justice to the strength of the case for partition. This alternative seems to be too easily disposed of by the argument that it is not immediately practicable because reference to the United Nations would be necessary.

Martin felt that partition, far more than provincial autonomy, offered the elements of finality, independence and control of immigration and should therefore be the goal. As for any reference to the UN, Martin was adamant:

> I regard this as far and away the worst possible alternative and suggest that it would be better not to mention the possibility. Those baffled by the other alternative may only too readily turn to this.

Martin recommended that the best course was

> to plump for partition as our ultimate solution, introducing provincial autonomy to cover the transition period ... We shall be doing no grave injustice to the Arabs but shall on the contrary be saving them from the real danger of creeping conquest by the Jews.

This forthright and vigorous response to the débâcle of the London Conference contrasts strongly with the vague thoughts under consideration in the Foreign Office. Martin carried the battle directly to the Foreign Office, writing to Baxter, the Head of the Eastern Department, on 4 November, and dismissing the problem of getting the permission of the United Nations for partition on the grounds that 'we have always assumed that, in fact, we should have to obtain international endorsement, in some form, for any scheme of partition'. Clearly Martin was prepared to take the worries of the Foreign Office about the difficulties of partition very lightly, and for good measure he told Baxter, in answer to the suggestion that the 1939 White Paper tied Britain's hands, that 'His Majesty's present Government do not regard themselves as bound by its terms'.[5]

The Eastern Department was not impressed, nor was it galvanised into further activity against the idea of partition. Beeley minuted mildly, 'I do not think we could claim, as Mr. Martin seems to imply, that partition is a measure within the general spirit of the mandate'. Within the Colonial Office, however, the pro-partitionists gathered momentum. On 19 November, Harris submitted another memorandum, more lengthy than before, arguing the case for persevering with provincial autonomy. This time Sir Douglas was answered yet more forcefully by Martin who minuted that partition should be 'our goal' for which the government should 'strive to obtain the necessary international endorsement'. On one point, however, Martin agreed with the Foreign Office:

> Nothing is worse than to remit to U.N.O. *without any recommendation*. If we can make no progress with provincial autonomy or partition let us think

again in the light of the situation disclosed by the discussion; but let us avoid prescribing at this stage, as a possible alternative, a counsel of despair.

This analysis of what was in fact to take place should be kept in mind for it is indicative of the extent of the British Government's eventual capitulation over Palestine. Gater concurred in Martin's support for partition, 'the only really satisfactory solution'. He continued:

> The Arab scheme is unthinkable. It is impossible to remain in Palestine as we are now. The autonomous area scheme is likely to be subjected to [the] strongest criticism from both sides ...

Gater evidently felt that Britain was running out of policy options, too. Gater agreed with Harris that referral to the UN would be necessary in the likely event of there being no agreement between the Arabs and Jews, but he argued that the government ought 'to be quite clear as to what is to be our destination': partition. Gater also stressed the importance of obtaining US support for partition, without which he felt the United Nations would have to adjudicate not only a British plan, but also the Jewish and Arab plans.[6]

Arguably of greater significance than these minutes by the officials of the Colonial Office in favour of partition was a detailed minute by Creech Jones himself, which now dismissed provincial autonomy because 'it is not practical politics for the reason that both Arab and Jew are utterly opposed to it, that America has denounced it and no side would work it'. Following the resumption of the London Conference, Creech Jones argued, the government would have to choose between offering some compromise scheme to the Arabs and Jews, and informing the UN that the Mandate was unworkable. The latter, he felt, would be open to such strategic objections as loss of British prestige, loss of Palestine and the opening of the area to 'other objectionable powers'. He argued that if a British compromise was rejected by the Arabs and Jews and a plan had to be referred to the UN, 'The scheme to be aimed at should move away from the Government's Provincial Autonomy Scheme towards Partition'. The Colonial Secretary further suggested that the conference should be steered towards partition, perhaps on the lines of the 1943 Cabinet Committee's proposal. Finally, Creech Jones suggested that the strength of the Arab League might be examined, together with the attitude of the constituent states in order to obtain 'appraisals of positive Arab reactions to partition'; furthermore, he added, partition would prove most satisfactory to parliamentary and public opinion in Britain.[7]

Eight days later, on 27 November, a lengthy discussion took place in the Colonial Office in which Creech Jones put his views across forcefully. A marginal note on the record suggests that Gater was present, but it is not clear who else was there. It was decided that, on his return from New York, Bevin should be told that it was agreed no overt concessions should be made to the Jews and that the conference should resume and discuss, in the first place, the provincial autonomy plan, but that, in addition, 'The attitude of [the] Cabinet and the move of opinion here towards partition should be made clear'. Creech Jones was evidently quite prepared to cross swords with the Foreign Office now, and the meeting concluded that if 'no agreement can be reached' with the FO, then the two points of view should be conveyed to the Foreign Secretary. Therefore, it appears that, by the end of November, the Colonial Office had given up provincial autonomy as a solution for the Palestine problem, retaining it merely as the opening point for the reconvened conference. In its place partition had been adopted in principle from the Secretary of State downwards, and the Colonial Office was as a result girding its loins for another battle with the Foreign Office on the subject.[8]

Interestingly, there is evidence to suggest that Bevin was less categorically opposed to the idea of partion than his officials were. For instance, on 3 October, the second Legal Adviser at the Foreign Office, Fitzmaurice, received a memorandum, apparently from one of Bevin's Private Secretaries, requesting a ruling on the legal position of the Mandate for the Foreign Secretary 'supposing he wished to proceed to partition the country into two independent States'. The note continued:

> The Secretary of State feels it is no use his trying to secure agreement on a policy of partition if it must be referred to U.N.O. and there be blocked by the Russian veto.

This note was endorsed by Dixon and by Bevin himself. The legal advice given suggested that Britain was probably bound, in the absence of the League of Nations, to continue to administer Palestine 'in the *general spirit*' of the Mandate. Beeley had minuted earlier that there was nothing in the final session of the League, held in April 1946, to suggest that future arrangements for Palestine might not cover partition; he warned, however, that the Arab states might challenge the creation of a Jewish state in the UN Security Council as a threat to the peace.[9]

Despite the weighty advice he was receiving about the legal, political and strategic difficulties raised by partition, Bevin evidently continued to entertain it as a possible course. He mentioned it in the Cabinet meeting of 25 October, and it featured during his visit to the United States in November. In a lengthy and important memorandum to the Prime Minister on 26 November, summarized also in a telegram for Cabinet distribution, Bevin described and pondered on his talks with Silver and other Jews, as well as 'several rather scrappy conversations with Mr. Byrnes'. The Zionists lobbied Bevin to adopt a policy of partition, and inevitably Bevin recorded that Inverchapel 'has pressed me to accept' this policy too. Bevin, wary of the US Government's equivocation on the subject and the forecasts of Arab reactions, contemplated the hurdles which partition would have to clear; there was the problem of obtaining a two-thirds majority in the UN General Assembly, then the difficulty of tying American opinion down. Finally, Bevin felt that if the Jews got wind of a move towards partition they would raise their price and press the US Government 'for the whole of Palestine'. Accordingly, Bevin felt that the Jews would 'have to make their position clear either at the [London] conference or in writing' so there could be no further bidding. Such thoughts about the feasibility of getting a scheme of partition adopted occupied a large proportion of the Foreign Secretary's memorandum, and apparently bulked large in his thinking, but he closed on an uncertain note:

> All this is very complicated ... especially having regard to the fact that we have had no consultation with the Arabs since October, I presume that I must proceed on the same lines as hitherto. I have no doubt you have been discussing it in London and if there is any different viewpoint or change ... I should be glad to be advised.[10]

Privately, then, Bevin seemed to be wobbling slightly towards partition. There was it seems a hint of bafflement and a sense of the exhaustion of possibilities in Bevin's thoughts which forced the consideration of such a scheme. Furthermore, there was a strong element of support for partition, which the Foreign Secretary could not fail to notice, evident in both the Colonial Office and the Cabinet. In the Cabinet discussion on 25 October, when the Foreign Secretry had advised against the consideration of the policy options on Palestine, the minutes record that nevertheless, 'several Ministers said that they were glad that the possibility of Partition was not excluded from consideration and expressed the view that this would

in the end be found to be the only practicable solution'. Such
sentiments showed themselves again in the Cabinet following the
tabling in the House of Commons by government supporters of an
amendment to the reply to the King's speech which criticised the
government's foreign policy. In Cabinet, Shinwell said that he did not
associate himself with this amendment but felt that it reflected a
prevalent uneasiness in the party, and he recalled that he had
'informed the Prime Minister of doubts which he entertained of
Government policy in the Middle East'. Apart from these pressures,
in New York Bevin was subjected to a colossal amount of Zionist
lobbying, and he also received further hints that the US Government
might support partition. On Bevin's instructions, Inverchapel sounded
Acheson out on the subject of partition on 22 November. According to
Acheson's account, Inverchapel came on rather strongly and
informed the Acting Secretary of State 'that Mr. Bevin is moving
rapidly toward acceptance of partition as the solution' but felt unable
to espouse it 'unless he knows with definiteness the attitude of the
United States'. Apparently Inverchapel's eagerness to see partition
adopted as British policy had caused him to bend his brief, for Bevin
had instructed him 'to find out from the State Department, as
Ambassador and not committing me, what their attitude really was'.
Perhaps Inverchapel over played his hand, for Acheson answered in a
cagey manner and merely picked his way through Truman's Yom
Kippur statement, giving nothing new away. Inverchapel felt unable
to report enthusiastically, and said that Acheson 'seemed to have no
doubt that the U.S. Government would "go along" with us if we
decided that it was best to favour partition'. Byrnes proved to be no
more forthright when Bevin tackled him, and the Foreign Secretary
gathered the feeling that 'he does not seem too keen on the matter
having to go to U.N.O. on the basis of partition'. This manoeuvre
was, of course, rather half-hearted, but Inverchapel was able to report
the view of Acheson's Middle East expert, presumably Henderson, on
the likely Arab reaction to partition which would be little beyond
rioting and protests without any military action, provided Britain and
the United States 'showed a very determined attitude'. It seems
probable that the US attitude to partition rather tantalized Bevin
while he was visiting the country and, although it did not provide a
decisive factor, it encouraged the Foreign Secretary to entertain
thoughts of a solution on the lines of partition, which was something
that his officials in Whitehall seemed unable to consider.[11]

There were limits to how far Bevin could follow this road, and these
limits were clearly evident in his dealings with the Zionists. The

Zionist leadership now seemed to be reconciled to the idea of partition provided a viable Jewish state could come into being. Ben Gurion told Weizmann at the end of October that the Zionists should demand that Britain implement her Mandate properly and facilitate without restrictions the development of the Jewish National Home. Silver also was, by the eve of the Zionist Congress in Basle, fully prepared in private to envisage a compromise from the old Biltmore Programme in favour of partition if it brought an immediate and viable Jewish state in Palestine. Bevin met Silver on two occasions, on 14 and 20 November, and on both days the Foreign Secretary refused to be lured into a discussion about partition. On 14 November, he dismissed partition as tricky because it would require the approval of the United Nations, and he went out of his way to urge the Jewish Agency's attendance at the reconvened London Conference. Failing an agreement there, Bevin warned frankly that the British Government 'would have to give up the Mandate', a warning he repeated, to Silver's evident consternation, on 20 November. There is nothing to suggest these were empty warnings, but plainly they were premature and delivered by the Foreign Secretary in order to fill his own silence on the subject of partition; a silence which, as he indicated in his memorandum to the Prime Minister, he felt unable to break before the conference reconvened or the Zionists had made it clear that they would rest content with a partitioned Palestine. In a telegram Bevin sent to the Prime Minister on 28 November, he explained that Byrnes wanted him to write a confidential note to Goldmann accepting the Jewish proposals, the old Goldmann partition plan, as the sole item on the agenda of the forthcoming London Conference. Bevin's reaction was identical with the line he had taken to a similar Zionist proposal months before, and he advised Attlee that:

> The Jews have not moved an inch from their position in the autumn which was to refuse to attend the Conference except to discuss their own plan. As you know I hold very strongly ... that His Majesty's Government having called a Conference of two parties cannot allow the agenda ... to be dictated by one of them.

Bevin argued that provincial autonomy should remain the first item on the agenda, and that it would be up to the participants to propose other items to the resumed conference; he suggested a reply to Byrnes on these lines. Perhaps the Jewish Agency was demanding too much, but the principal obstacle was the wretched business of the London Conference which, having already failed miserably to make any progress towards a compromise over Palestine, continued even durings its adjournment to provide a hindrance and a constraint upon the Foreign Secretary in his talks with the Zionists in the United States.[12]

Creech Jones evidently perceived the difficulty on this matter and considered that it provided a suitable opportunity to inject more enthusiasm from the British side for a scheme of partition. He minuted to the Prime Minister:

> I agree with the attitude which the Foreign Secretary proposes to take but think that his draft reply to Mr. Byrnes stresses the Government's provincial autonomy plan somewhat unduly and gives the impression that we are more deeply committed to that plan than is in fact the case.

Creech Jones suggested a comparatively minor change to Bevin's draft, deleting the reference to the Lord President's (provincial autonomy) plan as the first item on the agenda and the 'full opportunity' of other delegations to propose amendments or fresh proposals, instead saying:

> Proposals have already been laid on the table both by His Majesty's Government and by the Arab Delegations. The Jewish Delegation will have [the] opportunity either to suggest modifications ... or to advance other proposals.

This attempt to attract the Jewish Agency's participation in the conference and introduce a modicum of flexibility over partition by putting some little distance between the agenda for the reconvened conference and the provincial autonomy plan, which had already been torn to ribbons, was crushingly rejected by Attlee. He told the Colonial Secretary:

> I do not agree. I do not think ... [Bevin' draft] stresses the plan unduly. It merely states that it is the first subject on the Agenda[.] Your formula suggests that we have given a degree of support to the Arab proposals.

This interpretation was a curious one to place on Creech Jones' draft, but it seems that the Colonial Secretary made no counter and the Prime Minister sent Bevin a telegram on the same day approving his draft reply to Byrnes with a minor amendment only, adding that Creech Jones agreed![13]

Attlee's devotion to flogging the dead horse of provincial autonomy into yet another conference hall was reflected also in his attitude towards partition. Bevin's long account of his talks with Byrnes and members of the Jewish Agency was discussed in Cabinet on 28 November, and there the Prime Minister, while acknowledging the widespread feeling that partition offered the only solution, nevertheless stressed that it must emerge from the reconvened conference whose deliberations should not be prejudiced. Accordingly he advised the Foreign Secretary that the Cabinet would consider partition but should not be rushed, and for good measure he criticized the State Department's forecast of Arab reactions to partition, which Inverchapel had reported, as too rosy. It seems therefore that Attlee must be numbered among the many factors which held Bevin in check while he was in the United States, keeping before the Foreign Secretary the iron agenda for the forthcoming session of the London Conference, thereby helping to impose a constraint upon any discussion of partition.[14]

Returning now to the policy debate in London, Attlee was not alone in adopting a view opposite to that of the Colonial Office. The Chiefs of Staff, for so long silent on the subject of Palestine and their Middle Eastern strategic requirements, were at last goaded into action by the twin spurs of disorder in Palestine and the spectacle of the Colonial Office apparently appeasing the Zionists early in November by the release of the detained leaders of the Jewish Agency. Montgomery, who believed that the Colonial Office was the worst Ministry in Whitehall, told a meeting of the COS Committee on 20 November that the recent policy of appeasement in Palestine had failed. Between 1 October and 18 November, ninety-nine British soldiers and policemen had died, and the police force remained 50 per cent below strength. He wanted the High Commissioner to be issud with a new directive to impose 'strict law and order'. With the approval of his colleagues Montgomery raised the matter later in the day in the Defence Committee. It was a vigorous presentation, warning that the army had been placed in a defensive role by the recrudescence of terrorism following the release of the Jewish Agency leaders and suggesting that indiscipline might ensue. Creech Jones was, of course, less forceful. He admitted that the number of incidents in Palestine had increased, but alluded to their less serious nature. He suggested that 'the position of the armed forces in their capacity as an aid to the civil power' had not changed since the Cabinet's decision in June, and he pointed out that the High Commissioner had made it clear that there was no change in policy. The upshot was that the meeting called upon the Colonial Office, in consultation with the War Office, to examine the 'conditions governing the use of the armed forces in

Palestine' and to report to the Prime Minister. The implication was that the Colonial Office's ability to administer Palestine was being successfully interrogated by the Chiefs of Staff.[15]

Disorders continued in Palestine. On 26 November, a ship carrying nearly 4,000 illegal immigrants was escorted into Haifa, and on 2 December, another four soldiers were killed. On 29 December, Jewish terrorists abducted and flogged a British officer and three NCOs, an incident which made a considerable impression upon British opinion, Beeley telling Gallman of the US embassy that this flogging was having a greater effect that the bombing of the King David Hotel because 'it goes "right down through the ranks"'. Although the situation was fraught and highly charged, the Colonial Office attempted to follow a calm policy through. A report by Sir Charles Wickham endorsed Creech Jones' view that terrorism could and should be dealt with by police methods and not by unleashing the less discriminating force of the army. On 19 December, two memoranda were circulated to the Defence Committee, one setting out the War Office view on the need to take decisive military action, while the one by the Colonial Office argued that it was only the Irgun and Stern Gang who were responsible for the terrorist incidents and therefore reprisals against the whole population would be counter-productive, destroying the progress made in bolstering the moderates in the Jewish Agency. This progress was evidenced by a joint appeal from the Executives of the Vaad Leumi and of the Jewish Agency on 4 December for a cessation of terrorist activity. Beeley, minuting after the flogging incident, was utterly unimpressed; the Colonial Office's policy, he wrote, 'has already proved its bankruptcy. ... Sooner or later a strong policy will become unavoidable'. This attitude predominated in the Defence Committee's discussion on 1 January 1947, both Bevin and Attlee effectively siding with Montgomery, who presented a rather lurid case 'to see the country flooded with mobile columns' on the grounds that law and order had to be restored. Creech Jones was instructed to draw up a new directive for the High Commissioner to facilitate the application of military force. In Palestine the situation was to deteriorate over the coming months: further acts of terrorism claimed their victims, more ships arrived carrying a frustrated human cargo, and martial law was declared in areas of Palestine at the beginning of March.[16]

The importance of these events should not in themselves be exaggerated, for they contained three significant elements. First, the clash that began in late November 1946 between the Colonial Office and the Chiefs of Staff resulted from the CO looking for a compromise to the problem of Palestine and the COS, on the other hand, being preoccupied with carrying out a clear-cut military operation. The second grew out of the handling of the terrorism with the COS coming out heavily against the CO and partition: the COS came to believe that the retaining of Palestine by Britain was a strategic necessity. Alexander, the Minister of Defence, on 1 January in the Defence Committee made it known that,

> on the long-term issue he was convinced that the retention of our position in Palestine was a strategic necessity. On the short-term issue, he thought that all necessary discretion should be given to the Army to prevent and punish terrorism.

Finally, the COS realized that there was no use claiming the military value of Palestine, where by the end of 1946 Britain maintained one soldier or policeman for every eighteen citizens, if that place was manifestly in chaos and a military liability. Palestine was in danger of being written off. Dalton, reflecting in his diary at the end of the year on the wearisome and thankless nature of Britain's post-imperial burden, was as Chancellor of the Exchequer in a good position to notice how the erstwhile imperial assets became liabilities:

> It is quite clear that we can't go on holding people down against their will, however incompetent they are to govern themselves, for the whole pace, as determined in the East, has quickened in the war years, and it would be a waste both of British men and money to try to hold down any of this crowd.

Although it was India and Burma which had provoked these thoughts, their relevance to Palestine is obvious.[17]

During December the policy debate in London entered top gear. The adjournment of the London Conference on 21 November until January had allowed time for the Zionist Congress to make its decision in late December about the participation of the Jewish Agency, and for most of the Arab delegations to attend the UN session until mid-December.[18]

On 4 December, Gater wrote a long and rambling letter to his opposite number at the Foreign Office, Sir Orme Sargent, in which he turned over almost every conceivable option for Palestine and suggested that a joint note might be prepared urgently for Ministerial guidance. He thought it was

> inconceivable as a matter of practical policy that H.M.G. should embark on some entirely new line in Palestine without bringing the matter before

the United Nations at some stage, or should even continue indefinitely with the present regime (if this were possible on other grounds).

Possibly Gater intended his indefinite ideas as an olive branch to the Foreign Office, for he went on to mention that the 'inevitable' submission to the UN could be made to the Security Council 'if it were decided to declare Palestine a strategic area'. A proposal for British trusteeship, Gater felt, might not get a two-thirds majority in the General Assembly 'unless we can swing the Arabs to our side', whereas for any other scheme Britain might just inform the UN and thereby 'place the onus on our critics to get a two-thirds majority'. As for partition, Gater managed to raise an interesting difficulty, the retention of Jerusalem, envisaged in order to protect the Holy Places and 'retain strategic bases', meant that

> under partition, we should not be giving independence to the whole country but should be permanently annexing part of it for ourselves, with very mixed motives.

Gater was probably merely thinking aloud in a friendly way, but his letter seems to have inspired a fairly vigorous response within the Foreign and Cabinet Offices.[19]

Within the Cabinet Office a note was prepared, apparently by the Senior Assistant Military Secretary, Brigadier Cornwall-Jones, for Sir Norman Brook, the Secretary to the Cabinet, in which the pristine strategic analysis of the Chiefs of Staff was put forward in reply to Gater's letter: the COS required freedom to locate a joint Headquarters and 'such forces as we may consider necessary', as well as 'full control of the area'. 'On the other hand', the note continued, 'we have no military interest whatsoever in the Jerusalem enclave'. The COS perceived the dangers in referring Palestine to the United Nations because (a)' the opportunity might be afforded to the Russians to increase their influence in the Middle East' and (b) 'the intervention of U.N.O. might make it impossible to obtain our strategic requirements in Palestine'. The note preferred any submission to the UN to be upon Gater's non-trusteeship option of simply informing the UN of the new arrangements brought in by the government as this 'seems to be fraught with less risk'. As for any trusteeship arrangement, only if Britain was left as the sole administering power in Palestine would her strategic needs be met, but the difficulty was that 'it postulates the finding of a solution which we should have the military strength to see through'. So it would seem that Gater's letter

set the skeletons rattling, and the Chiefs of Staff, who wanted to
comment on any policy proposals, found that Norman Brook lent a
kindly ear to their calls.[20]

Brook and Beeley began collaborating on 4 December in the
drafting of a policy recommendation. The results of their labours were
eventually to be given to Bevin 'for Christmas reading' as three
papers, two together from the Eastern Department of the Foreign
Office and one from Brook. It is important to notice their common
origins, their parallel recommendations and the calculated echoing,
especially in Brook's paper, of points from Brigadier Cornwall-Jones'
note.[21]

The first paper from the Eastern Department, 'A Note On
Partition', was an exhaustive rehearsal of the arguments against
partition. It pointed out that any British compromise between the size
of state demanded by the Jews and, say, the token state offered by the
majority on the Woodhead Commission in 1938 'might result in the
alienation of both peoples'. In any case, the paper argued, the Arabs
would be inclined to regard the Jewish 'compromise' of partition as
temporary and the thin end of the wedge. Furthermore, there would
be colossal problems in drawing any frontier fairly, bearing in mind
the difficulties with minorities and cultivable land. Of course, 'The
Arabs of neighbouring countries would also refuse to accept a
settlement on these lines.' Finally, partition would require the
approval of the UN which, in the Foreign Office view, might not
provide the required two-thirds majority, while the British declaration of intent to partition Palestine 'would result in a decline of British
influence, and an increase of Russian influence, in the States members
of the Arab League'. The whole purpose of this paper was to
demonstrate that it would be 'impossible' to effect partition, and so
the opportunities for testing this path, such as some discreet pressure
on certain Arab states, or the indications by the US Government and
the Jewish Agency of their interest in partition which Bevin had felt
during his visit to America, were not mentioned. The second paper,
'A possible revision of the Arab plan', was the Department's policy
recommendation. The proposals put forward by the Arab delegations
at the conference, the paper began, 'cannot be accepted as they
stand'. Referring to Bevin's speech to the conference on 16
September, which laid down five criteria for a satisfactory settlement,
the Department argued that the Arab plan met these in principle
except over future Jewish immigration. Accordingly, it was suggested
that 'the British Delegation [at the reconvened conference] might
aim at agreement on ... 50,000 or 60,000—for the immediate future'

and acceptance of a small annual intake of Jews into Palestine thereafter. The other amendments suggested to the Arab plan were of a comparatively minor nature. The optimism in this paper, by comparison with the negative presentation of the case for partition, is striking, and it was felt that if the Arab plan was taken 'as the basis for negotiation' in the reconvened conference, 'there is no reason to suppose that in those circumstances the Arab delegates could not be induced to make substantial concessions.' Evidently the Eastern Department had still failed to perceive that obtaining concessions at a conference attended by delegates from the Arab states were contradictory concepts. These two papers went to the Secretary of State beneath a covering minute, dated 18 December, which summarized the recommendations. The choice lay between (a) reference to the UN and withdrawal, which would be perceived as a British abdication from the Middle East, (b) partition, which would 'so antagonize the Arab States that we should no longer be able to count on their goodwill', and (c) negotiating a settlement with the Arab states on the basis of their conference proposal. The resultant US hostility was 'doubtful ... [to] be either widespread or lasting' and was inevitable with any solution except one which fully satisfied the Zionists. Accordingly, a solution on the basis of the Arab plan was felt to be 'unquestionably the most advantageous'.[22]

Brook's paper for the Foreign Secretary, submitted on 20 December, was even more categorical. He reviewed the Arab position, noting that, 'For the Palestine Arabs and the Arab States the main objective of policy is to secure that Palestine shall remain a predominantly Arab country'. Brook, despite seeming to make an historical review of this Arab 'policy', nevertheless contrived to overlook the fact that the origin of the Arab states' involvement in Palestine was a consequence of British, or to be precise, Foreign Office policy. Furthermore, he ignored that this Arab 'policy' was no more than a symptom of the multifarious rivalries that existed between the Arab states, which had been reported by His Majesty's representatives in the Middle East. After setting this Arab policy alongside the Zionist demand for a state, Brook was able to draw the inevitable conclusion: 'the two peoples are, in fact, irreconcilable'. Hence Brook felt justified in advising that 'if we are to retain the Mandate we shall in the end be forced to impose a solution'. At this stage Brook referred to the old assessment by the COS, reechoed in Cornwall-Jones' note, that 'we cannot alone impose a solution which would be violently opposed by both peoples', and accordingly Brook moved on to propose, by clear implication, the pursuit of a solution acceptable to the Arabs. His argument, founded in what was intended to be a pragmatic approach, closed by seeking the sanction of a legality based in a different era:

> There is nothing in the Balfour Decleration or in the Mandate which is inconsistent with the essential requirements of the Arabs ... .
>
> The Jewish claim, on the other hand ... goes beyond anything that is promised ... The claim for an independent Jewish State ... is not warranted by anything in the text of the Declaration or the Mandate.[23]

On both documents Bevin merely indicated that he would be discussion Palestine with Creech Jones, whom he met on 22 December. Afterwards, Beeley drafted an account for his Secretary of State to send to the Prime Minister. Apparently the combined advice of the Eastern Department and the Secretary to the Cabinet did not dominate either Bevin's thinking or the feeling of the meeting. According to Beeley's draft the Ministers reflected ruefully that the decision to reconvene the conference was taken 'in full realisation that ... [it] has very little chance of success', and that in the event of its failure the choice would lie between imposing a solution against the opposition of either the Arabs or the Jews or both, and 'divest[ing] ourselves of all further responsibility for Palestine'. The military burden involved in the first alternative was viewed askance:

> It is doubtful whether we have the resources to sustain a burden of this kind, or whether public opinion would countenance the pursuit of a policy which did not seem to be leading to the pacification of Palestine and a substantial withdrawal of British troops ... There would also be a risk that we should be hauled before the Security Council.

Hence, to the Ministers, if not to their respective officials, the attractions of giving up in Palestine were strong, and a sense of frustration and exhaustion is apparent in their discussion. It was felt that Byrnes recognized the scale of Britain's problem, and it was suggested that the United States might be offered the Mandate, but that when this was refused,

> we have no alternative but to lay it at the feet of the United Nations. In so doing, we should not make any recommendation as to the policy which our successors should adopt.

The Ministers felt that severe criticism and loss of prestige would be Britain's inevitable lot in taking this course, but no real alternative was perceived. However, it was felt to be necessary to hear the views of the Chiefs of Staff on the strategic consequences. The next day Creech Jones proposed a few alterations to this draft account for the Prime Minister, because on

> two matters ... I do not feel myself so certain as the minute represents you as being. ... I am not yet satisfied that it is impossible to find a solution which, even if it did not secure the open approval of one or both ... communities, could not be imposed without the use of force greater than that which we ought to be prepared to contemplate. ... [secondly] I am very unwilling at this stage to shut the door on the possibility of devising some scheme of partition sufficiently fair to both Arabs and Jews to enable it to be supported to and possibly even to win the approval of the United Nations.

The Colonial Secretary, clearly, was following the line which Martin had advocated earlier. Accordingly, the most important amendment Creech Jones put forward was that if and when the matter was laid at the feet of the United Nations, the government should explain the various proposals on offer; significantly, however, he shrank from saying partition should be recommended, concluding the new passage rather lamely with, 'on balance it might be wiser to make no recommendation' for a successor to follow.[24]

Thus it seems that at this point there was now agreement between Bevin and Creech Jones; the Foreign Secretary did not appear antagonistic to his colleague's wish to have a go at partition, yet both seemed weary of the burden of Palestine and resigned to ultimate failure. During the coming weeks this incipient harmony was temporarily set aside by a barrage of advice from the Chiefs of Staff, Brook and the Foreign Office which engulfed the Foreign Secretary.

According to Beeley the account of the Ministerial meeting was not sent to the Prime Minister, but it seems probable that Bevin made him conversant with its contents when he saw him 'on this Middle East', as Bevin put it, soon afterwards. The Cabinet Office certainly became aware of it, for on Christmas Eve Cornwall-Jones was able to send Brook a detailed commentary upon Beeley's account. The proposal to hand Palestine to the UN after proferring it to the USA would, Cornwall-Jones explained, provoke a 'strong' reaction from the COS, 'inasmuch as both appear to endanger our whole position in the Middle East'. While he was relieved to see that the COS would be given the opportunity to comment, Cornwall-Jones was painfully aware

that whereas the Chiefs of Staff are firmly of the opinion that we must hold
on to the Middle East, as an essential element in our whole scheme of
Commonwealth defence, the Defence Committee and the Prime Minister
in particular, have so far declined to endorse that view. There may,
therefore, be more of an inclination to accept the Foreign Secretary's
present line of thought.

If the speed of his reaction is anything to judge by, Brook was
horrified by this prospect for he wrote a two-page minute to the Prime
Minister on the same day. He hoped Attlee would agree 'that a good
deal of further study is required' before Bevin's second option of
referral to the UN was accepted, and Brook warned of the
consequences that referral would have upon Britain's relations with
the Arab states, her strategic position in the area and upon the UN
itself. Brook pointed out that 'it is obviously necessary' for the COS to
comment on the policy options, closing with the comment that, 'the
Foreign Secretary in his minute does not develop his first alternative—of imposing a solution'. Brook referred to his paper of 20
December addressed to the Foreign Secretary, and continued:

> Before we decide to surrender the mandate, I think we should consider
> very seriously whether it would be practicable politics to enforce a solution
> which would be broadly acceptable to the Arabs ... Such a solution could
> perhaps be imposed without the approval of the United Nations: but we
> might hope, with that solution, to avoid a situation in which the Soviet
> Union would be ranged against us in support of the Arab States.

This was a remarkable document to send the Prime Minister, for
Brook seemed to be taking upon himself the combined role of Foreign
Office, Chiefs of Staff Committee and Defence Committee to weigh up
the policy options, and at the same time to be attempting to outflank
the Foreign Secretary in the policy debate. Naturally, Brook did not
breathe a word about considering the Colonial Office idea of
imposing a scheme of partition, nor did he pause to mention that the
dire scenario of Arab states and the Soviet Union being ranged
against Britain might place some of the Arab ruling families in an
unthinkable position.[25]
   Despite the gathering storm, Bevin and Creech Jones still
apparently found themselves on common ground. On 31 December,
Creech Jones sent the Foreign Secretary a lengthy paper which
attempted to set out the conclusions of their meeting on the day
before. Both Ministers were clearly in the depths of despondency
about the results of the World Zionist Congress in Basle. Weizmann

had not been re-elected to the Presidency, and Wise had also lost his office; Silver became the chairman of the American section of the Jewish Agency and championed the new shift towards militancy. By a vote of 171 to 154, the Congress rejected attending the reconvened London Conference 'in the existing circumstance', and Silver gained great emotional backing for his call for a state in an 'undivided and undiminished' Palestine. This public position was different from the policy actually pursued, for privately Silver was ready to consider partition, and in due course members of the Jewish Agency attended talks in London outside the conference arena. But for Creech Jones and Bevin the public posture of Zionism seemed to banish all hope and to defy the Colonial Secretary's earlier conciliatory efforts. Creech Jones' paper pondered the cancellation of the conference altogether, but felt that, on balance, cancellation would anger the Arab states needlessly. The conference was expected to fail, and two courses would then be open to the government: to impose a solution or to refer the problem to the UN. The former path was thought the least desirable, but if chosen then partition was thought to be the best scheme to impose since 'the Arab plan cannot be accepted' and the provincial autonomy plan was 'strongly opposed by both Arabs and Jews'. Hence, the Ministers evidently agreed that referral to the UN was the only alternative. There were, it was reconized, manifold pitfalls: the governance of Palestine during the intervening period, the loss of 'the special strategic advantages' in Palestine, the disappointment felt by sections of the Labour Party and public at the abandonment of the pledges for developing the Jewish National Home. However, 'After all, no other course seems now to be possible'. The matter should be referred to the UN with the three main plans but without a recommendation; in reaching this conclusion both Ministers had undoubtedly arrived at what their respective departments felt was a counsel of despair.[26]

There was no disposition in the Foreign Office or among the Chiefs of Staff to succumb. A paper prepared in the Eastern Department, probably by Beeley, was bitterly critical of the Colonial Secretary's paper and started by arguing that it

> conveys the impression that the principal aim of our policy in Palestine has been and should be to reach an agreement with the Zionists. Desirable as such an agreement would be, it is from the Foreign Office point of view far more important that we should avoid a quarrel with the Arab States over Palestine.

A detailed point-by-point critique followed in this vein over the next four pages. The 1939 White Paper was defended on the grounds that its authors believed that it was compatible with the Balfour Declaration and the Mandate, and it was suggested that the Chiefs of Staff should comment on the policy proposed. The Eastern Department took the opportunity to repeat its present policy recommendation for the amendment of the Arab plan, and argued that it was 'premature' to conclude that the Mandate should be surrendered. Bevin, perhaps, received this paper rather coolly, for Dixon noted on it merely that he had seen it.[27]

The barrage of advice continued from the Foreign Office. I. P. Garran, who had recently joined the Eastern Department as Assistant Head after a spell in the Western Department, quickly established his credentials with a draft memorandum that described at length in purple prose, 'The political consequences for His Majesty's Government of a solution to the Palestine question unacceptable to the Arabs'. Egypt would react strongly 'for prestige reasons, to justify Egypt's claim to be the leading Arab state', Syria and the Lebanon would react very strongly, while in Iraq the reaction would have 'most serious' repercussions for the British Government. The result of a settlement in Palestine unacceptable to 'the Arabs' would be 'a serious deterioration' in Britain's position in the area and would encourage Soviet penetration. Garran closed with his heartfelt admission that 'I am deeply impressed by the precarious character of our present position in the Middle East. ... I am anxious lest a decision be taken over Palestine which might nullify our whole endeavour' in the area. It is not clear whether the Garran paper was submitted, but it reflects the curious blindness that must have descended upon the staff of the Eastern Department, for even the newcomer Garran, while touching upon the evidence of the variety and disparity of interest felt by the Arab states in Palestine, was clearly incapable of considering that outside the process of reconvening the conference, the differences between the Arab states might be turned to good effect by the British Government in its efforts to find a solution for the country it ruled.[28]

Legal advice from Beckett served usefully to counter the attraction of partition and provincial autonomy, for after a discussion with the Lord Chancellor and the Attorney General Beckett advised that partition required the approval of the United Nations and that, although not strictly required, 'we should be politically most unwise' to attempt either provincial autonomy or partition without first taking the matter before the UN. This advice was circulated to the Cabinet.[29]

Making the maximum capital out of this advice, on 16 January Howe sent Bevin a paper prepared in discussion with the Colonial Office. The conclusions were stark. It was hard to forecast the result of

referring either partition or the scheme of provincial autonomy to the
United Nations but the chances of getting either through 'do not seem
to be very good'. Some days later Howe told the Foreign Secretary his
other fears about partition, arguing that it would be regarded by the
Arabs as a British surrender to the Zionists and would involve, during
the interim period, violence and ultimately the estrangement of the
Arabs. The next day Howe submitted a paper entitled 'Anticipated
Reactions in the Arab countries' which reviewed vividly and briefly
the anticipated 'violent' reactions to any settlement in Palestine
regarded as 'unacceptable'. Howe supported his paper with three
telegrams that Stonehewer-Bird had sent from Baghdad during May,
July and December 1946. Although this submission was the normal
Eastern Department axe-grinding, Bevin's reaction was not normal
but was significant. He scrawled:

> This means that we could never settle it. Must we go on in the present
> state? It is impossible.[30]

It was really from the standpoint of strategic requirements that Bevin
showed himself to be more inclined to part company with Creech
Jones and more ready to seek arrangements which would avoid
surrendering Palestine to the UN. For the Foreign Secretary the
niceties of Anglo-Arab diplomacy were a lesser consideration. For
example, in the Defence Committee on 1 January Bevin mentioned
his belief that 'the retention of Palestine was strategically essential to
the maintenance of our position in the Middle East', and that without
the region's oil 'he saw no hope of our being able to achieve the
standard of life at which we were aiming in Great Britain'. Beeley
briefed his Secretary of State on these lines for the Cabinet review of
foreign policy, adding that now Britain was committed to withdrawing her troops from Egypt, and as Cyrenaica did not offer a secure
alternative, 'our right to maintain troops in Palestine is of greater
importance now than at any previous time'. The military endorsement was fluent and delivered eloquently in a paper by the Joint
Planning Staff which was also circulated to the Defence Committee.
In reply to a paper circulated by the Foreign Secretary, the COS
argued, as usual, tht 'full military rights' were required in Palestine;
the submission to the Defence Committee emphasized the continuity
of thinking by referring to the earlier submission of 18 June 1946
'which subsequent events have reinforced'.[31]

The views were discussed not by the Defence Committee but at a
Staff Conference on 13 January attended by Attlee, Bevin, Alexander,

Brook, the Chiefs of Staff and General Hollis; Creech Jones was not a
participant. Bevin requested guidance on the options for Palestine,
mentioning his fear that partition would fail in the United Nations.
Provincial autonomy was attractive, however, 'since we should retain
the governing authority in the country until the time came for
independence' and thereafter forces could be retained in Palestine by
treaty arrangements with the successor states. Attlee was critical of
the idea of keeping forces in Palestine 'after stable conditions had
been created', but Montgomery, who had already warned that any
submission to the UN would risk forcing a British evacuation from the
country, replied that currently forces were needed for law and order
and that in future there would be no other place for the Middle East
reserve. Bevin sided with the military here, pointing out that any UN
enquiries about this could be met by explaining that the forces were
available to the United Nations. The meeting closed in a straightforward way, endorsing Attlee's suggestion that as the provincial
autonomy plan, with specific references to future independence,
would meet Britain's military needs it should be used as the basis for
discussions at the London Conference when it reconvened. It seems
quite likely that Montgomery got his way so easily, and that the COS
requirements for basing forces in Palestine passed almost unchallenged when they had been left on ice since the preceding summer,
because of the resignation threat he had conveyed privately to the
Prime Minister on behalf of himself and his colleagues 'in January' if
'the necessity to hold the Middle East' was rejected. It was, after all,
only a Staff Conference and not a decision of either the Defence
Committee or the Cabinet.[32]

The turn around on Palestine at the Staff Conference, however, was
more apparent than real. It was true that, for reasons of military and
strategic expediency, a species of provincial autonomy had been
brought firmly to the forefront. Bevin was, apparently, genuinely
impressed by the strategic arguments, and hoped they could be
satisfied. However, it is not possible to find any evidence to suggest
that Bevin had now abandoned the common outlook he evidently
shared with Creech Jones at the year's end about the eventual course
the government would have to choose. But his concern here was with
the immediate question of dealing with the forthcoming conference
session, and appropriately the Foreign Secretary let the Eastern
Department and the Chiefs of Staff have their way. Accordingly, on
13 January, Bevin 'called at short notice' for a Foreign Office paper on
the policy proposals setting out the Eastern Department's recommendations. The paper was dated 14 January but was circulated to the

Cabinet on 15 January, the day it was discussed, Bevin apologizing that there had not been time to consult the Colonial Office in its preparation. This was possibly an indication of the paper's short-term importance rather than an attempted slight to the Colonial Secretary. The submission to the Cabinet was in two parts, and in his preface to the Foreign Office paper Bevin set out the options because, 'The Cabinet is now called upon to determine the line of policy we must follow in the opening stages of the Conference'. This objective was crucial, for it reveals Bevin's immediate concern to be with managing the business of the conference; he was not concerned with the choices that would have to be faced by the Cabinet if the conference collapsed. For the time being the conference was the next step and the Foreign Secretary merely moved into line with his department's proposals for coping with it, proposals which also had the approval of the Staff Conference. Provincial autonomy in its present form was dismissed by Bevin as being unacceptable to both Arabs and Jews. Partition, to which Bevin said deliberately 'I would have no very violent objection', would nevertheless be unacceptable to the United Nations, and accordingly Bevin made a clear recommendation that the British delegation to the London Confer-ence should be instructed to inform the Arab delegations that their proposals were not acceptable, and that the objective should be the altering of the provincial autonomy proposals 'in such a way that they point towards an independent unitary State and incorporating into them as much as possible of the Arab plan'. This was exactly the recommendation contained in the papers Beeley and Brook had drafted for Bevin's Christmas reading. The Foreign Office paper for the Cabinet, annexed to Bevin's preface, was a powerful amalgam of everything the Eastern Department had been saying for weeks. Of course it made the same recommendations which the Secretary of State had summarized. It also mentioned, as the alternative to imposing some solution, the referral of the problem to the UN, possibly giving a date for the British evacuation:

> This possibility is not examined in the present paper, because at a recent Staff Conference it was decided that the maintenance of our right to station troops in Palestine is essential to the preservation of our strategic interests in the Middle East as a whole. If this opinion is accepted, then we must remain in Palestine.'

Hence, the combination of the immediate need to find a policy to pursue in the conference, the weight of advice from the Foreign Office and the power of Montgomery's counter-attack about Britain's strategic requirements in the Middle East together conspired to handle the London Conference in a traditional way, to postpone consideration of referring Palestine to the United Nations and to allow the Foreign Office paper to berate partition as 'a desperate remedy'.[33]

On 14 January, before this paper was circulated, Brook sent the Prime Minister a three-page memorandum setting down 'the points which, as I see it, ought to be made clear to the Cabinet' the next day. It was the usual argument, pointing out that retaining Britain's position in the Middle East was essential in terms of influence, resources and military strategy which became 'even more important at a time when we have abandoned very largely our position in Egypt, and may soon withdraw from India and Burma'. However, without these imperial possessions the nature of Britain's position and requirements in the Middle East was to alter fundamentally, yet Brook did not see matters that way. The requirements for retaining Arab goodwill and avoiding the Arab states making common causes with the Soviet Union when Britain's settlement for Palestine was submitted to the UN, which Brook now realized was 'inevitable', meant that a solution had to be found either by amending the Arab plan, as Brook had previously suggested, or as the 'next best' option, by modifying provincial autonomy to make it acceptable to the Arabs. However, the most significant part of Brook's paper was the first paragraph:

> The course of tomorrow's discussion in Cabinet will depend on the character of the Foreign Secretary's opening statement; and I have not been able to discover what line he intends to take.

This comment would indicate that Bevin's adoption of the Foreign Office view was recent and thus unknown to Brook. Hence, Bevin's position was the subject of some suspicion and investigation by the Secretary to the Cabinet who was waiting to see what the Foreign Secretary would recommend to the Cabinet, and whether, perhaps, he would adopt the policy proposed in the Foreign Office paper he had called for at such short notice on the previous day. As an outlet for his anxieties, Brook briefed the Prime Minister to act as the understudy in case the Foreign Office spokesman altered his lines.[34]

Brook need not have worried. Bevin circulated the FO paper on 15 January when the Cabinet discussed the problem at length. First, the Chiefs of Staff had their say, rehearsing their usual position. Tedder explained in detail that the retention of Britain's position in the Middle East, with the defence of the United Kingdom itself and the maintenance of sea communications, was one of 'the three vital props of our defensive position'. Retaining a foothold in the Middle East in peacetime was essential, according to Tedder, and made the more so by the withdrawal from India. Hence, it was vital to obtain military facilities in Palestine for the future, and the political solution there was immaterial so long as these facilities were procured. If one or other of the communities 'had to be antagonised, it was preferable, from the purely military angle, that a solution should be found which did not involve the continuing hostility of the Arabs'. No endorsement was made of the COS statement, and the Cabinet went on to consider the Foreign Office paper dated 14 January, but circulated only on the morning of the meeting. Bevin opened this discussion with a long review of the Palestine problem. He criticised Truman's intervention on the subject of the 100,000 immigrants following the Anglo-American Committee's report, and he argued also that partition would fail to get a two-thirds majority in the United Nations. However, Bevin suggested that an amended version of provincial autonomy might well secure UN support. He closed disarmingly, saying,

> he did not expect the Cabinet at their present meeting to reach final conclusions on this difficult issue. He would, however, be glad to have the advantage of hearing the views of his colleagues.

Creech Jones spoke next, pointing out that, following talks with Ben Gurion, the responsible members of the Jewish Agency Executive would assemble in London concurrently with the conference for private talks with the government. The Colonial Secretary referred to Cunningham's opinion that partition was 'the only practicable solution', and gently informed the Cabinet that he was 'more and more inclined to share this view' despite the possible difficulties presented by the United Nations Organization. There was no acrimony in the exchange, to judge from the minutes, which suggests that Creech Jones knew that Bevin was merely putting forward the proposals of his officials; their own fundamental understanding about what course to follow if the conference collapsed was left intact. During the Cabinet discussion which followed the likely voting patterns in the General Assembly were considered, Bevin concluding that there was 'no prospect' of obtaining the necessary majority for partition since the Soviet Union would oppose it. Considerable support was voiced for Creech Jones and partition by Dalton, Bevan and Shinwell, and the argument was pressed that the right policy should be selected and put forward before deciding on the ways and means for effecting it. At this point the discussion adjourned inconclusively.[35]

The next day Creech Jones circulated two papers for the Cabinet. The first annexed two notes from Cunningham in which provincial autonomy was severely criticized on the grounds that it did not bring the element of finality which the High Commissioner judged to be essential in any settlement; accordingly, Cunningham argued that it was of no value either in itself or as a transitional device preceding partition. Cunningham argued by clear implication that partition, notwithstanding its difficulties, offered the only satisfactory and final solution. The next paper contained the recommendations of the Colonial Office. Creech Jones began by referring to Bevin's proposal for amending the provincial autonomy plan, and confessed that 'I cannot see any hope of a settlement on these lines'. Proceeding 'from the point of view of the administration' of Palestine, Creech Jones examined the various options. Provincial autonomy would prove inoperative, the Arab plan was a repetition of the 1939 White Paper and therefore utterly antipathetic to Zionism and to 'the undertakings given by the Labour Party', while he felt partition was the only hope, since it offered the prospect of finality and it would be in harmony with domestic public opinion. Furthermore, it was likely to obtain the support of the United States and 'the endorsement of the Labour Party'. Referral of this plan to the United Nations was envisaged to be the immediate step, and if the UN failed to find an acceptable answer then 'it will be necessary to consider whether we should not announce our intention to withdraw'.[36]

The machinery of the London Conference featured nowhere in the Colonial Office's proposals—in a way, their most serious flaw. The Cabinet had been asked by Bevin to decide what to do with the conference when it reconvened, and the Foreign Office was of course entirely geared to this event; the Colonial Secretary's proposals could not, however, be fitted into this timetable. Arguably this was beside the point, since the idea of partition had seized a powerful hold on the Colonial Office, from the Secretary of State downwards, and with this momentum behind it the idea simply had to be placed before the Cabinet where, in addition, it had some strong supporters. Writing to James Callaghan in 1961 Creech Jones conveyed this sense of righteous inevitability, amounting almost to the call of destiny:

Bevin undoubtedly had influenced the cabinet along his line of policy and

in the broad it was the inevitable one. ... [On taking office I urged partition
which] my liberal and Jewish friends hoped might be a line of advance ...
It was too late and an impracticable policy at that stage in every respect,
but I felt, as a new boy in the cabinet, that it should be reviewed.

Even allowing for the wisdom and resignation of hindsight, the
suggestion that Creech Jones was acting his part in the Cabinet
discussions of January 1947 seems significant. The proposal he had
put forward lacked a certain edge, for it was not tailored to the
immediate requirements of conference diplomacy. There was
something of the academic exercise about it all, reflected strongly in a
draft Cabinet paper by the Colonial Secretary which submitted not
one but two schemes of partition, indicating Creech Jones' own
hesitancy. Of this characteristic Attlee was to write later that
'perhaps [he] is hardly strong enough for the position' he held in
Cabinet. But also it suggests that the Colonial Secretary and his
officials were alike eager to get the idea of partition off their chests, to
have their say before it was too late. In consequence, partition was
given an airing in the Cabinet but neither in concise form nor with a
ready application; this essential irrelevance in January 1947 was to be
confirmed, both by the absence of a Cabinet decision on partition and
Creech Jones' speedy abandonment of it early in February.[37]

Between the circulation of the Colonial Secretary's papers and the
subsequent Cabinet discussion, Bevin sought the views of the US
Government. Since early November, when the State Department had
announced Delphically that the Secretary of State was taking over the
handling of Palestine, a silence had descended upon Washington.
Acheson had shown himself wary of saying anything new to
Inverchapel in November beyond hinting that the US Government
quite liked the idea of partition as a solution. This tendency, as well as
a certain aimlessness in US policy, provoked another angry and
hard-hitting memorandum from Merriam, the Chief of the Division
of Near Eastern Affairs, at the end of the year. Merriam warned that
US policy was not only of no real help to the Jews, but also 'keeps us
constantly on the edge of embroilment' with Britain and the Arabs,
and hence, it was likely to allow the USA to fall between stools. He felt
that US policy 'is one of expediency not one of principle', which had
led to the spontaneous endorsement of such specific proposals as the
100,000 immigrants without any fundamental principle or direction.
Merriam proceeded to suggest some suitable aims such as the
independence of Palestine under any scheme which the Arabs, Jews
and United Nations could approve; he argued that the US

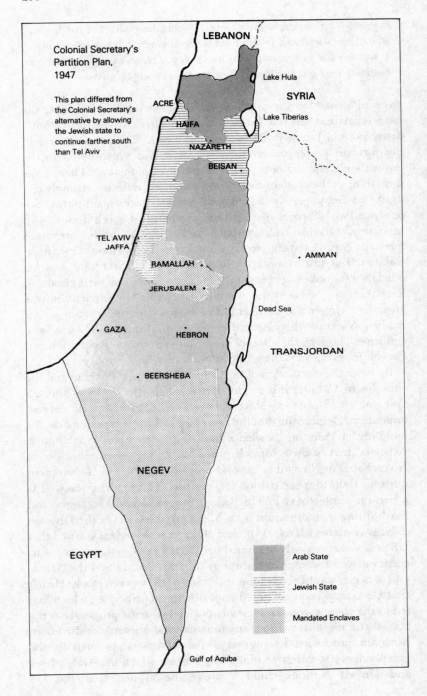

Colonial Secretary's
Partition Plan,
1947

This plan differed from
the Colonial Secretary's
alternative by allowing
the Jewish state to
continue farther south
than Tel Aviv

LEBANON

Lake Hula

SYRIA

ACRE

HAIFA

Lake Tiberias

NAZARETH

BEISAN

TEL AVIV
JAFFA

AMMAN

RAMALLAH

JERUSALEM

Dead Sea

GAZA

HEBRON

TRANSJORDAN

BEERSHEBA

NEGEV

EGYPT

Arab State

Jewish State

Mandated Enclaves

Gulf of Aquba

government should support such principles and that in the meantime, pending a settlement, Britain should administer Palestine under a UN trusteeship agreement. Whatever the merits or otherwise of Merriam's ideas, his paper indicates a malaise within the US Government on the subject of Palestine; policy was unresolved, the problem allowed to drift, senior staff were growing uneasy. Henderson admitted as much in a note to Acheson when he sent Merriam's paper on.[38]

Bevin was no less uneasy about US policy, but typically he sought to have it defined in January 1947 when the British Government was in the throes of makings its decisions on Palestine. Howe's minute on the draft telegram 'which the S[ecretary] of S[tate] has directed shall be sent in accordance with his notes' indicates clearly by whom the enquiry was prompted, for Howe scarcely thought the exercise worth taking:

> It is not going to be easy for Lord Inverchapel to send us anything sufficiently firm to enable Ministers here to make up their own minds, especially a[s] General Marshall has not yet arrived in Washington.

But Bevin's notes, and the more polished telegram which resulted, indicate a different attitude towards the US Government on Palestine from that adopted in the far-off days before the Anglo-American Enquiry. The corrosive effect of disappointment and the feeling of having been let down in the past rankled in the Foreign Secretary's mind, and he rumbled:

> the Anglo-American Committee, the ten points of which we would have adopted and carried through, the turning down of 9 of the 10 points ... and then the British–American experts' report which also was turned down by the United States Government very rapidly and almost without reason, and now we have to meet in conference and work up a solution. What solution does the United States favour; what solution would they be inclined to back?

Clearly any expression of preference by the US Government was going to be regarded sceptically and with the utmost wariness by Bevin and the Eastern Department.[39]

Inverchapel called on Under Secretary of State Acheson on 21 January with his enquiry, commenting that his instructions began 'with a somewhat plaintive review of United States participation in the Palestine problem'. Inverchapel said that the forthcoming London Conference was unlikely to produce an agreed solution, and he outlined the three options with which the British Government would then be faced; partition, cantonization on the lines of the Morrison–Grady plan, or surrender of the Mandate to the UN. Would the US Government support partition in the UN General Assembly? Acheson, who warned that he would have to consult the President and Secretary, nevertheless proceeded to give his own views that 'it would be easiest for the American Government' to support partition, but Britain's remained the ultimate responsibility. Secondly, Acheson felt that a solution combining the Morrison––Grady plan with partition might be a possible avenue of exploration, but that referral without recommendation to the UN

> did not seem ... to be a solution, but almost amounted to a confession that a solution was not possible ... [Acheson] thought that this course should be adopted only as a last resort and in the default of any suggestion other than the maintenance of the *status quo* by force.

Acheson's forthright views were all the more remarkable in the face of the advice he had been given. In a memorandum of 21 January, submitted under Henderson's name but evidently drafted by Wilkins, the desk officer for Palestine, it was suggested that 'we should avoid involvement at the present juncture' and merely inform Inverchapel that US policy was based upon Truman's Yom Kippur statement. By this process the US would avoid influencing the Jews beyond requesting the Agency, as they had already done, to attend the London Conference. Presumably, Acheson's devotion to the idea of partition, in evidence since Goldmann had persuaded him of its value, outweighed this departmental advice.[40]

Inverchapel reported Acheson's views to the Foreign Office, closing with the comment that his request for 'something rather more categorical' had been answered by Acheson's promise to consult the President and Marshall 'at once'. The Eastern Department received this with undisguised misgivings, Beeley minuting that Inverchapel's final comment

> is rather alarming. We wanted to know what line the American delegation to the U.N. Assembly would be likely to adopt ... [on] *any* of the recent proposals. We did not want to commit them at this stage, when the mind of H.M.G. is not made up, to support any particular plan.

The Eastern Department was of course the last place to accord a welcome to any expression of support for partition, but there was a genuine problem in the Americans waxing too enthusiastic as Beeley pointed out; partition to Acheson probably meant a boundary along the lines of the Goldmann plan, whereas the British Government would consider something rather different, rendering the consequent Anglo-American misunderstanding embarrassing. As the evidence which the Colonial Office submitted later to the United Nations Special Committee on Palestine showed, there was indeed a vast difference between the plan Creech Jones had drafted in January and the scheme which the Jewish Agency apparently had in mind; the Agency envisaged a state which embraced all of Palestine, including the Negev, and omitted only the central highlands, the West Bank area and Jerusalem, whereas the Colonial Secretary proposed a far smaller Jewish state. Apart from this difficulty, the Eastern Department showed no inclination to promote this American endorsement of a scheme it despised, and Inverchapel was told:

> I hope however that you will not press at this stage for the statement mentioned ... We are going into the Palestine Conference with an open mind.

Beeley drafted this telegram which contained at least cosmetic truth; an open mind at the conference was, however, unlikely to be open to the idea of partition for long.[41]

Acheson proved as good as his word and delivered to Inverchapel a 'Written Oral Statement' which set down the view he had expressed earlier to the Ambassador.[42] However there is no evidence to suggest that the US Government's stated policy preferences had any significant bearing upon the British Government's policy decisions. Bevin had sought the US view at a very late stage, almost as an afterthought, and there was a dangerous indefiniteness about the US concept of partition which Beeley had been quick to notice. Altogether, then, the impression is that the US Government had had its day in influencing British policy and that the Cabinet would now proceed to take its decisions without paying more than a passing regard to the American dimension.

The important Cabinet meeting which took place on 22 January was the last one before the conference reconvened. Brook, concerned that the ramifications of any decision should be fully explored by the Cabinet, wrote a paper for the Prime Minister which set out the questions 'which ought to be considered' in Cabinet the next day. Was a reference to the UN the accepted step to take before a solution was imposed? Brook warned that, whatever scheme was placed before the UN, obtaining the two-thirds majority was uncertain unless the

US Government could be persuaded to support a version of the Arab plan; a highly unlikely eventuality as Brook noted. What would the government do if the plan it proposed to the UN was rejected? Brook observed gloomily that there were 'obvious difficulties' about the only steps which could follow: carrying on with the Mandate or surrendering it. Most delicate of all, Brook felt the Cabinet should decide whether or not it accepted the COS view of the importance of maintaining Britain's position in the Middle East; if so, what would be the consequences of imposing a policy of partition and could military bases in a Jewish state compensate for estranging the neighbouring Arab states? Brook's paper was less partisan than his earlier submissions to the Prime Minister, although he closed with an obvious warning about proceeding too hastily towards partition; it is apparent from the concision and accuracy of Brook's probing analysis that he too perceived the corner that the government was in. Something somewhere had to give; the question whether it was to be the US attitude to the Arab plan, the COS's strategic requirements or Arab goodwill was begged. But the ordeal of decision was to pass the Cabinet by, and was destined to be reached by inches. On the very morning of the Cabinet meeting Brook wrote to Attlee to say that he understood that the Foreign Secretary would suggest that no decision should be taken in advance of the conference so that a maximum of flexibility could be allowed in the conference discussions, and accordingly the Cabinet could be spared the interrogation which Brook had prepared.[43]

The Cabinet discussion was something of an anticlimax, coming as it did after the argumentative submission by the Colonial Secretary in favour of partition. Although it was Creech Jones' two papers which were before the Cabinet, it was Bevin who spoke first. His was a comparatively brief and low-key performance in which he pointed out that: 'He himself was not opposed in principle to a solution by way of Partition', but was impressed by the problem of imposing it against opposition, especially as the resulting trouble might be brought before the Security Council as a threat to the peace. Bevin proposed yet another effort to negotiate the differences between the Arabs and Jews, and that if this failed the Cabinet would then decide how the matter should go before the United Nations. Creech Jones spoke next, and for the Minister responsible for the papers before the Cabinet his performance was grotesquely uncombative. The Colonial Secretary began by agreeing that

the Cabinet should not now be asked to decide what policy should be followed if the conversations broke down. He hoped that the Cabinet would leave the negotiators as much latitude as possible.

He argued gently that the object should be to move the Arabs and Jews closer together, and explained that he believed that partition held out the best hope of compromise. It was a brief submission, and it seems most unlikely that the Colonial Secretary had been suddenly overcome with shyness or had been overawed by Bevin, for he had demonstrated neither trait in submitting the papers to the Cabinet in the first place. Furthermore, Creech Jones most probably knew more about Palestine itself than anyone else in the room, with the possible exception of Brook, and his knowledge would lend a degree of confidence. In agreeing that the Cabinet should not decide its policy that day, Creech Jones was quietly acknowledging partition to be an unlikely hope. If he had really thought otherwise, the Colonial Secretary would surely have sought the Cabinet's immediate endorsement of it, for if he expected it to emerge from the conference hall he was blessed with more optimism than any Christian entering the lion's den!

Creech Jones' performance must have discouraged the pro-partitionists in the Cabinet from saying much, and only Shinwell made a brief sally to argue that the friendship of the Jews was of greater value than the friendship of the Arabs if a choice had to be made. The Cabinet minutes record that a general discussion took place in which 'Ministers agreed that, failing an agreed settlement, any solution ... would have to come before the United Nations'. The Cabinet morosely reflected that the resulting discussion

> was bound to be embarrassing. There would be much discussion of the various promises that had been made ... not all of which were easy to reconcile with one another.

Notwithstanding Bevin's attempted prohibition on discussing the future:

> Some Ministers felt that, if we were unable to secure an agreed settlement, there would be much to be said for leaving it to the United Nations to find a solution. On th other hand, we could not lightly take such a course, which might mean that we should be unable to secure the military facilities in Palestine which were necessary to our strategic position in the Middle East.

This was a percipient augury of the path which lay ahead, but for the moment the Cabinet concluded 'that it would be a mistake to decide at this stage what policy should be followed if the forthcoming conversations broke down'. The conference should strive to reconcile the parties, and the Cabinet should be consulted before any indication was given that the government would support any particular solution.[44]

So it was that the Cabinet members awaited, in a spirit of anxiety and hopelessness, the outcome of a conference which they all knew would fail. A curious orbital path had been followed by the British Government over the previous months. From the debris of the conference session which adjourned in October the Colonial Office had resurrected an old and preferred scheme for Palestine, partition, whereas the Foreign Office, having secured the destruction of provincial autonomy, had constructed from the rubble the framework of an amended Arab plan. At Cabinet level the path ahead was viewed with great misgivings and it was these, together with the momentum behind the consultative process, which sent the British delegation back into the conference hall in January 1947, without anything new to say except that the government was at the end of its tether.

The collapse of the London Conference

On 27 January the Arab delegations convened in St James's Palace for the first meeting of the resumed conference, the eighth of the series with the representatives of the British Government. The most significant alteration in the attendance was the presence of a delegation of the Palestinian Arabs led by Jamal Husseini. Creech Jones, following a discussion with Cunningham earlier in January, had suggested to Bevin that an invitation might be issued to the Arab Higher Committee to 'assist in dispersing any impression they may have that the Jews are having things all their own way'. Bevin agreed, but insisted that the Mufti should not come to London; Jamal Husseini was subsequently asked to nominate a delegation on this unspoken basis. There were some changes in the Arab states' delegations as well: Sanhouri, for instance, did not lead the Egyptian delegation, and the Saudi delegation was led by the Minister in London rather than the Minister of Foreign Affairs, Faisal, who had come to London in the autumn. Perhaps the most important absentee, however, was Azzam, the Secretary General of the Arab League, who excused himself on the grounds of ill health. These absentees cast something of a cloud over the reconvened conference, and Beeley told the US *chargé d'affaires* in London that Azzam and some other delegates 'did not come because they did not like [the] prospect of being associated with [a] conference which they felt was bound to fail'. Most probably there was some truth in Beeley's statement, for we have seen the despondency with which Azzam viewed the impending autumn session, and he might very well have felt that reconvening the conference was not only futile but courting disaster as well.[45]

Bevin wasted no time in telling the assembled delegates that the occasion 'must be, so far as His Majesty's Government is concerned, a final effort to settle the Palestine problem'. Jamal Husseini followed the Foreign Secretary and effectively proceeded to demarcate how far the Arab delegations could go in making a compromise. His position was clear: the Palestine Arabs wished 'to remain in undisturbed possession of their country' and cited the principle of self-determination in support. He continued, 'It is a foregone conclusion that the Arabs of Palestine are determined to reject partition, and resist it with all the means at their disposal'. El Khouri, the head of the Syrian delegation, speedily took the hint and commented portentously that he

> had no wish to refer to Partition, which had not been proposed by the United Kingdom Delegation last September. He felt confident that this solution would not be put forward.

Bevin soon brought the meeting to a close, remarking that the government would be meeting Jewish representatives shortly who, it was well known, favoured partition. He said bluntly that there were two problems with the plan which the Arab delegations had proposed in the autumn; it condemned the Jews in Palestine to a permanent minority status and it denied any further Jewish immigration. Finally, with more than a hint of exasperation, Bevin added, 'It might well be that, if no other solution to the Palestine problem could be found, the United Nations would ultimately have to deal with the situation'.[46] Bevin was embarking on a precarious path, and two days later, on 29 January, a gloomy minute was sent to the Foreign Secretary, apparently from Beeley:

> We have learned that the Arab delegates, after meeting together, have decided that if an attempt is made to draw them into discussion on the basis of partition, they will probably have to break up the Conference … .
>
> If any proposals for increased Jewish immigration were put to the Arabs at this early stage … they would probably have the same effect.

However, the Eastern Department felt that the Arab delegations were eager for the conference not to fail and believed that they could be drawn tactfully into a discussion after 'a statement from us that certain aspects of their plan are not acceptable'. Accordingly, Bevin was provided with the draft of a tactful speech with which he opened the meeting on 30 January.[47]

At the meeting Bevin mentioned the three types of possible solution: the Arab plan; partition, of which Bevin remarked the Jewish Agency had indicated they could support; and some intermediate scheme allowing 'a large measure of self-government' for both communities in Palestine 'which would be held together in some sort of federal unity'. The last was a reference to the Foreign Office plan to shape the old provincial autonomy scheme towards the Arab proposals. What happened next was a classic example of how to start an argument and is indicative not only of the futility of reconvening the conference but also of the inherent danger to the cause of Anglo-Arab amity. And it reflected the Foreign Secretary's mounting exasperation. Jamali, the Iraqi delegate, requested time in which to reply but then remarked that 'he hoped that the Arabs would not be expected to pay for Hitler's guilt'. Bevin answered that the whole world was paying, and Jamali replied that the Arabs seemed to be the only people being called upon to pay for what Hitler had done to the Jews. This undiplomatic exchange continued until the Egyptian delegate asked for the British Government's view on immigration; Bevin managed to avoid a direct answer but only at the cost of taking the bull by the horns and asking 'whether the Arabs wished to stop immigration'. Several delegates replied affirmatively, and Bevin answered 'that it would not be possible altogether to deny immigration to the Jews. Both sides had rights ...'. Bevin suggested a bi-national state allowing each community to have majority rights with its zone. Carried away either by his own confidence or exasperation, Bevin then begged the question: 'Was it too much to hope that eventually Jews and Arabs would meet in the same room?' Chamoun of the Lebanon thereupon said 'that would be too optimistic'.

Bevin, the master of many a turbulent trades dispute, pressed on regardless and outlined 'a bi-national basis of settlement' combining the Arab plan with the Morrison–Grady scheme. Creech Jones came to his assistance, saying that what he

wanted the Arabs to consider was not necessarily Partition and not necessarily even their own Plan. The Jews were determined to stay in Palestine and to increase there. If they could not do so by legal means, they would do so by illegal means. This fact must be reconciled with Arab aims ... if the Arabs wanted progress.

The Colonial Secretary's pragmatism seemed quite out of place in the conference hall, and merely provoked the Arab delegates to respond competitively with one another. Jamali referred to the fundamental injustice of the Jewish National Home promise, saying the 'Jews were intruders'. El Khouri raised the prospect of Jewish expansion from any bridgehead, for which Jamali later supplied some Biblical parallels and Jamal Husseini capped it all by pointing out that the Palestine Arabs rejected the idea of a Jewish state 'in any part of Palestine'. Obviously, to the Arab delegations the conference was not a forum for negotiation but a stage for display, and the meeting adjourned on this note.[48]

At the next meeting, on 4 February, the Syrian delegate delivered the agreed Arab reply to the British proposals. It was a lengthy and uncompromising reiteration of the Arab position that included the 'inflexible' demand that further Jewish immigration should be halted, the bald statement that partition would not be discussed, and the warning that, 'The Governments and peoples of the Arab States are determined never to allow the Arabs of Palestine to become victims of the Jewish minority'. Nothing less was to be expected from the bidding mechanism that operated in response to Arab rivalries, yet as Creech Jones had indicated at the previous meeting the interests of the Palestinian Arabs were likely to have been better served by moderation and compromise. But within the consultative process which the Foreign Office had engineered such moderation was utterly impossible. Bevin acknowledged that 'a solution of the problem seemed no nearer', and Creech Jones pointed out that the Arabs were arguing for the maintenance of the *status quo* which he said 'was quite impossible'. There was really nothing more that the British Ministers could say, and Bevin showed his exasperation at their predicament by a final desperate gesture in explaining that, 'He had been told that the Arab States might conceivably be prepared to acquiesce in the imposition of a solution by Partition, although they might not be prepared to agree to it in Conference'. By his own admission, therefore, the Foreign Secretary was asking of the conference what he knew was impossible, and the futility of the whole exercise must have occurred to him. Jamali replied that he was authorized to say on behalf of the Arab League that it was inflexibly opposed to partition, and in answer to Bevin's further interrogation all the delegates indicated agreement. In raising this subject Bevin was referring to the

indications which had first been reported to the Foreign Office during
the summer of 1946, that some Arab governments might be
persuaded to acquiesce in partition; Egypt, for instance, by a deal
with the Jewish Agency, Transjordan by the temptation of receiving
the Arab portion of Palestine, and Syria and the Lebanon by some
determined British diplomatic pressure. But to clutch at these
opportunities after an interval of six months and in front of the tenth
plenary session of a conference of all the Arab states was the gesture of
a drowning man. In bringing their Secretary of State to this pass the
Foreign Office was most clearly guilty of pursuing a bankrupt policy.
Bevin, thus discomfited, was left to bring the meeting to a close with
the warning that, 'some of the principal members of the Cabinet had
already reached a definite conclusion on what solution should be
adopted'. If the solution proposed was impossible, then past pledges
would have to be set aside and the matter referred to the United
Nations.[49]

The inordinately protracted nature of this cycle of meetings with
the Arab delegations was partly the result of the simultaneous
discussions which were taking place between representatives of the
Jewish Agency and the British delegation. Gallman, the US *chargé
d'affaires* in London, was well briefed by both sides in these
discussions, no doubt on the grounds that the US Government might
be able or be tempted to operate in some mediating capacity; both
Shertok and Neumann made suggestions on these lines after the first
meeting with the British delegation on 29 January. At this meeting
the Jewish Agency's delegation, which consisted of Ben Gurion,
Shertok, Goldmann, Neumann, Brodetsky, Locker, Horowitz, Eban
and Linton, refused to set forth its views on partition on the grounds
that it would then become committed to partition. However, Ben
Gurion said that on their interpretation of the Basle resolution, they
would be able to consider partition if it was proposed to them.
Instead, the Jewish delegation was prepared to give its written
objections to the provincial autonomy scheme. Ben Gurion asked why
the government could not return to the pre-White Paper regime, to
which Creech Jones 'replied with vehemence' that the government
was no longer prepared to rule Palestine through an autocratic system
without any democratic basis; Ben Gurion thereupon hinted
obliquely that the Jewish Agency would have no choice, if Britain
refused to operate the Mandate, but to press for a state. A second
meeting took place on 3 February when both sides fenced delicately
around the Morrison–Grady plan by swapping copies of past
speeches on the subject. Bevin warned that if the present series of talks

failed to produce a solution to which both Arabs and Jews could bring themselves to acquiesce and not to oppose with violence, then the British Government would refer the problem to the UN without recommendation. Bevin dismissed the idea of partition and went on to describe a scheme which allowed communal autonomy within a unitary state, and on this proposal Neumann gathered the distinct impression that Creech Jones envisaged a far larger degree of Jewish authority over immigration into the Jewish zone than Bevin proposed. No doubt the Foreign Secretary's wish to place a specific limit on Jewish immigration was founded upon his anxiety to make the scheme acceptable to the Arab delegations. The Jewish delegation said it would consider a paper setting out the unitary state proposals, but Neumann told Gallman afterwards that he felt the Jews had been too polite and should end the talks now, since the latest proposal was merely a version of the Morrison–Grady plan.[50]

The Government had at last succeeded in getting representatives of the Palestinian Arabs and Jewish Agency to London at the same time as delegations from the Arab states, but the consultative process was, by 4 February, in its death throes. The Cabinet had to be consulted before the new scheme, which the British delegation had mentioned in the discussions, could be presented to the Arabs and Jews in a detailed form because at their meeting on 22 January the Cabinet had, at Bevin's suggestion, avoided making a choice between the two rival suggestions of the Foreign and Colonial Offices. Instead, the Cabinet had agreed that the British delegation should seek to reconcile the differences between the Arabs and Jews and report back. In a paper for the Cabinet dated 6 February, Bevin and Creech Jones made their report and also removed from the Cabinet's shoulders the delicate task of choosing between rival Ministerial proposals. Brook had drafted the paper for the two Ministers, evidently on Bevin's instructions, and it would seem that the Colonial Office itself was little, if at all, involved. The Cabinet paper reported the position of the Arab delegations and the representatives of the Jewish Agency, and concluded that there was 'no hope of negotiating an agreed settlement'. Partition was rejected by Creech Jones and Bevin not only because of its 'intrinsic weaknesses', such as the demarcation of the frontiers and the consequent problem of minorities, but also because, if partition was advocated, 'we should have to face the resolute hostility of the Arab world'. Furthermore, it would be unlikely that Britain would get the support of the Jews for any scheme the government 'would feel justified in putting forward' because the Jewish Agency clearly expected to obtain 'a very substantial area of

Palestine' by partition. The paper then went on to outline in detail the original proposal of the Foreign Office for an amalgamation of the Arab plan and the provincial autonomy scheme with 'as its primary object the development of self-government in Palestine', an objective Creech Jones felt strongly about. The machinery of this plan was to be a five year period of trusteeship culminating in complete independence, even Britain's military position might be brought to an end. During the first two years of trusteeship 100,000 Jewish immigrants would be admitted, and continued immigration thereafter would be permitted by agreement between the two communities or 'failing that' by UN arbitration. This plan was commended to the Cabinet by the two Ministers on the grounds that it went some way to meeting some Arab and Jewish demands and that, 'if we concluded that it was possible to do so', it could be implemented forthwith without prior reference to the UN because it was within the existing terms of the Mandate. Accordingly, Creech Jones and Bevin annexed the details of the plan to their paper and asked their colleagues to approve its submission to the Arab and Jewish delegations in order to discover whether an agreement could be reached on its basis. If 'as is more likely' no agreement was possible, the Ministers undertook to report to the Cabinet and ask them then to decide whether the government 'would be justified in bringing it into operation on their own authority', but if there was no prospect of Arab and Jewish acquiescence, 'we believe that the only course then open to His Majesty's Government will be to submit the problem to the United Nations, explaining the efforts we have made to find a solution but making no positive recommendation'. The paper ended with these words, thus presenting the Cabinet not only with a united front by the two responsible Ministers about the next steps to be taken, but also adding this sober reflection of its likely destination. The Cabinet could be in little doubt; Britain's policy options on Palestine were nearly exhausted.[51]

The Cabinet discussed this paper on 7 February. Creech Jones made his confession that

> he had previously thought that Partition afforded the only way out of the present deadlock ... he had been confirmed in that opinion ... by the High Commissioner and by his advisers in the Colonial Office. He confessed, however, that the longer he had examined the detailed implications of Partition, the more he was impressed by its practical difficulties. ... He was also impressed by the difficulties of securing the assent of the United Nations. ... But perhaps the greatest difficulty of all was that the enforcement of Partition was, he was now convinced, bound to involve

conditions of rebellion and disorder in Palestine which might last for a considerable time and would involve a substantial military commitment from us.

No doubt the spectacle of the various Arab delegations vying with each other in the strength of their denunciations of partition had coloured the Colonial Secretary's impressions; therefore, the device of the conference, arranged by the Foreign Office, had made incarnate the Eastern Department's strictures against partition. However, it would be unreasonable to suggest that this performance provided anything more than the occasion for Creech Jones' apparent reversal of opinion. The evidence suggests that Creech Jones was no more convinced that his department's proposals would now prove workable than Bevin was convinced in the current viability of the Foreign Office plan. Both Ministers believed referral to the United Nations without recommendation would be the ultimate course, and until that desperate point was reached both were prepared to try anything. In abandoning partition Creech Jones had not undergone a fundamental reversal of view, but had merely struck from his short list one unlikely hope for Palestine in favour of another. Both he and Bevin knew and acknowledged in their submission to the Cabinet that the ultimate capitulation of a referral without recommendation to the UN was but a short distance away.

Having listened to the Foreign and Colonial Secretaries, the Cabinet had a short discussion in which some doubt was expressed as to whether the Jews and the Arabs would collaborate sufficiently to make the unitary state proposal feasible. Nevertheless, the 'general view' was felt to be that 'there was every advantage in putting forward these proposals'. However, the Cabinet seemed to understand and even to welcome the finality of this effort, the minutes recording that:

It was also agreed that the negotiations must be brought to a point within the next week or so. If there was no measure of acquiescence in the proposals, then it seemed that reference to the United Nations would be necessary.[52]

Armed with Cabinet authority, the British delegation now embarked on their final sally into the negotiating arena. The unitary state proposal was sent to the Arab delegations on 7 February, and communicated to the representatives of the Jewish Agency as well. On 10 February, the Arab delegations sent their rejection of the proposal that disregarded fundamental Arab principles and suspended Arab independence due to the presence of Jewish 'foreigners'; the local authority powers were dismissed as 'another guise for partition', which was rejected in all its forms. It was an utterly uncompromising document that reiterated yet again the Arab opposition to all further Jewish immigration, and further reminded the British Government that its proposal on the matter 'cannot well go with Anglo-Arab friendship'. On the same day the British delegation was told by Ben Gurion that the present proposals moved away from the Morrison-–Grady plan, which the Jews had already rejected, towards the White Paper, and he objected to the immigration provisions and the proposal, after trusteeship, of an independent Palestinian state. There was no chance of the Agency agreeing to the proposals, and on the evening of 12 February a further meeting took place at which the map drawn up by the Anglo-American expert delegations, showing the provincial boundaries, was revealed. In the words of the report sent to the High Commissioner, the Jewish representatives rejected the area assigned to the Jewish province as 'a mockery of their just claims. ... In other words, they claimed the whole of Palestine except the central Judaean hills'. This meeting confirmed the British delegation in their assessment that 'any scheme of partition which we could defend in the United Nations as not being demonstrably unfair and unreasonable to the Arabs would be unacceptable to the Zionists'.[53]

Thus it remained only for the conference and the discussions with the Jewish Agency delegation to be brought to an end. On 12 February, Bevin informed the Arab delegations that 'agreement was as distant as ever' and that the Jews had rejected the recent proposals for the opposite reasons to those which the Arabs had advanced. Creech Jones, referring to the next step of submitting the problem to the United Nations, asked the Arab delegates whether they wished Britain 'to wash her hands of the Palestine problem and take it to the United Nations or withdraw completely from Palestine'. Several delegates expressed the wish to see Britain leave, and Bevin then sought further confirmation that 'they now wished Great Britain to surrender the Mandate':

> Arab Delegates agreed that they would wish British administration to continue for the transitional period provided for in the Arab Plan, but, if Britain decided not to do so, the Arabs would make themselves responsible for the administration of the country.

This meeting, the penultimate in the series, closed with Bevin's promise to report the results to the Cabinet. The next day the final meeting took place between the British and Jewish Agency delegations at which the Jewish position was summarized. The requirements were either for a Jewish state in western Palestine, or for Britain to administer the Mandate as had been done prior to the White Paper, or for a scheme of partition which allowed a viable Jewish state. These demands were all rejected by the British delegation, and the meeting closed in sombre mood.[54]

On this note of irreconcilable division and hopelessness, the consultative process expired. Its genesis lay with the policy of involving all of the Arab states in the affairs of the British Mandate, which the Foreign Office had established before the Second World War and resurrected during 1946. Its achievement was as conspicuous as it was doomed; it had succeeded in engaging, unifying and orchestrating the attitudes of the various Arab states on Palestine to such an extent that even the Foreign Office's own scheme for Palestine, based obviously and avowedly on the Arab plan but with some small amendments, was unceremoniously rejected by the assembled Arab delegations. In such an environment it was ludicrous to expect to discover a scheme in which not simply the Arab delegations and the British Government could acquiesce, but the representatives of the Jewish Agency as well. And indeed there is no evidence to suggest that Bevin and Creech Jones had any faith in the attempt by the end of 1946; they felt merely that they ought to see it through. As a result of following the guiding light of the Foreign Office, the responsible Ministers and their Cabinet colleagues had no alternative now but to accept what Martin had called 'a counsel of despair'.

Referral to the United Nations

By mid-February, therefore, events had about them that remorseless and automatic quality which was the inevitable product of the exhaustion of alternatives. Bevin and Creech Jones reported to the Cabinet the fate of their recent proposal at the hands of the Arab and Jewish delegations, and recommended the referral of the Palestine question to the judgement of the United Nations.[55] This recommendation and the failure of the conference which engendered it had been foreshadowed to the point of tedium, and indeed it was the outcome anticipated by Bevin and Creech Jones since December at the latest. In the Cabinet discussion on 7 February, when the unitary state proposal had been approved for submission to the conference, the rejection of this proposal was confidently anticipated and Ministers had resigned themselves with an almost uncanny fatalism to the next step of referring the matter to the UN. Now that moment had arrived, and on 14 February Bevin ushered the subject before the Cabinet as merely the second item before the meeting that day. Although the decision was made to refer the Palestine problem to the General Assembly of the United Nations, and to announce this step, the course of the discussion in the Cabinet in fact raised matters which blurred the clarity of the decision and added to the difficulty of judging its significance.

In his introductory account to his colleagues, Bevin said that he felt

> the representatives of the Jews had not believed that we should in fact refer the matter to the United Nations. He thought that both Jews and Arabs were anxious to avoid discussion of the problem in that forum, and it might be that, if we now announced our firm intention to take the matter to the United Nations Assembly, this might bring them to a more reasonable frame of mind. Even after such an announcement had been made, he would certainly continue his efforts to find a solution ...

Bevin concluded by pointing out that 'we could subsequently withdraw ... [Palestine] from the agenda of the Assembly if between now and September a solution could be found which was acceptable to both parties'. On the face of it, this suggestion by the Foreign Secretary lends an important qualification to his proposal and the Cabinet's decision to refer the problem of Palestine to the United Nations. Suddenly this step had been down-graded from being a turning-point into merely a negotiating device. In fact this analysis does not bear scrutiny. Consider first the record of the preceding few months: the process of referring Palestine to the UN had been mentioned by Bevin in his conversations with the US Secretary of State and with Creech Jones, to his colleagues in the Cabinet and to the assembled Arab and Jewish delegations, always as the final act of capitulation, the last irretrievable step. It seems unreasonable to regard this consistent record as an exercise in calculated mendacity simply on the grounds of the construction placed upon certain of Bevin's comments in Cabinet on 14 February.

There are also other explanations for Bevin's remarks, which were in evidence during the Cabinet discussion that day. Two thrusts from different quarters proposed deferring the decision to send the problem to the United Nations, and Bevin's suggestion that Palestine might not reach that forum seems to have been made partly to give their protagonists a crumb of comfort to savour. One objector was Tedder, the Chief of the Air Staff, who warned somberly on behalf of the COS: 'If the future of Palestine were left to the decision of the United Nations, we could not be sure that we should be able to secure there the military facilities which we required'. It is apparent that Bevin, by implying that Palestine might not be left to the decision of the UN, cast in doubt Tedder's hypothesis and thereby diminished the force of his argument in Cabinet. A rather more subtle thrust came from the Lord Chancellor, Viscount Jowitt. As soon as Bevin had finished speaking, Jowitt told the Cabinet about his interview with Ben Gurion, at the instigation of Sir Simon Marks and with Creech Jones's knowledge, that had taken place late the previous day. Jowitt reported Ben Gurion's wish that a final solution to the Palestine problem should not be forced at present by a referral to the UN, that for the time being the government should administer Palestine as it had done before the 1939 White Paper and that 100,000 immigrants should be admitted during the next two years. If this was done and subsequent immigration permitted in accordance with the economic absorptive capacity of Palestine, and if the land purchase restrictions were ended, then the Yishuv would co-operate in ending terrorism and curbing illegal immigration. Jowitt had reacted jubilantly on hearing this from Ben Gurion, and his ebullience was reflected by his prominent efforts in the Cabinet. But Jowitt's enthusiasm was clearly unjustified and derived from his partial view of the conference proceedings; he had not sat through meeting after meeting of the Arab delegations' competitive intransigence, nor was he a party to the conversations with the Jewish Agency representatives.

Ben Gurion's proposals to the Lord Chancellor were not new; the British delegation had heard them before. Creech Jones had previously replied to them that a return to the pre-White Paper regime in Palestine would mean maintaining the *status quo* of an autocratic government, which was wholly unacceptble. But Ben Gurion reiterated his suggestion to the British delegation on 13 February by which time both Bevin and Creech Jones were more acutely aware of how utterly unacceptable further Jewish immigration was to the assembled Arab opinion and accordingly this scheme was given a very dusty answer. Yet when Jowitt heard of it later in the day from Ben Gurion himself, he not unnaturally felt a breakthough was at hand: his was the idle optimism of the newcomer.

Jowitt's incursion, however, threatened to delay the Cabinet decision to refer the problem of Palestine to the UN, and accordingly Bevin answered it in two ways. He explained to his colleagues, in reply to Jowitt, that the Jewish Agency had already advanced its idea, but that to continue the Mandate as before 'was bound to excite the active hostility of the Arabs in Palestine'. In addition, the Foreign Secretary had already made it clear that if both Jews and Arabs became more amenable to compromise, then Palestine could be subsequently removed from the agenda of the General Assembly. Therefore it would seem that this latter suggestion of Bevin's was made principally with the requirements of the Cabinet discussion in mind, for by pointing out that if the deadlock changed the matter could be withdrawn from the UN agenda, the Chiefs of Staff were lent an olive branch and Jowitt and his supporters were left with an opening for their breakthrough if and when it materialized.[56]

Bevin and Creech Jones got their way in Cabinet on 14 February, notwithstanding the efforts of Tedder, Jowitt and his supporter Strachey, and Ministers well realized the step they were taking. The minutes record that in discussion it was agreed that the whole problem should now be referred to the UN on the basis proposed by the Foreign and Colonial Secretaries, without the government recommending any particular policy. It was understood that,

> This submission would not involve an immediate surrender of the Mandate; but His Majesty's Government would not be under an obligation themselves to enforce whatever solution the United Nations might approve. If the settlement suggested ... were not acceptable to us, we should be at liberty then to surrender the Mandate and leave the United Nations to make other arrangements for the future administration of Palestine.

There was a note of indifference about this 'Further discussion' which suggests that, excepting those Ministers and Chiefs of Staff who had particular interests, Palestine had been written off by the Cabinet, which could contemplate with equanimity the eventual surrender of the Mandate in these circumstances. This decision had the strong flavour of finality, notwithstanding Bevin's sanguine expression of hope that the Arabs and Jews might reach an agreement before the UN grappled with the problem. Finality and resignation are also apparent in the unquestioned policy of referring the problem to the United Nations without recommendation; acquiescence came partly because the Cabinet would have found it virtually impossible, in the wake of the conference, to make any particular recommendation and, hence, the decision to offer none met with the acceptance even of those who still clung to partition, such as the Chancellor of the Exchequer who queried whether the proposals now before the Cabinet did not exclude the possiblity of a decision by the United Nations in favour of Partition. *The Foreign Secretary* confirmed that Partition was not excluded.

But Brook had rationalized the matter of reference without recommendation for the Prime Minister in traditional Foreign Office style, saying that

> it appears from our discussions that—although neither side likes the idea of reference to the United Nations—we shall not incur the active hostility of either party if the matter is put to the United Nations on this objective basis.

The fact that Attlee had been briefed in this way also helps to explain why, under his chairmanship, the Cabinet discussion did not ponder the policy of referral without recommendation.[57]

On the subject of the timing of the reference to the UN, Brook's advice to Attlee proved less acceptable to the Cabinet. Bevin and Creech Jones had proposed that the matter should be handled by the General Assembly which met in September, and Brook, in his brief for Attlee, agreed because a Special Session could not be convened until the Foreign Ministers' meeting in Moscow ended:

> as that would mean waiting until June, we might as well wait until the next regular meeting in September. For the general irritation caused by the convening of a special Session would produce an unfavourable atmosphere for discussion.

In discussion on 14 February, the Cabinet certainly felt differently but the official minutes do not record who the prime movers were who asked whether Palestine could be considered by the UN before the General Assembly convened: 'It was admitted that this further delay would be most unfortunate'. The problems involved in convening a Special Session were discussed, and Bevin brought the matter to a conclusion by undertaking to enquire whether 'there were any means by which the United Nations could set in train preliminary enquiries and other preparatory measures with a view to ensuring that the General Assembly could proceed at once to a definitive discussion of the problem at its next regular Session in September'. The feeling in the Cabinet was not the only factor which operated to encourage some preparatory work to be done by the UN on the subject of Palestine. However, it seems a significant indicator, especially when considered with Bevin's prompt and compliant attitude, of the spirit of resignation and finality in which the Cabinet handed Palestine over to the UN and which is impossible to equate with an ulterior motive.[58]

After the Cabinet meeting, Bevin attended the final session of the conference with the Arab delegations where the proceedings also had that aura of finality. Bevin informed the delegations of the Cabinet's decision to refer the problem to the UN without recommendation. 'They would leave this to the decision of the United Nations and they would accept that decision'. Bevin regretted his government's failure to resolve the matter. In the midst of his speech, without any special prominence, the Foreign Secretary asked the Arab governments to consider 'whether the problem could not be solved between now and the time when the matter was brought before the United Nations'. Indirectly, the meeting provided the answer, for the Arab delegations were evidently still smarting from Bevin's desperate interrogation of 4 February when he had quizzed them about their real attitude towards partition. As soon as Bevin had finished speaking, the Egyptian delegate referred to this exchange of ten days ago and said he 'had been instructed to declare publicly and emphatically that Egypt would not be a party to any solution ... based on a plan in which the idea of partition was given effect'. Even the Foreign Office's unitary state plan had smacked of partition because of its arrangements for communal autonomy, according to the Arab delegations, so this rather unnecessary incantation by Amr Pasha of the old formula merely had the usual effect of provoking similar denunciations of partition and further Jewish immigration from the other seven Arab delegations in turn. Afterwards Bevin informed the delegates that the British Government would maintain the *status quo* in Palestine until the UN made its recommendation. The meeting and the conference closed on this familiar note, its final session serving only to emphasize how unlikely was Bevin's mild hope in some belated agreement. The Arab chorus had never been in better voice.[59]

The formulation of policy on Palestine for the interim period until the United Nations dealt with the problem followed a protracted cycle, beginning with optimism but speedily descending into a grim and final chapter of the Mandatory government trying to maintain the *status quo*. According to a minute by Martin, the paper which the Cabinet considered on 14 February, circulated above the signatures of Bevin and Creech Jones, was originally drafted by Beeley in discussion with Brook and other officials:

The draft as agreed by officials included a recommendation that the immigration rate of 1500 [per month] should not be altered pending submission to U.N.O.; but Ministers have altered it on this point and added a sentence ... which envisages the possibility of some relaxation of the restrictions.

Brook, however, was not disposed to accept such tampering without fighting back, and he advised the Prime Minister prior to the Cabinet's discussion that:

> If any such concession [on the immigration rate] were made, the Arab States would react sharply and might, I fear, take the matter at once to the Security Council. The Cabinet are not asked to take any decision on this point today. It would, however, be wise to make it clear that no concession about the interim period should be offered to either side without further reference to the Cabinet.

In Cabinet, Attlee clearly acted upon Brook's advice, for when the idea was mooted in discussion that some interim concession on Jewish immigration might ease the situation in Palestine, Attlee went on record as saying:

> that in his view the right course ... would be to make every effort to maintain the *status quo* ... including the restriction on Jewish immigration to the present rate of 1,500 a month. Any concession on that point would excite the opposition of the Arabs.

Evidently Brook had a willing pupil to chair the Cabinet.[60]

Apparently Creech Jones was the Minister chiefly responsible for urging the consideration of a larger immigration quota, and he was in company with the US Government. The Colonial Secretary's attitude might appear inconsistent with the experience he had shared with Bevin in witnessing the orchestrated barrage of protests at Jewish immigration from the Arab delegations, especially as he had apparently been impressed by the Arab antagonism towards partition. The explanation for his position is evident from the draft of a Cabinet paper on interim policy prepared in the Colonial Office, despite Attlee's statement to the Cabinet on 14 February. From its wordy argument, clear recommendations emerged that the Jewish immigration quota in the interim period should be raised to 4,000 per month, but that the existing restrictions on land transfer should remain. The principle reason advanced for this increase in the quota was the recommendation of the High Commissioner. In his telegram to the Colonial Secretary of 20 February Cunningham warned bluntly that Jewish institutions were unable to control the dissident terrorist organizations and therefore outrages would continue despite the referral of Palestine to the UN. Cunningham continued with peculiar emphasis, by underlining the following:

> The two alternatives are either to increase the immigration quota which gives the only chance of getting co-operation from the Jews or to embark on a period of military repression. In regard to the latter, I am not sanguine that however much latitude the Army gets it will produce the required results.

The draft for the Cabinet quoted this passage and added that General Barker, the General Officer Commanding in Palestine, endorsed Cunningham's view. The paper continued, saying that Cunningham did not consider the Arab reaction to increasing the immigration quota would be serious. Faced with this cogent advice from the men on the spot, Creech Jones's preparedness to take the recommendation for an increase in the quota to the Cabinet is understandable; indeed it follows the same pattern as his support for partition which the Colonial Secretary had put forward in Cabinet with the High Commissioner's support. The Colonial Office draft advanced other reasons for increasing the quota, arguing that the Jewish Agency would be fully occupied in coping with the numbers and therefore indisposed to countenance additional illegal immigration which, in the absence of a larger quota, would persist. US support for an increase in immigration was mentioned, and so too was a motive Creech Jones had advanced before: 'The Jews have not hesitated to remind the Government of the Labour Party resolutions and of its repudiation of the White Paper Policy'. However, the general tone of the draft was a little defensive, and took grim cognizance of the difficulties in raising the immigration quota.[61]

These difficulties were to overwhelm this draft for the Cabinet, and it was never to be submitted. Making a concession on immigration was awkward in the absence of change in the attitude of the Jewish Agency, and became impossible in the face of terrorism. The draft paper alluded to the first problem in its closing recommendation:

> in connection with the Foreign Secretary's statement that there was still room for discussion of a settlemnt before the United Nations dealt with the problem, note should be taken of the latest submission of the Jewish Agency, who should be informed that His Majesty's Government do not consider that any useful purpose would be served by further discussions on the basis proposed in the submission.

Apparently the submission referred to was the one made by representatives of the Jewish Agency to the British delegation on 13 February, and repeated by Ben Gurion to Jowitt later on that day. Yet there was no sign that the Jewish Agency would alter its position in the face of the British Government's rejection of its proposals and the reference to the United Nations. On the contrary: at a meeting on 27 February, Goldmann, Locker and Linton confirmed the Agency's position to Bevin, Creech Jones and other officials. The Colonial Secretary began by asking whether the Agency could make any fresh proposals and, hence, postpone the consideration of the problem by the UN. Locker replied that the Agency would be satisfied if the Mandate was administered in the spirit prevailing before 1939; as before, Bevin answered that this would not be possible since Britain required the Arabs and Jews to agree before she could continue the Mandate. The meeting closed inconclusively, but it had demonstrated the lack of movement, which provoked Mathieson of the Colonial Office to minute: 'The draft Cabinet paper ... will require revision in the light of [the] discussions'. But within a few days of these events, the situation was to be changed drastically.

A series of terrorist outrages including the destruction of the Officers' Club in Jerusalem claimed twenty lives, while on 1 March a ship carrying 1,416 illegal immigrants ran ashore near Haifa. Cunningham instantly reversed his opinion, advising the Colonial Secretary on 2 March, 'After the events of yesterday, it is clear that any move to ... [increase Jewish immigration] would be taken now as surrender to terrorism and that it could only be done after a period of quiet'. On the same day the High Commissioner made use of his recently revised powers and declared martial law in Tel Aviv and the surrounding area, but the troubles continued and two ships arrived during the next ten days carrying about 1,400 illegal immigrants. Concessions on the quota were felt to be impossible now, Bevin telling Creech Jones on 3 March that he felt Britain's line

> should be a firm one but when the situation is easier H.M.G. should concert with all sections of Jewry ... to indicate that H.M.G. was prepared to consider an increase in the immigration quota on humanitarian grounds, but it should be clear that the Jews must do their utmost to stop illegal immigration and co-operate ... in dealing with terrorism.

This attitude was not surprisingly in contrast with that of the Eastern Department of the Foreign Office, which argued in a minute, probably by Beeley, on the same day that any increase in the quota while the problem of Palestine was *sub judice* would provoke a strong Arab reaction and subject Britain to severe criticism if violence resulted. But the Foreign Office officials need not have worried; Sir Thomas Lloyd, the new Permanent Undersecretary at the Colonial Office, endorsed the wisdom of Cunningham's latest advice against increasing the quota, advice which the High Commissioner reiterated on 16 March. On 12 March, the Defence Committee discussed the situation in Palestine and *inter alia* agreed that the quota should not be changed 'for the present'; accordingly, the Colonial Secretary circulated a paper to the Cabinet on 19 March with this recommendation. The earlier Colonial Office draft for the Cabinet was scrapped, having proved itself ill-suited to the troubled waters of the Palestine problem; the concessions it had proposed were out of joint with the times.[62]

In making an assessment of the significance of the British Government's referral of Palestine to the United Nations, this outcome of the debate about interim policy serves only to emphasize still further the finality of the step. No concession was possible on the immigration quota because of the irreconcilable deadlock between the position of the Jews and the Arabs which the London Conference had highlighted, and also because the British Government and Mandatory authorities found it utterly impossible, as always, to make concessions in the face of terrorism. As a result, the Mandate staggered on for the interim period as before. A continuation of the Mandate on this basis was precisely what the Cabinet had decided to avoid by the hand-over to the UN.

Did terrorism and its concomitant illegal immigration help to destroy the prospects of compromise and thereby force the British Government into a corner? Before March 1947, terrorism had already restricted the government's options on two notable occasions: following the report of the Anglo-American Committee it had resulted in the insistence on the disarmament of the Yishuv before the 100,000 were admitted to Palestine, and the murder of Lord Moyne had provoked Churchill's Cabinet to shelve the Morrison Committee's partition plan. If the terrorists' objective was like that of their analogues in Tsarist Russia to destroy moderate measures, they clearly achieved some success in Palestine. But of equal importance was the effect of terrorism, illegal immigration and the general burden of ruling Palestine on the public mind; Ministers, parliamentarians, journalists and electors alike were aware that the Mandate bestowed a thankless and expensive task, consciousness of which contributed a certain haste and carelessness in terminating it. A few examples from early in 1947 illustrate this effect. On 14 January Bevin submitted to the Cabinet the Foreign Office proposal for the forthcoming conference, suggesting that provincial autonomy might be amended to point towards the Arab plan, warning that 'the local situation in ... [Palestine] makes it imperative that the decision of His Majesty's Government on future policy should be announced with the minimum of delay'. In view of the time-consuming rigmarole which the Foreign Office was responsible for, this interest in speed because of the situation in Palestine seems of some importance. Dalton's diary provides evidence of a certain hasty carelessness, born out of weariness with the burden of Palestine, even when due allowance is made for his preference for partition and his reservations about Bevin's abilities. For instance, on 17 January he typed or dictated, and perhaps crossed out, this comment:

> The present state of things cannot be allowed to drag on. There must be a Jewish State ... even if it is quite small, at least they will be able to let lots of Jews into it—which is what they madly and murderously want.

On 5 February he noted with mounting exasperation that 'E.B[evin] goes doddering round and round with the Arabs and the Jews and nothing ever happens except a long and rising series of outrages in Palestine which are rapidly producing anti-Semites'. Finally, on 24 February, Dalton rationalized the idea that Palestine was fast becoming a liability and it was best for Britain to cut her losses there; he recorded this view of India:

> If you are in a place where you are not wanted and where you have not got the force to squash those who don't want you, the only thing to do is to come out. This very simple truth will I think, have to be applied to other places too, e.g. Palestine.

Soon after penning these reflections, Dalton wrote to Bevin, warning that Britain was running through the dollar credit 'faster than is at all pleasant'. He wondered whether the Americans could be persuaded to shoulder a larger share of Britain's dollar expenditure in Germany and in the Mediterranean 'e.g. Palestine. Would not Truman like to take the mandate? I wonder!' Evidently, although concessions in the face of violence were impossible, an almost nonchalant surrender was not. When Bevin announced the Cabinet's decision to refer the Palestine question to the UN in the House of Commons on 18

February, Churchill's highly critical reply fastened upon a very similar point as its main thrust:

> Are we to understand that we are to go on bearing the whole of this burden, with no solution to offer, no guidance to give—the whole of this burden of maintaining law and order in Palestine ... not only until September, which is a long way from February ... but until those United Nations have solved the problem. ... How does he justify keeping 100,000 British soldiers in Palestine, who are needed here, and spending £30 million to £40 million a year from our diminishing resources upon this vast apparatus of protraction and delay?

This ringing question testifies to the absolute weariness felt by many with the Palestine Mandate, and there can be no room for doubt that terrorism and the thankless task of intercepting illegal immigrants contributed a telling and corrosive influence over Britain's will to rule in the Holy Land.[63]

At this important stage in Britain's Palestine policy the part played by the US Government must also be assessed. During his visit to the US during November 1946, Bevin had sounded out the government on its attitude towards Palestine, but he had returned without any very strong impressions. Bevin's efforts to elicit some US response were entirely consistent with his general policy of working in harmony with the US Government, and for this reason he had given Byrnes an elaborate Foreign Office memorandum, twenty-seven pages long, describing the problem and the options facing the British Government, but without obvious results. The clearest indication of the US Government's attitude emerged in January when, following Inverchapel's enquiries, Acheson had produced the 'Written Oral Statement' which showed a preference for partition as the best policy. It seems significant that Bevin regarded these intimations as insufficient to affect British policy at this desperate stage when the conference was on the brink of collapse. On 6 February, Bevin and Creech Jones submitted their recommendation to the Cabinet that partition would be impossible, and that the amalgam of provincial autonomy with the Arab plan should be proffered to the conference as the final proposal. In his instructions to Brook on the 'Points to be stressed' in the draft for the Cabinet, Bevin now discounted the US Government's influence:

> I do not feel, after Acheson's [views conveyed by Inverchapel's] telegrams, that we are going to get any support from America. They

have accentuated this situation and now the State Department appear to be leaving it for us to carry the whole burden.

Although the Foreign Secretary had struggled hard in the past to obtain a useful US involvement in the Palestine question, there are signs that Bevin thereafter merely tried to prevent further trans-Atlantic disruption of Britain's Palestine policy rather than win active US co-operation. For example, on 7 February, the new Secretary of State, Marshall, had steadfastly refused to be drawn on the subject of Palestine at a press conference, except that he made a few remarks designed to calm American Zionist anxieties about an impending military crack-down in the country; Bevin responded speedily and with gratitude, explaining in detail the final proposals being placed before the London Conference and tactfully requesting the US Secretary of State's steadfastness in not succumbing to Zionist protests.[64]

The records would suggest that Bevin was probably wise to discount the US from British policymaking. The State Department possessed no clear policy and no sense of haste; for instance, McClintock, special assistant to the Director of the Office of Special Political Affairs, noted to his superior, Ross, on 3 February, that Loy Henderson 'said that until we perceive what line the British are going to follow … our own policy will remain undetermined'. In response to Bevin's detailed description of the final proposals to the conference, Henderson's memorandum for Acheson was vague and for some reason he commented first that 'the British Government is endeavoring gradually to reduce Palestine from a world to a local issue'. He concluded, sagaciously in the circumstances, 'We feel that it would be unwise for us to comment on the merits of the plan until the storm which its announcement will raise has subsided'. Not until 15 February is there any hint that the drifting might end, when Acheson wrote to Henderson 'with concern' at the collapse of the London Conference and 'in the hope of provoking some thoughts from you'. Acheson considered whether a higher interim immigration quota for Palestine might be useful, and enquired anxiously what US long-term policy should be when the problem came before the United Nations; he felt the Department should get its views 'crystallized'. US policy remained uncertain, and in response to the British decision to refer the question to the UN, Henderson's memorandum to Acheson was shot through with caution:

I feel that we should move slowly in committing ourselves in any direction. … We cannot afford in the forum of the United Nations to retreat from

a position once taken as a result of pressure ... from highly organized
groups in the United States.

Backed by such irresolution, Marshall was able to respond to Bevin
merely with the remark that referral to the UN 'does not render ... [the
Palestine problem] any less complicated or difficult'. Marshall,
however, added two suggestions; that an increase in the interim
immigration quota should be considered, and that in his announcement of the referral to the UN Bevin 'might consider not referring to
G[eneral] A[ssembly] specifically since on further reflection
preparatory work in Trusteeship Council might be helpful'.[65]

The Eastern Department of the Foreign Office was again massively
against Marshall's first suggestion and the quota remained as before,
but Bevin altered his announcement in the Commons on 18 February
in accordance with Marshall's second suggestion and avoided
mentioning which organ of the UN would receive the problem from the
Mandatory government. However he told Marshall that the
Trusteeship Council would not be appropriate since its consideration
of the Palestine question would pre-empt the General Assembly's
handling of it as a trusteeship matter. The US Government did exert
some influence over the procedure of reference to the UN, and in the
process encouraged that feeling, already clear in the Cabinet
discussion on 14 February, that early steps should be taken to prepare
the ground for a definitive consideration by the General Assembly in
September. The British Permanent Representative at the UN, Sir
Alexander Cadogan, spoke to the Secretary General on 26 February;
Trygve Lie confirmed Cadogan's feeling 'that any Assembly will
simply *wallow* on Palestine unless some preparatory work has been
done, [and] he proposes he sh[oul]d convoke an *ad hoc* Commission. I
think this is quite right'. Cadogan reported this conversation to the
Foreign Office, which agreed to any procedure 'most convenient
provided it is practicable'. When the State Department heard of this
procedure, Acheson informed the US representative at the UN,
Austin, that it was 'legally of doubtful validity'. The upshot of these
American misgivings, after a short period which left the Foreign Office
nonplussed about the US attitude, was that Cadogan received
instructions to present a formal request to the Secretary General,
placing Palestine on the agenda and asking for a Special Assembly to be
convened in order to set up a special committee to prepare a report for
the next General Assembly to consider in September. Cadogan
presented his request on 2 April, and to this extent the US Government
succeeded in influencing the matter of Britain's reference to the UN.[66]

There was another aspect to the influence of the United States on Britain's policy, adding that note of rancour to Anglo-American relations on the subject of Palestine which Bevin's utterances illustrated. One component was the blatant fund-raising activity of Zionist organizations in the United States. The American League for a Free Palestine ran a massive campaign; on 30 November 1946, Creech Jones drew Bevin's attention, while he was in New York, to an advertisement in the *New York Post* of 7 October that solicited contribution to a $5 million fund 'with the thinly veiled implication that the money will go towards illegal immigration'. A particular source of annoyance was that the advertisements frequently boasted that the donations were tax-free, which gave these dubiously charitable organizations a flavour of official approval. Instructions were sent to Inverchapel to make 'strong representations', but the Ambassador replied that he had just sent a second *aide mémoire* in response to an advertisement in *PM* which appealed for contributions to a Palestine Resistance Committee, and felt that it would be best to await an answer to this and the three previous ones! This answer from Inverchapel was not appreciated in the Foreign Office, Beeley noting that the embassy 'appears to attach more importance to the embarrassment caused to the official Zionists by terrorism than to its consequences for the administration of Palestine', while Rundall of the North American Department thought the *aide mémoire* 'a lamentably weak document' which would have no effect. Rundall was quite right; the matter continued in this ineffectual way and, as late as 18 March 1947, Henderson briefed Acheson for an interview with Inverchapel that there 'is nothing we can do to prevent these advertisements':

> the only thing we can do is to ask Treasury to look into the question of the tax-free status of gifts of this kind. A communication to Treasury along this line was drafted sometime ago but we understand it has not gone out.

Probably Inverchapel's representations wanted a cutting edge, but like the State Department's inertia the problem continued to rankle throughout 1947 and made its contribution to the unhappy state of Anglo-American relations on Palestine.[67]

Bevin's own bitterness had deeper roots and emerged in public when, on 25 February in the House of Commons, he described *inter alia* how he felt: the President's past interventions on the subject of the 100,000 had destroyed the prospects of finding a solution to the Palestine problem and his Yom Kippur statement had wrecked the

talks with the Jewish Agency leaders in Paris. The State Department
memorandum noted that the Foreign Secretary's words were greeted
with cheers in the House. The response from the White House was
measured and mild, drawing attention to the widespread interest of
the American public in the Palestine problem, an interest which the
US post-bag reflected. The exchange was a sad commentary on
Anglo-American relations on Palestine. Whatever the past failures,
the evidence suggests that Bevin went out of his way, later in 1946 and
at the beginning of 1947, to elicit a firm expression of policy from the
State Department, an expression which might help the British
Government at its time of decision. But there was no policy to elicit
until, after the Cabinet had made its decision to refer Palestine to the
UN, the State Department brought its views to bear and influenced
the manner of this referral. It was a trivial achievement.[68]

But if this time of decision for the British Government passed the
United States by, for the Chiefs of Staff it was climacteric and serves
to highlight the significance of these events. The Staff Conference on
13 January had given a sympathetic hearing to the COS view of the
necessity of retaining control of Palestine and had consequently
endorsed provincial autonomy as a satisfactory plan to put before the
London Conference. However, it was conspicuous that the Chiefs of
Staff's strategic requirements in the Middle East, unaltered since
their submission to the Defence Committee in the summer of 1946,
had never been endorsed by the Defence Committee nor by the
Cabinet. Furthermore, although Bevin often lent a kindly ear to
military requirements in Palestine, he was out of sympathy with the
general level of military involvement in the Middle East and grew
angry at the number of troops still on Egyptian soil at the end of 1946.
On this particular matter, the Cabinet avoided any resolution and
merely 'took note' of the position—this avoidance of direct confrontation was to be repeated in its decisions over Palestine. For instance, on
22 January, at the final meeting before the conference reconvened, the
Cabinet decided not to decide between the Foreign and Colonial's
Secretaries' rival plans but to wait to see how the talks progressed;
this meeting also shelved the question posed by Brook to the Prime
Minister the day before:

> Do the Cabinet accept the views of the Chiefs of Staff on the importance of
> maintaining our position and influence in the Middle East?

This question was left in the air and the COS paper entitled
'Palestine—Strategic Requirements' circulated to the Defence Committee early in January was never considered.[69]

Willy-nilly, events moved on, and on 6 February, Bevin and Creech Jones circulated their joint paper to the Cabinet confessing that the London Conference was on the brink of failure and asking the Cabinet's approval to present the unitary state plan as a final British proposal before taking the decision to refer the question to the UN. On the same day, Tedder, Cunningham and Simpson, the COS Committee, met in morose and unanimous session; Tedder began by saying that

> if the problem of Palestine was referred to the United Nations without any recommendation ... we should be faced with the loss of our military rights there in a very short time. ... the grave military implications of such a course, should be submitted to the Minister of Defence.

Cunningham suggested that the conclusion of the Defence Committee paper should be reiterated: 'The preservation of our strategic position in the Middle East as a whole would be gravely prejudiced if our right to station British forces in Palestine were not retained'. However, the only authoritative endorsement of this position mentioned was the Staff Conference of 13 January. The meeting agreed that the Minister of Defence should be told of the Chiefs of Staff's unaltered strategic requirements in the Middle East and the grave risk of losing these completely if the Palestine problem was referred to the UN, and that the period of trusteeship proposed in the Foreign and Colonial Secretaries' scheme should be extended from five years to an indefinite period in order to safeguard matters 'from the military point of view'. In Cabinet the next day Alexander, the Minister of Defence, did his best and suggested a ten-year period of trusteeship; the Cabinet's 'general view' brushed this aside and strongly favoured the shorter period, adding for good measure:

> As to our strategic needs, we must in any event rely on a military Alliance with an independent State when the period of Trusteeship ended.

Thus discomfited, the Chiefs of Staff returned to the subject on 14 February, shortly before the Cabinet met to take its decision to refer the problem to the UN. Alexander chaired the meeting, and gently asked the Chiefs' opinion of various points arising 'on the assumption' that the course proposed by Bevin and Creech Jones of referral to the UN would be approved in Cabinet. The meeting felt that this step would, in the short term, lower the morale of the troops in Palestine, that it would eventually 'destroy our military position in Palestine,

and hence in the Middle East, since our ... forces would only have the
right to be present as a policing force to ensure that the United Nations
policy was followed'. This comment on the best outcome envisaged
betrayed the outlook of an ancient imperialism. The COS felt it would
be best to make a recommendation to the UN for future policy on the
lines of the latest British proposals. In the Cabinet meeting Tedder put
in a strong statement of the COS 'considered view', but according to
the minutes it was virtually ignored; no Minister mentioned or
answered it. In view of this, Brook's wary briefing to the Prime Minister
on the subject was probably important for he had advised that, 'The
Chiefs of Staff have already given their views on the long-term strategic
effects of losing our position in Palestine; and it is unlikely that they will
have any more to say on that point'. Accordingly the Cabinet took its
decision to refer the problem to the UN in the teeth of the Chiefs of
Staff's opposition—opposition, it should be noted, which was based on
a strategic appreciation of the Middle East that had never been
endorsed nor rejected at an appropriate level. Instead it was to be
eroded by inches.[70]

It must be said, however, that the Chiefs of Staff's strategic
requirements in the Middle East and Palestine were, by early 1947,
virtually museum-pieces. They were clearly derived and little altered
from detailed requirements laid down by the COS before the end of the
Second World War, yet during the early months of 1947 it became
blindingly obvious, with the collapse of the negotiations with Egypt
over treaty rights, the impending withdrawal from India and the
termination of aid to Greece and Turkey, that Britain's will, ability
and, indeed, her rationale for upholding such strategic ambitions in the
Middle East were passing. Despite this, the Chiefs of Staff persisted in
forwarding their obsolescent analysis. For instance they circulated to
the Defence Committee on 7 March a paper which recognized these
changes in Britain's position, but argued it was therefore all the more
essential to have facilities in Egypt and Palestine in order to have bases
from which a counter-attack could divert pressure from the United
Kingdom, and from which communications could be maintained
'through the Mediterranean'. Their tenacity in argument annoyed
Cadogan when he suspected that it was responsible for a series of
alterations in the draft statement he was to make in April before the UN
Special Assembly, and he informed the Foreign Office ironically,
referring to the COS requirements in Palestine:

I assume that this is the main reason why you do not wish to propose that
His Majesty's Government should commit themselves absolutely [over

accepting any UN policy]. ... I do not know what these requirements are though I presume that Chiefs of Staff were consulted before decision was taken to refer matter to United Nations.

But the tide of events had inexorably turned against the Chiefs of Staff. The process began in the summer of 1946, and reached its turning point with the Cabinet's decision of 14 February 1947, to refer the problem of Palestine to the UN. The COS continued, however, to spit into the wind; when, on 20 September 1947, the Cabinet decided against enforcing the United Nations Committee's plan for Palestine, and instead to withdraw, Dalton's diary records that at his suggestion the three Service Ministers and the Chiefs of Staff were left waiting outside the room. Noel Baker, the Secretary of State for Air, came in during the discussion. When Bevin was informed that the Air Staff wanted to stay in Palestine, he remarked, 'Tell them that, if they want to stay, they'll 'ave to stay up in 'elicopters'. With this avuncular remark the Foreign Secretary kicked out the last support from beneath the Chiefs of Staff and their strategic requirements in the Middle East.[71]

Returning to the Cabinet's decision to refer the Palestine problem to the United Nations without recommendation, the overwhelming weight of evidence suggests this decision to be the conscious beginning of the end of Britain's rule in the Holy Land. In this decision, terrorism and the awareness of the burden of the Mandate helped to sour and make careless the gesture of abdication, the submission without recommendation. The influence of the US Government was by this stage peripheral, but memories of its turbulent past still angered the Foreign Secretary when he had reason to recall what he saw as wasted opportunities; Bevin was never able to countenance nor forgive the electoral component in US foreign policy. But the reason why this decision had to be taken, and was taken in February 1947, was that by then the Eastern Department of the Foreign Office had secured an iron hold over Britain's Palestine policy and it had then made use of this authority to compound its pre-war mistake. Despite warnings, the Foreign Office had convened another conference to discuss with all and sundry British Mandatory policy in Palestine. As the evidence shows, this process rendered hopelessly complex and irreconcilable a situation which the holocaust had already made acute. Writing in January 1947 from his pro-partitionist standpoint, Dalton could perceive the bankruptcy of the Foreign Office policy:

[Bevin's] Palestine talks with the Arabs—a great geographical mistake in my view ... are making no progress. I have tried several times in Cab[inet] to get them all to agree to Partition ... I have urged that, instead of trying to make a synthetic glue of all the Arab States, including Egypt, we should try to split them and, in particular, should try to make Transjordan want Partition.

But, as both Creech Jones and Bevin evidently realized from their thoughts of handing Palestine to the UN, it was now much too late to change course. The Foreign Office's achievement was too deep rooted; in 1944 and 1945 it had edged out partition and contrived to defer consideration of another current preference of the Colonial Office, provincial autonomy. Bevin's involvement of the USA in the Committee of Enquiry was tolerated but, with Sir Norman Brook's able assistance, the Report of the Committee was heavily criticized to the Foreign Office specification in 1946, and the subsequent discussions with Grady's delegation turned into a triumph for Foreign Office wishes. Thereafter, with the American component excluded from British policymaking on Palestine, the Foreign Office contrived to negotiate a settlement at a conference from which, initially, representatives from both the Palestinian Arabs and Jews were absent. This machinery eventually turned against its maker, and the Foreign Office, rather like the sorcerer's apprentice, witnessed the second phase of the conference reject even the pro-Arab scheme tailored specifically for the occasion by the Eastern Department. The consequence was to drive Foreign Secretary and Cabinet alike into a corner. Hobson's choice faced the government which had become the victim of its own, Foreign Office policy. It had no choice but to throw the burden down, for continuing to rule in Palestine indefinitely and without hope in the future was utterly rejected. But for criticism or signs of awareness about this extraordinary cycle of events, about the utter and complete failure of policy, the reader of the Foreign Office files will seek in vain. Minuting on 1 March 1947 on a suggestion of the Jewish Agency's that British military bases in a Jewish state would allow the government to support partition, Beeley wrote:

> The Zionists believe that Palestine itself is of first-class strategic importance to us. What is important, I think, is the effect upon our Middle Eastern position generally of our policy in Palestine.

Thus unchanged and unchanging, the Foreign Office proceeded on its way.[72]

6

The United Nations Special Committee on Palestine

Naturally the traditional preoccupation of the Foreign Office affected the actual procedure of referring Palestine to the United Nations. In this, Foreign Office concerns to minimize the damaging effects of this step on Anglo-Arab relations combined with the continued exertions of the Chiefs of Staff to remind the government of its view on Palestine's strategic importance. The result was an elaborate effort to hold the UN Special Committee on Palestine (UNSCOP) at arm's length, to ensure that it was disinterested and to avoid any British commitment to enforce its recommendations lest these upset the Arabs. Yet the process of resolving the submission to the UN Special Assembly also showed clearly the government's anxiety to ditch the burdens of the Mandate, as well as the FO's anxiety to minimize the Anglo-Arab reaction; the COS's interest in retaining Palestine was in the process of being by-passed. A consequence of this range of interests was to help render British efforts in New York futile. The British Government failed to get its gently preferred composition for UNSCOP, but this failure did not seem to matter. The greater British efforts to halt illegal immigration and terrorism under the auspices of a UN enquiry were a conspicuous failure. And finally, the British Government failed to impress upon UNSCOP its utter weariness with Palestine and its plain determination to avoid enforcing a solution there which the Foreign Office felt would wreck Anglo-Arab relations. Here the problem was not merely one of woolly decision-making in London but that the government had failed to enunciate clearly its wish to leave Palestine. UNSCOP itself, elaborately sensitive to all the demands placed upon it by Jews, Arabs and by the Palestine Government, forgot to weigh up the attitudes of the third corner of the Palestine triangle properly: the British Government's attitude was overlooked, clearly, in part, the result of the British

Government shielding its inexplicit policy and bankrupt ideas behind the guise of disinterested neutrality. But the result and UNSCOP's error was to be a fatally impaired Majority Report.

Sir Alexander Cadogan's Statement to the UN

The interval between the Cabinet's decision of 14 February to refer Palestine to the United Nations and Cadogan's statement in the First Committee of that organization on 9 May has about it something of the nature of an amusing interlude. The actual words Cadogan was to use to explain his government's position were the subject of inordinate discussion and redrafting in London; the antics themselves are less important than the motives and circumstances behind them. Basically the Cabinet's decision had been vague on two important points. The Cabinet had avoided deciding explicitly to surrender the Palestine Mandate, although it is quite clear that surrender was regarded as the expected, and, to some Ministers, welcome outcome of the reference to the UN. After all, as Lord Bullock has pointed out (1983), during the second half of February the Empire seemed to be in the process of dissolution since, besides taking the decision on Palestine, the Cabinet agreed to end British aid to Greece and Turkey and to pull troops out of the former, while Attlee announced that the end of the British Raj would transpire by June of the next year.[1] The Cabinet had also been vague over the COS requirements in the Middle East; we have noted the unflinching articulation of these requirements from 1945 well into late 1947 by the COS themselves. But since July of 1946 neither the Defence Committee nor the Cabinet had approved nor rejected these requirements specifically, so they lingered on in a twilight world of their own until, in September 1947, the Cabinet made its decision to withdraw from Palestine explicit. But the consequences of this woolliness prompted the Foreign Office to produce some interesting draft statements for Cadogan, drafts which are not only quite revealing in themselves but which prompted a retort from Bevin of considerable importance.

It was Cadogan himself who set the ball rolling in his telegram from New York to the Foreign Office on 6 March. He debated the value of declaring Britain's intention to carry out any UN recommendation passed by a two-thirds vote in the General Assembly and showed an awareness of 'the odium of implementing' an 'objectionable recommendation'. But he went on with tongue firmly in cheek:

I presume however that since His Majesty's Government have decided to refer Palestine question to United Nations they are in fact prepared to abide by the latter's decision whatever it may be.

This statement simplified the issue gracefully, avoiding the distinction between acceptance of and implementation of any UN decision by the British Government, but Cadogan hit his mark and his former junior, the now Permanent Undersecretary, was suitably galvanized into action. Bevin was in Moscow at the Foreign Ministers' Conference, and Sargent's advice to him was clear:

> We do not understand the Cabinet's decision as meaning that His Majest's Government are prepared to commit themselves to accepting any recommendation ... it follows that it would not be possible to give the Assembly a blank cheque such as Sir Alexander Cadogan submits....

Sargent was understandably concerned lest the British Government place itself in a corner, with the UN requiring her as Mandatory to implement recommendations which were judged unworkable in London, and he sought his Secretary of State's confirmation of his attitude.[2]

Bevin's reply was clear and supportive. Regarding the future status of Palestine, Bevin said 'I would be prepared to agree in advance to accept the recommendations of the Assembly' but the British Government could not bind itself in advance to carry out either by itself or in association with other powers 'a recommendation which would involve them in the use of military force'. This attitude of the Foreign Secretary's is important in that it helps to confirm that the government had accepted the relinquishment of its control over Palestine, while his reservation was to be expected and was, ultimately, to govern Britain's policy during the closing months of the Mandate. Yet, strangely, Satgent was still unhappy and he warned that the government's freedom of manoeuvre may be restricted by any agreement in advance to accept a UN recommendation. With the support of the Colonial Office behind him, Sargent proposed that Cadogan should make only the blandest of promises to the UN and say that HMG

> will of course give the most serious consideration to the Assembly's recommendations. They must however reserve their freedom to refuse the task of themselves administering any policy of which they do not approve.

Bevin's reply of 30 March showed some exasperation and he doubted whether the Permanent Undersecretary understood the argument that the Palestine question had been referred to the UN because 'we have reached a point where the Mandate can no longer continue.' The Foreign Secretary continued with asperity, 'In the circumstances it seems to me that we are bound to accept the recommendation of the Assembly since we have declared that we ourselves can do no more but that some new solution must be found.' There is no doubt that this reiterated attitude is significant as yet further evidence of the government's intent to quit Palestine. Beeley, in fact, minuted his approval, 'making a virtue of necessity' and allowing Cadogan to announce in advance 'that we would not oppose the implementing of any recommendations ... though we might have to refuse to carry them out ourselves.' His rationale was simple; this British position would encourage the UN to consider the implementation of its recommendations 'with a sense of responsibility' and it would also refute the irritating Zionist scepticism about the sincerity of Britain's handover to the UN. Sargent accordingly responded on 4 April with another draft statement for Cadogan which mentioned that all proposals hitherto made for Palestine had aimed at one of three broad goals: an Arab controlled state, a Jewish controlled state, or some division of authority between the two peoples. Adroitly avoiding Bevin's fourth option for the UN that it could 'propose some other course', Sargent's draft merely pledged British acceptance of whichever of the three courses received the backing of two-thirds of the General Assembly while reserving Britain's 'freedom to refuse the task of themselves administering any policy of which they do not approve'. Bevin failed to mention the alteration in Sargent's draft, but Henniker's minute (Bevin's Assistant Private Secretary) indicated that the third option of a division of authority in Palestine could include a unitary or partitioned country. Bevin agreed to the draft statement with a clarifying change to its final sentence, but the matter did not end there.[3]

Why was the Foreign Office being so wary about making what even Bevin considered a banal commitment? It seems that the FO was eager to avoid taking any step that might jeopardize Britain's relations with the Arab states and was therefore eager to disassociate Britain as far as possible from any UN recommendation in case that recommendation went against the Arabs. Baxter's attitude strongly suggests that this was indeed the FO's underlying rationale, for he minuted anxiously on 24 March; 'It is worth noting that the Arabs seem to take it for granted that the setting up of a new [UN] Committee [of enquiry] would favour the Zionists.' Eyres' report from Damascus captured the consequent sense of being on a knife edge as the Syrian President intimated mysteriously that if things went against the Arabs, 'the reason would be clear for all to see; if, on the other hand, the decision [of the UN] was in favour of the Arabs, they would know that His Majesty's Government were largely to thank.' Other reports emphasized the potentially adverse Arab reaction to events; Campbell conveyed the Arab League's resolution to establish a committee to defend Palestine while Stonehewer-Bird reported Iraq's touchy attitude to the Egyptian leadership in all this. Campbell himself interpreted the signs in a telling comment on 25 March:

> I fear that our friends ... are afraid of standing up for us and that in this they have been influenced not alone by considerations of interests of Arab League but also by anti-British attitude of the Egyptian Government ... [which] we have apparently not succeeded in checking....

Bearing in mind the attitude of the Foreign Office displayed over the preceding decade, it seems that it was painfully aware of the dangerous possibilities and most anxious to avoid incurring for Britain further ignominy in Arab eyes by being too accommodating to anything which the UN might say.[4]

The saga of Cadogan's draft statement was not yet ended, for before the British Representative to the UN could utter a word Sargent advised Bevin, who was still in Moscow on 24 April, of the misgivings expressed by Butler (who superintended the North American department in the FO), Beeley and by the UN department. Sargent now felt that the UN General Assembly might dislike the limited choice implied in the three alternative solutions mentioned for Palestine and the Arab states may take offence at Britain's preparedness to accept a Jewish state. Accordingly, he proposed a new draft simply deleting mention of the three courses, but then muddied the whole effect by recommending that this draft be held in reserve and a less 'sweeping' statement made by Cadogan to start with. Cadogan was not amused. The day before he had been asked at Harvard to explain his government's intentions even as Lord Hall, the former Colonial Secretary, was commenting in the House 'I cannot imagine His Majesty's Government carrying out a policy of which it does not approve'. Baxter noted angrily that Lord Hall went 'quite outside his brief', but Cadogan was already acutely aware of the suspicions he had to allay in New York about the sincerity of Britain's reference to the UN and he warned the Foreign Office that the less commital statement now proposed to start with would simply provoke further questions.[5]

The reasons for the chopping around this time were, as Cadogan commented, the COS strategic requirements. Cadogan indignantly presumed that the COS 'were consulted before decision was taken to refer matter to United Nations.' He warned, 'Clearly we cannot explain a refusal to accept Assembly recommendation on grounds that it is contrary to our strategic requirements.' This was indeed the nub of the problem. On 21 April the COS had reaffirmed to the FO the principle in their submission to the Defence Committee that, 'We should retain our essentail strategic requirements in Palestine.' Consequently the COS were 'unable to agree' to any statement 'that does not safeguard' these requirements. The warning bells were by now ringing piercingly in the Foreign Office, for on the same day as they received this reminder from the COS the Egyptian Government requested the inclusion of a new item on the agenda of the UN Special Assembly, convened originally to set up a Committee of enquiry. The new item was; 'the termination of the mandate over Palestine and the declaration of its independence'. The response was for Sargent to advise a retreat into generalities, Cadogan being given the unenviable task of fronting for the COS in New York in order to preserve the government's freedom of manoeuvre.[6]

The whole matter was becoming utterly ludicrous, the resolution and good intentions of the government's referral to the UN being jeopardized by the COS's repetition of views which had never been endorsed by the Cabinet. Furthermore it had been agreed at the Cabinet meeting on 3 April that the period of National Service should be reduced from eighteen to twelve months, and that the army would be redeployed by 1950, mainly to the UK and Germany, as Montgomery had said at the preceding Defence Committee meeting 'on condition that certain overseas commitments such as those in Palestine and India were liquidated by 1949 or 1950'. The Chief of the Imperial General Staff repeated this formally to the Minister of Defence on 9 April so it would appear that in the spring of 1947 the COS were thinking double—on the strategic necessity of keeping Palestine and on the strategic necessity of liquidating military commitments there. The problem went before the Cabinet on 29 April with Sargent repeating to the Prime Minister the advice he had given Bevin on 24 April. The Colonial Secretary supported him but Bevin, most probably fed up with the FO's delicate footwork, was now reportedly in favour of sticking to the least commitment for the time being until the UN General Assembly met in September. The

Cabinet wisely sidestepped the problem and agreed that Attlee should discuss the matter with Bevin on his return.[7]

But events in New York overtook the agonizing in London. The Special Session of the UN General Assembly had convened on 28 April, and on the 29 April, Cadogan was obliged to explain Lord Hall's remarks before the General Committee. So, he informed the Foreign Office, he could not avoid repeating the reservation about enforcing any UN recommendation, even though this laboured the distinction between enforcement and acceptance and would thus highlight the British avoidance of commitment. He went on to explain with deliberation and authority the consequences should the British Government's hearing fail to carry conviction:

> I must warn you however that this is not just a question of local Jewish pressure. My concern is rather with the general feeling among the delegates ... there is even a risk that unless we can allay their suspicions the Latin Americans may well combine with the Slavs and for example the Indian delegate in opposing our request for the setting up of a preparatory committee.

The minutes show that Cadogan's point went home. As a result Cadogan was able to make a full statement of his government's attitude to the UN First Committee which was deliberating on the actual creation of the preparatory committee of enquiry. The crucial passage in his statement of 9 May ran:

> Having failed we now bring ... [the Palestine problem] to the United Nations in the hope that they can succeed where we did not. If they can find a just solution which would be accepted by both parties it can hardly be expected that we should not welcome ... [it].
>
> All we say is that *we* should not have the *sole* responsiblity for enforcing a solution which is not accepted by both parties and which we cannot reconcile with our conscience ....
>
> But if this question is addressed to us concerning our acceptance of any recommendation that the Assembly may make, I suggest that it should be addressed ... to all other members of the United Nations.

Thus adroitly and honestly Cadogan presented the government's position, a position which was of course to have momentous consequences by the end of the year. For the time being it apparently satisfied everyone, Bevin noting his agreement on the text and Garran observing that he had 'not seen any press reports of any adverse reactions to ... Cadogan's statement which is very cleverly phrased'.[8]

The Special Session of the UN duly went on to create the Special Committee on Palestine to imvestigate and report back later in the summer, but Cadogan plainly felt that his government's reluctance to act with manifest sincerity had risked the whole submission of the problem. The rigmarole of drafts, redrafts, and reconsidered drafts of Cadogan's statement is significant beyond the level of humour. Despite the explicit Cabinet decision to refer Palestine to the UN and the implicit decision to give up the Mandate, the Foreign Office continued its quest to preserve the government's freedom of manoeuvre. This objective, was, of course, perfectly reasonable, but it was performed from motives that were discreditable. These motives were an excessive sensitivity to the attitude of the Arab states over Palestine, despite Palestine having become a UN concern and not a purely British one, and an extraordinaary loyalty to the outmoded strategic requirements of the Chiefs of Staff, although these strategic requirements had not been approved by the Cabinet and Defence Committee. It would of course be too much to expect these attitudes of several years' longevity to have evaporated from Whitehall as soon as the Cabinet had decided to throw down the burden of the Mandate; clearly there was a mighty sense of tradition at work. The response to these traditional attitudes is of importance because it emphasizes the real break in Britain's Palestine policy. Bevin's earlier reply to his department's pussyfooting that 'we are bound to accept the recommendation of the Assembly' as 'we ourselves can do no more' represented accurately the spirit of the government's decision. Cadogan's actual statement had to be a good deal more ingenious to satisfy the by then multilateral demands being placed upon him, but it did convey the fact that the government had reached the end of its tether on Palestine and was giving the problem to the UN with the necessary reservation that Britain would not alone enforce an opposed policy. The comic interlude contained a serious meaning after all.

The creation of UNSCOP

The decision, made largely thanks to US wishes, to convene a Special Session of the General Assembly in order to set in motion a preparatory investigation of the Palestine question had ramifications beyond Cadogan's statement. For instance there was the well-founded worry, felt in both London and Washington, that the discussions at the Special Session would develop beyond the procedural level into a substantive debate on Palestine. There was also the question of which countries, and indeed which personalities, would be chosen to serve on the preparatory committee. Besides these issues the British Government also exercised itself over the questions of terrorism in and illegal immigration to Palestine pending the General Assembly's next meeting in the autumn, as well as over the terms of reference of the preparatory committee.

Just two days after Cadogan formally requested UN Secretary General Lie to convene a Special Assembly to set up a committee to investigate Palestine preparatory to it being discussed by the autumn General Assembly, on 4 April, Acheson (Acting Secretary of State) circularized US diplomatic posts, asking them to press that the Special Assembly's agenda be 'confined to this question alone'. The State Department energetically forwarded this line and briefed the US delegation to the UN accordingly. However, it was not to be so easy to pre-empt the much practised Arab eloquence on the subject of Palestine. On 21 April, Egypt requested the addition of another item on the Special Assembly's agenda; 'the termination of the mandate ... and the declaration of ... independence' for Palestine. Iraq, Syria, Lebanon and Saudi Arabia obligingly made the same request over the next few days. On 1 May, Bevin received a report from Richard Stokes, who was Minister of Works with a long-standing interest in the Middle East. Stokes had just completed a tour of the Arab states, and he discomfortingly warned that:

I am convinced that all expect the opportunity to present objective statements at the [Special Assembly] meeting now taking place in New York. Any attempt at suppression ... will be regarded as due to Anglo-American Jewry ... everyone is assuming ... that the British Delegation [to the UN] will show sympathetic understanding of the Arab case ... Fact finding commissions have no (repeat no) buyers.

But Beith of the Eastern Department minuted cooly, 'Our own attitude must be one of neutrality'. However he wrote this on 6 May after the crisis was partially over, for on 1 May the Special Session of the General Assembly had rejected the inclusion of the Arab item by twenty-four votes to fifteen with ten abstentions. On the same day, and without a vote, the Assembly approved the inclusion of the British item and referred it to the First Committee. But by this stage, the possibility of broadening the discussion had moved away from the Arab item to consideration of whether the Arab Higher Committee and Jewish Agency should appear before the UN. This was, however, a lesser problem.[9]

The choice of which countries would serve on the preparatory committee naturally engaged the thinking of both the British and US governments, but it is noteworthy that the degree of influence Britain exerted in the UN was negligible. On 11 April, Inverchapel questioned the Foreign Office on the delicate business of defining what a 'neutral' committee would in fact be neutral over; between Arab and Jewish claims, or by reference to Britain. Referring to the early State Department listing, Inverchapel commented that Brazil, Mexico and the Philippines were hardly neutral under the first definition since they would be more likely to follow a US lead than to pay attention to Palestine itself, whereas India, Czechoslovakia and Poland, also on the State Department's list, were likely to be against anything which they thought HMG might favour. The FO's reply seems significant for it began by concurring in the first definition of neutrality; that is, Inverchapel should strive to obtain a committee which was neutral over the Arab and Jewish claims irrespective of its members' attitude to Britain.

As to the size of this committee, Bevin had instructed from Moscow that Inverchapel should be authorized to approve either the larger committee (of about twenty-six) or a smaller one (of about eleven) 'on the understanding that it is put forward by the United States'. He warned that any lobbying should be left to the USA. Bevin did however express a preference for the larger committee which, according to the State Department's briefing paper for Truman, should comprise members of the Security Council, the Economic and Social Council and the Trusteeship Council. The memorandum for the President expressed dislike for this option, pointing out that the list included three Arab states and averred that it would have to create a less committed sub-committee to do the spade work. The preferred option, which Truman concurred in, was a 'disinterested' committee comprising Canada, New Zealand, Sweden, Belgium, Czechoslovakia, Brazil, Mexico, Colombia, Norway and Siam. Cadogan, regarding an earlier edition of this US list, commented briskly that Britain would be lucky to get both Canada and New Zealand, would prefer Denmark and Turkey to India and Persia (none of which featured on Truman's list) and found the others all right except that Siam and the Philippines were 'rather fantastic', but one may be good 'in deference to Asiatic feelings'. Again the Foreign Office reply was remarkably unhasty and disinterested, agreeing generally with Cadogan but proposing to leave the matter until the Special Assembly began. So it was that on the day the UN First Committee was instructed to consider the British request, Cadogan reassured the Foreign Office of the position; the US delegation, he said, now 'fully understand that we expect them to make proposal regarding committee and we shall discuss membership with them in due course'.[10]

Generally therefore the British Government was content with leaving the initiative to the Americans and standing by its wish for a disinterested committee, while at the same time softly articulating preferences of its own regarding the membership. This was the important message contained in the brief for Britain's delegation at the UN which Attlee himself approved on 24 April. The brief avoided repeating Bevin's earlier preference for a large committee and apparently left committee size up to discussions with the State Department. It continued to put the British dilemma succinctly:

> While the attitude of His Majesty's Government ... will be one of neutrality as between Arab and Jew, every effort should be made to prevent unnecessary damage to Anglo-Arab relations as a result of the reference of Palestine to the United Nations.

This desire not to damage Anglo-Arab relations was indeed the principle underlying much of the saga over Cadogan's statement, as well as the very discreet preferences expressed by the British Government over the composition of the committee.[11]

Hence the Foreign Office replied to a planitive request from Turkey for 'guidance' with the firm advice that Britain wanted those attending the Special Assembly to be motivated purely by the merits of the issue and to help to set up the committee 'in as businesslike a way as possible'. Similarly, when Campbell reported Azzam's fears of an impending clash with Britain, Garran (Assistant Head of the Eastern Department) minuted firmly that HMG had decided to pursue neutrality in the proceedings 'and we can send no instructions to the Delegation in New York'. The US State Department was equally wary of making any commitment, the British Embassy reporting that:

> They also do not wish to influence in any way the choice of members for the smaller committee which they still favour, as they want to meet Arab objections that ... the U.S. Government ... will in fact exercise considerable influence.

This stance of neutrality remained the position of both governments until after the Special Assembly convened.[12]

On 3 May, Cadogan reported the US delegation's suggested membership of a committee of only seven: Canada, the Netherlands, Sweden, Czechoslovakia, India, Peru and Uruguay. Cadogan commented:

> If U.S.S.R. presses for another satellite then we must include another neutral.
>
> It is doubtful whether India can be considered a 'neutral' but the only other Far Eastern candidate would be Siam. Persia is a possible alternative ...
>
> Peru and Uruguay are the nominees of the President of the Assembly. [Aranha]

These remarks clearly show the powerful multilateral forces at work in the UN First Committee, and against these it was to prove vain for the Foreign Office to suggest gently that Cadogan considered putting Turkey forward to balance another Soviet satellite. Cadogan reported on 5 May that the US delegation 'are quietly supporting ... [Peru and Uruquay] share our doubts with regard to the personal qualifications of the Uruguayan representative.' Senator Fabregat, Cadogan explained, only knew Spanish and believed that the government was endangered by a popular movement which favoured the Jewish Agency. At Cadogan's suggestion, the Foreign Office instructed the Ambassador in Montevideo to urge another choice. Fabregat was in fact nominated despite British representations. But the real surprise came in the First Committee on 13 May when the US list, now with Iran replacing India, was discussed finally. Cadogan, who thought that the matter was a foregone conclusion, complained furiously to the FO over the American

> surrender without consulting us to Soviet insistence upon enlarging committee of investigation, has added Yugoslavia, Guatemala, India and Australia to original seven on United States list. Except for Australia all these additions were [Soviet representative] Gromyko's favoured candidates. Their election was adroitly rushed through in full committee to fill the vacuum created by Australian insistence upon a committee of eleven; without any apparent thought on the part of Australia as to who, other than Australia, was to be added to the previously well-balanced list.

Cadogan's diary entry for 13 May makes it plain that Austin (the US representative on the committee) had promised to stick to his own resolution for a committee of seven, but then proceeded to change his mind without a word and to suggest Guatemala and Yugoslavia, leaving Cadogan to try to re-balance matters by adding Australia and India. So it was that the UN First Committee recommended the eleven-nation Special Committee on Palestine to the Special Session of the General Assembly, which in turn adopted it on 15 May by forty-seven votes to seven with one abstention. Two things are quite plain from this affair. The British Government proved unable to secure its preferred committee at the UN despite close liaison with the US delegation, but it did not exert itself much to influence things. Secondly, Cadogan's real fear that UNSCOP may prove 'unbalanced' focused upon the Soviet success in getting its preferred nominees on the committee.[13]

Cadogan suggested to the Foreign Office a way of partially retrieving the situation by pressing the governments concerned to nominate representatives 'who will as far as possible resist Soviet manoeuvring ... for a biased or unworkable report'. He amplified his earlier warning about Fabregat (of Uruguay) that 'he was in the Soviet and Zionist pockets', while he warned that Granados (of Guatemala) 'is generally accused by his Latin-American colleagues of being a Soviet stooge and his anti-British bias would make him a most unsuitable choice'. These remarks suggest that Cadogan was rather more alive to a pro-Zionist bias in Soviet policy than were his colleagues in London when it came to the voting on UNSCOP's recommendations. At Cadogan's suggestion the British representative in Guatemala did his best, but Granados was indeed nominated, as was Fabregat, and the former in particular proved himself to be a staunch Zionist in his behaviour while a member of UNSCOP.[14]

There were other less traumatic matters for Cadogan to deal with in New York. The Polish proposal to grant a hearing to the Jewish Agency before the Special Assembly was defeated, but the First Committee was obliged to grant it a hearing on 6 May together with the Arab Higher Committee, after some manoeuvring. Although there were dangers that the various procedural wrangles would spill over into a general discussion of the Palestine question, Cadogan, Austin and the First Committee successfully contained the debate to the business of setting up UNSCOP. The terms of reference for UNSCOP presented surprisingly little difficulty. The Jewish Agency failed to write into the terms some basic premise about a Jewish National Home in Palestine. A Polish proposal to require that UNSCOP visited the DP camps in Europe was defeated in a sub-committee on 10 May, as too was an Australian notion that HMG should be given policy recommendations for the interim pending the next regular session of the General Assembly. Finally, on

13 May, the First Committee rejected the Soviet resolution that UNSCOP should submit proposals 'on the question of establishing without delay an independent State of Palestine' twenty-six to fifteen (with two abstentions and two absences); Johnson spoke against the Soviet proposal, warning that it would prejudge the issue. Accordingly, on 15 May, the Special Session of the General Assembly adopted the terms of reference for UNSCOP proposed by the First Committee; these terms granted the widest powers of investigation, subject matter and procedure 'relevant to the problem of Palestine' and required that the Secretary General had its report by 1 September containing 'such proposals as it may consider appropriate for the solution of the problem'.[15]

Cadogan felt the terms of reference were satisfactory, and Garran briefed Sargent to this effect on 23 May. The Arab delegations were unhappy, however, at their failure to disconnect the DP issue from UNSCOP's terms of reference and had warned the First Committee on 12 May that any recommendations incompatible with Arab demands would not be accepted. Accordingly Cattan of the AHC intimated to Cadogan that the Palestine Arabs favoured a boycott of UNSCOP, which was indeed to be the way of it. It is important to remark the British Government's private expressions of satisfaction with terms of reference which allowed for a wide-ranging enquiry without preconditions, despite the very evident Arab dislike of these terms. In fact Cadogan realized that he had crossed the Rubicon to some extent, for he confided in his diary on 13 May after mentioning the decision on the terms of reference:'I shall be stuck in the back by the Arabs'. This outcome accorded with the priorities set out in the brief for the British delegation which Attlee had approved on 24 April.[16]

The final meeting of the Special Assembly approved a resolution calling upon all and sundry to refrain 'from the threat or use of force or any other action which might create an atmosphere prejudicial to an early settlement' for Palestine pending the General Assembly's decision. This was an attempt to forestall terrorist action, illegal immigration or assistance with either and was of special importance to the British Government. As early as 12 March, the Defence Committee had urged an approach to the UN Secretary General to obtain an appeal against aiding further illegal immigration, while on 19 March, Creech Jones admitted in the House of Commons that during 1946, 19,500 entry certificates had been granted to Jews coming to Palestine of whom 11,976 'had attempted to enter the country as illegal immigrants'. The British authorities were finding it extremely difficult to control the problem, especially following the sabotage of two large ships which had been used to take illegal arrivals in Palestine over to camps in Cyprus, and the COS feared they would be swamped by a further influx. Terrorism itself also concerned the Cabinet where, on 20 March, criticism was voiced of the apparently meagre effect of imposing martial law in Palestine between 2 and 17 March. The upshot of these concerns which preoccupied the British Government far more than the likely size, membership or terms of reference of UNSCOP was that Baxter issued instructions to Cadogan, with Attlee's approval, on 29 March. Cadogan was asked to approach the Secretary General in order to elicit some pronouncement against any action by member states while Palestine was *sub judice*; it was suggested that this would be best accomplished after the Special Session convened. Cadogan was also provided with an interesting brief drawing attention to the fact that 'the headquarters of this [illegal immigration] traffic would now appear to be in the south of France' and consequently 'strong representations' were being made to the French Government. Other concerns and US wariness at the Special Session impeded Cadogan from obtaining early satisfaction and it was left until the final meeting before the UN took cognizance of the British Government's worries, providing a further indication of Britain's lack of leverage in New York even on a matter of such concern to her authorities.[17]

At this same meeting Gromyko pointed out that an equitable solution to the Palestine problem required consideration of 'the legitimate interests of both' Arabs and Jews. He felt that 'an independent, dual, democratic, homogeneous Arab–Jewish State' would be 'one of the possibilities' for recognizing these interests, but if such a State proved impossible because of poor Arab–Jewish relations, partition into two autonomous states should be considered. One interpretation of Gromyko's statement was to see an emerging bias in Soviet policy towards the Zionist goal of statehood, a tendency implicit in Cadogan's remarks about the attitudes of Grenados and Fabregat. However, the Foreign Office did not see it that way, Beith of the Eastern Department minuting automatically that the Soviets 'are clearly at pains to keep on the fence', which was a curious accolade for what was a significant and gratuitous Soviet comment entertaining quite favourably the idea of a Jewish state. It suggests that the FO held preconceived notions of how the USSR would exploit British difficulties in the Middle East, that is by currying favour with the Arabs. These notions relegated the Soviet support for partition and the creation of a Jewish state to the very fringes of the remotest possibility in May, yet this support was to be a reality in October. Beith's comment does suggest that the Foreign Office was slow to wake up to this direction in Soviet policy.[18]

Concluding now from all the evidence, it is clear that the actual way Britain referred Palestine to the UN was important. The concerns which most exercised the British Government were the statement Cadogan was to make and the onerous and immediate business of containing terrorism and illegal immigration. It was these issues which most occupied the Cabinet, the Defence Committee and the Foreign Office. Matters such as the terms of reference for UNSCOP were practically unconsidered even within the Foreign Office, while the size and composition of the committee was the subject of modest concern and Cadogan's instructions pressed on him a very low-key approach to try to ensure a neutral investigation. This emphasis is in diametric contrast to the British atitude in 1945, when the Anglo-American Committee was instituted; then every concern focused upon the terms of reference, whereas little if any attention was paid to the immediate situation in Palestine or to undertakings about what to do with the eventual recommendations. This points to a simple truth. The passage of time had wrought a vast change in British policy. No longer was her government confident in its ability to handle the situation and prepared to await recommendations before considering long-term policy. In 1947 Britain was eager for a helping word from the UN to contain the turmoil in Palestine and most desperately anxious to avoid extending her responsibilities by having to enforce a future UN policy for the Holy Land. All other concerns were definitely subordinate. Therefore we can see that the decision to quit Palestine was implicit not only in the decision to refer the matter to the UN in the first place, but also in the actual concerns during the process of that referral. It is clear, too, that the Foreign Office hoped to salvage the bedrock of its Palestine policy, the retention of Arab goodwill, by avoiding any commitment to enforce a UN plan. Accordingly, although Britain's Palestine policy had changed, her Arab policy had not. Strangely, some Zionist observers at the time and since have been convinced that Britain's referral to the UN constituted a smoke-screen behind which her hold over Palestine was to be maintained. The argument runs that the British Government was calling the Americans' bluff, saying effectively that she would pull out of Palestine regardless of the consequent Soviet gain unless the US Government put up with and shut up about her Palestine policy. The evidence to support this contention is slender, and mention is usually made of some remarks of Beeley's to David

Horowitz, an official, no less, of the Jewish Agency.[19] Apart from this being a curious way of exposing the innermost intentions of the British Government, this version of the truth appears to be utterly unsubstantiated by anything in the British documents, instructions, memoranda or in the minutes of officials, which show plainly that all of the British Government's concerns at this time revolved around the speedy liquidation of the burdens of the Mandate, if necessary by leaving Palestine, while aiming to accomplish this with the minimum damage to Anglo-Arab relations.

UNSCOP's Report

UNSCOP convened for the first time in New York on 26 May, but adjourned quickly since only five of the eleven members were represented by their principal nominees. It met in public on 2 June with only Fabregat absent, and proceeded to elect Justice Sanstrom of Sweden to be Chairman with Dr Ulloa of Peru as Vice-Chairman. Soon afterwards the Committee embarked for Palestine where it began formal hearings in Jerusalem on 16 June, the decision to quit the charged environs of New York at this early stage being made in an attempt to pacify Arab feelings by distancing the Committee from the hub of Zionist advertising.[20] We shall look briefly at the evidence heard by the Committee and at its deliberations in order to try to explain why it made the recommendations it did, but first we must establish the attitude of the British and US governments to its investigations.

The attitude of the British authorities to UNSCOP was one of paternal neutrality. The authorities were quite prepared to lavish any amount of information upon the Committee, a desire no doubt encouraged by the initial appraisal of its members by the First Secretary of the Palestine Government, H. L. Gurney. He confided to Martin:

> I should perhaps add that we are astounded at the complete ignorance of [on] the part of the Committee of anything concerning Palestine. They indeed have a lot to learn and I do not see how they are going to do it in so short a time. When I talked to them for three hours I was reminded of the verse in the 'Snark' [by Lewis Carroll] which begins: 'The indictment had never been clearly expressed'.

Besides the verbal evidence of officials in Palestine, the British authorities submitted a vast quantity of written data such as the 'Supplementary Memorandum by the Government of Palestine' of 17

July, which included notes on oral evidence the Committee had heard, and also a memorandum entitled 'The Political History of Palestine under British Administration' by Beeley. Both documents were comparatively anodyne and avoided suggesting any future course of action. On 7 July, MacGillivray, an officer of the Palestine Government who had been appointed at UNSCOP's request in a liaison role, supplied Mohn (Sandstrom's alternate) with a copy of Sir Douglas Harris's analysis of past partition plans. This copy was strictly for the use of Mohn, Sandstrom and Bunche, the American member of the UN Secretariat detailed to UNSCOP, and it was handed over because it had become clear that the Committee was studying forms of partition. Harris had prepared this material in March to help the UN 'adjudicate speedily' between various partition ideas on the basis of proper data; it scrupulously avoided expressing any British preference. Beeley felt that its submission at this stage was all right, and on 24 July, the Foreign and Colonial Offices agreed formally to the submission but to remain uncommitted as to the acceptability of any hypothetical plan. One of the plans described in Harris's memorandum was coyly referred to as the 1943 'revision' of the Peel Commission's partition plan. This revision was in fact the first version of the partition scheme approved by the Morrison Committee of the War Cabinet, but was naturally kept a dark secret as Mathieson pointed out to MacGillivray on 15 August:

> It will be most undesirable ... to give a public indication at this stage that in 1944 a scheme of partition ... was approved by a ministerial committee of the War Cabinet which was predicated upon an arbitrary adjustment of Arab sovereignty.

The FO would find such a revelation of previous dalliance with and rejection of partition a matter of the 'liveliest regret'! This serves to highlight the considerable efforts made by the British authorities to avoid expressing any preference to UNSCOP about the future. On 5 July Cunningham reported his vacant response to Sandstrom's idea of obtaining HMG's view even through 'underground' channels:

> He [Sandstrom] particularly mentioned that they would like to know in this manner whether there was any likelihood of His Majesty's Government accepting any proposals they had in mind and also ... [HMG's] views on the practicability of any scheme ... I made no comment.

Beeley minuted showing that he was tempted to give the Committee the benefit of our 'twenty-five years' experience' in this way, but there is no evidence to suggest that it happened and the deliberations of UNSCOP strongly suggest that it did not. The final word seems to have been said by Martin, Assistant Undersecretary at the CO, to Butler, his opposite number at the FO. Martin felt that it would be undesirable to incur suspicions of influence and it would be most awkward also because HMG 'have themselves failed to make up their minds and there is no clear policy' on a solution for Palestine. Accordingly, no representative of HMG travelled to Geneva to give evidence before UNSCOP, and the Committee, having been showered with well-meant, well-balanced and well-written material by the British authorities, was left appropriately and disastrously in the dark about any preferred solution.[21]

The Delphic and verbose species of neutrality assumed by the British authorities contrasted curiously with the US Government's tongue-biting efforts to say or imply absolutely nothing while UNSCOP was at work. This extended even to the nomenclature of things Palestinian, as the State Department's circular telegram of 13 June showed:

> Dept concerned by current tendency ... to describe various solutions which have been suggested in recent years as, for example, 'the Arab plan', 'the Jewish plan', 'the British plan for provincial autonomy', or 'the American plan for a partition of Palestine'.
>
> Dept realizes many persons ... use such descriptions as labels. Dept is convinced however that others may reiterate such descriptions for propaganda reasons, thereby conveying impression that those to whom proposed solution is attributed favor one solution as opposed to another.

Accordingly, Marshall's telegram instructed diplomatic posts to 'make clear that this Govt has not at any time put forward or supported any plan for future of Palestine and at this stage it is not supporting any solution in preference to another'. Marshall explained to Austin something of the State Department's rationale for this attitude, arguing that UNSCOP's speedy departure from New York without any hearings made any governmental statement superfluous, while the problem of enforcing any solution made it desirable to review the matter carefully before taking a public position. This perception of treading on eggshells was reflected too in Henderson's important and reflective memorandum of 7 July which *inter alia* recommended that the US government avoid taking any 'public, definite position with regard to the future government of Palestine' until UNSCOP had reported and the British, Jews and Arabs had given their reactions. Clearly the State Department was doing its best to avoid either prejudicing the Committee or exposing itself and Truman to another spate of Zionist lobbying. It is interesting to remark in passing how much Henderson's views had changed, for according to McClintock of the office of Special Political Affairs, on 21 May, Henderson was hoping to head off Zionist pressure by an early official communication to UNSCOP proposing that:

> Palestine be placed under temporary trusteeship, either with Britain as the administering authority or with a joint United Nations trusteeship made up of several powers. Immigration would be carefully controlled ... Independence ... would only be achieved after there was a clear consensus of feeling among the inhabitants.

This view, which McClintock understood was in preliminary draft from, vanished for reasons that are not clear from the records but, one must surmise, because it was felt that such a position would expose the US Government to more, rather than less, Zionist presure. After all, Truman was clearly eager to pour oil onto troubled waters, for he made a statement on 5 June, urging all US citizens 'meticulously to refrain' from encouraging passions or violence in Palestine. Memories of his earlier futile exertions on behalf of the 100,000 Jewish DPs still rankled, as Forrestal records, when Palestine was discussed in Cabinet on 8 August:

> The President interjected that he proposed to make no announcements ... until after the United Nations had made its finding. He said he had stuck his neck out on this delicate question once, and he did not propose to do it again.

This attitude certainly helps to account for the fanatically non-committal stance of the State Department on the subject of Palestine, as well as the brusque tone and calculated equivocation in the reply Truman made on 6 August to Wise's request that he should intervene to halt the cycle of violence: 'there seeems to be two sides to this question. I am finding it rather difficult to decide which one is right'. Accordingly the US Government betrayed by neither a flicker nor a whisper any viewpoint of its own about Palestine's future, so, with the cautious neutrality of the British authorities too, this left UNSCOP to deliberate in a deceptive, pregnant tranquillity which contrasted strangely with what Bunche jokingly called 'the monotony of daily bombings, shootings, kidnappings, sirens, security checks and ducking ... barbed wire' of the Committee's sojourn in the Holy Land.[22]

The Arab Higher Committee's decision to boycott UNSCOP was a curious mixture of petulant protest and paranoia. Jamal Husseini's explanation, conveyed to the State Department on 11 June, enumerated the various objections to UNSCOP's membership and terms of reference which had manifested themselves in the Special Assembly, denouncing the 'Policy [of] procrastination through investigating committees well understood by Arabs; their rights need no bargaining or confirmation.' UNSCOP's reply to this boycott was restrained, Sandstrom commenting to journalists on his arrival in Palestine that: 'It would be easier and more correct, if they were right, to come and give their opinions'. The next day, coincidentally with an Arab strike in Palestine, he broadcast an appeal evidently directed at reassuring the Arabs of the committee's impartiality, while on 17 June, UNSCOP decided in secret session to reject the proposal of the Yugoslav alternate to issue a statement censuring the AHC's attitude and to let the matter alone for the present. On 10 July, the AHC turned down the Committee's final appeal. The AHC's attitude was carried to such extremes as evacuating an Arab village through which the Committee passed during its tour of Palestine; there can be no doubt that this attitude damaged the Arab case to some extent.[23]

In his analysis of the Palestine Arabs' thinking, Cunningham reported to the Colonial Secretary that the Arabs regarded the Special Assembly as an

> elaborate Anglo-American–Zionist conspiracy. ... They are consequently evincing pronounced symptoms of political paranoia; all the world seems banded together to deny Arab rights ... even Ibn Saud, so long sacrosanct, is suspected of amenability to dollar persuasion.

In fact, if Prince Faisal's comments to the British embassy in Washington were an honest reflection of Saudi views, then these coincided closely with those of his brothers in Palestine, for Faisal felt that the Committee's conclusions would inevitably be pro-Zionist owing to the US involvement in Palestine. There were other signs besides the suspicions of the Palestine Arabs that Arab solidarity was not all that it might be, for Abdullah conveyed to the British Government on 30 July that he had rejected partition before UNSCOP for tactical and political reasons only; he really favoured it and wanted to take over the Arab sector of Palestine. Beeley commented drily that 'His Majesty seems to have missed the bus' in view of the 'resolute opposition of the Mufti' and the elements of economic unity contained in the scheme of partition currently being considered by UNSCOP. Abdullah's was not the only Arab testimony heard by the committee which eventually travelled to Beirut to hear the views of Lebanon, Egypt, Iraq, Saudi Arabia and Syria on 22 and 23 July. Arab solidarity was insufficient even at this point to react uniformly to UNSCOP, and apparently there was no British diplomatic lobbying to help ensure the boycott was not universal.[24]

But of more importance is the effect on UNSCOP itself; there is no evidence to suggest either that the Arab case went by default, or that the Committee resented the attitude of the Palestine Arabs. However it is clear that, in these circumstances, the Arabs made a more fragmented and less effective submission to UNSCOP than the Jews, and perhaps symbolic was the heated and unusual questioning by the Moslem Sir Abdur Rahman (of India) of Ben Gurion before a vocal and committed Jewish audience in Jerusalem. Rahman wanted Ben Gurion to 'be precise' about the basis of the Jewish claim to Palestine, and it was of course upon this historical legalism that the Palestinian Arabs based their claim to determine their own future. In its final deliberations the Committee was to accord this aspect no more than equal weight alongside the political and contemporary demands being made upon Palestine by the Jews. Perhaps this was the result of the bias in the testimony the Committee heard, a consideration which the US representative in Jerusalem encouraged; on 3 August he wrote to Merriam:

> In the five weeks of the UNSCOP inquiry, when the Jews enjoyed 100% of UNSCOP's time and attention, we have been unable to discover ... [except in Weizmann's and Magnes' testimony] a single word showing on the Jewish side recognition or even realization that the primary interest of the UN in the Palestine problem is the preservation of peace. The Arab side was treated as non-existent, except when prodded into existence by UNSCOP delegates.[25]

The US representative was certainly correct about the Jewish monopoly of UNSCOP's hearings while it was in Jerusalem, although of course the Mandatory Government had a good say as well. The Jewish Agency put forward a powerful case for a Jewish state, Shertok making it plain on 19 June in a private hearing that it would be acceptable to establish a Jewish state by a partition of Palestine.

Subsequent testimony by Horowitz sought to show that Jewish settlement had not displaced the Arabs but had improved their economic position, and that the economic absorptive capacity for further Jewish immigration was vast. On 8 July the Committee heard Weizmann's evidence and, although Ben Gurion afterwards made it plain that he did not speak for the Agency, it was clear that he urged a Jewish state be created on the basis of the Peel partition plan plus the Negev, and in this matter his testimony was similar to that of the Agency's officials. Apart from these formal hearings, clandestine meetings also took place between some members of the Committee, its Secretariat and, in Bunche's words, 'with the High Command of Hagana and with some prominent Arabs who were willing to talk if they could keep up the appearance of observing the boycott'. There was also one between Bunche, Sandstrom, Hoo (the personal representative of the UN Secretary General to UNSCOP) and Begin of the Irgun, probably on 4 August. The meeting provided evidence that the Irgun, Stern Gang and Hagana co-operated from October 1945 until August 1946 when the latter broke off the agreement, but for the Committee the significant passages, marked on the transcript in the UNSCOP files were those which spelt out the Irgun's claim to the traditional land of Eretz Israel both east and west of the Jordan, and that 'Irgun rejects partition and will fight agianst it'. For light relief from these activities the Committee toured various parts of Palestine, including Tel Aviv and the Jewish settlements in the Negev where they were fêted; inevitably, perhaps, in these circumstances individual members of the Committee became identified with certain views. Granados and Fabregat were both considered pro-Zionist and both later received the distinction of having Tel Aviv streets named after them, whereas Rahman was conspicuous by his absence from the tour of Tel Aviv.[26]

But, to judge from Bunche's remarks and from the Committee's ready agreement that the Mandate was unworkable, the abiding impression the Committee members carried away with them was not so much of Zionist talk but of Zionist terror and illegal immigration. On 16 June, the very day that UNSCOP began its hearings in Jerusalem, the British authorities passed a sentence of death on three members of the Irgun convicted of raiding the prison at Acre. The Committee unwisely became embroiled in what was a rather run-of-the-mill matter for Palestine and by a vote of nine to one with one abstention expressed concern to the British Government at the possible unfavourable repercussions of this sentence, although Cunningham later reported Hoo's comment that several delegates would not have voted for this step had they realized that it was up to the High Commissioner to confirm or commute the sentences of death. The affair escalated unpleasantly, for on 12 July the Irgun kidnapped two NCOs and held them hostage for the lives of their comrades; on 31 July, the day after the executions were carried out, the NCOs were found hanged and the site mined. Troops in Tel Aviv went on the rampage as a consequence. The Jewish Agency deplored the action of the extremists, but it escaped no one's notice that its military organization the Hagana continued to promote illegal |immigration which in turn raised the tension between Arabs, Jews and Mandatory Government. UNSCOP was present in Palestine when this promotion reached its climax with the arrival of 4,554 immigrants on board the *Exodus*, formerly the river-steamer the *President Warfield*, which had embarked from the south of France. The *Exodus* was a propaganda coup of the first order as Lord Bethell's account makes clear; what better symbol of Zionist determination and British brutality could there be than the night-long radio broadcasts from the ship as the Royal Navy struggled to board it at sea, and the much-photographed spectacle of the battered vessel with its overcrowded, bloodstained human cargo being escorted into Haifa on 18 July? Although it undoubtedly went down well with Zionist sympathizers in the USA, there is evidence to suggest that it proved counter-productive for impressing the Committee. Sandstrom and Simic (the Yugoslav delegate) witnessed the transshipment of the would-be immigrants onto vessels that were to take them back to Europe; MacGillivray reported Sandstrom as saying he sympathized with their plight but was sickened by the capital made out of it by Zionist propaganda. He noticed a bloodstained British soldier carrying a suitcase down the ship's gangway for a crying boy, comforting him with the words 'Cheer up laddie, it won't be long before you're back here'. Sanstrom wondered aloud why the newspapers didn't report that. The incidents of the *Exodus* and the NCOs, together with the continuous pattern of security precautions, alerts and the Palestine Government's helpful attitude left the Committee favourably impressed with the British efforts in the face of difficulties and provocation; Gurney noted the growing friendliness of most of the Committee (the exception being Granados and Fabregat) which developed during mid-July. It was at this time that Bunche wrote to a friend in the UN Division of Trusteeship, repeating a witticism of Atyeo's (the Australian alternate) as amended by himself; they proposed:

'Give Palestine back to the Turks with a substantial bonus to them for taking it.' Since they had it once before they can't be easily fooled.

Somehow this attempt to make light of the Palestine question betrays exasperation and a weariness with the passions involved, and indeed it would seem that, as with the Anglo-American Committee, the Zionists were in danger of overplaying their hand and tiring their audience.[27]

Replete with these impressions of Palestine under the Mandate, the Committee proceeded to Beirut and from there to Geneva where, Bunche hoped, 'the Committee's genius will reveal itself'. At the beginning of August a sub-committee including Hood (the Australian delegate), Granados and Fabregat visited some of the DP camps in Germany and Austria. MacGillivray, who accompanied the Committee to Geneva where he spoke with members of Hood's sub-committee, reported that they had been impressed by the 'stark determination of nearly 100% of the inmates ... to get to Palestine', by the evident success of the Jewish Agency 'in inducing this state of mind', and by the vast numbers involved, estimated at 250,000. But already by this stage the Committee had begun its Herculean labour of thrashing out and writing up a plan for Palestine's future, a process in which Bunche played a crucial role in timetabling, co-ordinating and drafting.[28]

As soon as the Committee was settled in Geneva its members received a 'Memorandum by the Chairman on the Future Work-Program', probably drafted by Bunche. It proposed, in view of the 'very limited time at our disposal', a series of discussions focusing upon various options for Palestine's future, and based upon memoranda submitted 'by the Chairman with the assistance of the Secretariat and by such of the Committee members as may choose to do so'. According to MacGillivray's intelligence, Rahman insisted that the discussions should be informal and that no records be kept, but there are records of some of these 'informal private meetings' in the UN archives. The first such discussion on 6 August reached the conclusions that, as Lisicky (of Czechoslovakia) told MacGillivray, the Mandate could not continue and 'that it should be replaced by a form or forms of government which would give independence ... at the earliest possible moment'. Most of the delegates showed an acute awareness of the new political demands being placed upon Palestine by the Zionists and in consequence of the holocaust, and drew their conclusions from what they had seen of the results:

Entezam (Iran): ... [Mandate] has become impracticabie. Obligations imposed on Mandatory involve National Home. Mandate must end and independence be given ....

... one part of population of Palestine cannot be submitted to another ....

Sandstrom (Sweden): Mandate unworkable and must be abolished.

Independence in one form or another must be granted.

Mandate only a statement of policy which can be changed. ... Jews cannot claim an absolute right to the country on the basis of the Mandate, the Balfour Declaration, or on any other grounds.

Cannot accept either extreme claim—all Arab or all Jewish state.

Must find a compromise between basic aims—immigration on Jewish side and independence of Arab.

It would seem the Committee had formed the impression from the evidence it had heard and seen that the basic problem was not with an imperial power's effort to stay where it was not wanted, nor with a corruption of some legal right, be that Arab self-determination or promises given to the Jews; rather the problem was seen very much as the unhappy child of the times, of irrepressible Zionist aspirations, resentful Arab reactions and a floundering Mandatory Government.[29]

At this first meeting Justice Rand, the Canadian delegate, put forward a scheme for territorial partition of Palestine with 'some economic inter-relationship'. His memorandum, evidently handed to Bunche on 12 August, expanded this idea carefully. He proposed 'three independent states'—a Jewish state, an Arab state and a state of Jerusalem. In the latter Jews, Arabs and Christians would have an equal say in the government, but no state was to be allowed any military forces. The memorandum went into considerable detail of this sort, but the salient elements in Rand's proposal were a tripartite partition with a Central Authority, the whole to operate under the auspices of the UN. Economic union would be possible under this limited species of independence, but nevertheless immigration into the Jewish state was to be up to 'the Jewish Agency'. Britain was to preside over the transitional period and was to be allowed base rights in future. Now this whole scheme was most important for it represented the genesis of the Majority Report of UNSCOP. Rand had hatched his plan early in the Committee's time at Geneva, and it contained elements which attracted not only the pro-partitionists but also those who favoured some sort of confederation and others who had reservations about the economic viability of any completely independent state carved out of a land as small as Palestine. Bunche clearly identified the plan as a potential winner, since his files contain a lengthy and critical analysis of it which proposed various alterations. Bunche was particularly critical of the curious status of the Central Authority *vis-à-vis* the states, warning that: 'It is useless to propose granting independence with one hand and taking it away with the other'. Significantly it was this feature of Rand's scheme which was to disappear, while the tripartite partition and economic union was retained. It was to prove sufficient of a compromise to attract eventually the backing of the majority of the Committee.[30]

Meanwhile the Committee's fourth informal meeting had taken place on 8 August, and was important because it showed a clear division opening up between those who favoured some sort of partition and those who opposed it. Entezam and Rahman figured amongst the latter, principally on the grounds of the substantial Arab minority which would be left in any Jewish state, while the others whose views were recorded favoured some sort of partition with the exception of Hood (of Australia) who questioned its enforcement and finality. He was ultimately to abstain from both the Majority and Minority Reports. Both Rahman and Simic (of Yugoslavia) submitted memoranda proposing a unitary state with safeguards for minorities, Simic expressing the opinion that immigration would be possible on the basis of a common agreement. Entezam appartently did not submit a memorandum but was to join Rahman and Simic in the Minority Report which recommended a Federal state.[31]

On 13 August Bunche had 'a casual conversation at dinner' with Crossman. It must have been a good dinner, for Bunche's three-page memorandum showed Crossman's views to be wild in the extreme; for instance:

> Mr. Bevin, alleges Mr. Crossman, is definitely anti-Semitic and pro-Arab.
> Mr. Attlee ... is mildly anti-Semitic only because he regards the Zionists and the Palestine question as a terrible nuisance. Mr. Eden ... tends to be pro-Arab primarily because he had the unusual honour of gaining a first at Oxford in Oriental studies.

These allegations, one might presume, were jocular exaggerations; certainly there is no evidence that Bevin was anti-Semitic, as Lord Bullock (1983) and Michael Cohen (1982) agree, whereas Attlee evinced no such racialism and Eden's intellectual debt to the Eastern Department of the Foreign Office passed unacknowledged. However,

Crossman did press the case for a clean-cut partition 'with no strings attached', and warned of the importance of getting the transitional arrangements right because, in his view, otherwise Bevin would use the threat of immediate British withdrawal and refusal to assume any responsibility for enforcement as a way of defeating partition 'to perpetuate British occupation of Palestine'. The evidence shows that Crossman was no more accurate about the government's wish to stay in Palestine than he was about Bevin's outlook, and one suspects his judgement was clouded by considerable, mutual personal animosity. Crossman's views were important, however, because the next day he appeared at the Committee's seventh informal meeting. Quite why this happened is not clear from the records, but presumably his experience as a member of the Anglo-American Committee was felt to make him a valuable witness. The Committee 'studied partition maps' with Crossman on 14 August, and heard his opinion on partition and his strictures on the 'need for national contingents other than British for enforcement'. Later in the day, evidently spurred but not convinced by Crossman's warning, the Committee discussed the interim period and agreed: 'Request to UK to assume responsibility alone or with assistance of one or more other states'. Simic reserved his position on this point, but all agreed to the termination of the Mandate.[32]

In retrospect this was a fateful set of decisions, and there is nothing to suggest that the Committee was in fact aware of their incompatibility. The delegates had seen to the point of utter weariness evidence showing the Mandate to be unworkable and degenerating. The British Government had agreed in handing the problem to the UN. Yet all but Simic seemed to think that the British Government would be willing to continue its responsibility for Palestine in circumstances likely to be more trying than merely continuing the Mandatory *status quo*, namely for an interim period while a new plan was put into effect. It was precisely in order to avoid such an inference that so much energy had been expended on drafting Cadogan's statement, and Sir Alexander's carefully measured words before the UN First Committee had been designed to disabuse anyone of such an assumption. But nowhere is there any reference in the records of UNSCOP to this attitude or to Codogan's statement; the British authorities had insulated the Committee too thoroughly from their views. It is possible that UNSCOP's crucial line of reasoning is contained in an undated memorandum, probably written by Bunche a few days before this meeting. On the subject of enforcement of any solution the paper argued that, 'The difficulties in creating an international force

... are enormous.' It elaborated briefly on the process of the General Assembly deciding who should send what, the resulting fragmented force and the problem of who should pay. Inevitably the paper concluded 'the most practicable course might well be to designate the United Kingdom' to enforce the solution, with UN assistance if Britain so desired. It recognized however that:

> The current attitude of the Palestine population toward the British would make this an extraordinarily difficult task, which might well be accentuated by Arab and Jewish dissatisfaction with the final solution proposed.

Despite this pertinent observation, no mention was made of 'the current attitude' of the British Government towards Palestine either in this paper or in the records of the Committee's discussion; Cadogan had laboured in vain.[33]

However the Committee was, by mid-August, only feeling its way towards proposing any final solution. The files indicate the efforts made by Bunche to find the common ground of a majority. Apparently following the tenth informal discussion on 15 August, Bunche summarized the views of the Committee; all agreed on the termination of the Mandate, the importance of the transitional period and the desirability of Britain assuming enforcement responsibilities during this under UN auspices and, if the government desired, with help. But it was the actual solution which Britain was to be asked to enforce that still divided the Committee even at this stage; however, Bunche noted hopefully that, 'The gap would seem to be very narrow between those who favour partition without any enforced economic collaboration ... and those who envisage the necessity of such measures.' Working groups were formed to thrash out this problem, and also to draw up a plan for the Federal scheme preferred by the non-partitionists. Although the evidence in the UN files is not definite it suggests very strongly that it was Bunche who drew up the resulting drafts and also the Majority and Minority Reports themselves, a view which Wilson confirms.[34]

The Report was finished and signed on 31 August, just within the deadline, but it is not surprising in view of the painfully slow coalescing of the majority around the partition idea that this plan presented many weaknesses. The entire Committee was in agreement that the Mandate should be ended; their unanimity was to be expected after the evidence they had seen and heard. All but Granados and Fabregat concurred that Palestine could not provide a solution to 'the Jewish problem in general'. As for the future, a

Summary of UNSCOP Representatives' views at informal private meetings and the memoranda submitted during August 1947.

Source: UN arch. UNSCOP 1947 DAG 13/3.0.1. Boxes 1 and 2.

COUNTRY Representative Alternate	1st meeting, 6 August	4th meeting, 8 August	Memoranda handed to Bunch, 12 August	5th meeting, 13 August	8th meeting, 14th August	10th meeting, 15 August	Outcome
CANADA Rand Mayrand	Partition. Economic union.	Trusteeship not a solution.	Partition into 3 with political sovereignty (including immigration) and economic unity. UK to run transition.	Economic and social unity vital.	*ALL* informally agree: 1. termination of Mandate; 2. creation of an interim regime; 3. request UK to assume responsibility during this, with UN help if desired.	Partition with economic cooperation.	MAJORITY REPORT
INDIA Rahman Viswanathan	Independence.	Opposes partition; would cause war.	Unitary state with minority safeguards. Federal structure possible. Arabs and Jews would learn to cooperate.			Unitary state. Would consider a federal state.	Minority Report
PERU Ulloa Salazar	Independence, but Jews not to live under Arab rule. (Salazar)	Partition. Minorities a problem. Jerusalem to be international. (S)	Partition, with Negev to Jewish state. Economic cooperation needed. Jerusalem to be international. (Salazar)			Partition with economic cooperation. (Salazar)	MAJORITY REPORT
YUGOSLAVIA Simic Brilej	Independence.		Unitary independent state. Bicameral system for racial equality. Some local autonomy, including over immigration.	Agrees with Rand; unity vital.	Reserved position on point 3.	Federal state.	Minority Report
CZECHOSLOVAKIA Lisicky Pech	Independence; form to be discussed.					Confederation.	MAJORITY REPORT

GUATEMALA Granados Gonzalez	Independence with Jews' 'land of their own' in Palestine.	Partition. Minorities and economic problems.		Prefers unity; will consider partition. (Gonzalez)		Anything which gives independence and Jewish immigration.	MAJORITY REPORT
AUSTRALIA Hood Atyeo	Independence. Partition problems. Trusteeship possible.	Questions finality and enforcement of partition.		Partition and unlimited immigration impossible. (Atyeo)		No preference. Enforcement a crucial problem.	Abstained
NETHERLANDS Blom Spits	Independence after transitional period.	Interest in Rand's scheme. Problems in partition.	Prefers partition or federation. Enforcement a crucial problem; UK trusteeship with UN help.			Confederation preferred.	MAJORITY REPORT
IRAN Entezam Ardalan	Independence, but no Jew or Arab to be subject to other race.	Generally opposes partition; minority and economic problems.	Opposes partition; unity favoured.		Unitary state.		Minority Report
URUGUAY Fabregat Ellawi	Independence of both Arabs and Jews.					Partition with economic cooperation.	MAJORITY REPORT
SWEDEN Sandstrom Mohn	Independence with compromise between Arabs and Jews. Prefers partition.	Partition most practical, boundaries a problem.	Partition; will appease Jews and Arabs may accept. Firm enforcement needed.				MAJORITY REPORT

Minority Report (signed by the delegates from India, Iran and Yugoslavia) proposed a Federal State after a three-year transitional period under an authority to be designated by the General Assembly; this plan was, of course, still-born. The Australian delegate abstained from backing any proposal, leaving the Majority Plan of seven delegates to propose a tripartite partition creating a Jewish state, an Arab state and an internationalized Jerusalem under UN administration. There was to be an economic union of the states, since neither was felt to be viable on its own, and a two-year period of transition under British administration and UN auspices during which period 150,000 Jewish immigrants were to be admitted into the proposed Jewish state. The partition arrangements were justified on the grounds it was necessary to compromise between two legitimately based but now quite irreconcilable demands; partition was argued to be final and would remove the Arab fear of further Jewish immigration. But the drawbacks were enormous. Economic unity required some co-operation, as did the immensely complicated boundaries which, for example, left Arab Jaffa deep within the Jewish coastal plain and internationalized Jerusalem in the middle of the Arab state. Nothing the Committee had heard justified its sanguine expectations that such co-operation would be forthcoming. Worse still, the projected Jewish state was to contain some 498,000 Jews and between 407,000 and 497,000 Arabs (depending upon how many Bedouins there were), hardly a sound basis for Jewish self-determination on democratic lines.[35]

But the fatal limitation of the Majority Report was in its uncritical assumption that Britain would hold the ring during a two-year transitional period; the only crumb of comfort the Committee offered to the British authorities was that they could operate under UN auspices and, if they so desired, call upon the assistance of other unspecified members of the UN. Seemingly, the Committee members had not listened to Cadogan's statement carefully, nor had they allowed Crossman's warning to jog their memories, for it required no particular alertness to be aware that the British Government was unlikely both to overcome its evident exasperation with ruling Palestine and also to reverse its anti-partitionist policy, all at the say-so of seven out of eleven. It is hard to avoid the conclusion that the British authorities had allowed their own case to go by default. The Majority Report, responding to the Zionist case, the Balfour Declaration's promises and the DP situation, had proposed a Jewish state and the entry of 150,000 refugees within two years. The Arab attitude had been noted by the seven who had decided that the principle of self-determination did not entitle the upholding of the Arab view that there should be no Jewish state. The burden on the Mandatory Government had been noted to the extent that all the members of UNSCOP agreed the Mandate must end, yet the attitude of the British Government had not been considered. Nowhere in the Committee's deliberations is there an acknowledgement of HMG's efforts to avoid antagonizing 'the Arab world', nowhere is there recognition of her dislike of partition for this reason, and nowhere is there any acknowledgement of the mounting political and popular repugnance at shouldering the burdens of Empire in general and of the Palestine Mandate in particular. After all, it was these factors which had forced Britain to refer Palestine to the UN at the beginning of the year, and it was these factors too which had shaped the delicate phraseology of Cadogan's statement of 9 May. The Committee should have been alive to these pressures. However, it should have been possible for the British Government to assert itself more effectively too. Its record had been feeble. The ineffective British effort to regulate the size and membership of UNSCOP was an example, but with the possible exceptions of Granados and Fabregat, the British Government's fears over the question of the Committee's neutrality seem to have been groundless. Britain's effort to impose some sort of a moratorium on terrorism and illegal immigration had proved a conspicuous failure with the French authorities actually allowing the *Exodus* to depart even while UNSCOP was at work. Finally, it is clear, Cadogan's attempt to ensure that his government was not saddled with the unwelcome burden of enforcing a UN policy also failed. There is a simple explanation. First of all, the British Government was eager to maintain a strictly neutral and impartial stance towards UNSCOP because neutrality offered the best hope of extrication from Palestine without damaging relations with 'the Arab world'. Secondly, British policy had been suspended in a dangerously vague mode. The decision to leave Palestine was as yet unarticulated, due to the Chiefs of Staffs' position, and Britain had no helpful or coherent suggestion to make for Palestine's future. As Martin had reminded Butler in July, His Majesty's Government

'have themselves failed to make up their minds and there is no clear policy'

on a solution for Palestine. As a result UNSCOP unwittingly and insensitively fulfilled the role of janitor, merely opening the door and obliging the Mandatory power to collect itself together and to shuffle out of the Holy Land.

7

The Aftermath of the UNSCOP Report

The Majority Plan for the partition of Palestine realized the worst fears of the Foreign Office, the State Department and the Service chiefs on both sides of the Atlantic, but their influence on the policies of the British and US governments was diminishing. The reaction in London was predictably but absurdly prolonged and badly articulated. Having already abandoned hope of ruling Palestine by referring the problem to the UN without recommendations in February, it was to take a series of pronouncements and until the year's end for this British policy to reach its logical, inescapable conclusion in the enunciation of a date for the termination of the Mandate. The reasons for this protracted and unconvincing performance were firstly the elaborate effort to act the honest supplicant before the UN and remain 'neutral', and secondly the length of time taken postponing and then overruling the various weighty military objections to withdrawal. The end result was that Britain lost what was left of her leadership role over the Palestine problem. She stuck to a dogged abstentionist policy not only over the vote in the General Assembly on 29 November but also in her developing opposition to the idea of a UN Commission arriving in Palestine to arrange partition before her administration ended. The underlying rationale was simple: the pristine Foreign Office doctrine of seeking to maintain good relations with the Arab world which meant having nothing to do with partition even if partition was recommended by the UN.

That this salvage operation was to have some success was due more to the policy of the US Government than to any positive qualities. In stark contrast to the abnegation of responsibility by the Mandatory power for the future of Palestine, the US Government assumed a clear leadership role. By late November 1947 not only had the USA become the clear backer of the plan of partition, but also, so the evidence suggests, the White House had been instrumental in securing a two-thirds majority vote in the General Assembly. This White House stance was despite the wholehearted opposition of the officials in the State Department who must surely have envied their opposite numbers in the Foreign Office as Britain prepared to flit out of Palestine. To Loy Henderson and the Joint Chiefs of Staff it looked as though the poisoned chalice was changing hands and that the US Government was the gullible recipient.

His Majesty's Government's policy on the UNSCOP Report

There is nothing surprising about British policy on Palestine either during or after the deliberations of UNSCOP. Inevitably, the pattern was of consciously but artificially avoiding any decision which would anticipate UNSCOP's report, while all around the pressures on the Labour Government and the Mandatory authorities grew remorselessly. When the report appeared at the end of August it precipitated the lightning rehearsal of official, Service and Ministerial views which had changed little over the past nine or ten months. But this time, with no further options available, the conscious decision to withdraw from Palestine was actually taken by the Cabinet with anticlimatic ease, and made explicit by Creech Jones at the United Nations on 26 September. It had by then taken the British Government nearly eight months to conclude the logical sequence of policy decisions and to resolve the period of agonized uncertainty seen at its highest stage in the London Conference.

While UNSCOP was at work, the tone was set in London by the meeting on 24 July between Wright (who had just replaced Butler and was Superintending Undersecretary of both the Eastern Department and the North American Department), Garran (Assistant Head of the Eastern Department) and Beeley for the Foreign Office and Martin (Assistant Undersecretary), Trafford Smith and Mathieson for the Colonial Office. Martin mentioned that it was impossible for UNSCOP to be told what arrangements the government might find acceptable, and then proceeded to ask the FO representatives a leading question about the future. Martin enquired whether the department

> ruled out partition as a tenable solution. Mr. Wright said that in the Foreign Office view, HMG could not oppose any decision of the General Assembly, but on the question of assuming responsibility for such a decision the position was very different.

There was general agreement at the meeting that the government could refuse to have anything to do with a decision of the UN General Assembly. This attitude is significant for two reasons. First, it shows some apprehension on the part of the Foreign Office that UNSCOP and subsequently the General Assembly might indeed fasten upon the judgement of Solomon and recommend partition, and secondly it presaged accurately the response which Britain was to make to that recommendation when it actually appeared. Yet this attitude was in complete accord with all that had gone before. The FO's antipathy to partition had an impeccable and ancient pedigree. Furthermore, the British Government's anxiety to avoid the burden of enforcing any troublesome or controversial policy had been made explicit by Cadogan on 9 May, and it had of course been at the heart of British concerns for much longer. So British policy on Palestine was held in a state of suspended animation during the summer of 1947, frozen in mid-stride between the despairing gesture of surrendering the issue to the UN and the inevitable outcome of this step, withdrawal to avoid continuing along such a difficult path.[1]

While this official meeting talked only of refusing to implement any UN decision and avoided discussing withdrawal as the only option remaining under such circumstances, other pressures and opinions were more explicit. First among several resolutions on Palestine before the Labour Party Conference at the end of May was one calling for Britain to hand over responsibility for Palestine to the UN, and although Bevin fended off the matter by pleading that it was *sub judice* he sounded less than eager to continue to grapple with the problem of Palestine when he addressed the Conference:

> I cannot speak for the Government because we have not decided, but I personally would want to know whether all the other United Nations would accept the [UN] solution as well. ... I shall want to know, whether this thing is settled once and for all.

This statement failed to satisfy many members of the Parliamentary Labour Party and, on 23 July, nineteen of them, including Crossman, Foot, Callaghan, Mikardo and Castle, wrote to the Prime Minister proposing that Britain should announce a date for her withdrawal from Palestine in order to 'induce a sense of reality' as the same step over India had done. This group apparently took for granted the inevitability of such a withdrawal, but Dalton provided the telling rationale for it in his minute to Attlee on 11 August:

> I am quite sure that the time has almost come when we must bring our troops out of Palestine altogether. The present state of affairs is not only costly to us in man-power and money, but is, as you and I agree, of no real value from the strategic point of view—you cannot in any case have a secure base on top of a wasps' nest.[2]

Dalton was quite right. In May, Creech Jones had submitted a paper to the Cabinet which showed that the cost of terrorism to the public funds of the Palestine Government during the last two years had been five million pounds, while the current annual cost of security measures was eight million pounds. Although this expenditure was not a direct burden on the British Exchequer, other charges were, as Ovendale mentions in his study (1984). Together these certainly diminished the attractiveness of Palestine as a strategic investment, while the pressures of illegal immigration had a similar but still more corrosive effect. At the beginning of May the Cabinet had pondered the interception on the high seas of ships carrying illegal immigrants, but interception had been rejected because of practical difficulties and the invidious precedent which would have been established. Instead an official Inter-Departmental Committee was proposed to co-ordinate action to prevent the embarkation of would-be immigrants. Despite such exertions and the most vigorous, repeated and well-informed representations, the French Government failed to prevent the departure of the *President Warfield (Exodus)*. Consequently, both Bevin and Duff Cooper delivered resounding protests to Bidault on 12 July, but, although the latter gave his assurance that France would receive the passengers back and assist with the disembarkation of the Jews on board, the DPs were not disembarked onto French soil. The British Government eventually ferried the would-be immigrants back to Germany in three transport ships, amidst widespread condemnation, in a vain attempt to halt the flow by this example. In fact, the British Government's efforts to stop the tide were no more successful than Canute's, as a report from the British embassy in Warsaw reflected. Broad noted that the exodus of Jews from Poland peaked in July and August of 1946 when, in the wake of the Kielce pogrom, an estimated 40,000 had left. However, a probable 50–60,000 Jews were currently in Poland, the high figure possibly resulting from an influx from the East, and he noted pertinently that there was nothing illegal about their departure from Poland:

the illegal part of their trip only starts when they reach Palestinian ... waters. I gather, however, that there is a good deal of 'shanghai' business about all this and that Jews who say they want to leave Poland have very little chance, once they are taken over by one of these bodies [American Joint Distribution Committee, Jewish Agency Office, Hebrew Immigration Aid Society of Warsaw and another organisation in Lodz], of deciding their ultimate destination for themselves.

If diplomatic representations to halt the traffic were debilitating and futile, the effects on the Government of Palestine were worse. Obviously the sympathies of the Yishuv were with those would-be immigrants who attempted to run the blockade of the Royal Navy, but, in addition, terrorist action such as the murdering of the two NCOs by the Irgun at the end of July and the subsequent police riot showed that the security situation was almost out of control. Cunningham admitted as much to the Colonial Secretary on 7 August when he urged that troop numbers should be maintained at a level which enabled martial law to be imposed. His telegram continued, 'This measure now seems the only shot left in our locker. I cannot gruarantee that the situation will not deteriorate to such a degree that the civil government will break down'. Inevitably such perceptions and fears about the situation in Palestine contributed to Ministerial, parliamentary and public distaste for continuing with any British role in the country and helped to make easy the path of withdrawal.[3]

By August 1947, Ministerial and parliamentary indications of being fed up with Palestine are easy to find. According to Dixon's memorandum, Bevin told the US Ambassador bluntly that

the United States Government must not be surprised if matters went wrong when the Palestine question came up at the United Nations. We were disillusioned and disappointed by our thankless task as Mandatory, and might be forced to give up the charge.

Such sentiments were correctly noted by the US Secretary of State Marshall, and Forrestal records his saying the following in Cabinet on 8 August

Aside from the normal British doggedness in sticking out a difficult and unpleasant situation, he thought there was no particularly strong British desire to retain the mandate over Palestine.

Bevin nursed a particular grievance towards the US Government at this time which highlighted the ineffectiveness of diplomatic pressure in diminishing illegal immigration, for which funds were raised in the USA. The advertisement campaign was highly offensive to Britain; for instance *PM* on 5 June reprinted Ben Hecht's 'Letter to the Terrorists' which included the memorable travesty:

> Every time you blow up a British arsenal, or wreck a British jail, ... or let go with your guns and bombs at the British betrayers and invaders of your homeland, the Jews of America make a little holiday in their hearts.

Usually such advertisments, in this case 'to speed medical relief' to the 'Palestine Resistance Fighters' boasted that as charities they were exempt from US taxation, thus imparting an aura of official sanction. British diplomatic efforts to ensure that Americans and, indeed, European governments were disabused of this impression had met with partial success when Truman made his statement on 5 June urging restraint all round, but it took most of 1947 for the tax-free status of contributions to be called into question publicly despite repeated pressure on the State Department which was eventually conveyed to the US Treasury Department.[4]

Parliamentary reaction to the burden of the Mandate was highly vociferous and reached its peak in the adjournment debate on 12 August. There were powerful demands for a speedy British withdrawal. Former Colonial Secretary Stanley argued that if partition was impractical, Britain had to evacuate. Lever warned that nothing remained for Britain in Palestine 'except grief and suffering'. Foot demanded that the government 'make an act of policy for the first time in two years, and declare now that whatever decision is arrived at by U.N.O. we are going out of Palestine'. The Colonial Secretary himself acknowledged the public antipathy towards the Mandate and the questioning of the burden. Edelman conjured up a telling image of the vascillation in office of his party and its predecessors:

> I cannot help feeling that in dealing with Palestine successive Governments have been rather like a man suffering from a disease—a Palestine ulcer—who has gone from one doctor to another seeking not a diagnosis but the assurance that he is perfectly well and that all he needs is a rest and to leave matters exactly as they are.

Edleman hoped that the UN would give the final opinion which the government would accept, but it must be quite clear that Britain's disenchantment and abject inability to find a rest-cure for Palestine had become even more acute since the referral to the UN. It was with something of an effort that the guise of disinterested calm was maintained until UNSCOP reported, but with the majority recommendation for partition the policymaking machinery lurched ponderously into action once again. However, its conclusion was inevitable.[5]

Just three days after the UNSCOP report became available the Joint Planning Staff delivered their judgement. Their report, virtually unaltered, was made into a paper for the Cabinet and circulated by Alexander on 18 September. It had nothing good to say about the prospects which UNSCOP had opened up. If Britain were to implement the Majority Plan, reinforcements would be needed, whereas the Minority Plan could be implemented provided 'there was no appreciable Arab resistance' and that forces were kept at the present level. Either option was likely to 'entail a drastic revision of our Defence Policy' on the grounds both of the commitment of forces needed and because implementation of the Majority Plan 'would be at the immediate and lasting expense of our overriding strategic requirement of retaining Arab goodwill'. The future of these requirements under the Minority Plan was problematical. The only other option (short of annexation) was withdrawal without implementing either plan, but this too was unacceptable and the Cabinet was informed:

(i) The decision [to withdraw] might be impossible to implement. It would in any case present considerable military difficulties.

These 'difficulties' were in fact the root of the problem and were destined to take many weeks of haggling to resolve. The paper continued:

(ii) It may be taken as a further sign of weakness and lack of determination to maintain our position in the Middle East.
(iii) The only way to secure our long term strategic requirements will be by Treaty with the Successor States. Our demonstration of weakness ... may well convince these Successor States, and the Arab world as a whole, that Treaties with us are of little practical value.

To guard against Ministerial forgetfulness the appendix to the Cabinet paper comprised an extract from a paper submitted to the Defence Committee at the beginning of the year which outlined the 'Strategic Importance of Palestine'. It should come as no surprise that these requirements echoed faithfully the words of that paper's predecessor, which had been submitted to the Defence Committee on

18 June 1946 and merely noted, but not accepted, at the behest of the Prime Minister. By their seemingly unshakeable commitment to requirements which were becoming economic and political anachronisms the Chiefs of Staff were not only condemning themselves to the role of military Cassandras but also appearing to overlook what could be salvaged from a British withdrawal from Palestine. Their third point, quoted above, could have been adapted to a different purpose; a British withdrawal made apparently in order to avoid the implementation of a plan unacceptable to the 'Arab World' might in fact redound to the everlasting credit of Britain, and her strategic requirements, in Arab eyes. This Arab favour was the consolation which the Foreign Office was to grasp over the coming months, but seemingly the doom-laden report which the Minister of Defence laid before his colleagues was devoid of all hope.[6]

In considerable contrast to the military's attitude, the Colonial Office, faithful to its old position, regarded the Majority Plan as workable provided the boundaries were modified to reduce the number of Arabs in the Jewish state. This view was expressed in a memorandum submitted on 16 September to Bevin with a covering letter from Ivor Thomas who was at that time in charge of the Colonial Office while Creech Jones was away, delayed, according to Dalton, by a hurricane in the West Indies. The paper argued that Britain, by remaining neutral in the UN but by accepting UNSCOP's unanimous recommendations and even suggesting a date for withdrawal, could obtain a workable solution, avoid an Arab revolt and obtain military facilities into the bargain. Not only was this view inordinately optimistic and in stark contrast to that of the Services, but it had not been cleared with Creech Jones. In fact, Martin recorded the following June that on his return Creech Jones joined the Foreign Office and the Cabinet in eschewing the delicate footwork suggested by the CO and instead accepted the option of a straightforward withdrawal with all the enthusiasm that could be mustered.[7]

The Palestine Government initially embraced the Majority Report of UNSCOP with alacrity, informing the Colonial Secretary on 8 September that it envisaged a Jewish State in about six months' time; 'speed, finality and firmness' were seen to be vital and it was felt that martial law should contain the Arab reaction until ameliorated by the prospect of independence. Beeley was flabbergasted. He felt that the Palestine Government 'are already packing their bags' and regarded the effect of the suggested policy on Anglo-Arab relations as 'too obvious for comment'. The Palestine Administration was gently brought back to a consideration of the obvious, but the Foreign Office was not to rest content with a withering silence when it came to evaluating the UNSCOP report for the Cabinet.[8]

The crucial paper for the Cabinet was prepared in the Eastern Department and circulated over Bevin's initials on 18 September. Interestingly, Attlee saw it at the draft stage but his insubstantial suggested alterations were not incorporated and the final form of the paper was unchanged. After summarizing UNSCOP's report, the lengthy document reminded Ministers of the statement Cadogan had made on 9 May and went on to conclude:

> The majority proposal is so manifestly unjust to the Arabs that it is difficult to see how, in Sir Alexander Cadogan's words 'we could reconcile it with our conscience'. There are also strong reasons of expediency for declining the responsibility for giving effect to this proposal.

These reasons included the likely Arab rising in Palestine, the everlasing hostility of the Arab states alongside which any treaty rights in a Jewish state 'would be poor compensation', and the future tensions generated between Jews and Arabs. The Minority Plan was felt to be fundamentally marred by its requirement that Arabs and Jews should co-operate. The stress on the element of expediency suggests a new and more detached view of Palestine, which is indeed the tone of the final paper. An adjustment of partition to reduce the size of the Arab minority in the Jewish state was considered, as the CO had done, but Bevin's paper dismissed the idea because there was no prospect of making the scheme acceptable to both Arabs and Jews. The paper proceeded remorselessly towards its conclusion:

> The present situation in Palestine is intolerable and cannot be allowed to continue. His Majesty's Government have themselves failed to devise any settlement which would enable them to transfer their authority to a Government representing the inhabitants of the country. If the Assembly should fail, or if it were to propose a settlement for which His Majesty's Government could not accept responsibility, the only remaining course would be to withdraw from Palestine, in the last resort unconditionally.

Despite the consequent chaos and bloodshed, British lives and resources would be saved thereby. Here at last was expressed the logical and inescapable conclusion of the British Government's policy on Palestine. Bevin's final recommendations for the Cabinet were for the earliest possible announcement of Britain's intention to withdraw because 'there is a chance' that this statement might produce a UN solution or an Arab–Jewish agreement for which the government 'would feel justified in accepting responsibility', but the paper had made plain that such an outcome was a highly unlikely eventuality. Hence, Bevin warned that a further announcement would be necessary before the UN Assembly ended in order to give the date of the British evacuation.[9]

Bevin and the Foreign Office had argued a powerful case for withdrawal in the light of UNSCOP's report and in the expectation that the General Assembly would not improve upon its recommendations. Expediency was indeed the keynote, for by withdrawing and avoiding the responsibility for the enforcement of any plan Arab goodwill could be salvaged: 'we should not be pursuing a policy destructive of our own interests in the Middle East'. Understandably the Eastern Department had not found it easy to adopt this standpoint on withdrawal. Beeley wrote an early draft of this paper, dated 3 September, which considered the option of withdrawal only in one sub-paragraph, and gave it another mention at the end. Garran minuted that withdrawal was one point which would require careful consideration. Presumably Bevin himself instructed the clear adoption of the withdrawal option. Beeley's draft was extensively rewritten, and the final paper culminated in a six-paragraph analysis advocating withdrawal.[10]

The Services were less easily persuaded that withdrawal would be anything short of an unmitigated disaster for Britain's strategic requirements. The Joint Planning Staff paper of 19 September morosely pondered the problem of evacuation, then went on to list yet again the likely damage to British interests. The paper did, however, acknowledge: 'If, by convincing them [the Arab world] that our withdrawal is dictated by our refusal to implement a solution unjust to them ... there is some hope of recovering a part of our strategic position and requirements'. Someone had seen the Joint Planning Staff and he told the Eastern Department of the Foreign Office about an earlier draft which warned of a total collapse of Britain's position in the Middle East. In his own words, 'I persuaded them to take all this out, and as you will see the brief is not now altogether hostile to the Secretary of State's proposal'. So Bevin's withdrawal recommendation went before the Cabinet unchallenged, but in any case the Service Ministers and the COS were excluded from the Cabinet meeting on 20 September, although the Secretary of State for Air came in later. The cost of their military requirements, currently the subject of a strenuous debate in the Defence Committee, enabled

Bevin to brush aside the Air Staff's wish to stay in Palestine with the dismissive joke about helicopters, recorded by Dalton and quoted before.[11]

This Cabinet meeting in fact passed off smoothly, and the policy which Bevin had proposed in his paper was approved with an air of anticlimax. Creech Jones, Bevan, Shinwell and Cripps all spoke in favour of a British evacuation. Dalton repeated the views which he had conveyed to the Prime Minister on 11 August. Attlee concurred and drew a careful comparison with the withdrawal from India. He hoped that an announcement of Britain's intention to evacuate would have 'salutary results' but directed that the proposed statement for the UN should avoid any commitment to co-operate with other powers in implementing a solution and any reference to the points mentioned by the Secretary of State for Air.[12]

So it was that the British Government completed its final important act of policy for Palestine. The automatic and virtually uncontested nature of the step highlights the point that withdrawal from Palestine had been implicit in the earlier decision to refer the question to the UN without recommendations. Furthermore it was the inescapable consequence of the government having followed the Foreign Office's policy and staging a bewildering series of consultations with the Arab states over the preceding decade. As Edelman had described in the adjournment debate in August 1947, the advice which successive British governments received about the treatment of the 'Palestine ulcer' merely rendered a difficult situation insoluble. Withdrawal was now the only way. To remain in Palestine had become utterly unthinkable because of the burdens of the Mandate, the costs and the mounting public and parliamentary pressure. The Chiefs of Staff no longer exerted any suasion on the matter both because of the impossible costs of their plans to an economically beleaguered nation and because the United States was beginning to take up the job of containing any Soviet threat in the Eastern Mediterranean following the 'Truman Doctrine'. Hence the Cabinet embraced the policy of withdrawal with an unclouded sense of relief after its long and thankless efforts. Any sense of failure was overpowered, for the moment at least, by the belief that the *Pax Britannica* was not about to explode from any shortcoming in the policy pursued by His Majesty's Government.

Cadogan was told of the Cabinet decision by Creech Jones, who had travelled to New York to make the statement to the UN General Assembly. He was somewhat aghast, recording in his diary that: 'It is an ultimatum to the U.N.' He foresaw 'great difficulties' but shared a sense of relief. Marshall was also informed and reacted in a 'friendly and understanding' way, according to Cadogan's report, thus clearing the way for Creech Jones's statement to be made on 26 September before the Ad Hoc Committee which the UN General Assembly had set up to consider the UNSCOP report. The Colonial Secretary duly built up to the burden of his message that to avoid any possible misunderstanding he had been instructed by his government to announce 'that in the absence of a settlement they must plan for an early withdrawal'. He made it plain that the only 'settlement' which Britain would help to administer was one which her government felt was just and which would not require force. Cadogan noted the reaction in his diary: 'Well received by Arabs, but no one had thought it out.' This last was indeed to prove the problem. Creech Jones reported to London that the Jewish reaction seemed to interpret the move as one designed to perpetuate the British hold on Palestine, Garran noted on 1 October that there was widespread doubt in the Arab countries about the sincerity of Britain's withdrawal intention, but worse still was the Acting US Representative's comment on 11 October. Herschell Johnson told the Ad Hoc Committee of US support for the Majority Plan, an important decision, but what alarmed Creech Jones was the commonplace interpretation of the speech, the assumption of British responsibility for enforcement, albeit with some UN and US assistance. Bevin, concerned that the US Governmnet 'have not fully appreciated our determination to withdraw', quickly secured Attlee's approval for another statement by Creech Jones who was told to 'rub in the implications' of the Cabinet's decision.[13]

The British Government seemed to be taking part in a dialogue of the deaf, but one reason for there to be doubt about the sincerity of her intentions was the simple fact that she had not named a date for her withdrawal. In a personal telegram to Creech Jones sent at the same time as the instructions for issuing a further statement, Bevin noted, 'the difficulties everywhere which make it impossible for us to indicate publicly even a target date for our withdrawal.' Accordingly Bevin could only urge his colleague to press the earnestness of Britain's intention to quit and then express some hope that perhaps, in the absence of any considered plan to implement partition, then the US, the Jews and the Arabs 'may feel very differently' and reconsider their attitudes. This was a forlorn hope, but the difficulties in naming a date to which Bevin referred were more tangible. First, the initial timetable for withdrawal, drawn up by the Joint Administrative Planning Staff, and sent to the FO as an expression of the COS view, argued that the evacuation of forces from Palestine

> could be completed in some fifteen months from the date of authority being given. This time is dictated by the length of time required to build tented camps with hutted ancillaries in Cyrenaica.

This presupposed the development of Cyrenaica as a base in advance of any decision about its political future, and a high priority being accorded to shipping, building materials and finance. However it was felt that a 'most rapid withdrawal' could be effected within eight months of authority being given by accepting 'severe living conditions' for the soldiers. Either timescale with the various and elaborate preconditions set forth boded fair to stimulate a lively wrangle in the Defence Committee and certainly threatened to blunt the clarity of the Cabinet's withdrawal decision. However, other problems arose in the UN to further complicate matters.[14]

The second problem arose on 13 October when Tzarapkin, the Soviet delegate on the Ad Hoc Committee, announced that his government supported the partition plan and with it the creation of a Jewish state. The significance of this decision was not lost on the Chiefs of Staff. Indeed the most sinister ramifications were considered at their meeting on 22 October when the Chairman, the Chief of the Naval Staff Admiral Sir John Cunningham, argued that this made 'it most likely that any body succeeding British authority in Palestine would hold a Russian element', consequently the meeting re-emphasised that 'in future it would be essential to locate our forces in Libya, Cyprus and the Sudan in order to be able to get back into Egypt and Palestine in an emergency'. While the COS were clearly counting on shouldering the burdens of the world, the analysis from the British Ambassador in Moscow was refreshingly accurate and down to earth:

> Primary object of the Russians is ... to debar us and the Americans from establishing ourselves strategically in the eastern Mediterranean.
>
> Best method of achieving this seems to them to lie in encouraging partition since either party is thereafter likely to resent and oppose the establishment of bases in the territory of the other.
>
> Soviet Government no doubt also have in mind possibilities offered by continued unrest in Palestine as affecting whole Middle East.

Although certainty and Soviet foreign policy do not go together, this analysis seems valid and is substantially endorsed by Krammer's study (1973). Yet it involved a complete re-appraisal in the Foreign

Office. W. R. Louis (1984) has drawn attention to the perceived impossibility, in the FO's view, of Soviet support for partition which would effectively wreck any chance of UN support for such a solution when the matter was referred to the UN earlier in the year, and mention has been made earlier of the currency of this view in reaction to Gromyko's speech in May. Now there was no doubt of the Soviet attitude, but in a sense British policy on Palestine was past caring and there was nothing which could be done to counter the situation. Accordingly, Bevin responded vehemently to a US suggestion for manoeuvring theUSSR out of any UN peace-keeping force: 'But it must be made absolutely clear to the Americans that they cannot frighten us with this bogey into assuming responsibility ourselves for enforcing partition'. This reply was made on 5 November, some three weeks after Tzarapkin's statement, and two days later the Defence Committee took the decision to withdraw from Palestine by 1 August 1948. This decision followed the protracted labours of the Cabinet Official Committee on Palestine, created under Luke's chairmanship on 30 October especially to co-ordinate withdrawal plans, the duration of its deliberations reflecting faithfully the difficulty of its task amidst the various departmental views. Bevin in the Defence Committee postponed deciding whether the Mandate should end earlier pending the UN decision.[15]

Cadogan was not to announce this until 13 November, the further delay being attributable to a joint Soviet–American proposal in the UN Sub-Committee One that the British Mandate should end on 1 May 1948, that her armed forces be withdrawn by then and that a UN Commission should assist the Mandatory Power and subsequently run the country until partition by 1 July. To Bevin, this prospect was alarming because it appeared that British troops would be manoeuvred into acting as a screen for the UN Commission and continue to bear the burden of maintaining law and order. Consequently he confided to Cadogan that it would be preferable for the UN to make no recommendations, and for Britain 'to withdraw in our own way thus possibly influencing the *de facto* settlement' rather than avowedly underwriting a UN partition. As a result of all this Cadogan on 13 November pointed out that 'British troops would not be available as the instrument for the enforcement of a settlement in Palestine against either Arabs or Jews', that the withdrawal of troops would be effective by 1 August 1948, that responsibility for law and order would be accepted only for areas still occupied in the run-up to that date, and that the right to terminate the civil administration earlier was reserved. This statement was entirely consistent with the policy the

British Government had embarked upon early in 1947 and the single most remarkable feature of it was the length of time it had taken to articulate its attitude. It was not until after the UN Ad Hoc Committee had voted in favour of partition on 25 November that Cadogan was told of Ministerial approval for a withdrawal plan involving the termination of the Mandate on 15 May 1948, and this was not made public until 11 December when Creech Jones announced the decision to the House of Commons, long after the historic vote in the UN General Assembly on 29 November.[16]

Both at the time and since, the multiple and apparently grudging nature of the British Government's policy decisions cast in doubt the sincerity of her intention to quit Palestine. The decision to refer the matter to the UN had been taken in February in the full knowledge of all that this implied. Yet it had not been until September that the withdrawal decision had been made explicit, while actual dates were not filled in until November and December. Was Britain hoping that the UN would fail or that some miracle would unite Arabs and Jews into agreeing a compromise? The evidence for the existence of such a hope is slim indeed, confined to some expressions of pious optimism from Bevin and the Colonial Office. Nor does it make sense from the evidence to invest the Foreign Office misconception of Soviet policy with central significance. The overwhelming weight of evidence points to the decision to refer the Palestine problem to the UN without recommendations as the crucial and conscious turning point, itself the product of an erroneous and indecisive policy pursued over many years and culminating in the absurd stalemate of the London Conference. Throughout 1947 the British Government acted hesitantly and with no outward conviction; anxious to appear neutral while UNSCOP deliberated, at the same time her administration in Palestine was tottering, her Chiefs of Staff were strident and uncompromising in their articulation of strategic needs in the region, and her senior Ministers and parliamentary supporters were equally but conversely adamant in their demands for withdrawal. To these many-sided policy considerations must be added the curious pressures from the discussions in New York. Inevitably the consequence was less a decision to quit but rather a series of decisions, each following logically behind the next like a line of circus elephants, but amounting in the end to the terminally decisive act of British policy on the Holy Land. Britain's Palestine ulcer was about to be cured.

US policy on the UNSCOP Report and the vote in the UN

To say that US policy during the autumn of 1947 was fragmented is a truism. Beeley's report of 4 October from the United Nations is apposite:

> the attitude of the U.S. Delegation is still shrouded in obscurity. There is at least artistic truth in the rumour that they received from Washington a draft of a statement to be made in the [Ad Hoc] Committee, and rejected it as having no ascertainable meaning.[17]

The State Department was of course a dedicated opponent of partition, repeatedly going on record to this effect during the second half of the year, yet by late November the US Government had not only committed itself to supporting the UNSCOP Majority Plan of partition but also had exerted itself to obtain the votes of other delegations in the UN in favour of this line. Clearly the State Department was outmanoeuvred on this occasion. It was destined to have a Napoleonic return the following March when the US delegation at the UN proposed that a scheme of trusteeship should be substituted for partition and the creation of a Jewish state, only to meet its Waterloo in May when the creation of the state of Israel was met with a Presidential benediction in the form of *de facto* recognition. This second defeat highlights the underlying reason for the first; Trunam was favourably disposed towards the scheme of partition and this, together with other factors, ensured that the persuasive efforts of Loy Henderson's division were in vain.

In an important memorandum to the Secretary of State on 7 July, Henderson outlined four possible schemes for Palestine as envisaged by his division and by the Office of Special Political Affairs. Henderson argued that the scheme for a 'uninational Palestine state' coincided best with the principles of the UN Charter, but confided later to Lovett that it may prove too idealistic and that the second scheme for a 'binational' state (a species of provincial autonomy) would be preferable to partition with or without the Negev going to the Jewish state. Now clearly it was no good facing the rising clamour for partition merely with preferences for outmoded plans, and Henderson clearly had in mind another option; some form of international trusteeship for Palestine. Henderson had proposed as much to McClintock in May, but then kept quiet about these 'preliminary draft' views.[18]

Three weeks after the UNSCOP Report was out, Henderson returned to the fray with a powerfully argued memorandum for Marshall stating 'that it would not be in the national interests of the United States for it to advocate any kind of plan at this time for the partitioning of Palestine or for the setting up of a Jewish State'. The reasoning was careful; support for partition would estrange the Arab states, consequently eroding not only US and British interests in the region to the benefit of the USSR, but also damaging the European Recovery Programme. Furthermore, given Britain's attitude to enforcing partition, US support for such a plan would raise the expectation of an American troop commitment to implement it. Further judicious criticism of partition in general and of the Majority Plan in particular were added before Henderson drew forth his final recommendations that the US Government should be seen to have an open mind on the whole matter because 'there is a possibility that the moderates in both camps might be led to acquiesce in a sufficient number of points to enable the setting up of a trusteeship for a period of years which would be instructed to function in such a neutral manner as not to favor either partition or a single state.' But already by this time the ground was slipping from beneath Henderson's feet. On 17 September Marshall had informed the General Assembly that the United States 'gives great weight' to the Majority Plan, while an important meeting on 3 October between Marshall and the US delegation to the UN decided to support the plan 'in principle' and to work for some modifications to it. Johnson announced this in the Ad Hoc Committee on 11 October. [19]

Henderson had a valuable ally in the Joint Chiefs of Staff who were as apprehensive as his own division about the dangers involved in American backing for partition. In a memorandum for the Secretary of Defense, sent with a covering note from Admiral Leahy (for the JCS) dated 10 October, the objections to partition were rehearsed in detail before the real problem was raised: a British refusal to enforce a solution which the USA had backed in the General Assembly. The consequence of the British refusal might be either a Soviet involvement in the region through the medium of the UN or strong pressure for the USA to become militarily committed to upholding the solution she had advocated. Such a commitment by the US would

invalidate entirely current estimates of required strengths of the Army, Navy and Air Force. It would place upon United States troops the dangerous responsibility of preventing or quelling disturbances which, in all probability, will be serious and widespread, while at the same time depriving the United States of the extremely small strategic reserve it now possesses. From the military point of view the risk involved is very grave.

With the decline in the US armed forces' personnel over the two years since the war from 3.5 million to half a million, the concern of the JCS is understandable and indeed Marshall was at pains to avoid committing any of the remnant to Palestine. In another memorandum for Lovett dated 22 October, Henderson argued:

> On the assumption that we are going to follow our present policy of supporting partition without waving the flag, we agree that partition will probably fail of a two-thirds vote [in the General Assembly].

In this event Henderson proposed a 'compromise plan'; 'a temporary trusteeship with fairly substantial immigration, ending in a plebiscite in Palestine'. But Henderson's initial premise proved wrong; the US not only supported partition but also 'waved the flag', the General Assembly voted on 29 November for partition and the scheme of trusteeship, the champion of the Office of Near Eastern and African Affairs, would have to wait a few months before it had its day at the United Nations.[20]

Why had the skilful and persistent advocacy of Loy Henderson proved ineffective in guiding US policy? Most probably an earlier statement by Britain about her withdrawal date would have helped the Office of Near Eastern and African Affairs and the JCS to amplify their strictures about enforcement of partition, but it seems unlikely that British dithering was the decisive factor here. Since the days of the Harrison Report on the plight of the DPs, Truman's sympathy had been with the Jewish survivors of the holocaust. Certainly he was no wholehearted Zionist, but his disposition was to support a UN backed scheme which looked likely to settle the humanitarian problem. Consequently he was easily persuaded to make the necessary moves to support the Majority Plan for partition. For example, Truman accepted Niles' suggestion that General Hilldring should be appointed to the US delegation to the UN because, Niles advised, 'it is most important that at least one of the advisers be a vigorous and well-informed individual in whom you ... and American Jewry have complete confidence.' Evidently Niles did not feel they had confidence in Wadsworth, the Ambassador to Iraq, who was the State Department's man on the US delegation. Hilldring, formerly the State Department's Assistant Under Secretary for Occupied Areas, had acquired a lively sympathy for the Zionist cause and his appointment on 10 September opened a direct channel of communication between the White House and the delegation of which E. M. Wilson (1979) later complained: 'The Department often did not know what was being reported to the White House or what instructions Niles was passing on to Hilldring.' Mrs Eleanor Roosevelt was also on the delegation and lent her vigorous support for the Majority Plan as well. The upshot was that the State Department's case against partition came under heavy fire in the deliberations of the delegation; one specific instance was immediately before Marshall's announcement on 17 September that the US 'gives great weight' to the Majority Plan. Of course Marshall wasn't the hapless victim of advice concocted by a delegation 'picked' by Niles, and W. R. Louis (1984) rightly points to Marshall's efforts to be fairminded to all the parties concerned. In fact his speech itself makes this clear: 'We realize that whatever the solution recommended by the General Assembly, it cannot be ideally satisfactory to either of the two great peoples primarily concerned.' Notwithstanding this, US public support for the partition scheme and the defeat of the State Department can be dated from this time, but other factors besides the composition of the US delegation and the mind of the Secretary of State were involved in the final outcome.[21]

Zionist lobbying of the White House built up remorselessly during the second half of 1947 with the aim of securing unequivocal US backing for partition. In the third quarter of the year the White House received over 65,000 items, ranging from telegrams to petitions, relating to Palestine, the vast majority supporting partition. The number increased to over 78,000 in the final quarter of the year. This well-orchestrated lobbying campaign achieved a dramatic success following Weizmann's meeting with the President on 19 November. He successfully impressed upon Truman the need for the future Jewish portion of Palestine to include the Negev, and Truman telephoned Hilldring in New York apparently indicating his support for Weizmann's position. It could scarcely have come at a more embarrassing juncture for, as McClintock noted in his memorandum, Johnson 'was poised to enter the 3 p.m. meeting of the Subcommittee' and carry out the State Department instructions to press for the inclusion of the Negev in the Arab state. The upshot was ultimately that the Subcommittee awarded the Negev to the Jewish state in its report to the Ad Hoc Committee, but the President's intervention was variously interpreted as a direct repudiation of the State Department and as a spur to the US delegation to retain a flexible negotiating position. What is quite clear, however, is that given such pressures from the top Henderson's case against partition had no chance of success. Furthermore, the by then current State Department alternative of trying to amend the Majority Plan to make it acceptable to the Arabs and standing by with a trusteeship scheme, in case the whole thing failed to obtain the necessary support in the General Assembly, appeared a sanguine exercise, to say the least.[22]

The direction of Truman's policy was entirely consistent with that pursued, for example, over the 100,000. Basically humanitarian sympathies were intermingled with a commonplace American perspective which tended to see the Jews as the great pioneers in the Holy Land, making the desert bloom and promising to do the same with the Negev, while the Arabs were regarded as the old, backward race which, rather like the plains Indians, should give up part of their hinterland to the cause of progress. After all, the Arabs stood to gain from such progress in a Palestine politically partitioned but economically unified as the Majority Plan proposed. However it seems unlikely that Truman was motivated solely by such considerations. Niles' efforts helped, as did Marshall's approach. Moreover the whole matter of Palestine was heavily politicized and on at least two occasions, on 4 September and 6 October, the matter was brought up at Cabinet meetings. According to Forrestal, Hannegan, the Postmaster General, reminded Truman that 'very large sums were obtained a year ago from Jewish contributors and that they would be influenced in either giving or witholding by what the President did on Palestine', and a month later he returned to the subject. Such considerations, along with the overpowering lobbying by the Zionist machine, must have helped shape Truman's response and clearly doomed Forrestal's suggestion that the Palestine question be lifted out of politics. Of course, Truman faced his own election battle in 1948. Clark Clifford advised him in a memorandum dated 19 November that he could in fact win the election despite losing New York, the only state in which the Jewish vote was important, but, as Ganin points out, pursuing a Palestine policy in defiance of electors in such a plum constituency was highly unattractive and furthermore inconsistent with the Democratic Party's fund-raising concerns being pressed by Hannegan. Willy-nilly party and Presidential politics were involved and so Henderson's original hope of seeing US policy eschew the partition plan was about as naive and improbable as Forrestal's suggestion for depoliticizing the Palestine question.[23]

There is another factor which may have played a part in the eclipse of the State Department's preferred policy in the autumn months of 1947. In common with the Foreign Office, the State Department incorrectly forecast Soviet intentions despite Gromyko's statement at the UN in May. In September, at Henderson's request, a report on probable voting patterns in the General Assembly was prepared and forwarded by Babbitt (Assistant Director of Reports and Estimates). In part it read:

> It is impossible to predict how the 3 Soviet states [USSR, White Russia, Ukraine] and Poland will vote. ... If the three Soviet states and Poland support partition, it will probably be carried; if they oppose partition, it will almost certainly be defeated.

Despite this analysis, Henderson continued to pedal his view that partition would fail to obtain sufficient support in the General Assembly, and the general consensus amongst the US delegation to the UN in September remained that the USSR would back the Arabs for obvious reasons. Only Mrs Roosevelt disagreed. When Tzarapkin made his announcement on 13 October that the USSR supported partition, it came as a great surprise and, in view of the narrowness of the final vote on 29 November, it was a crucial development. Some efforts were made to fathom Soviet intentions, Gallman reporting an informal conversation with Garran on 15 October in which the latter registered surprise at the turn in Soviet policy and opined that, 'either USSR envisaged partition as opportunity for Soviet troops to help implementation or USSR still regards M[iddle] E[ast] as having low priority.' A month later the US Ambassador in Moscow suggested a more considered version of this analysis which closely paralleled that of his British counterpart: 'Soviet policy and tactics toward Palestine question are deliberately calculated to ensure unsettlement, rather than settlement, and to create maximum difficulties for British and Americans in Near East.'

In the short term unsettlement is precisely the effect Soviet policy had. First of all, on 10 November, in UN Subcommittee One, the Soviet and US delegates together propounded a compromise plan for advancing the termination date for the British Mandate. They proposed that a UN Commission should assist the Mandatory and then run Palestine for a brief interval at the end of which independent Arab and Jewish states would emerge. It was this arrangement which provoked Bevin's angry reassertion that British troops would not act as a screen behind which any UN Commission could operate and partition Palestine. In fact the disruptive effect of this whole business of the UN Commission on Britain's standing at the UN and on her relations with the USA was destined to feature heavily during the final months of the Mandate, and it seems significant that it received such an important and early boost from its Soviet and American backers. Secondly, Soviet support for partition exploded the Office of Near Eastern and African Affairs' earlier premise to the contrary, thus upsetting a fixed point in their calculations about the chances of the Majority Plan's progress. Furthermore it served to alarm the JCS which was already highly suspicious of Soviet intentions in the area, as Admiral Leahy's memorandum to the Secretary of Defense had shown. Altogether then the Soviet policy of supporting partition helped diminish the credibility and effectiveness of the State Department's line of resistance, its wish to see partition defeated in the General Assembly and replaced by a scheme of trusteeship.[24]

The State Department was therefore written out of US policy on Palestine during the autumn of 1947 principally because of Truman's attitude and his political concerns, but also to a lesser extent by David Niles' clever Zionist lobbying and by a fundamental misapprehension about the direction of the Soviet policy. The dénouement came between the 25 and 29 November. On 25 November the UN Ad Hoc Committee voted on a slightly amended version of the partition scheme laid before it by Subcommittee One; it received the support of twenty-five votes to thirteen against, with seventeen abstentions, which was one vote less that the two-thirds majority the proposal would require for adoption in the General Assembly. On 29 November the partition proposal was adopted by the General Assembly. Thirty-three nations voted in favour, thirteen against and ten abstained. During the four day interval Chile had changed her vote from being in favour to abstaining, Siam, who had originally voted against the plan, absented herself, Greece changed from abstaining to vote against, while Belgium, France, Haiti, Liberia, Luxemburg, the Netherlands and New Zealand all changed from abstaining to vote in favour.[25] Much evidence points to the direct intervention not only of leading US citizens but also of the White House during the last couple of days to help secure a majority in favour of the creation of a Jewish state; it is intervention that had considerable consequences not only for the State Department's position but also for the status of the partition plan itself.

The 'official' US position was that no lobbying for votes in favour of partition should be undertaken, made explicit in a telephone conversation on 24 November in which Acting Secretary of State Lovett conveyed Truman's instructions to the US delegation at the UN. By this stage, however, Arab states were grumbling that US pressure was being placed on South American states. Inverchapel reported from Washington the State Department's denial which argued that the representatives of the South American states, when

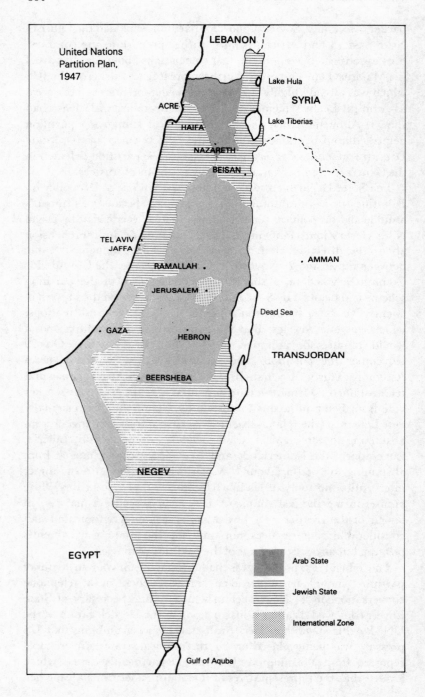

United Nations
Partition Plan,
1947

LEBANON

Lake Hula

SYRIA

ACRE

HAIFA

Lake Tiberias

NAZARETH

BEISAN

TEL AVIV
JAFFA

. AMMAN

RAMALLAH .

JERUSALEM .

. GAZA

Dead Sea

HEBRON

TRANSJORDAN

. BEERSHEBA

NEGEV

EGYPT

Arab State

Jewish State

International Zone

Gulf of Aquba

challenged by the Arabs about pressure, 'had preferred to say that it was the United States Government rather than the Zionists who were doing this'. Beith minuted drily; 'The explanation is ingenious, but I think there *has* been canvassing by the Americans'. Confirmation arrived at the Foreign Office in two telegrams on 24 November, the very day on which Truman's instructions were telephoned through to New York. In one telegram the Minister of State reported the 'American attempt to stampede the Assembly' partly by pressure which seemed to be having an impact on the Chinese delegation, while in another Cadogan told Sargent that; 'the US Delegation are now undoubtedly putting pressure on other delegations to support partition'. However, it was after the indecisive vote in the Ad Hoc Committee that the really crucial US lobbying took place, and M. J. Cohen's study (1982) has surveyed the somewhat incomplete evidence admirably. Niles had evidently already pressed Johnson to 'get all the votes they could'. He went on to mobilize unsuccessful commercial pressure on Greece to change her abstention to a positive vote and successful pressure via former Secretary of State Stettinius and the Firestone Rubber Company to dragoon Liberia into casting a positive vote on 29 November. Niles also exerted pressure on the French delegate but apparently it was Weizmann's telephone call to Leon Blum which procured the necessary instructions from Paris to vote in favour of partition. Pressure was applied on the Philippines by Supreme Court Justices Murphy and Frankfurter, and also by ten senators. Haiti's vote was also secured. Now plainly much of this successful lobbying was a result of the Zionist machine running at full throttle, but there is incontrovertible evidence to suggest that Truman, despite the denial in his memoirs, did allow the White House to become involved and instrumental in securing sufficient votes in the General Assembly for partition to be adopted. Consider, in the first place, Niles' important and continuous instigating role in procuring pressure on delegations in New York, a feat he could not have accomplished without at least the tacit approval of his chief. Secondly, evidence of Truman's role is provided by the thanks he received on 3 December from Congressman Celler 'for the effective work you did with regard to the Palestine resolution passed by the U.N. General Assembly', and the next day from Congressman Klein 'for your magnificent work' in obtaining the UN's approval for the creation of a Jewish state. Finally, there is the evidence of the accounts of contemporaries, among them Goldmann, Comay (who was in charge of the Jewish Agency's New York office) and Silver, which clearly attribute to Truman himself the decisive motivation and involvement. Beeley, writing up the whole affair in January 1948, recorded that 'the United States Government was persuaded to use its influence with Governments which were for one reason or another dependent upon it, and which if left to themselves, would either vote against partition or abstain'. He cited as particularly ludicrous the consequent *volte-face* of the Philippine and Haitian delegates 'who were obliged to vote in favour of partition three days after they had spoken against it'.[26]

The US Government's role was highly important, for it had helped the plan to create a Jewish state obtain international backing which was as essential to its implementation as the League of Nations' Mandate had been in making the Balfour Declaration anything more than a pious hope expressed for ulterior political motives. It was important too because both the Presidentially sanctioned lobbying and the vote itself represented a conspicuous defeat for the State Department, Henderson repeating his views to Lovett as late as 24 November that

> the policy we are following in New York at the present time is contrary to the interests of the United States and will eventually involve us in international difficulties of so grave a character that the reaction throughout the world ... will be very strong.

Clearly then the influence exerted by the official levels of the State Department was as negligible at this point as it had ever been at the crucial junctures of US policy on Palestine.[27]

Finally, as M. J. Cohen (1982) has pointed out, by not only backing partition herself but by actively working to secure the support of other nations for this plan, the US Government had succeeded in making what was originally the UNSCOP Majority Plan into the American plan. This incidentally meant the concerns expressed by both the Joint Chiefs of Staff and by Henderson's division that US troops might be required to help enforce the scheme became more real. More importantly, the USA had now become the leading influence over the future of Palestine, in contrast to Britain whose imperial sunset in the Holy Land had left her policy there shrouded from the outside world in impenetrable and virtually irrelevant gloom. In this context the weighty deliberations of Wright, the Superintending Undersecretary of the Eastern Department at the Foreign Office, make interesting reading. On 22 November he was pondering whether Britain should abstain in the UN vote, which would be logically in accordance with the non-committal policy to date and was expected by the Arabs, or should vote against the Majority Plan with 'the courage of our convictions' because 'we believe the Majority plan to be a bad one and unfair to the Arabs, and that its adoption will entail risk of disturbances on a large scale'. Wright felt such a negative vote would be quickly forgiven by the USA 'particularly since we should have voted against the Russians' whereas, naturally, 'our position throughout the Arab world would be strengthened and fortified'. Beith quickly passed on the news that Creech Jones did not agree with voting against the plan of partition, and Burrows minuted that Bevin wanted Cadogan merely to abstain. This he duly did to a suitable chorus from the Zionist supporters who packed the public gallery at the General Assembly Hall on 29 November.[28] Wright's view was really no more than a pipe dream. Certainly it is true that he stated what the Foreign Office hoped to salvage from the whole débâcle of Palestine and reflected the policy Britain was to pursue in the coming months. But the idea that at such a point and in such a public way the British Government could cast aside its ragged mantle of neutrality and raise with a leader's courage the banner of the Eastern Department's conviction was just a shade whimsical.

8

The End of the Mandate

Neither the British nor the US Government found it possible to pursue credible, let alone creditable policies between the UN vote in November 1947 and the proclamation of the State of Israel in May 1948. During February and March, the USA reversed its support of partition at the behest of the State Department and the Joint Chiefs of Staff on the grounds that it would have to be enforced, but it failed to establish any alternative successfully, even a truce. The process destroyed the credibility of US policy on Palestine and provoked serious disagreements with the British Government, yet even while this was going on President Truman was moving towards recognizing the Jewish state which was simply awaiting the British departure from Palestine to come into being. The prompt US recognition of Israel restored US policy to its earlier direction, but the excursion showed plainly the real quality of US leadership in the matter.

British policy was yet more convoluted. Consistent in its attitude to partition, Britian refused the UN Commission early entry to Palestine for fear that otherwise Arab opinion would identify Britain with its purpose to implement the General Assembly's resolution. The undoubted inadequacy of the United Nations in considering how partition was to be effected was rendered utterly irredeemable by Britain's policy which inevitably attracted severe criticism. Furthermore, Britain's withdrawal from Palestine proved ignominious indeed, for the authority of the Mandatory government and the ability of its forces to maintain law and order quickly vanished. Long before the Mandate expired a civil war was raging, and effective partition, which the British Government was so fearful of sanctioning, had become a manifest reality. The British Government accepted that war between the Arabs and the Jews was inevitable; not only inevitable but desirable in so far as it was the only way that any stable settlement could be reached. In thus placing faith in war as a continuation of diplomacy, the British Government made a serious error. This abnegation of responsibility was the inescapable outcome of Britain's surrender of authority over Palestine, a process which had begun at the hands of the Foreign Office before the Second World War and reached a peak in the London Conference of 1946–7. Furthermore in early 1948 it resulted in a refusal by the British authorities to oppose the intention of King Abdullah of Transjordan to invade and annex the Arab portion of partitioned Palestine, notwithstanding the fact that this action would precipitate a multilateral invasion of Palestine by other Arab states, war with the newly established Jewish state, and would damage the delicate façade of Arab unity. The consequences of Israel having to establish its existence through war and the result its success had on the Arab states in the Middle East are still very much in evidence.

British policy during the last months of the Mandate

There was a ragged, one might say a rattled consistency about British policy between the UN vote in November 1947 and the termination of the Mandate the following May. Despite criticism in the United Nations and considerable American pressure, the British Government stuck doggedly to its opposition to the arrival of the UN Commission more than a fortnight before the Mandate terminated, fearing that otherwise it would be saddled with the blame from the Arab states for sanctioning the UN partition plan. This plan of partition had one glaring deficiency; the lack of provision to enforce it peacefully. However, it was Britain's policy towards the UN Commission which rendered this deficiency irreversible. In the spring of 1948 the position became further complicated, first by the US espousal of a trusteeship scheme for Palestine to stave off the conflict which partition would bring, and secondly by variations on the theme of a truce in Palestine. Britain's policy towards all these complications was, to borrow a phrase of Cadogan's, one of 'manful abstention' in order to preserve her 'neutrality' and her relations with the Arab states, although by May the Foreign Office was bringing pressure to bear to secure a truce. As for the British Government's resolve in sticking to the dates for the termination of her Mandate and the evacuation of her forces, it seems that here a considerable nervousness was displayed and the idea of advancing both dates was repeatedly discussed. But the most destructive dimension of British policy lay in its attitude to Abdullah, for there is evidence to show that his aspirations to absorb the Arab portion of partitioned Palestine were viewed sympathetically and indeed winked at in London despite clear evidence that not only would the resulting aggrandisement of Transjordan do harm to the cause of Arab unity so beloved of the Foreign Office, but would also precipitate an Arab scramble for Palestine and war with the newly formed Jewish state. These then are the issues of British policy to be considered here.

During the early months of 1948 Britain's Palestine policy, and indeed many of the deliberations in the UN, entered a new degree of irrelevance. For one thing the USA had seized back the initiative in November 1947 and went on to retain an initiative, albeit in a highly confused way, first by proposing a scheme of trusteeship in Palestine and then by promptly recognizing the newly emerged state of Israel on 14 May 1948. Furthermore, events in Palestine itself outdistanced the ability of Britain or the United Nations to control them. Hostilities between the Jews and the Arabs began in earnest early in December 1947 and for the next few months the Arabs retained the initiative against defensive Jewish tactics. In January the Palestinian Arabs were supplemented by units of the Arab Liberation Army which entered Palestine from Syria. During April the Hagana moved onto the offensive, accomplishing, for example, the temporary opening of the road to Jerusalem, and the capture of Tiberias (by 19 April) and Haifa (22 April). Consequently by the time Britain's virtually meaningless Mandate expired on 14 May the Jewish forces had, in M. J. Cohen's words, 'managed to secure most of the areas designated to become the Jewish state'.[1] In these circumstances it had long since become ludicrous to look to the United Nations either to implement or to repudiate partition; it was a fact as plain to see as the complete atrophy of the *Pax Britannica*.

It is clear, too, that during 1948 events in Palestine came to be seen as part, and a comparatively minor part, of an increasingly menacing Cold War confrontation which focused on Europe. The crisis in Czechoslovakia prompted Bevin to advise the Cabinet in March that economies in the armed forces were

> in foreign affairs a very grave disadvantage. If we are strong we shall have friends, and if we are not strong our friends will make the best terms they can with our enemies.

On the same day he confronted his colleagues with another paper whose title told all: 'The Threat to Western Civilisation'.[2] Two days later General Clay dispatched to Washington his famous augury of confrontation, before the end of the month the Brussels Treaty was signed and in June the crisis over Germany culminated in the closure of surface routes to Berlin. The effect of these developments was twofold. They distracted the attention of governments and help to account for a quality of haste and petulance glimpsed sometimes, especially in Bevin and Truman, towards the comparatively local difficulty in Palestine. Secondly, as Bevin's advice to the Cabinet suggests, these concerns enhanced the importance attached to the recommendations of the Services, for instance over the Chiefs of Staff's strategic requirements in the Middle East and their interest in rescuing valuable stores and equipment from Palestine even though a protracted and embarrassing evacuation timetable resulted. This then comprised the background; the final actions of British policy towards Mandated Palestine were enacted as tensions in Europe developed and as a civil war was fought in the country.

The Eastern Department of the Foreign Office established at an early stage British policy towards the successor authority in Palestine. Burrows, the departmental head, submitted a paper to Bevin during October advising; 'if an alternative adminstration is set up, we should hand over to it, but should not delay our withdrawal to do so'. At this stage it was, of course, unclear what type of government or interim adminstration would succeed Britain's, but the attitude expressed here became axiomatic. The paper went on to Attlee and was taken, amongst others, by the Defence Committee on 7 November which felt that the UN would be the residuary authority after Britain surrendered the Mandate. They put off a final decision pending events in New York. Here the plan for a UN Commission to act as the transitional authority to give effect to partition emerged, leading to categorical instructions being issued on 18 November to the British delegation at the UN: if partition was approved by the UN, Britain should hand over authority in Palestine to the Commission and was entitled to relinquish responsibility from the moment the Commission arrived in Palestine. The instructions continued; 'We should therefore try by all possible means to delay despatch of UN Commission until we are ready to hand over to it.' These instructions seem to have been issued in advance of proper Cabinet consideration. On 25 November, a week later, a paper went to the Defence Committee advocating such a course, adding that the UN Commission should not reach Palestine before May when the withdrawal plan envisaged the end of the Mandate. On 27 November the Defence Committee agreed and instituted appropriate action to delay the arrival of any UN Commission. However, two days before the

Cabinet in discussion had suggested that 'a more positive attitude' may be needed in the UN and that a decision on 'whether we intended to facilitate the establishment of alternative authorities to whom we could hand over' was needed. It was not until 4 December, that is, after the vote in the General Assembly, that the Cabinet endorsed the FO and Defence Committee line on the UN Commission; but already on 27 November further instructions had been sent to the delegation in New York. These instructions pointed out that it was essential for the arrival of any UN Commission to fit into the withdrawal plan, which meant arriving in Palestine no earlier than May. More than a fifteen-day overlap with the British Mandate would cause Arab disturbances, Cadogan's team was told, necessitating a switch to a faster evacuation plan involving 'disastrous losses of stores' which were unacceptable to Ministers.[3]

What lay behind such zeal to exclude the UN Commission, a policy in some contrast to the tone of the Cabinet discussion of 25 November? As Cadogan's instructions suggested, it was as ever considerations of Anglo-Arab amity allied with fears of chaos in Palestine which prompted these efforts to distance Britain from any programme of partition. On 19 November Cunningham, the High Commissioner in Palestine, concurred emphatically with the earlier instructions sent to New York, adding that the handover of authority 'should be completed willy nilly within a fortnight of Commission's arrival in Palestine'. This attitude was echoed by Creech Jones and Bevin in the paper put up to the Cabinet before its meeting on 4 December which warned the earlier arrival of the Commission 'would provoke serious disturbances amongst the Arabs'. Apart from this, the Foreign Office eagerly collected signs that British policy in New York was working to preserve her relations with the Arab states. Commenting on 25 October about Arab governments' reactions to Britain's statements in the UN, Brigadier Clayton noted that they read into them, 'a refusal to impose what they consider an unjust settlement and a disinclination even to take any part in imposing it.' Evidently, the right message was getting through. Clayton continued hopefully; 'there now appears a chance of disentangling ourselves from the thorny Palestine tangle without forfeiting the good will of the Arab States.' Further optimistic messages arrived in December following the meeting of the Arab League Council in Cairo. Clayton reported Nuri Pasha talking on 16 December of Arab military plans to 'occupy areas as we evacuate them both in Arab and Jewish zones' with 'regular forces of Transjordan and Iraq', but that there would be 'no interference with our military facilities'. Clashes with British forces would be avoided. On 23 December, Clayton reported that the Iraqi delegate, Salih Jabr, told him he had said in the meeting that originally he wanted all concessions cancelled, but that Britain's stand had changed his opinion. 'The enemy was now the United States'. These Arab statements helped the Foreign Office to grin and bear what it knew would be severe criticism in New York for Britain's attitude to the UN Commission, Burrows minuting succinctly for Bevin:

> the essence of the question is that we should be able to complete our withdrawal from Palestine according to plan without becoming involved in repressive measures which will endanger our position throughout the Middle East. Everything must be subordinated to this requirement, even if it involves an appearance of non-cooperation with the United Nations. The Arab disorders which have already broken out, though they should perhaps not at this stage be taken too seriously, add point to this argument.

The Head of the Eastern Department here encapsulated the guiding principle of British policy during the final months of the Mandate. This policy triumphed over the earlier feeling within the Cabinet that a more positive attitude to the UN may be desirable, and its pursuit proved painful and destructive.[4]

Naturally it fell to Cadogan to bring home to the British Government how its policy was regarded in New York. On 24 January, he reported a conversation with Lisicky, now the unhappy chairman of the UN Commission, in which he told of the Commission's conviction that a neutral force would be required to enforce partition and that a two-week overlap with the retiring Mandatory Government was much too short. Cadogan was apprehensive that Britain may be blamed if the Commission failed in its job. Later he confided to his diary that London was 'being silly on this', and again pressed his government to extend the overlap to a month if the consequent flare up was likely to be only brief. Sargent felt Britain could oblige if the military evacuation was halted so as to 'maintain' law and order, but the Official Committee on Palestine was damning. It saw no grounds for altering its earlier recommendations and concluded its advice to the Colonial Secretary with derision:

> The United Kingdom Delegation repeatedly pointed out to the General Assembly, and to the Palestine Committee, the implications of adopting any scheme not acceptable to both sides. Nevertheless, no provision for implementation was made. The fact that the Commission are now

beginning to understand the difficulties involved seems to us no ground for
modifying our policy ....

The Cabinet considered the matter on 5 February and, while
reaffirming their attitude to the UN Commission's arrival in
Palestine, conceded that the precise period of overlap could be
discussed with the Commission in London and that a nucleus of the
Commission's staff may proceed to Palestine 'well in advance of 1st
May'. This concession was indeed meagre for Creech Jones to carry
with him to the United Nations. Cadogan fumed at his pleas about
Britain's evacuation problems, confiding to his diary that these were
'nothing like so difficult as what the wretched Commission have to do,
in picking up the threads and rebuilding everything we have
destroyed, *in a fortnight.*' On 19 February he noted:

> Our Government seems to be completely wooden. ... Creech made a
> statement to the Commission, and was then cross-examined. I hope he
> made a better impression on them than he did on me. He's much more
> terrified of London than he is of New York.

There was to be no shifting the British Government on this issue, but
it must be said that 'most' members of the UN Commission itself
(consisting of members from Bolivia, Denmark, Panama and the
Philippines, under the chairmanship of the Czech Lisicky) 'were
firmly resolved not to stir from New York', to quote the view of
Azcárate (the Assistant Principal Secretary to the Commission) who
actually led the advance party to Palestine on 2 March. Furthermore,
some criticism of Britain's position was deflected as a result of clear
indications that the US Government was retreating from the whole
idea of partition, which, in turn, raised new problems for Britain's
policy of glorious neutrality.[5]

Between February and May of 1948, several different schemes for
dealing with the crisis in Palestine emerged in turn, and held the field
for a short while before being replaced by others. Until the eleventh
hour the British Government fought shy of expressing an opinion on
any of them, but ultimately did become committed to supporting
arrangements for a truce and UN mediation.

Later in February and with the obvious intention of calling into
question the plan to partition Palestine, Austin proposed that a
Committee of the Security Council should consider the threat to the
peace in Palestine and give guidance to the UN Commission.
Cadogan 'manfully abstained' on the issue throughout the discus-

sions, and when he was later summoned before the Committee he insisted on giving factual information only and refused to express an opinion on 'whether there was a "threat to the peace"'. When Austin disclosed the American scheme of temporary UN trusteeship to replace the immediate partition of Palestine, the Foreign Office promptly instructed the British delegation on 19 March that they could neither support nor oppose the proposals without deviating from neutrality. In Cabinet discussion three days later this serene course was confirmed. There was to be no change in British policy. It was felt highly unlikely that trusteeship would prove acceptable to the Arabs and Jews, and for good measure the Cabinet agreed that the authorities in Palestine 'should make no effort to oppose the setting up of a Jewish State or a move into Palestine from Transjordan, but should now concentrate on the task of withdrawing.' Altogether this attitude amounted to a withering repudiation of the new American policy. Although Cadogan was able to vote in favour of other US resolutions in the Security Council on 1 April, calling for a truce in Palestine and the convening of a Special Session of the Assembly, pressure on Britain to go along with the trusteeship plan grew menacingly. In reply to reports of this pressure, the Foreign Office merely insisted that the delegation in New York make plain that while Britain would not veto the plan, this 'does not commit us in any way' to participating in it. The Anglo-American confrontation peaked on this issue in mid-April. Bevin was given a briefing paper on 14 April prepared by the Eastern Department, probably by Burrows himself. It was a thorough, strongly argued defence of Britain's policy and withdrawal programme. It rejected the idea of altering either in order to support US proposals for trusteeship or truce which were both felt unlikely to win the approval of the Arabs and Jews. For good measure it pointed out:

> It is unfair that we should be asked at this late stage to reverse our policy
> ... in order to retrieve a situation which need never have arisen if we had
> been allowed to seek a settlement in Palestine without interference from
> outside.

One must assume that this reference to interference was to American interference, although as we have seen the situation had been rendered irretrievable long before by the involvement of the Arab states at the hands of the Foreign Office. Such ironies were incidental; Bevin was duly primed with righteous indignation for when he saw the US Ambassador on 15 April and warned him that if the contents of the US note pressing for British support became publicly known 'it would endanger relations' between the two countries. Partly due to the British Government's attitude, partly due to the reality of the situation on the ground in Palestine, and partly due to Truman's anger at the way trusteeship had been proposed, the scheme soon faded and it was formally abandoned by the US delegation on 11 May. With bitter irony, the previous day the British delegation had been instructed that if the Americans still insisted on their trusteeship proposals 'you have discretion to express general approval in the last resort' and without commitment. Evidently it was now felt safe, with just a few days of the Mandate still to run, to prejudice Britain's neutrality to this extent.[6]

British policy was more supportive to the truce proposals. Adamant in resisting US pressure to prolong the Mandate to help effect a truce, the British Government did exert itself to bring pressure to bear upon the Arab states to agree to a truce. On 23 April the Security Council voted on a US resolution and established a Truce Commission, and at the end of the month Bevin promised to Douglas that he would use his influence to presuade the Arabs to accept a truce 'provided', as he told the Cabinet, 'that the terms were fair'. This lobbying seems to have been held up by a new US proposal to suspend the Assembly and prolong the Mandate for ten days while a truce was worked out on the spot. Predictably, Bevin refused to extend the Mandate when he saw Douglas on 4 May, and told the British delegation in New York that 'I cannot help being very nervous' of making any concessions in view of the 'many different proposals' and heavy pressure coming from the Americans. The idea of prolonging the Mandate and suspending the Assembly was dropped—the Jewish Agency rejected the former—and on 6 May Bevin instructed the Ambassador in Damascus to press the Syrian Government and representatives of other Arab states to accept the US truce proposals. The instructions were to convey the substance of the telegram, which did not mince its words. It was 'extremely unwise of the Arabs not to accept the United States proposals for 10 days cease-fire and Azzam's reasons against this ... are particularly foolish. Object of the cease-fire would be precisely to stop the Jewish activities of which he complains.' Bevin went on: 'if they continue their present policy of holding out for 100% of their demands ... they will once again lose every advantage which they might gain by early and realistic decisions, just as they did by refusing to accept my proposals at the London Conference.' Broadmead did his duty before the Syrian Minister of Foreign Affairs who was apparently 'surprised at the forcefulness of the language used'. However the reply he received was that 'public opinion would prefer that reversals should be suffered than that nothing should be done to help the Arabs in Palestine.' Persuasive but less trenchant representations were made to Ibn Saud, replete with the warning that war in Palestine may have 'incalculable' effects both there and 'on the internal situation in the Arab States'. On 8 May the Foreign Office instructed all British posts in the Middle East to reiterate that the truce proposals were fair and reasonable, and should be accepted if only to avoid blame for any breakdown. The response was flat. The Syrian Prime Minister explained that no Arab country could by itself accept the truce, the President of Lebanon said he would continue to advocate a truce before the Arab League but was worried about Abdullah's attitude, the Egyptian Prime Minister felt it was very necessary and promised to think it over, Abdullah and his Prime Minister appeared evasive and eager to preserve Transjordan's freedom of action whether the Arab League accepted or rejected the truce, and Ibn Saud replied tartly that either Britain should reassert her responsibility 'or that matters must take their course'. Clearly the situation now was hopeless; the Arab states were locked into a deadly course of action by a mixture of domestic pressures and rivalry with each other which together provoked a paranoid attitude to the progress of the Hagana's offensive. Broadmead summarized:

> 'anything is brought out to support the conviction that the Jews, having already effected partition, ... are not going to stop anywhere even if they sign a truce. Pleas about doing nothing which would put the Arabs in the wrong with world opinion did not seem to carry any weight.[7]

Besides this belated and ineffective effort to press the Arabs to accept the American inspired truce, the British Government toyed with a couple of ideas of its own. On 5 March, Bevin broached to Creech Jones the idea of an 'interim settlement' in Palestine, 'giving time for tempers to cool' after Britain's withdrawal. This idea had taken firm shape by about mid-April. The scheme was basically to freeze the situation in Palestine by an agreed truce, policed by the Hagana, the Arab Legion and an international volunteer force which might also require stiffening with US troops. Britain would consider providing joint naval forces to restrict immigration. The whole was to be run by a Governor and it was argued that it had the advantage over the US trusteeship scheme because it 'leaves the final solution entirely open' whereas trusteeship seemed 'to prejudice it'. Creech Jones advised Bevin on 20 April that these proposals assumed the success of the truce, but there was 'virtually no prospect' of this 'with the Jews strongly determined to proclaim their state on May 15th'. Bevin, probably after discussion with the Prime Minister, dropped the whole idea and advised Creech Jones 'that it would be too risky to give the Americans my plan'. Bevin's plan for an interim government was stillborn, the victim both of the situation in Palestine and of Britain's inscrutable neutrality.[8]

By early May it looked as though all attempts to stave off chaos and war in Palestine were futile. It was in tacit acknowledgement of this danger that Creech Jones suggested to the UN Political Committee on 3 May that 'some neutral authority at the centre' should be considered to help mediate 'until the communities can resolve their conflict'. Cadogan thought the Colonial Secretary had made 'a perfectly flatulent speech'. However, as the American hopes for making their truce proposals work faded, they came round to accepting the idea of mediation as the next best thing. Instructions to the US delegation at the UN to adopt the proposals were approved by Truman on 12 May but with one UN Commissioner to mediate rather than the commission which Britain had been proposing. On 14 May the General Assembly approved a resolution to this effect and the UN Mediator was created. Britain had inspired the idea and voted in favour of it, a rare phenomenon indeed in these abstentious months.[9]

The same resolution which created the Mediator also relieved the UN Commission of its former reponsibilities to implement the plan of partition. This purpose was of course now quite superfluous in view of the civil war and the actual partition which had taken place in Palestine by mid-May, but the way in which the instrument of the UN's original purpose was quietly thanked and relieved helps to explain how Britain's earlier opposition to the Commission's arrival in Palestine had by May long since ceased to be controversial. The British Government was distanced from responsibility for the failure of the UN Commission to effect its task peacefully not only by the passage of time and events in Palestine, but also by the currency of other schemes for resolving the crisis such as the American trusteeship plan. Undoubtedly there was much in the continual British assertion that the General Assembly had approved a plan of partition but failed to create proper machinery to implement it, but Britain did little enough to try to remedy this deficiency during the final months of her Mandate. The British policy of straining by all means to stay neutral in order to salvage the goodwill of the Arab states rendered her position in New York uncooperative and open to severe criticism, as well as tarnished the real quality of her neutrality. The British attitude to the UN Commission resulted, for instance, in the belated nature of the pressure brought to bear on the Arab states to accept the truce proposals. It showed too in Britain's policy of continuing to supply arms under existing agreements as a result of treaty obligations with some Arab states in February 1948, notwithstanding the continuation of the US embargo imposed the previous November.[10] But by 1948 the heart of the problem was how or whether peace could be imposed on Palestine under one guise or another. The Joint Planning Staff estimated on 1 April that the UN would require 200,000 soldiers to impose the scheme of temporary trusteeship![11] Under these circumstances, and as effective partition took place in Palestine with a Jewish government standing by to claim sovereignty, the belief grew that conflict and stalemate were the unavoidable and necessary next steps before any compromise could obtain. Beeley had suggested this theory in a letter to Burrows as early as 23 October 1947 and he reported it seemed to be the general opinion in New York in April 1948. Consequently, well before Britain's Mandate expired, there was the widespread conviction that peace in Palestine would come only by ordeal; Ibn Saud's reply to the truce reflected this belief, while on 6 May, Kirkbride commented perceptively from Amman:

> When both Arab and Jewish forces face each other and possibly after a few trials of strength it might be possible to secure a general truce.[12]

The British Government apparently accepted this slide into war. Having already committed itself to refusing the UN Commission early access to Palestine, Britain's ability to spare Palestine her ordeal was severely limited. Britain's real problem was a paralysis of leadership, which led to her abnegation of any responsibility by the spring of 1948. Authority does not wait upon a dying king, and Briain's real authority over Palestine's future had expired long ago.

The dithering which took place during early 1948 about advancing the dates for the Mandate's termination and the evacuation of British forces was symptomatic of this lack of authority in Palestine. The original withdrawal plan, outlined in a Cabinet paper on 3 December, envisaged the termination of the Mandate 'by 15th May' and the evacuation of British forces from their final enclave around Haifa by 31 July. The Cabinet endorsed these recommenedations the next day. Apparently there were at least three occasions when significant advances in these dates were considered. In December, Kirkbride

sent Burrows a report by Pirie-Gordon of his recent impressions of the
security situation in Palestine. They were not reassuring. Wright,
who superintended the Eastern Department, minuted, 'We are
unwise to stay so long in Palestine'. Sargent added; 'The soldiers
showed a complete lack of imagination when they argued that the
civil administration could be maintained until May 15.' Cunningham
felt similarly, to judge from a draft telegram he prepared, but it is not
clear whether his views were communicated to London at this stage.
Bevin prompted the COS to consider an earlier termination of the
Mandate, which they did in January. Montgomery's comments in the
COS Committee on 14 January epitomized the verdict:

> there was no military reason whatsoever for terminating the mandate
> earlier than 15th May. He was firmly opposed to it. ... Conditions were
> certainly not easy ... but in his opinion the [Palestine] Administration
> should by firm leadership retain control of the situation. To discharge this
> task they needed firm backing from the United Kingdom, and not
> indications of wobbling.

Despite the lack of advice as to how mere firm leadership was to
control the situation, and Cunningham's obvious anxiety, the date
remained fixed evidently out of a military distaste for 'wobbling'.[13]

In March and April the possibility of advancing the date of the
evacuation of British forces was discussed. It was the US trusteeship
proposal which had evidently rattled the Cabinet. The COS were
instructed that the acceleration of the evacuation should be
considered 'in the light of the new situation', which was that British
forces would probably be roped into enforcing the new American
scheme. At this stage the COS felt there was no reason to change
plans to the emergency 'Plan B', but altered their minds in April
following advice from the Commanders-in-Chief, Middle East. This
showed that it was possible to advance the present evacuation plan
and Ministers approved this on 21 April. Accordingly, 1 July became
the new target date for the final evacuation from Haifa and the price
for thus lowering the British profile in Palestine was accepted: 'the
disposal of ... 20,000 tons of low priority army stores'.[14]

Soon after this the question of advancing the termination of the
Mandate to 5 May was raised. Evidently the British decision, taken
on the spot, to allow the Jewish forces to take over Haifa from the
Arabs on 22 April prompted this reconsideration. The British Consul
in Haifa commented on 25 April about the dilemma: 'The fact is that
our forces have been so run down that we cannot maintain law and

order in addition to ensuring our safe evacuation'. This situation prompted the local military authorities to propose the evacuation of Jerusalem on 5 May and the transference of the garrison to Haifa. Consequently the High Commissioner proposed ending the Mandate on 5 May, too. Creech Jones told Cunningham immediately from New York that this 'would bring dismay, a very serious loss of reputation here with intensification of malicious criticism', and on 29 April the Cabinet confirmed instructions to the High Commissioner to maintain the position. When the situation in Jerusalem itself deteriorated further, reinforcements were sent back into Palestine, in the words of Alexander's memorandum to Bevin

> to enable the administration and the forces to maintain themselves there until the 15th of May, and to maintain 100% control of Haifa. This ... does not also mean that British forces can maintain 100% control of law and order of the other towns in the areas of their withdrawal.

This last sentence was of course a considerable understatement, and indeed another instance was the acceptance by the Cabinet the previous December that 'it may not be possible effectively to limit' immigration after 1 February. As immigration was a perpetual source of Arab resentment, it was another tacit acknowledgement by the British authorities of their inability to control the situation. Although the Mandate's termination was not advanced to 5 May, at a very late stage it was set for midnight on the night of 14–15 May, the very earliest instant that Britain could divest herself of her responsibilities without going through any public palaver about advancing the date. It was in fact some twenty-four hours earlier than expected, and necessitated Cunningham's inglorious departure from Jerusalem early on the morning of 14 May, so that he could be on board the Royal Naval ship which took him beyond Palestine's territorial waters on the stroke of midnight. British forces followed soon afterwards, completing their evacuation from Haifa on 30 June. Beith of the Eastern Department minuted with, one suspects, an audible sigh; 'The fact is that we have held on to the Mandate too long, not through any lack of Foreign Office advice to the contrary.'[15]

The pattern which emerges from the evidence so far is one of Britain's resolute determination to avoid alienating the Arab states, despite thereby impeding the UN Commission, provoking criticism in New York and difficulties with the Americans, accompanied at the same time by a collapse of authority in Palestine which provoked nervous 'indications of wobbling', to use Montgomery's memorable phrase, about advancing the withdrawal plans. It is in British policy towards King Abdullah of Tansjordan that a damning dimension is added to this pattern.

Abdullah had considerable ambitions in the Middle East and speedily sought to turn UNSCOP's partition plan to his advantage, announcing his intention to absorb the Arab portion of Palestine to Golda Meyerson of the Jewish Agency when they met in November 1947. Given the rivalries which existed between the Arab states there was a considerable possibility that Abdullah might find it necessary to show his fidelity to the cause of the Arab League by attacking any Jewish state as well; Beeley recognized this and briefed Bevin accordingly on 16 December. There was considerable sympathy with the idea of Abdullah absorbing the Arab portion of partitioned Palestine. As M. J. Cohen (1982) has shown, Kirkbride, the British Ambassador in Amman, was Abdullah's most consistent advocate, repeatedly arguing the benefits in terms of regional stability for allowing Abdullah to absorb the Arab portion. He also pressed the case for non-interference with an ally's use of its own force, in this case the Arab Legion—something of a fiction for the Arab Legion was heavily subsidized by Britain under the terms of her treaty with Transjordan. But there were other temptations for Britain in Abdullah's dynastic aggrandisement, as the Joint Planning Staff well knew. On 24 October the JPS argued that Transjordan would require 'extensive development' for it to be of value in easing the military problems consequent upon the withdrawal from Palestine, but significantly it was felt that if Transjordan was enlarged as Abdullah envisaged then its 'economic and strategic strength ... would be considerably increased'. So there was a British strategic interest at stake, and in the gathering chill of the Cold War furthering these interests appeared alluring. However the British Government had to be cautious in furthering these and Abdullah's interests out of deference not only to the delicate unity of the Arab League but also in order to retain the guise of disinterested neutrality about Palestine's future. Accordingly, Beeley minuted on 2 March that 'while we should not go so far as to discourage proposals for the incorporation of large parts of Palestine in Transjordan, we should not at present commit ourselves to this definite proposal.' Beeley argued cautiously that efforts to find a common approach with the Americans and to press a conciliatory attitude on the Arabs should proceed as the first priority. Certainly British policy sought to avoid any confrontation with regular forces from the Arab states before her Mandate expired, even if this meant that the warnings delivered to Arab governments required an element of bluff after the Cabinet's decision on 22 March to oppose neither the creation of a Jewish state nor a movement into Palestine from Transjordan. Britain's caution also extended to making arrangements in April to withdraw British officers from their secondment to the Arab Legion if this was to re-enter Palestine after the Mandate terminated, but perhaps the best example of this caution is evident in the reports of Bevin's meeting with the Transjordanian Prime Minister in February. According to the British record of the meeting, Tewfiq's statement that the Arab Legion would take over the Arab portion of Palestine when Britain left but would not enter the Jewish portion (unless the Jews entered the Arab area) was met by a simple reply from Bevin that he would study this. On the other hand, Glubb, who attended the meeting as Tewfiq's military advisor, records in his memoirs Bevin's response; 'It seems the obvious thing to do, but do not go and invade the areas allotted to the Jews'. The difference between the two records is revealing, for while the British policy meant to say the former it really wanted the latter, but without committing itself.[16]

There were considerable complex ramifications to this policy. Plainly it carried forward with Abdullah's aggrandisement the risk of disrupting not only the Arab League but also the Foreign Office's long-standing efforts to unite 'the Arab world' and to treat it as a single entity. The importance of this to the Foreign Office, as well as its absurdity and adverse consequences for Palestine, have been seen in the affair of the London Conference of 1946–47. The danger was recognized, as Beeley's remarks showed, but it does not appear to have weighed heavily upon British policy during the last months of the Mandate. The second complication in this British attitude to Abdullah lay in what it implied about the British attitude to Palestine's future. Did Bevin's reply as recorded by Glubb signify an acceptance of partition? While there is much evidence to show that the Foreign Office anticipated some kind of partition taking place on the British withdrawal, there is nothing to suggest that a Jewish state there was viewed as a blessing for British interests. Indeed the Joint Planning Staff were aware that any treaty rights obtained in such a state would run the risk of imperiling the goodwill of the Arab states.[17] Nor did the British authorities expect that much of a future lay in store for a Jewish state, at least before the Hagana's April offensive; in March the Eastern Department of the Foreign Office believed that after the Mandate ended the Jews would be confined to the coastal plain, losing Galilee and the Negev.[18] In fact it seems that Bevin's attitude was rather one of resignation to the prospect of some sort of partition; certainly there is much evidence to show that the attitude in the Foreign Office about actually 'accepting' partition was not benign. It has been seen how, amongst the multiplicity of proposals being considered at the UN, the perception grew that war in Palestine was not only inevitable but also the necessary ordeal through which the communities had to pass before compromise was possible. The Foreign Office endorsed this notion early, as the important paper prepared, probably by Beeley, for the Foreign Secretary in March, shows. Having dismissed the chances of compromise or trusteeship obtaining in Palestine, the paper went on:

> It might be preferable to permit civil war to break out on the 15th May rather than to inaugurate a period of so-called truce in which Palestine would be a centre of international intrigue and which would only postpone a probably inevitable crisis.

The expected result was some sort of partition.[19] But in thus envisaging that partition would be reached only by civil war and presumably with the annexation of part of Palestine by Abdullah, the British authorities were compounding their responsibility for war following their departure from Palestine, a responsibility partly acquired already by their attitude to the UN Commission. Indeed there was something to be gained by it, for Transjordan was expected to become strategically more valuable. On the other hand, the fatally disruptive consequences of such a war upon the unity of the Arab world were evidently ignored. British policy as a result was not only culpable, but so muddled that it failed to safeguard the unity of the Arab League despite an awareness of the dangers implicit in an Arab scramble for Palestine.

Therefore the British Government winked benevolently at Abdullah's ambitions, and was in due course to witness the consequences of the first Arab–Israeli war on the stability of Arab governments and the unity of the Arab League. But in all probability there are other reasons to explain British policy besides a confidence in war as the necessary continuation of diplomacy to settle the Palestine problem. Strategic interests were attractive, Kirkbride's advice persuasive. In addition there are suggestions that this policy was in some way an angry response to American pressure, coupled with the more familiar British problem of not showing the necessary leadership to the Arab states. On 28 April, Attlee and Bevin saw the US Ambassador. The official record of their conversation shows a most extraordinary and aggressive defence by Bevin, in particular, of Abdullah's projected invasion of Palestine. Douglas was concerned that such an invasion would be regarded as aggression and was answered roundly:

> what was Abdullah to do? First of all, he had never been admitted to the United Nations. ... how did the Charter ... apply to him?

Thus ignoring Transjordan's heavy dependence upon Britain, a member of the UN Security Council, no less, the reply continued with rising anger:

> were the Jews to be allowed to be aggressors on his [Abdullah's] co-religionists and fellow-Arabs in the State of Palestine while he had to stand idly by ... ? Would America do nothing if a similar struggle was going on over the borders in South America? Had they not actually intervened ... in Costa Rica ... ?
> ... I [Bevin] said that it seemed to me that United States policy was to allow no Arab country to help their fellow Arabs anywhere, but for the U.S. themselves to assist the Jews to crush the Arabs within Palestine and to allow the slaughter to go on, and then to ask the British Government to restrain Abdullah. Did this not seem a very illogical position?

Clearly His Majesty's Principal Secretary of State for Foreign Affairs was at his brow-beating best that day, boiling over with accumulated resentment at US policy and pressure on Britain. To Bevin it seemed that the US Government was pursuing its own interests in its Palestine policy; why should Britain assist by putting pressure on her ally Abdullah? Bevin's perception of American selfishness encouraged in him an angry, devil-may-care defence of what the Foreign Office defined to be Britain's interests in supporting Abdullah. The only note of agreement came later when Attlee and Bevin promised to use Britain's influence with the Arabs to secure a truce and to prevent Abdullah invading if, and only if, 'the Jews did not indulge in disorder'; the conversation implied this would require US pressure to be brought to bear on the Jews. Plainly the condition was not fulfilled to the satisfaction of the British, for although the government did lobby the Arabs for a truce it did not press Abdullah to stay put.[20]

Throughout the final months of the Mandate Britain avoided confronting the Arab states with maximum pressure to secure a peaceful aftermath to her rule. Obviously to do this publicly and with the utmost vigour would conflict head-on with her efforts to retain the goodwill of the Arab states by avoiding any commitment to the UN partition plan. But there were opportunities to exert strong discrete pressure, just as there had been before the London Conference. For instance, on 17 December Cairo reported, 'Clayton thinks Salih Jabr [Iraqi delegate to Arab League] sees in Ibn Saud's refusal on oil sanctions [on US] a handle to turn Arab world away from him, and [for] bolstering Hashimites.' Burrows minuted significantly:

> I am sure there is a great deal in ... this .... Most Arab leaders would be much more ready to be moderate over Palestine if they could claim that other Arab leaders' pusillanimity made more drastic action impossible.

Of course when it came to invading Palestine, Abdullah was the least pusillanimous Arab leader, equipped as he was with the best trained Arab army, a tame British Ambassador and the sympathy of the British authorities for his dynastic ambitions. To a considerable extent, his was a client state of Britain's. Why did the British Government not bring decisive pressure to bear to prevent Abdullah from invading Palestine, thereby obviating the necessity for the other Arab states to follow suit? The explanation is simple. Kirkbride was keen to see Abdullah pursue an independent course, and London was sympathetic to his taking over the Arab portion of Palestine. As the months passed and 14 May approached, new factors came into play, such as a disinclination to do to Transjordan what the US Government would not do to the Jews. Furthermore, British power was waning fast in Palestine, the COS confirming on 30 April that 'no effort could be made by the British Civil and Military Authorities in Palestine to resist an attempt by the Jews to set up a Jewish State before the 15th of May or by the Armed Forces of Transjordan to enter Palestine before that date.' Kirkbride made certain that the FO realized the pressure Abdullah was under from his brothers in the Arab League to be seen to be striking a blow against the Jewish state, as shown in his telegram of 2 May, while the next day he reported his own narrow success in obtaining the cancellation of Abdullah's message that he was proceeding at once to Jerusalem with a force to protect the Holy Places. Naturally this helped deter the issuance of any belated instructions by London to dictate to Abdullah, but the underlying reasoning against this course was the by then current faith that a settlement could come only through war, which is confirmed following Houston-Boswall's interesting analysis from Beirut on 8 May:

> Impression given to us here by telegrams from Amman ... is that in his heart of hearts King Abdullah does not propose to attempt more than

occupation of Arab areas. Lebanese Government ... now appear to have higher hopes.

Houston-Boswall advised that if this was the case, nothing should be said to Abdullah, but that if he intended to occupy Jewish areas he should be told of the likely dire consequences (military and political) of Arab 'foolhardiness and lack of preparation'. If Abdullah pursued the first course and when the Arab states' fuss had died down, Houston-Hoswall felt that

> if the King were to invite other Arab States to do something about it [partition] themselves, the time might be propitious for ... some settlement between the Jews and the Arabs, especially if latter were able to establish themselves in area occupied on a sound military basis.

Bevin's comment was simply; 'This is what I have believed all the time and I am convinced the Jews know.' Clearly then it was felt safe and convenient to allow Abdullah to invade the Arab portion of Palestine as the necessary precursor for any final settlement between the Jews and the Arabs. War in Palestine was accepted by Britain as the alternative to dictating to Abdullah.[21]

Consequently the end of Britain's Mandate was ignominious indeed. Following the vote in the UN General Assembly in November the British Government had sought to distance itself from partition by resolute opposition to the early arrival of the UN Commission in Palestine. The rationale had been the preservation of British interests in the Arab world. The ploy was undeservedly successful, for long before the Mandate expired, the consequences of Britain's original non-cooperation with the UN had been diminished by the dramatic impact of the change in US policy to trusteeship, and the *de facto* partition of Palestine through the efforts of the Hagana. But Britain's disinterest towards the UN partition scheme was indeed a ploy. The British Government consistently favoured the idea of Abdullah invading the Arab portion of Palestine, and strongly resented American pressure to prevent it. Inevitably such an invasion by Abdullah would be the signal for other Arab states to take action, and they certainly did not intend to stop at the border of the Jewish state. Therefore, war in Palestine was not merely the result of inadequate planning by the UN, nor of Britain's nerve-racked withdrawal schedule. It was rather the inevitable consequence of the British Government's policy towards Abdullah and its cynical acceptance of the view that a settlement could only come by war. The Jewish state would have to earn its right to exist on the battlefield.

The USA, Trusteeship and the recognition of Israel

By comparison with the complexities and delicate nuances of British policy during the final months of the Mandate, US policy appears simple if confused; the State Department achieved a temporary triumph in securing the abandonment by the US of partition, only to be defeated when Truman decided to recognise the newly established state of Israel. US policy was dangerously indecisive during these months and failed to live up to the quality of leadership promised during the vote on partition. Understandably, the US Government was apprehensive about committing troops to Palestine; it was this apprehension which above all else relegated the US role to one of persuasion and gesture. America sought to persuade the UN to change its mind on partition, it sought to persuade Britain to keep the peace in Palestine, and finally, when persuasion failed to have any impact on the actual situation in Palestine, the President took the opportunity open to him and recognized Israel. This gesture involved no troop commitment and did permit Truman to retain the credit for supporting the humanitarian objectives of Zionism during the past few years.

Well before the vote in favour of partition the JCS had warned Secretary of Defense Forrestal of the alarming consequences for the strategic reserve of making a commitment of troops to Palestine. On 24 November, Royall, the Secretary of the Army, sent a report to the Executive Secretary of the National Security Council which stressed such consequences meant that any decision taken by the UN would be a matter for the NSC to consider. Following the vote on partition, the JCS became highly exercised, General Gruenther (Chairman of the JCS) telling Forrestal in January that

> the strategic planning of the Joint Chiefs of Staff had been substantially altered by the Palestine decision. That it pretty well 'spiked' any consideration of any military operations in the Middle East and ... disposed of the idea that the United States would continue to have access to the Middle East Oil.

The ramifications of this analysis were apparent at the NSC meeting on 12 February. Providing troop units for Greece would involve partial mobilisation, the JCS had argued, as would sending troops to Palestine. According to Forrestal's account, Marshall commented with exasperation that 'we are playing with fire while we have nothing with which to put it out'. The result of these concerns may be seen in the NSC's draft report dated 17 February, which concluded that US support for partition should continue 'by all measures short of the use of outside armed force'. But even this was too much for the military members of the NSC staff who proposed instead that the US 'should alter its previous policy of support for partition and seek another solution to the problem.' The US should propose to the Security Council that the changed conditions necessitated a Special Assembly to reconsider the matter. The military was destined to have its way, more or less, in March. It does seem important to note the uncompromising tone of the JCS advice, which added considerable weight to the efforts made by the State Department to abandon partition, for the views of the services and the Department of Defense were taken seriously in the NSC. With the Communist success in Czechoslovakia by 25 February, tension building up over Germany and the 'Northern tier', and General Clay's ominous warning arriving on 5 March, the National Security Council was arguably the crucial arena for US policy-making by this stage, making its dislike of partition of telling importance.[22]

The case for abandoning partition was ably developed within the State Department as well. On 11 December, Merriam, the chief of the Division of Near Eastern Affairs, sent his superior, Henderson, a memorandum proposing that 'to restore the situation following the recent shambles in New York' the President should issue a statement disavowing the unauthorized pressure brought to bear in the UN vote. The proposed statement continued:

> the US does not consider that UN has or should have the right to enforce a settlement ... of Palestine without the free consent of the majority of both ... communities; that if such consent cannot be obtained then it is clear that the problem should be reviewed.

Under these circumstances the UN should make arrangements for a government of Palestine to continue 'until the two communities can agree upon what the future government ... should be', with Britain carrying on, with assistance, until the UN arrangements were complete. No such Presidential statement was made, but Merriam's proposal was to become US policy in the UN in February and March. Merriam's argument was shrewd, for he focused on the highly questionable authority of the UN to impose a settlement, authority which to become a reality would almost certainly require a commitment of troops from the USA. In place of such a course of action he proposed, by implication, Henderson's old standby—a scheme of UN trusteeship pending an agreed solution.[23]

Merriam's arguement was given vigorous support by the State Department's Policy Planning Staff, headed by Kennan. In a preliminary report of 17 December, the PPS proposed that the US should announce the abandonment of partition on the grounds that it was 'impossible of implementation' and should urge the convention of a UN Special Assembly to seek a compromise solution or, failing that, the US should propose a temporary UN trusteeship for Palestine. Alternatively, and here the paper proposed a different line to Merriam's, the US should simply propose that nothing be done to implement partition in view of its 'manifest impossibility'. It was this latter proposal which found favour with Kennan's team when the final report was prepared for the NSC in January. It was a closely reasoned argument that began by establishing the strategic ramifications of the Palestine question and noted the internationally perceived responsibility of the United States in getting partition through the UN. Already, the paper noted, there was a 'loss of U.S. prestige and disillusionment among the Arabs'; if the US followed up its support of partition and contributed troops to the UN to enforce it, it would result in 'deep-seated antagonism for the U.S.' with severe consequences in the region such as the imperilling of the Marshall Plan due to oil sanctions and the loss of both US and British strategic facilities. Beside, the USSR would share in any enforcement action. It concluded that US support for partition had been premised on its workability, which required 'cooperation between the parties concerned'. The premise was invalidated. No US forces were to be sent to implement partition. The paper recommended that the US 'should take no further initiative in implementing or aiding partition', and, most significantly, should 'divest ... [herself] of the imputation of international leadership in the search for a solution'. When it became abundantly clear that the UN's partition plan was not feasible, the US might agree and take the position that her government would 'cooperate loyally' in working out proposals to encourage a compromise or to investigate some other solution like a federal state or trusteeship 'which would not require outside armed force for implementation'. Thus the whole emphasis in PPS/19 was on lowering the US profile on Palestine and rigorously avoiding any further leadership on the matter; partition should be dropped without drama, and the US should just help with anything proposed in its place. In this respect it differed from

Merriam's proposal which retained a high degree of US leadership on the Palestine problem.[24]

W. R. Louis (1984) has drawn attention to the impact of Kennan's analysis and recommendations, and shown the difficulty which confronted Rusk in adopting them. In January, Rusk became head of the Office of UN affairs, and his immediate concern was how such a major reversal in US policy could be presented in the UN. On 26 January, he submitted a memorandum to Under Secretary Lovett on PPS/19. While agreeing that 'the paper appears to be accurate from the factual point of view', he argued such a change of policy would require Presidential approval. The President, in turn, would require an explanation as to how a 'new situation' had come about, what had been done to increase the chances of partition's success, and what alternatives to it were to be put forward. Defining the 'new situation' would clearly be fraught with embarrassment for the US in Rusk's analysis, for he attached much blame to 'the present irresponsible attitude' of Britain in seeking 'to shift the Palestine problem to the United States', while he also noted that armed Arab intervention to prevent the implementation of the General Assembly's resolution would constitute aggression; to spell out either publicly in the UN would be difficult. In addition Rusk advanced various ideas for helping partition to work, including the 'Exploitation of Differences of View Among the Arabs' and lobbying the British Government. Rusk warned that:

> The United States will not be able to avoid responsiblity for a Palestine solution. A completely hands-off policy (even if politically possible from the domestic point of view), coupled with British determination to withdraw ..., would leave Palestine in a state of violence which would inevitably come before the Security Council.

Rusk felt that here US prestige would suffer heavily. Kennan dismissed Rusk's objections to a fundamental change in US policy, arguing that Rusk's proposals were aimed only at obtaining short-term relief and this 'at the expense of our relations with the British and Arabs'. Furthermore Kennan feared, 'if we continue to temporize ..., it would not stop short of a point where we would finally hold major military and economic responsibility' for maintaining the peace in Palestine. It was precisely this military obligation which so alarmed Forrestal and the JCS, and indeed on 4 February, Wadsworth, the US Ambassador to Iraq, received 'a categorical ejaculation of concurrence' from Truman himself when he asked whether he could say that no American troops would be used to impose partition. The risk of US military involvement was the critical flaw in the case Rusk made for persisting for the time being with partition, objectionable though he felt it to be. Henderson argued straight away that 'it is self evident that a "new situation" has existed since the 29th November when it became ... clear that the Arabs of Palestine would not cooperate.' US support of partition had been 'toward securing the adoption of a plan which would not require implementation by force'; clearly force would be needed, the plan was 'manifestly unworkable' so the reasons behind the US Government's original backing for it were invalidated. Henderson's unspoken but basic assumption was the one already adopted by the Services and the President that no US troops should be used to enforce partition. He was fearful also of the consequences of pressing the British or the Arab states in furtherance of partition. Altogether, then, Rusk's lively defence of continuing for the time being to pursue a policy supporting partition, which really he felt to be an indefensible solution, was heavily challenged.[25]

Rusk's assistant, McClintock, did the necessary and drafted a paper entitled 'Shift to New Position on Palestine'. The paper accepted the premise that partition 'is unworkable without resort to war' and followed exactly the line proposed by Merriam in December. The Security Council was empowered to use force to preserve international peace but not to enforce partition, so the US representative could point this out and call for a Special Assembly to reconsider the matter. There the USA would support a UN trusteeship arrangement for Palestine. While all this was going on the Security Council would require everyone to 'keep the peace' and Britain to oblige by continuing with her Mandatory responsibilities. Accordingly, there were now just three alternative lines of policy being proposed, and these were summarized in a paper by the Policy Planning Staff: to support partition, including the use of armed force under the UN; to 'adopt a passive or "neutral" role' and take no further steps in support of partition; to change policy, call a Special Assembly and seek a new solution. The second proposed policy was Kennan's preference, while the third was the State Department's, now united around NEA's proposal with Rusk's line dropped.[26]

The NSC met on 12 February but, according to Forrestal's account, Marshall merely outlined the three options and noted that he approved none as yet. The indecision continued, the staff of the NSC recording on 17 February the clear division between the view that the US should continue to support partition short of sanctioning enforcement action and the military members' view that policy should be changed. The option of using force had gone, but there was still no decision and this cryptic message from Marshall to Lovett on 19 February suggests that the real indecision was with Truman:

> In my conversation with the President today, I followed the understanding you and I had this morning.
> The President assured me whatever course we considered the right one we could disregard all political factors. I told him ... we would send to his ship the proposed statement for Austin.

The drafting of this statement proceeded immediately. McClintock's first draft was most ingenious for, after rehearsing the powers of the General Assembly and the Security Council, he came to the crucial section and obligingly bracketed the sentence upon which US policy hinged:

> The Council's action, in other words, is directed to keeping the peace and not to enforcing partition. (It is undeniable, however, that the establishment of internal order in Palestine by the Security Council in pursuance of its duty to maintain international peace might establish conditions under which the Palestine Commission could succeed in carrying out ... the resolution of November 29, 1947.)

Marshall took part in the final drafting of the speech which was sent to Truman on 21 February—with the bracketed passage omitted. In addition the President was invited to consider and approve for the future the submission that, if the Security Council could not come up with an alternative acceptable to the Jews and Arabs, a Special Assembly should be convened. The State Department recommended UN trusteeship as the best solution until Palestinian self-government by consensus became possible. McClintock knew, as he told Lovett, that the draft as sent 'knocks the plan for partition ... in the head', yet even after such a protracted delay Truman's approval for 'this basic position' failed to recognize the fact properly. Truman's condition was that:

> I want to make it clear, however, that nothing should be presented to the Security Council that could be interpreted as a recession on our part from the position we took in the General Assembly.

Evidently this condition was ignored, for Austin's lengthy statement in the Security Council on 24 February was universally interpreted as 'a recession' from partition. Some of the dithering had been obvious, the well-informed columnists Joseph and Stewart Alsop commenting on 27 February on 'The Wriggling President' that he had put off his decision until he was in the Virgin Islands and his late approval caused the cancellation of plans for 'a very necessary briefing of the press on the legal niceties' of Austin's speech. The Alsops complained of the lack of resolution in US policy, yet they could not have known of the dire condition Truman had attached to his belated decision which rendered the policy contradictory. It was to remain so for some time to come.[27]

Not until 19 March did Austin make his second important speech to the Security Coucil in which he proposed that 'a temporary trusteeship' be established for Palestine under the auspices of the UN Trusteeship Council. The delay, the inevitable product of procedure in New York, does not seem to have afforded Truman and the State Department with the time to resolve the contradictions in US policy. Austin was told on 8 March that Truman approved the trusteeship statement 'for use if and when necessary'. On 16 March Marshall instructed Austin that as soon as the Security Council had drawn the obvious conclusion that partition could not be effected peacefully 'you should make statement'; 'the time factor is imperative', Marshall warned. Notwithstanding this pressure, Austin was unhappy and at one stage wished to clear the policy change with Truman. Rusk reported from New York that finally Austin had contented himself with some modifications to the statement to stress that trusteeship 'would be a temporary measure and without prejudice to whatever future settlement were arrived at by agreement', thus avoiding a complete repudiation of partition at some future time. Austin went ahead and dropped his bombshell, and Truman felt very badly let down by the timing of this announcement which amounted to a complete reversal of the US position of the previous November. W. R. Louis (1984) points to the other weighty concerns in Europe which must have preoccupied the President at this juncture and distracted him from thoroughly monitoring the policy on Palestine. Although such distraction is probable, the evidence shows a long-standing lack of resolution over Palestine of which Truman's flabbergasted reaction was merely the latest and inevitable symptom.[28]

What precisely was Truman's position? Since the vote the previous November the President had sought to contain his irritation with Zionist pressure by avoiding seeing anyone who might prove to be a lobbyist. However, amongst his staff in the White House were such able and influential advocates of partition as David Niles and Max

Lowenthal. Ganin points to Lowenthal's role from March 1948 in analysing State Department documents on Palestine for the President. But clearly Truman found the advice of these two men rather emotional and complained to Ewing, another aide, that:

> I am in a tough spot. The Jews are bringing all kinds of pressure on me to support the partition of Palestine ... the State Department is adamantly opposed ... I have two Jewish assistants on my staff, David Niles and Max Lowenthal. Whenever I try to talk to them about Palestine, they soon burst into tears ... so far I have not known what to do.

The evidence certainly upholds this last remark. It was Clark Clifford, Special Counsel to the President, who apparently rescued Truman from his indecision. His efforts began rather late which explains the dominance in February and March of the State Department's proposals for Palestine. On 8 March, Clifford submitted a powerfully argued memorandum to Truman. He drew attention to the US record going back to Wilson's approval of the Balfour Declaration which showed support for partition to be consistent with US policy. He dismissed the problem of estranging the Arabs by arguing that a Jewish state would be a valuable friend and that 'the Arab states must have oil royalties or go broke'. Crucially Clifford continued:

> We 'crossed the Rubicon' ... when the partition resolution was adopted by the Assembly—largely at your insistence. A retreat now will be a body-blow to the United Nations.

Accordingly he advocated strong US leadership 'to take the immediate initiative in the Security Council to implement the General Assembly's Palestine resolution.' Truman's response to this advice is unknown but it may be significant that he made an important concession to the Zionists soon afterwards. In mid-March he saw Eddie Jacobson, his former partner in the Kansas City menswear store enterprise, at the White House. Jacobson had been mobilized to plead with the President to see Weizmann. A. J. Granoff, a Kansas City lawyer and close friend, recalled what happened:

> Of course, he [Jacobson] claimed that he was a great admirer of Weizmann. Now whether this was an exaggeration I don't know. ... I don't think Weizmann's name ever passed our lips before this....
> I think Truman inwardly laughed about it. ... And I think his reply ...

was clever and humane, 'All right, you baldheaded son-of-a-bitch, let him come'.

Accordingly Weizmann saw Truman on 18 March and by all accounts received an assurance that the US still backed the UN partition plan. Mere susceptibility to Weizmann's undoubted persuasiveness cannot account for Truman's assurance, and there is much in Granoff's reference to Truman's essential humanity. Since becoming President, and after the revelations of the holocaust, he had shown his consistent support for the humanitarian aims of Zionism; his comments to Weizmann were in accordance with this support. Unfortunately, they were inconsistent with Austin's announcement the very next day when he proposed a trusteeship for Palestine.[29]

Weizmann and those who knew of his mission felt devastated, but kept their counsel; a public condemnation would have made Truman's position doubly difficult. As it was the President reacted furiously, noting on his calendar:

> The State Dept. pulled the rug from under me today. ... This morning I find that the State Dept. has reversed my Palestine policy. ... I am now in the position of a liar and a double-crosser.

The result was a rigorous internal enquiry, led by Clifford. It emerged from this that Truman had clearly approved Austin's statement but expected prior notice of it, and probably believed that it would not in fact be used for a while until the Security Council's deliberations had unequivocally ruled out partition as a feasible solution. Following this hiatus, US policy pursued the State Department's trusteeship scheme but with little enthusiasm or chance of success.[30]

Within a week of Austin's speech both Marshall and Truman made statements which stressed the temporary nature of the trusteeship proposed and that it would not prejudice the eventual solution; as Truman put it, it 'is not proposed as substitute for partition plan'. These pronouncements reflected the President's discomfiture at being saddled with this new policy. Trusteeship was destined to fail not only because of Truman's attitude and the fact that during April he began to move towards prompt recognition of a Jewish state, but also because of the situation in Palestine. Trusteeship was rejected by the Jews on the grounds that it would postpone the establishment of the state, and Azzam Pasha found nothing good to say about it. Furthermore it would require a truce in Palestine for it to be made effective, or alternatively it would have to be enforced—just like partition. On 4 April the JCS argued that, even with a truce, trusteeship would require a minimum force of some 104,000 troops to cope with the opposition of the extremists. Forrestal's account recalls the JCS estimated that for the US to supply even 15,000 troops would require partial mobilization; could the British 'hold the fort alone' pending the adoption of Selective Service? The British Government's reply to such a suggestion was a resounding negative and the USA inevitably shrank from the consequences of contributing to any enforcement action, although eventually a readiness to help maintain a truce by contributing to a UN force was shown. The essence of the matter was that it became clear trusteeship would have to be enforced, not merely policed, and to enforce it meant preventing the establishment of a Jewish state. If the authorities in Washington, D. C., disliked the idea of using US troops to help enforce the UN partition resolution, it became farcical to consider now using US troops to prevent *de facto* partition in Palestine. Trusteeship accordingly vanished from the realms of debate before the state of Israel was proclaimed.[31]

By this stage US efforts at the United Nations were directed at obtaining a truce and later at furthering the British suggestion to create some machinery for mediation. These efforts, valuable though they were, scarcely compared with the clearly identifiable policy and leading role of the United States the previous November. Truman's speedy recognition of the newly formed state of Israel to some extent corrected the drift in US policy.

Truman's motives for recognizing Israel have been studied extensively; Ganin's account is particularly thorough and clear. Truman committed himself to recognizing the Jewish state promptly if the UN continued to support partition later in April in response to a moving letter from Weizmann which pointed out, 'The choice for our people, Mr. President, is between Statehood and extermination'. Secretly and orally Truman sent his promise to Weizmann through his advisor Sam Rosenman; it reached him on 23 April. W. R. Louis (1984) points out the perils of the President so acting without the knowledge of the State Department; had this been known he argued it 'would probably have strained even Marshall's allegiance'. Certainly US policy was contradictory, with the delegation in New York energetically pursuing trusteeship even as the President promised recognition for a Jewish state, but Roosevelt had shown a comparable capacity in his dealings with Palestine, although he had not kept these secret from the State Department. What were Truman's motives? Resentment at the State Department's 'striped-pants boys' for their action over trusteeship may well have been a factor, coupled with Truman's evident respect for Weizmann and his acute embarrassment over letting him down. But Truman was not the kind of President to make policy based solely upon such local and personal emotions. Of far greater importance was the attitude he had shown consistently since the war towards the survivors of the holocaust; it was in accordance with these humanitarian considerations that in 1948 Truman came around to endorsing the idea of Jewish statehood by the simple gesture of promising recognition. After all, it would be doing no more than recognizing the reality of the situation that had developed in Palestine.[32]

The evidence points to another motive of Truman's; the desire to win the 1948 Presidential election. There was considerable evidence, as the *New York Times* puts it, of

> The possibility of a revolt among New York Democrats against the nomination of Harry S. Truman. ... It drew its impetus from the Truman Administration's switch on Palestine partition.

Already there had been signs of an electoral revolt, for on 17 February, in a predominantly Jewish electoral district in the Bronx, the American Labor Party candidate had triumphed over the Democrat. Risking the loss of New York because of the policy on Palestine was one thing, but having Truman's nomination jeopardized by it was infinitely more serious. Furthermore, the previous autumn there was the matter of Jewish contributions to the Democratic Party to consider as well. It was these pressures which when combined with Truman's earlier record together provided the decisive incentive for the President to make his promise to Weizmann. However it required a mighty effort from the White House staff to overcome the opposition of the State Department to recognizing the new Jewish state.[33]

On 6 May Niles sent Clifford a draft of a proposed Presidential statement which argued that; 'The partition solution which could not be enforced by external means has now become a practical reality in Palestine.' Accordingly, the US was recognizing this reality and with it the Jewish state. The statement was never issued but undoubtedly this was a strong argument and both Niles and Lowenthal helped to prime Clifford for the critical encounter with the State Department on 12 May at the White House. Marshall and Lovett spoke strongly against precipitate recognition, Marshall recalling his warning to Shertok on 8 May that it would be dangerous for the Jews to base their claim to statehood 'on temporary military success', while Lovett felt such a move 'was a very transparent attempt to win the Jewish vote'. Clifford presented his point of view strongly, but the meeting ended inconclusively. Clifford told Lovett later that the debate had caused Truman 'to change his mind and agree to a "postponement of recognition"'. However, it was not to be and Truman accorded US recognition *de facto* to the state of Israel at 6.11 p.m., Washington time, just minutes after the state had been proclaimed following the termination of the British Mandate at midnight in Palestine, 6.00 p.m.,Washington time. The final hours before this pronouncement had been hectic ones in the White House, Clifford telling Lovett during the afternoon Truman had decided prompt recognition would help to stabilize the situation. Lovett requested a delay, at least until after the General Assembly session in New York had finished later in the evening. Clifford was against this, pointing out that the timing of recognition was 'of the greatest possible importance to the President from a domestic point of view'. Lovett felt very bitter, recording angrily in his note of these conversations:

> My protests ... and warnings ... appear to have been outweighed by considerations unknown to me, but I can only conclude that the President's political advisers, having failed ... to make the President the father of the new state, have determined at least to make him the midwife.

Of course, Lovett did not know of Truman's earlier commitment to Weizmann, but it seems unlikely such knowledge would have assuaged his feelings in any way. As for the US delegation at the UN General Assembly, their circumstances could not have been more embarrassing. Rusk had telephoned Austin at about 5.45 p.m. and informed him of the impending announcement, but according to E. M. Wilson's account (1979), Austin was 'so upset' that he went 'straight home without informing anyone'. Soon after 6.00 p.m. rumours began circulating in the Assembly hall of US recognition; Jessup of the US delegation sent a secretary to find out what the news tickers were saying and 'she returned with a crumpled piece of paper, taken from Secretary-General Lie's wastepaper basket, with the President's announcement'. Inevitably several members of the US delegation had to be dissuaded from resigning, and it would appear that Truman had unwittingly had his revenge on the very delegation which had caused him such embarrassment some two months before.[34]

Somehow the crumpled piece of paper is symbolic of US policy pronouncements over the months past. They all had about them a certain temporary and insubstantial quality, while Truman's recognition of Israel in May really went back to the position the US had adopted at the UN the previous November, a position which had been discarded when trusteeship was adopted. It seems only fitting that news of its reinstatement should be recovered from Trygve Lie's wastepaper basket. Truman's recognition of Israel was indeed consistent with his previous policy. Truman had not in the past identified himself with the Zionist objective of statehood but merely with the humanitarian aim of 'a national home for the Jewish people in Palestine'. But by supporting, indeed by obtaining the passage of the UN partition resolution in November 1947, the United States had moved forward and identified itself with the Zionist aim for a state. Given the change in US policy to supporting trusteeship, and given the real situation in Palestine, Truman was faced with a stark choice by May 1948. Either he could adhere to the State Department's cautious line of awaiting developments and pursuing truce initiatives, which meant paying a political price, or he could reaffirm the earlier policy by now extending prompt recognition. The latter meant he could salvage the political credit which he had built up over the previous years by his careful support of pre-Zionist initiatives. Clearly there was a significant political component in Truman's motivation; it could scarcely have been otherwise in election year. But equally apparent is the underlying consistency of his action not only with his previous policy but also with the major consideration which affected any US proposals for Palestine: the anxiety to avoid sending troops to implement or police any solution.

This consideration was the acid test not only for US policy but also for US leadership on the question of Palestine. The State Department successfully engineered the abandonment of partition by showing that it would require enforcement action and pose a threat to international peace. Enforcement action would require a US component, and the JCS had shown the dire consequences of such action. Temporary trusteeship was the alternative most convenient to hand in the State Department, but it seems to have been put forward with the purblind faith that it would be acceptable and not subject to exactly the same objections which partition had raised. US troops, it was inferred, would, as part of a UN force, help to police a scheme of trusteeship accepted by both Arabs and Jews, but there was no question of their being used to enforce it against the wishes of the inhabitants of Palestine. Partly as a result of these considerations and partly because of opposition to trusteeship both in Palestine and at the UN, the US initiative proved a dismal failure.

Extending US recognition to the state of Israel was not subject to this military constraint. It was a gesture. To a certain extent it again acquired for the US 'the imputation of international leadership' (Kennan's phrase) in the matter, but this role had been badly tarnished during the preceding months. The damage had been done by the public reversal of policy, the impression that decisions were delayed or badly co-ordinated, and by the evident anxiety of the US Government to avoid committing troops to Palestine. The credibility of US policy suffered, nowhere more than in the eyes of the British Government. Relations between the two governments over Palestine became very strained. Not only did the reversal of US policy on partition make Bevin nervous and all the more anxious to quit Palestine fast, it also led to considerable pressure being placed on Britain to extend her Mandate and to help, both diplomatically and physically, to obtain both trusteeship and truce in Palestine. This pressure was keenly resented and led Bevin to warn Douglas on one occasion that relations between the two countries may become endangered. The resentment felt was not merely at being pressed to alter British policy, but rather at the perception of American hypocrisy. Bevin, having so often felt goaded by the Americans over Palestine in the past, reacted angrily to the idea of more British soldiers dying in order to further an American solution in the absence of American soldiers. He recorded what he and Attlee told Douglas on 28 April: 'We feared that we would be left to carry the whole weight again, and this we would not and could not undertake to do.'[35] Furthermore the British Government felt that it had more to lose in the Middle East than had the US. Britain's still pre-eminient position, expensively nurtured in the past by such Foreign Office initatives as the 1939 White Paper, the Arab League and the 1946–47 London Conference, meant there was no prospect of her budging on a Palestine policy which by 1948 was clinging to its single fond rationale of salvaging relations with the Arab states. By contrast, the US Government was perceived as secure in Saudi Arabia and having a relatively low profile elsewhere; indeed in August 1947, the working party of the Official Cabinet Committee on the Middle East concluded that 'opposition to the U.S. [in the Middle East] arising from its Palestine policy will not be effectively sustained in the face of her material strength.'[36] Accordingly, from the perspective of London it appeared the US Government was in a comfortable position on the sidelines, able to interfere, reluctant to intervene, and quick to take political advantage. The US recognition of Israel confirmed this analysis; the Americans evidently had less to fear from the Arabs and had cashed intheir Jewish investment.

The US view of British policy was highly coloured by the dreadful impression Britain's conduct had made at the United Nations. Rusk was particularly critical, Henderson disppointed by the British reception of trusteeship. Only Kennan defended the Anglo-American community of interests in the Middle East, urging strongly in PPS/19 the strategic need of both powers to retain facilities in the Arab world; his proposed 'hands off' policy on partition followed exactly the line he saw Britain taking over the matter. Later on, although the British Government's apparent acceptance that war was inevitable found many in agreement within the State Department, the attitude taken towards restraining Abdullah provided another point of argument.

Altogether it is a matter of some considerable surprise that Anglo-American disagreements over Palestine did not spill over and mar relations generally. In 1948 the Cold War escalated dangerously, which seems most likely to have helped keep Palestine in perspective. Instead of it becoming the cause of a major division between Britain and the US, as it would most probably have done in more tranquil times, it was merely a rather remote point of controversy and contention. It failed to interfere with the process which aligned the US with Western Europe. Britain and Bevin in particular played a major role in this process; notwithstanding his low opinion of Truman's policy on Palestine, Bevin was most eager for the United States to have a policy committing herself to Europe.

Conclusion

The last years of Britain's Mandate in Palestine constitute a considerable imperial failure. At a time when her government was preoccupied with domestic concerns and no longer in possession of the power or will to govern a far flung empire, a withdrawal from Palestine seems, on the face of it, unremarkable. However, the Chiefs of Staff, the terms of the original Mandate and the acute problem in Palestine following the holocaust all provided telling reasons for British rule to continue there, or at least for Britain to arrange for a peaceful settlement to the problem before leaving. Yet the last British High Commissioner departed with a war raging about him and the problem entirely unresolved. Why did Britain leave, and why did Britain fail in Palestine?

These two questions have the same answer, for the British Government decided to leave because it knew that it had failed in Palestine. There were many stages on this journey towards realization. For instance, the failure to secure American co-operation in a Palestine policy in 1946 proved serious, for it again left Truman free to make gestures of support for Zionist objectives which served to anger Bevin and discredit US policy in the eyes of his colleagues and officials. Another failure from the British Government's standpoint was reflected in the UNSCOP Majority Plan and the subsequent UN vote in favour of partition, for this plan proposed a similar solution to that which had twice been considered and rejected by the British authorities during the previous ten years. Disorder and illegal immigration in Palestine provided a continual reminder of failure, and, furthermore, British lives and resources seemed to be expended without hope of procuring thereby a better future. Public and parliamentary pressure reacted to the shortcomings and criticism of British policy with the unmistakable demand for Britain to leave

Palestine. Certainly, such events and considerations helped bring home to the British Government the failure of its Palestine policy and influenced the careless quality of its surrender: a referral to the United Nations without recommendations, followed by a withdrawal in the absence of either a solution or peace.

But these factors and influences were only symptoms of the underlying failure of Britaish policy, a failure not so much of her Palestine policy but rather of her Arab policy. This policy went back to the interwar period. It was preoccupied with the burden of guilt arising from the view that 'the Arabs' had been cheated out of Palestine during the First World War. It resulted in the convention of the St James's Palace Conference in 1939 which accorded formal recognition to the notion that the Arab states should have by right a decisive say over what policy Britain pursued in Mandated Palestine. This Arab policy led inevitably to the rejection of partition as a solution and the publication of the 1939 White Paper; war and the perceived need to appease the Arab states merely added to the rationale for recognizing their right to meddle in Palestine. Furthermore, Britain's Arab policy sustained the notion of a united 'Arab world' friendly to Britain, despite the evidence to the contrary supplied by dynastic rivalries and wartime treachery. Nevertherless, the British authorities lent active encouragement to the fiction of the Arab League and before Churchill left office they saw to it that this Arab policy was not disrupted by another scheme to partition Palestine. It was the Foreign Office that proved to be the creator and leading protagonist of this Arab policy, a policy which the Chiefs of Staff endorsed for strategic reasons.

During the final years of the Mandate the Foreign Office retained both its policy and its pre-eminence. It was challenged early on by Bevin's initiative to involve the US Government over Palestine, but the Anglo-American Committee's report proved flawed, the initiative lost the confidence of the Cabinet and was duly emasculated by Foreign Office counter-proposals and the Brook–Grady discussions. Accordingly the Foreign Office was able to reaffirm its belief that the Palestine problem could be settled through the medium of its Arab policy; again the Arab states were invited to send delegations to convene in London, again their demands were uncompromising, again their right to intervene was acknowledged. Dedication to the belief in maintaining the unity of 'the Arab world' precluded the Foreign Office from making use of the rivalries and differences among the Arab states to bring diplomatic pressure to bear over Palestine. Anachronistic strategic thinking by the Chiefs of Staff about safeguarding routes to the East even as the British Raj was ending and resources diminishing merely confirmed the rectitude of Foreign Office policy and prevented a fresh approach. Instead of discarding Arab unity as a fiction, denying Arab states the right to meddle in Palestine, and treating the problem as a small one, the Foreign Office merely reaffirmed its prewar tenets. The result was the complete atrophy of British policy on Palestine seen in the irreconcilable deadlock of the London Conference, which ended early in 1947.

The consequences of this atrophy of British authority over Palestine were considerable. In the first place the Foreign Office had left the government early in 1947 with no options for the future. Accordingly, the decision was taken to throw the problem at the United Nations with no suggestions as to how it might be solved. This step was the conscious beginning of the end of the British rule in Palestine, but the decision-making capacity of the government had been so worn down that even now it took months to articulate the inescapable decision to withdraw. Always the government showed itself to be indecisive, slow to reconcile strategic demands with political necessity, and above all concerned to act the neutral and disinterested party. The rationale for this concern was plainly to show to 'the Arab world' that Britain was distanced from anything which the UN might decide. When the United Nations backed partition and the creation of a Jewish state, the utter bankruptcy of Foreign Office policy over the previous decade was self-evident; even this despised solution had not been averted.

It could be argued that up to this point when the UN voted for partition, Britain's policy for Palestine had been shown to be bankrupt, her authority and leadership long since surrendered. What followed in the closing months of the Mandate was the abnegation of British responsibility for Palestine as well. This abnegation was far deeper than evidenced merely by the disorder and civil war in the country which existed, apparently beyond British control, during the final months. It was the abnegation of a democracy's responsibility to believe in and to pursue peace. Britain failed to co-operate with the UN Commission, and, although its chances of effecting a peaceful partition were slim indeed, the British attitude nullified them entirely. For the sake of retaining 'Arab goodwill' the British Government preferred non-cooperation with the United Nations Organization and its efforts to keep the peace. Furthermore, there is much evidence to show the British authorities accepted that war in Palestine was inevitable and the only way through which a solution could come. In addition, the government lent its tacit approval to

Abdullah's intention to invade and absorb the Arab portion of Palestine even though it was obvious such action would escalate Arab–Jewish hostilities. Clearly all this amounted to writing off Britain's rule in Palestine as a complete, irredeemable loss. Instead, the effort was directed at salvaging what could be salvaged from the débâcle — some standing with the Arab states. Selfish and arrogant as this course was, it also proved destructive of the goals for which the Foreign Office had striven so ardently — Arab unity and stability perished on the same battlefield which established Israel's right to exist.

On the other side of the Atlantic, policy was made differently. Certainly the State and Defense Departments well understood the considerations that dominated British policymaking; indeed they shared many of them such as a lively regard for the need to keep Arab goodwill. But the record shows that the crucial decisions on Palestine were made in the White House, and as a result electoral considerations entered the process. Policy was to a high degree the creation of sporadic Presidential initiatives. Instances abound: for example, the Harrison mission, the rejection of the so-called Morrison–Grady plan, the support of partition in the UN and above all the decision to recognize the newly formed state of Israel. Zionist pressure, which transferred itself from London to Washington, D.C., during the Second World War, played a significant part in stimulating Truman's initiatives but does not alone explain them. Truman undoubtedly supported the aims of the 'humanitarian Zionists' for a national home. His support was provoked by the revelations of the holocaust and was a typical American reaction. Ultimately, however, Truman went further. The UN provided the mechanism through which his support for a national home became US endorsement of Jewish statehood; it was the Majority Plan of the new world organization, and the USA could support it as a loyal member rather than as a nation whose government paid excessive heed to a pressure group. There were limits to this support; US troops would not be used to enforce partition against the wishes of the inhabitants of Palestine. Another limit to this support was the US bureaucratic system, for in early 1948 the State Department succeeded in reversing Truman's policy. Its achievement proved short-lived and was overturned by the President's recognition of Israel—a highly significant gesture and one which was entirely in keeping with the direction and style of US policy on Palestine. It involved doing nothing, but it did retain for the USA her leading role in furthering Zionist aspirations.

US policy on Palestine proved something of a catalyst for Britain, but remarkably, the strained relation between the two governments on this issue did not affect their co-operation elsewhere. Truman's pressure had encouraged Bevin to press ahead with the Anglo-American Committee of Enquiry, and after it failed, US criticism had encouraged the Cabinet to ditch the problem of Palestine. Signs of American indecision early in 1948 only stimulated this attitude. But, arguably, the interest of the US delayed the conclusion of the Mandate. The attempt to formulate an Anglo-American policy consumed one precious year. There was nothing to show for it. Another year passed during which the Foreign Office failed to solve the problem and UNSCOP investigated. As the time went by the situation in Palestine deteriorated, the Arab states piled threat upon threat, and the unhappy army of Jewish DPs in Europe swelled. Perhaps an earlier exhaustion of alternatives and an earlier British withdrawal would have proved less susceptible to a violent aftermath. Steps to deny the involvement *en masse* of the Arab states would almost certainly have avoided such violence. As it was, it is difficult to imagine that Britain's rule in the Holy Land could have ended with greater ignominy.

THE UNCOVERED WAGON, by Vicky in the *News Chronicle*, 28 April 1948. Reprinted with permission of the Bodleian Library, Oxford, and the Associated Newspapers Group.

Notes

To avoid overburdening the text, the notes have been grouped together as far as possible to relate to paragraphs of the text. Multiple sources are cited within each note in the same order as they are used in the text. Unless otherwise stated, all documents cited in the notes are deposited in the Public Record Office, London.

Chapter 1. 1945: the Legacy from the Past

1. FO 371/68621 E7834/8/31 despatch, Beaumont, Jerusalem, to Foreign Secretary, 29 May 1948.
2. CAB 23/4 WM(17)261 in Fraser, p 18; Weizmann, pp 142–5; Gilbert, pp 103–4; UNSCOP Report, vol III, Weizmann's evidence at 21st (public) Meeting, 8 July 1947, in Fraser, pp 18–20; Vereté.
3. CAB 23/4 WM(17)227 and 245 in Fraser, pp 14–15; A. Cohen, p 124.
4. Mandate conferred by Council of League, in Crossman, appendix II.
5. Kedourie, *Islam*, pp 308–9; Gilbert, p 89.
6. CMD 5957, March 1939; Rendel, p 121; Bentwich, p 57; Kedourie, *Islam*, p 310 & *Labyrinth*, pp 267–70, 271 citing FO 371/23221 E764/6/31, 285, 311, 319.
7. FO 371/45380 E7522/15/31 memorandum circulated by McGhee, Price, Reid, Stokes, Thurtle, September 1945.
8. Gilbert, p 160; Monroe, p 85; CO 733/342F Parkinson to Oliphant in Kedourie, *Islam*, pp 97–8; FO 371/20026 E6010, 6169 & 6256/94/31 & FO 371/20027 E6296/94/31 in Kedourie, *Islam*, pp 107–9; M. J. Cohen, *Retreat*, p 29; FO 371/20811 E4597/22/31 Baggallay to CO in Kedourie, *Islam*, p 112.
9. CMD 5479, July 1937; FO 371/21862 minute, Baggallay, 16 March 1938 and Ormsby Gore to FO, 22 March in M. J. Cohen, *Retreat*, p. 45; Cmd 5854, October 1938; FO 371/21864 note of Ministerial meeting, 23 September 1938 and CAB 23/96 Cabinet meeting, 19 October in M. J. Cohen, *Retreat*, pp 71–2; Cmd 5893, November 1938; Cmd 6019, May 1939.
10. Kedourie, *Islam*, pp 113, 145–6, 160–1, 166–8 & *Chatham*, pp 386–7, 391.

11. FO 371/21879 E4464/10/31 minute, Baxter, in Kedourie, *Islam*, p 133; USNA OSS R&A Report 1666, 2 March 1944.

12. Weizmann, p 140 in Laqueur, p 527; Edelman, p 115; Ben Gurion, p 17 in Ganin, pp 1–2.

13. Bauer, p 352.

14. Halperin, pp 25–6; Ganin, pp xiii, 3–4; Schechtman, p 63.

15. Ganin, p 7.

16. Sykes, pp 236–7, 240–1; Baram, p 257.

17. FRUS 1945 VIII, p 699 memorandum, Alling, 6 April 1945; USNA RG 165 Records of War Dept General & Special Staffs OPD 336 ME Section 1 case 4 memorandum, Hull, Ast. COS to COS, 7 September 1943.

18. Ganin, p 14; FO 371/23236 E3875 in Ilan, p 24n; Baram, p 288.

19. Baram, p 51, 246–8.

20. Baram, p 80, 234; Kedourie, 'Pan-Arabism and British Policy' in *Chatham*.

21. Polk, p 262; Baram, pp 16–19, 55–8, 105, 158, 267; FRUS 1945 VIII, pp 34–9 Report by Coordinating Committee of St Dept, 2 May 1945 and pp 85–7 memoranda, British Embassy to St Dept, 6 September and reply 18 September.

22. Louis, *Imperialism*, p 53, 55–8.

23. Ilan, p 166; Ganin, pp 13–15; FO 371/44535 AN 49/4/45 Halifax, Washington to FO, Supplement to Weekly Political Summary, 18 December 1944, reporting on letter from F.D.R. to Wagner.

24. USNA 867N.01/1-845 Box 6750 NE Div memorandum by E.M. Wilson (desk officer for Palestine) and M.W., 'Suggested Procedure Regarding the Palestine Question', 8 January 1945; FRUS 1945 VIII, pp 690–1 letter, Hoskins (Economic Advisor to US Legation), Egypt to Alling (Deputy Director, NEA), 5 March 1945; USNA 867N.01/3-545 Box 6750 Letter, Merriam to Hoskins, 23 March 1945.

25. Louis, *Imperialism*, p 544; *New Palestine*, 31 January 1945, p 1 in Ganin, p 16; FRUS 1945 VIII p 679 memorandum, S/S to President, pp 680–2 letter, Landis to President, 17 January 1945, p 687 telegram, Eddy Jidda to S/S, 1 February; *New York Times*, 2 March 1945 and Rosenman, pp 527–8 both in Halperin and Oder, pp 338–9.

26. FRUS 1945 VIII, p 693 note of *New York Times* report, 17 March 1945, pp 693–7 telegrams, Damascus to S/S, 20 & 22 March, memorandum, Murray to Grew, 20 March, telegram, Acting S/S to *chargé* in Iraq, 24 March, pp 703–4 letters, S/S to President of Lebanese Council, 11 April, President to Regent of Iraq and President of Syrian Republic, 12 April, p 698 letter, President to King Ibn Saud, 5 April.

27. Morgenthau Diaries vol 707, p 2, F.D.R.'s remark to Stimson, in Ilan, p 28; FRUS 1945 VIII, pp 690–1 letter, Hoskins to Alling, 5 March 1945; Bowman Papers, Bowman to F.D.R., 22 May 1943 in Louis, *Imperialism*, p 55.

28. TL OF 204 Box 771 letter, Wagner to Truman, 18 April 1945; FRUS 1945 VIII, pp 704–7 letter, Stettinius to Truman, 18 April 1945,

memorandum, Grew to President, 1 May, letter, President to Abdullah, 17 May, p 709 memorandum, Grew to President, 16 June; FRUS 1945 I pp 972–4 Briefing Book Paper No 646 'Palestine', 22 June 1945; Ganin, p 29; Baram, p 305.

29. M. J. Cohen, *Retreat*, pp 88, 90, 98.

30. Gilbert, pp 230–2; M. J. Cohen, *Retreat*, pp 124, 160–1.

31. FO 371/34955, minute, Churchill, in M. J. Cohen, *Retreat*, p 162, 165–71, 222n.

32. CAB 65/45 WM(44)11 item 4 Confidential Annex, 25 January 1944.

33. *Ibid*; Wasserstein, p 196.

34. PREM 4/52/1 Eden to ME Ambassadors, 1 February 1944 and WO 216/121 despatch, MacMichael, July 1944 in M.J. Cohen, *Retreat*, pp 172, 174.

35. CAB 95/14 P(M)(44)14 Second Report of the Committee; FO 371/45377 E1834/15/31G minute, Morrison to Churchill, 26 February 1945; *The Times* report of Churchill's speech of 17 November 1944 in M.J. Cohen, *Retreat*, p 179; CO 733/454 Part I 75113 minute, Eastwood, 13 December 1944 on PM's conversation with Weizmann on 4 November; FO 371/45378 E5665/15/31 letter, Churchill to Weizmann, 9 June 1945.

36. CAB 66/45 WP(44)46 'British Strategic Needs in the Levant States', COS Committee, 22 January 1944; CAB 119/147 JP(44)227 (Final) 'The British Needs in the Levant States', JPS, 2 November 1944; CAB 119/147 COS(44)952(0) COS Committee, 7 November 1944 annexed to above and approved at COS (44)359 meeting, item 5, 6 November.

37. CAB 119/105 COS(45)63(0) 'Internal Security in the Middle East', COS Committee, 23 January 1945; CAB 119/105 COS(45)23 meeting, item 11, 23 January.

38. CAB 66/63 WP(45)197 'Future Defence Policy in the Suez Canal Area', Suez Canal Committee, 20 March 1945; CAB 66/65 WP(45)256 'Defence of the Middle East', Eden, 13 April 1945.

39. FO 371/45376 E435/15/31G 'Comments', manuscript note on copy initialled by Butler, dated 4 November 1944.

40. FO 371/45376 E435/15/31G minutes, Baxter, 4 November 1944, Butler to Eden, 9 November and Butler to Cadogan, 30 November.

41. FO 371/45376 E435/15/31G minute, Law to Cadogan, 3 December 1944; FO 371/45376 E1725/15/31G minutes, Butler, 20 February 1945, Jebb, 5 March, Hankey, 2 April, Butler to Campbell, 10 March, Hankey, 29 March; CAB 66/64 WP(45)229 'Palestine', Eden, 10 April 1945; FO 371/45376 E435/15/31G draft paper, 1 November 1944; FO 371/45376 E1725/15/31G minute, Baxter, 17 April 1945.

42. FO 371/45376 E1716/15/31G telegram, Grigg, Cairo to FO, 11 March 1945, minutes, Baxter, 15 March and Campbell, 16 March.

43. FO 371/45377 E2453/15/31G minutes, Baxter, 14 March 1945, Campbell to Eden, 14 March, A.E.[den] on Law's of 15 March, Dixon, 25 March.

44. CO 968/162/14814/11A memorandum, Boyd, 6 November 1944 in

Louis, *Imperialism*, pp 400–1; FO 371/45376 E1725/15/31G minute, Hankey, 29 March 1945; FO 371/45376 E1716/15/31G minute, Baxter, 15 March.
45. FO 371/45377 E2453/15/31G minute, A.E., 30 March 1945; FO 371/45377 E3090/15/31G P(M) (45)1 memorandum for Palestine Committee, Colonial Secretary, annexing Gort's telegram of 15 March, with Eden's minute; FO 371/45377 E2453/15/31 minute, A.E., 8 April.
46. FO 371/45377 E2263/15/31G WP(45)214 'The Future of the British Mandate for Palestine', Minister Resident, 4 April 1945; FO 371/45377 E2297/15/31G telegram, Grigg, Cairo to Bridges, 4 April; FO 371/45377 E2298/15/31G telegram, Killearn, Cairo to FO, 6 April and minute, Baxter, 10 April.
47. CAB 66/64 WP(45)229 'Palestine', Eden, 10 April 1945.
48. FO 371/45377 E2615/15/31G P(M) (45)2 'Some first thoughts on Sir E. Grigg's note' for Cabinet Committee, S/S for India, 9 April 1945; FO 371/45406 E3006/834/31G JIC(45)151(0), 2 May and minute, Wikeley, 13 May; FO 371/45377 E3091/15/31G 'Draft Memorandum' sent to FO on 7 May, copy letter, Law to Stanley, 11 May and minute, Baxter, 9 May; FO 371/45377 E3092/15/31G minutes, Baxter and Campbell, 12 May; FO 371/45377 E3093/15/31G WP(45)306 'Palestine', Colonial Secretary, 16 May.
49. FO 371/45377 E3975/15/31G memorandum by Campbell to HM Representatives in Baghdad, Beirut, Cairo & Jedda, 11 June 1945; FO 371/45378 E5139/15/31G memorandum, 'Top Secret', D.H[arris], 11 July, sent to Baxter, and various replies from ME posts in E4690, E4853, E4846, E4775, E5140/15/31G.
50. FO 371/45378 E4939/15/31G M679/5 personal minute, Churchill to Colonial Secretary and COS Committee, 6 July 1945 and minute, Beeley, 10 July; FO 371/45378 E5141/15/31G JP(45)167(Final) 'Future Control of Palestine', JPS, 10 July.

Chapter 2. Labour in Power; the Creation of the Anglo-American Committee

1. Gorny, pp 168–72; Bullock, *Foreign Secretary*, p 165.
2. RH, Fabian Colonial Bureau Papers Box 176 file 1 Labour Party International Dept. No 160A, Report of Palestine Sub-Cmte of Advisory Cmte on Imperial Questions, February 1936 and No 179C, Report … on a proposed long-term policy, April 1937; RH, Creech Jones Papers Box 30 file 3 letter, Creech Jones to Capt V. Cazalet, MP, 9 April 1937; RH, Creech Jones, Papers Box 30 file 1 typewritten draft, 1964.
3. Sked & Cook, p 62; BLPES, Dalton Papers Part IIB 7/10 letter, Locker to Dalton, 7 June 1944.
4. BLPES, Dalton Papers Part IIB 8/1 copy letter, Dalton to Morrison, 28 October 1944.
5. Kirk, pp 190–1; Barker, p 40; also Goldsworthy, p 13, and Gupta, p 283.

6. Northedge, p 34; Bullock, *Life and Times*, vol 2, pp 393–4; Churchill Coll. Cambridge, Attlee papers ATLE 1/17 draft autobiography, pp 1–2.

7. Bullock, *Life and Times*, vol 2, pp 109, 340–7; Hansard vol 413 Col 312, 20 August 1945 in Frankel, p 185.

8. See also Morgan, p 87; M. J. Cohen, *Great Powers*, p 18.

9. FRUS 1945 VIII, pp 716–17 memorandum, Truman, Babelsberg, to Churchill, 24 July 1945; p 719 memorandum, Attlee, Berlin, to Truman, 31 July; p 722 telegram, Byrnes, Washington, to Pinkerton, Jerusalem, 18 August; FO 371/45379 E6062/15/31 telegram, Balfour, Washington, to FO, 19 August; *New York Times*, 30 September 1945, pp 1, 38 on Harrison Report in Dinnerstein, pp 283–4; Ganin, p 32; FRUS 1945 VIII, pp 737–9 letter, Truman to Attlee, 31 August; FO 371/45399 E6878/265/31 telegram, Halifax, Washington to FO, 15 September; FRUS 1945 VIII, pp 741–2 telegram, Moreland, Baghdad to Secretary of State, 18 September; p 739 telegram, Attlee to Truman, 14 September; pp 740–1 telegram, Attlee to Truman, 16 September; p 741 telegram, Truman to Attlee, 17 September.

10. Truman, *Year of Decisions*, p 72; USNA 867N. 0 1/5-1745 Box 6751 Report by Princeton Office of Public Opinion Research, submitted to Henderson 5 May 1945; USNA 867N.01/7-345 Box 6751 letter from 54 Senators and 250 Representatives to Truman, 2 July; TL OF 204 Box 771 memorandum, Rosenman to Truman, 7 September.

11. Truman, *Years of Trial and Hope*, p 148; FRUS 1945 VIII, pp 710–14 memorandum of conversation between Goldmann, Henderson, Merriam and Wilson, 20 June 1945 and memoranda, Henderson to Acting S/S Grew, 22 June and of conversation between Ben Gurion, Kaplan, Goldmann, Henderson, Merriam and Wilson, 27 June; *Palestine Year Book*, vol 2, p 408 in Ganin, p 37; USNA 867N.01/7-845 Box 6751 telegram, Winant to S/S, 8 July 1945.

12. FRUS 1945 VIII p 722 telegram, Byrnes, Washington to Pinkerton, Jerusalem & repeated to Cairo, Baghdad, Jedda, Beirut, Damascus, 18 August 1945; pp 734–6 memorandum, Henderson to S/S, 31 August, annexing Merriam's memorandum of same date; pp 745–8 memorandum, Merriam to Henderson, 26 September; pp 745–6 minute, Allen to Henderson attached to above memorandum; pp 751–3 memorandum, Henderson to Acting S/S, 1 October; pp 753–5 memorandum, Acheson to President, 2 October; Acheson, p 169; Truman, *Year of Decisions*, p 72.

13. FO 371/45378 E5452/15/31G FO appreciation submitted under Baxter's minute, 11 July 1945; FO 371/45379 E6562/15/31 minute, Beeley, 29 August; FO 141/1021 129/33/45 memorandum, Smart, Cairo, 29 August — telegram in this sense sent to FO on same day.

14. BLPES Dalton Diary Part I, 34 entry for 25 February 1946; Shlaim, Jones & Sainsbury, pp 32–3; Williams, p 245; CAB 129/2 CP(45)174 'Middle East Policy', Bevin, 17 September 1945; CAB 128/1 CM(45)38 item 6, 4 October; Labour Party, Report of Annual Conference, p 115 in Gupta, p 281, also pp 284, 388–9; Gorny, p 217.

15. CO 733/455 75113/82 memorandum, Intergovernmental Committee on

Refugees, Emerson, 2 January 1945; *ibid* letter, Eastwood to Paul Mason, FO, 22 March; FO 371/45391 E882/119/31 telegram, Gort, Jerusalem to CO, 26 January & minute, Wikeley, 10 February; CAB 65/53 CM(45)16 item 2, 20 July; FO 371/45378 E5474/15/31G minute, Beeley, 27 July; FO 371/45382 E8047/15/31G P(M) (45)11 Palestine Committee of the Cabinet, Scheme for local autonomy, GHH, 1 September; Nachmani, pp 15, 17.

16. CAB 119/148 COS(45)555(0) 'Middle East Policy', COS Committee, 30 August 1945; CAB 79/38 COS(45)214 meeting, item 15, 4 September.

17. CAB 66/64 WP(45)240 'Manpower in the Middle East', S/S for War, 12 April 1945.

18. FO 371/45382 E8047/15/31G P(M) (45) 11 Palestine Committee of the Cabinet, Scheme for local autonomy, GHH, 1 September; CAB 95/14 P(M) (45) 1 meeting, 6 September 1945. Membership: Morrison, Bevin, Dalton, Lord Pethick-Lawrence (S/S India & Burma), Hall, Lawson (S/S War), Viscount Stansgate (S/S Air); also present, Gater PUS at CO; Secretaries Sir G. Laithwaite & Sir D. Harris.

19. CAB 129/2 CP(45)156 'Palestine Committee', Lord President of the Council, 8 September 1945; CAB 129/2 CP(45)165 'Security Conditions in Palestine', Colonial Secretary, 10 September; CAB 128/3 CM(45)30 item 7, Confidential Annex, 11 September; FO 371/45380 E6966/15/31G draft memorandum, 'Palestine. Short-term policy' submitted with letter, Hall to Bevin, 14 September and minute, P.D[ixon] (Bevin's Private Secretary) to Eastern Department, FO, 16 September; FO 371/45380 E6957/15/31G minute, Baxter, 26 September; CAB 21/2277 48/37/1 Part I minute, Hall to PM, 19 September; CAB 129/2 CP(45)196 'Palestine', Hall, 28 September; CAB 129/2 CP(45)200 'Palestine — Move of Reinforcements', COS Committee, 1 October; CAB 128/1 CM(45)38 item 7, 4 October; Hansard vol 415 no 37 cols 1930–8, 13 November.

20. FO 371/45393 E6947/119/31 telegram, Adams, Jedda to FO, 17 September 1945; FO 371/45393 E7195/119/31G telegram, FO to Grafftey-Smith, Jedda, 25 September; FO 371/45393 E7258/119/31G telegram, Grafftey-Smith to FO, 27 September; FO 371/45396 E9306/119/31 telegrams, Shone, Damascus to FO and Cairo, 30 November, FO to Cairo and minute, Beeley, 1 December; FO 371/45396 E9419/119/31 telegram, Killearn, Cairo to FO, 3 December; FO 371/45396 E9488/119/31 telegrams, Killearn, Cairo to FO, 5 December.

21. CAB 128/1 CM(45)38 item 7, 4 October 1945; CAB 129/3 CP(45)216 'Palestine', Lord President of the Council, 10 October.

22. CAB 128/1 CM(45)40 item 1, 11 October 1945.

23. See also Nachmani, p 32; Kirk, pp 188–9; Dinnerstein, p 299.

24. CAB 95/14 P(M)(45)1 meeting, 6 September 1945; CAB 128/3 CM(45)30 item 7, 11 September; CAB 129/2 CP(45)196, 28 September.

25. AIR 20/4962 125/10 Part 1 brief, CP(45)216 'Palestine', unsigned, 11 October 1945.

26. FO 371/45380 E7479/15/31G first draft 'Note on the Cabinet decision regarding the establishment of an Anglo-American commission ...',

unsigned, submitted to the S/S on 5 October 1945 (pages 1, 2 & 4 of this four-page note are in file).

27. FO 371/45380 E7479/15/31G note, Howe to Foreign Secretary, 6 October 1945; *ibid* minute, Sargent to Foreign Secretary, 6 October; *ibid* minute, Bevin, & reply, Sargent to Bevin, 8 October.

28. USNA 867N.01/8-2845 Box 6751 memorandum of conversation, Hoskins, Clayton, at Cairo, 28 July 1945; USNA 867N.01/8–2745 Box 6751 information airgram, Byrnes to certain diplomatic & consular offices, 27 August.

29. FO 371/45381 E7757/15/31 telegram,S/S to Halifax, 12 October 1945.

30. FRUS 1945 VIII, pp 771–5 memorandum, Halifax to S/S, 19 October 1945; FO 371/45381 E7757/15/31 contains the draft of the proposed communication to the US Government.

31. FRUS 1945 VIII, pp 775–6 Informal Record of Conversation, British Embassy to Dept of State, 19 October 1945; FRUS 1945 VIII, pp 777–9 memorandum of a conversation between S/S and Halifax, 19 October; FO 371/45381 E7932/15/31 telegram, Halifax, Washington to FO, 19 October; FO 371/45380 E7230/15/31G the same, 20 October.

32. FRUS 1945 VIII, pp 779–83 memorandum of conversation between S/S and Halifax, 22 October 1945; FO 371/45382 E8013/15/31G telegram, Halifax, Washington to FO, 22 October; FRUS 1945 VIII, pp 785–6 communication, S/S to Halifax, 24 October.

33. TL Rosenman Papers Rosenman to Truman, 23 October 1945 in Ganin, p 52.

34. FO 371/45382 E8013/15/31G Howe's draft telegram, 23 October 1945, initialled P.D[ixon] and sent to Washington, 25 October; FRUS 1945 VIII, pp 788–90 communication, Halifax to S/S, 25 October, pp 794–5 copy of FO telegram, 26 October, sent by British Embassy to Dept of State.

35. FRUS 1945 VIII, pp 799–800 copy of FO telegram, 27 October 1945, sent by British Embassy to Dept of State; FO 371/45382 E8162/15/31G telegram, Halifax, Washington to FO, 27 October; FRUS 1945 VIII, pp 800–1 communication, S/S to Halifax, 28 October.

36. FO 371/45382 E8177/15/31G telegrams, Halifax, Washington to FO, 28 October 1945 and S/S to Halifax, Washington, 29 October; FO 371/45383 E8266/15/31 telegram, Halifax, Washington to FO, 30 October.

37. FRUS 1945 VIII, p 812 memorandum of a conversation between S/S & Halifax, 6 November 1945, p 814 memorandum, S/S to Halifax, 7 November, pp 815–16 letter, Halifax to S/S, 9 November, pp 819–20 telegram, S/S to US Ambassador, London, 13 November; FO 371/45386 E9001/15/31 transcript of Truman's radio announcement; FRUS 1945 VIII, pp 827–8 memorandum of conversation between S/S and Halifax, 19 November, p 833 copy of FO telegram, 27 November sent by British Embassy to Dept of State.

38. FRUS 1945 VIII, pp 15–18 Replies of the President, annexed to memorandum, Henderson to S/S, 13 November 1945.

Chapter 3. The Collapse of the Anglo-American Initiative

1. FRUS 1945 VIII, p 838n Statement released from White House, 10 December 1945; pp 822–3 copy letter, Bevin to Byrnes, 14 November, enclosed with letter, Halifax to Byrnes, 14 November; pp 830–1 letter, Halifax to Secretary of State, 24 November; pp 831–2 letter, Byrnes to Halifax, 25 November; Schechtman, p 146 citing Crossman's view; FRUS 1945 VIII, p 838 telegram, Byrnes to Winant, 6 December 1945; Ganin, p 57; Nachmani, pp 159–64; Sachar, p 20; Wilson, p 70.

2. Minutes of AZEC, 14 November 1945, pp 4–5, in Ganin, p 55; FO 371/45402 E8848/265/31 telegram, Halifax, Washington to FO, 17 November 1945; Minutes of Inner Zionist Council, 11 December 1945, S5/363, Central Zionist Archives, in Ganin, p 56; FRUS 1946 VII, p 576 airgram, Pinkerton, Jerusalem to Secretary of State, 9 January 1946.

3. McDonald diary, p 2 in Ganin, p 57; Wilson, p 69; FO 371/44539 AN3788/4/45 Supplement to political summary, Halifax, Washington to FO, 10 December 1945; FRUS 1945 VIII, pp 841–2 State Department Memorandum, Concurrent Resolution, 17, 19 December 1945.

4. FRUS 1945 VIII, telegrams, Charge in Damascus & Baghdad to S/S, 21 December 1945, Chargé in Baghdad to S/S, 28 & 29 December, Minister in Jidda to S/S, 31 December; FO 371/45389 E9969/15/31 telegram, Halifax, Washington to FO, 19 December.

5. Nachmani, p 121; Wilson, pp 71–2; St Antony's Coll. Oxford, MEC, Crossman Papers 'R.H.S. Crossman (Private)', Diary, 30 December 1945; Crum, pp 36–40.

6. Crossman, p 66; also FO 371/52522 E4268/4/31 telegram, Halifax, Washington to FO, 9 May 1946 & memorandum, Howe to Sargent, 10 May; Wilson, p 73; Sykes, pp 284, 288; St Antony's Coll. Oxford, MEC, Crossman Papers cited above.

7. FO 371/52504 E389/4/31G letter, Martin, CO to Howe, FO, 10 January 1946; minutes, Baxter, 14 & 15 January & Howe, 15 January; CO 537/1754 75872/138/4 note of a meeting, D.G. Harris, 23 January; minutes, Martin, 26 January & 1 February, & Harris, 28 & 29 January.

8. Crossman, p 18; FO 371/52505 E537/4/31 telegram, Colonial Secretary to Cunningham, 13 January 1946 referring to telegram, Cunningham to CO, 23 December 1945; Nachmani, p 242; USNA Records of Anglo-American Committee of Inquiry, RG43, Box 12 Report of Leslie Rood on sub-Committee visit to Poland, 7–13 February 1946.

9. Sykes, p 289; Wilson, pp 73–4.

10. AIR 20/4963 125/10 Part 3 JP(46)15(Final) 'Palestine: Anglo-American Committee of Enquiry' with annex 'Military Implications of the Maintenance of Law and Order in Palestine', 21 January 1946; CAB 79/43 COS(46)12 meeting, item 2, 23 January; USNA Records of Anglo-American Committee of Inquiry, RG43, Box 10 Notes of Meeting at

Military Headquarters, Cairo, 5 March; FO 371/52507 E802/4/31G telegram, COS to GHQME, 23 January.

11. USNA Records of Anglo-American Committee of Inquiry, RG43, Box 11 Notes of Meeting in Jerusalem (in camera), 14 March 1946.

12. Wilson, p 77; also St Antony's Coll. Oxford, MEC, Crossman Papers, DS.126.4 'Notes on Palestine Report of Anglo-American Committee', sent by Crossman to McNeil (Parliamentary Undersecretary, FO), 22 April 1946.

13. Nachmani, p 187; Wilson, pp 77–8; St Antony's Coll. Oxford, MEC, Crosssman Papers, DS.126.4 'Notes on Palestine Report of Anglo-American Committee', sent by Crossman to McNeil, 22 April 1946; PREM 8/302 letter, Crossman to PM, 7 May; D. Horowitz, p 91; Ilan, p 248 cites interview with Crossman in 1973; Nachmani, p 308; Wilson, p 78 cites interview with Beeley in 1974; Niles papers, memorandum of telephone conversation between Goldmann, Geveva & Weisgal, 5 April 1946, submitted to Niles and telegram, Truman to Hutcheson, c 18 April 1946, both in Sachar, pp 24–5; Nachmani, p 310.

14. Cmd 6808 'The Report of the Anglo-American Committee of Enquiry'; USNA Records of Anglo-American Committee of Inquiry, RG43, Box 12 Report of Leslie Rood on sub-Committee visit to Poland, 7–13 February 1946; Bullock, *Foreign Secretary*, p 297.

15. Ganin, p 43; Cmd 6873 'Palestine: Statement of Information Relating to Acts of Violence'; CAB 69/7 DO(45)12 meeting, item 2, 5 November 1945; Sykes, p 283.

16. CAB 69/7 DO(45)12 meeting, item 2, 5 November 1945; CAB 79/41 COS(45)267 meeting, item 7, 7 November and COS(45)269 meeting, item 4, 9 November; CAB 119/105 telegram, GHQME to Cabinet Offices, 14 November; CAB 79/41 COS(45)272 meeting, item 5, 16 November and COS(45)273 meeting, item 11, 19 November; CAB 69/7 DO(45)31 'Situation in Palestine', COS, 19 November; CAB 79/42 COS(45)291 meeting, item 5, 31 December; CAB 128/5 CM(46)1 item 3, 1 January 1946.

17. CO 537/1703 75113 telegram, Cunningham, Palestine to Colonial Secretary, 18 January 1946; CO 537/2346 75872/154/10 'Supplementary Memorandum by the Government of Palestine', submitted to UNSCOP, 17 July 1947.

18. CAB 119/105 telegram, Cs-in-CME to COS, Cabinet Offices, 1 January 1946; *ibid* COS(46)97(0) 'Palestine — Illegal Arms', COS, 26 March 1946, Annex II telegram, Cunningham, Palestine to Colonial Secretary, 19 February, Annex III reply, 28 February and Annex IV response, 4 March.

19. CAB 84/80 JP(46)69(Final) 'Anglo-American Committee of Enquiry', JPS, 7 April 1946 annexing letter, FO to COS Committee, 2 April.

20. AIR 20/4963 125/10 Part 2 briefing paper, 'Anglo-American Committee of Enquiry. JP(46)69(Final)', ACAS(P), 8 April 1946; AIR 20/4963 COS(46)55 meeting, item 21, 8 April; AIR 20/4963 COS(46)57 meeting, item 4, 11 April; CAB 79/47 COS(46)60 meeting, item 1, 15 April; AIR

20/4963 125/10 Part 2 briefing paper, 'Anglo-American Committee of Enquiry. Military Implications. JP(46)83', ACAS(P), 17 April; AIR 20/4963 draft telegram annexed, Cabinet Offices to Cs-in-CME; CAB 79/47 COS(46)61 meeting, item 5, 17 April.

21. CAB 128/5 CM(46)1 item 5, 1 January 1946; FO 371/52503 E200/4/31G minute, Howe to S/S, 3 January; FO 371/52504 E257/4/31 telegram, Grafftey-Smith, Jedda to FO, 8 January; FO 371/52505 E498/4/31G draft minute, Colonial Secretary to PM, submitted for Foreign Secretary's approval, 14 January; FO 371/52507 E879/4/31 minute, Creech Jones to Bevin, 23 January; CAB 21/2277 48/37/1 Part 1 minute, Attlee to Foreign Secretary, 25 January; FO 371/52507 E879/4/31 telegram, FO to Cairo & other posts, 28 January; FO 371/52510 E1512/4/31 despatch, Grafftey-Smith, Jedda to FO, 11 February and minute, Baxter, 22 February.

22. FO 371/52572 E56/46/31 note of meeting held at FO, 3 January 1946; FO 371/52574 E2502/46/31G CP(46)112 'Proposed Treaty with Transjordan', 14 March; FO 371/52573 E2393/46/31 telegram, Grafftey-Smith, Jedda to FO, 16 March; FO 371/52574 E2490/46/31 telegram, FO to Jedda, 23 March and E2705/46/31 reply, 25 March; FO 371/52574 E2490/46/31, minutes, Wikeley, 26 March, Baxter, 28 March, Howe, 1 April and memorandum, Wikeley & Howe to S/S, 14 April; FO 371/52574 E2639/46/31G telegram, FO to Cairo, 29 March; FO 371/52575 E2899/46/31G telegrams, Grafftey-Smith, Jedda to FO, 31 March and E3384/46/31 15 April; FO 371/52575 E3404/46/31 minute, Wikeley, 19 April.

23. FO 371/52574 E2693/46/31G telegram, FO to Baghdad, 29 March, 1946; CO 537/1853 79238 Part 1 minute on meeting at FO attended by Trafford Smith, Reilly, Bennett, Baxter, Cornwallis, 22 March and minute, Bennett, 25 March.

24. FO 371/52514 E3057/4/31G report, 'Procedure in Connection with Palestine Policy', Harris, 21 March 1946 and report of meeting at FO, 6 April.

25. PREM 8/284 note, PM to Ismay (Secretary, COS Committee), 21 August 1945; PREM 8/284 note, PM to Lawson, 23 October and reply, 15 January 1946; CAB131/1 DO(46)5 meeting, item 1, 15 February; CAB 129/7 CP(46)65 'Defence Policy in 1946', PM & Minister of Defence, 15 February; CAB 128/5 CM(46)16 item 6, 18 February.

26. CAB 128/5 CM(46)1 item 1, 1 January 1946; CAB 128/7 CM(46)14 item 1, Confidential Annex, 11 February; CAB 128/5 CM(46)20 item 2, 4 March; CAB 128/5 CM(46)25 item 3, 18 March; PREM 8/285 letter, Gallman, US Embassy to Bevin, 9 March; CAB 128/5 CM(46)23 item 4, 11 March; CAB 128/5 CM(46)27 item 1, 25 March.

27. CAB 131/2 DO(46)27 'Future of the Italian Colonies', PM & Minister of Defence, 2 March 1946; CAB 131/2 DO(46)40 'Defence' annexing 'Memorandum by Secretary of State for Foreign Affairs', 13 March; BLPES Dalton Diary, Part I 34 entry for 22 March; CAB 79/46 COS(46)51

meeting, item 4, 29 March; CAB 131/2 DO(46)47 'Strategic Position of the British Commonwealth', COS, 2 April.

28. CAB 131/1 DO(46)14 meeting, item 2, 24 April 1946; CAB 131/2 DO(46)67 'Strategic Requirements in the Middle East', COS, 25 May; CAB 79/48 COS(46)82 meeting, item 1, 24 May; CAB 131/1 DO(46)17 meeting, item 1, 27 May; CAB 131/3 DO(46)80 'British Strategic Requirements in the Middle East', COS, 18 June; CAB 131/1 DO(46)22 meeting, item 1, 19 July.

29. CAB 128/5 CM(46)41 item 1, 3 May 1946 and CM(46)42 item 2, 6 May.

30. FO 371/52515 E3492/4/31G minute, Wikeley, 19 April 1946; FO 371/52517 E3840/4/31G note for Secretary of State's discussion with Defence Committee, Wikeley, 23 April; CAB 131/1 DO(46)14 meeting, item 1, 24 April.

31. PREM 8/627 Part 1 minute, Bevin to PM, 24 April 1946.

32. AIR 20/4963 125/10 Part 2 briefing paper, 'Examination of Report by AACE', ACAS(P), 26 April 1946; AIR 20/4963 COS(46)67 meeting, item 7, Confidential Annex, 26 April 1946.

33. FO 371/52517 E3757/4/31G minute, Wikeley, 26 April 1946; CAB 129/9 CP(46)173 'Palestine', Brook, 27 April.

34. FO 371/52520 E4013/4/31 memorandum, Butler for Howe, 26 April 1946 and minute, Beeley, 3 May.

35. FO 371/52521 E4133/4/31G record of discussion between Bevin and Byrnes, 26 April 1946; FO 371/52517 E3815/4/31G telegram, Bevin, Paris to FO, 27 April.

36. CAB 128/5 CM(46)38 item 1, 29 April 1946.

37. FRUS 1946 VII, pp 588–9 telegram, Acheson to Byrnes, Paris, 30 April 1946, giving text of President's statement; Williams, p 260; FO 371/52519 E3921/4/31G telegram, Bevin, Paris to PM, 1 May 1946; FO 371/52519 E3980/4/31 note of exchange in Commons between Hall & Stokes, 30 April; FO 371/52519 E3967/4/31G telegram, delegation, Paris to FO, 1 May, giving text of letter sent to Byrnes; FO 371/52520 E3933/4/31 Attlee's statement to Commons, 1 May.

38. FO 371/52515 E3492/4/31G telegram, FO to Halifax, Washington, 17 April 1946; FRUS 1946 VII, pp 584–5 memorandum, Byrnes to Truman, 19 April & Truman's marginal note; Silver Papers, Silver's notes for 28 & 29 April 1946 in Ganin, p 63; Sachar, p 27.

39. FO 371/52521 E4175/4/31 telegram, Halifax, Washington to FO, 7 May 1946; FRUS 1946 VII, pp 591–2 memorandum, Hilldring to Under S/S Acheson, 3 May, pp 597–9 memorandum, Merriam to Acheson, 8 May.

40. FRUS 1946 VII, pp 595–6 memorandum, Acting S/S Acheson to President, 6 May 1946, p 595n draft, Henderson to Acheson with marginal note, 3 May, pp 596–7 telegram, Truman to Attlee, 8 May; FO 371/52522 E4305/4/31G minute, PM to Foreign Secretary, Paris, 8 May; FO 371/52522 E4317/4/31G telegram, Bevin, Paris to FO for PM, 9 May; FRUS 1946 VII pp 601–3 telegram, Byrnes, Paris to Truman, 9 May; FO

371/52523 E4324/4/31G telegram, Bevin, Paris to FO for PM, 9 May; FRUS, 1946 VII, p 606 telegram, Attlee to Truman, received 13 May.

41. FO 371/52524 E4482/4/31G extract from note on Chequers meeting 12 May 1946; CAB 128/5 CM(46)46 item 5, 13 May; FRUS 1946 VII, p 606 telegram, Attlee to Truman, received 13 May; FO 371/52524 E4482/4/31G telegram, FO to Washington, 14 May; FRUS 1946 VII, pp 607–8 telegram, Truman to Attlee, 16 May, pp 608–8 telegram, Attlee to Truman, 18 May, pp 612–15 telegram, Attlee to Truman, received 27 May.

42. FRUS 1946 VII, pp 617–18 telegram, Truman to Attlee, 5 June 1946; AZEC Minutes, 9 May 1946 in Ganin, p 68; TL OF 204 Box 771 letter, Taylor to President, 15 May and memorandum, Niles to President, 27 May; Niles papers, letter, Truman to Taylor, 27 May in Sachar, p 31; TL OF 204 Box 771 memorandum, Niles to President, 27 May.

43. FO 371/52527 E5213/4/31G telegram, Inverchapel, Washington to FO, 6 June 1946; FO 371/52528 E5400/4/31G telegram, FO to Washington containing message PM to President, 10 June; FO 371/52528 E5401/4/31G telegram, Inverchapel, Washington to FO, 10 June 1946; FRUS 1946 VII, pp 624–25 telegram, Byrnes to Harriman, Ambassador in London, 10 June.

44. FRUS 1946 VII, p 624n Executive Order 9735, 11 June 1946; FO 371/52528 E5352/4/31 telegram, Inverchapel, Washington to FO, 12 June; FRUS 1946 VII, p 625n memorandum, Henderson to Acheson, 18 June.

45. FRUS 1946 VII, pp 624–5 telegram, Byrnes to Harriman, 10 June 1946, pp 626–7 telegrams, Truman to Attlee and reply, 14 June 1946; FO 371/52529 E5446/4/31 telegram, Inverchapel, Washington to FO, 13 June; FO 371/52530 E5628/4/31G minute, Sargent to PM, 16 June.

46. FO 371/52533 E6026/4/31 memorandum on results of discussions 17–27 June on Anglo-American Committee's second recommendation, 21 pp, undated; FRUS 1946 VII, pp 638–9 telegram, Harriman, London to Byrnes, 27 June 1946; FO 371/52533 E5496/4/31G CM(46)61 item 3, 24 June; FRUS 1946 VII, pp 636–7 telegram, Attlee to Truman, 25 June, pp 643–4 the same and reply, 4 & 5 July; FO 371/52536 E6364/4/31 telegram, Inverchapel, Washington to FO, 5 July.

47. FO 371/52530 E5671/4/31G telegram, Bevin, Paris to FO for PM & Cabinet distribution, 20 June 1946 and minute, Beeley, 20 June; FO 371/52531 E5844/4/31G telegram, FO to Paris, PM for Foreign Secretary, 20 June.

48. FRUS 1946 VII, pp 592–94 telegram, Tuck, Cairo to S/S, 3 May 1946; FO 371/52519 E3869/4/31G telegram, Stonehewer-Bird, Baghdad to FO, 27 April and minute, Beeley, 1 May; Niles papers, note, Truman to Niles, undated, in Sachar, p 28; FRUS 1946 VII, pp 605–6 memorandum of conversation between Ministers & Acheson, by Henderson, 10 May, pp 609–10 circular telegram, Acheson to ME posts, 19 May, p 615 telegram, Pinkerton, Jerusalem to S/S, 27 May; CAB 129/10 CP(46)220 'Arab Reaction in Palestine to the Report of the Anglo-American Committee', 6 June; FRUS 1946 VII, pp 615–16 telegram, Eddy, Jidda to S/S, 28 May, pp 628–31 telegram, Wadsworth, Beirut to S/S, 19 June.

49. FO 371/52526 E4922/4/31G telegram, Shone, Beirut to FO, 27 May 1946; FO 371/52529 E5441/4/31G telegram, Inverchapel, Washington to FO, 12 June; FRUS 1946 VII, pp 620–22 letter, Balfour, Washington to Henderson, 7 June; FO 371/52527 E5227/4/31G telegram, Campbell, Cairo to FO, 7 June.

50. FRUS 1946 VII, p 635n despatch, Damascus to S/S, 19 June 1946; despatch, Beirut to S/S, 16 October.

51. FO 371/52532 E5897/4/31 copy of Note Verbale, MFA Baghad to US Legation, 19 June 1946.

52. FRUS 1946 VII, pp 590–1 telegram, Pinkerton, Jerusalem to S/S, 2 May 1946; FO 371/52522 E4268/4/31 telegram, Halifax, Washington to FO, 9 May; FRUS 1946 VII, pp 627–8 telegram, Pinkerton, Jerusalem to S/S, 17 June; Sykes, p 299; FO 371/52529 E5444/4/31 telegram, Inverchapel, Washington to FO, 13 June.

53. Niles papers, letter, Wise to Niles, 18 June 1946 in Sachar, p 33n; Ganin, pp 73–3; FO 371/52536 E6342/4/31 telegram, Bevin, Paris to FO, 7 July 1946; CAB 128/6 CM(46)66 item 5, 8 July.

54. FO 371/52523 E4328E4/31G COS (46)72 meeting, item 3, 8 May 1946; CAB 21/2277 48/37/1 Part 1 minute, Attlee to Ismay, 10 May.

55. FO 371/52526 E4913/4/31G telegram, C in C, ME to WO, ?24 May 1946; CO 537/1768 75872/142 telegram, Cunningham, Palestine to Baghdad, 5 July; FO 371/52528 E5405/4/31G COS(46)154(0) circulating letter from Gater, CO, 1 June and COS(46)88 meeting extract, 5 June; FO 371/52526 E4914/4/31G COS(46)148(0) 'Illegal Immigration into Palestine', War Office, 23 May; FO 371/52627 E7702/7656/31 despatch, Vice-Consul, Stettin to Ambassador, Warsaw, 1 July; FO 371/52528 E5403/4/31G telegram, Peterson, Moscow to FO, 12 June; FO 361/52525 E4774/4/31G CO(46)77 meeting, extract, 15 May.

56. CO 537/2346 75872/154/10 'Supplementary Memorandum by the Government of Palestine', submitted to UNSCOP, 17 July 1946; Meinertzhagen, p 211; CAB 79/49 COS(46)95 meeting, item 6, 19 June 1946; CAB 129/10 CP(46)238 'Palestine', Colonial Secretary, 19 June; FO 371/52530 E5671/4/31G telegram, Bevin, Paris to FO for PM & Cabinet, 20 June; CAB 128/5 CM(46)60 item 3, 20 June; FO 371/52531 E5747/4/31G telegram, Colonial Secretary to Cunningham, 20 June.

57. FO 371/52532 E5846/4/31G telegram, Cunningham, Palestine to CO, 20 June 1946; CO 537/2346 75872/154/10 'Supplementary Memorandum by the Government of Palestine', submitted to UNSCOP, 17 July; FRUS 1946 VII, pp 642–3 Press Release by White House, 2 July; FO 371/52535 E6206/4/31G telegrams, FO to Washington, 28 & 29 June & telegram, Inverchapel, Washington to FO, 28 June; CAB 128/6 CM(46)67 item 3, 11 July.

58. CAB 128/6 CM(46)64 item 2, 4 July 1946.

59. CAB 129/11 CP(46)258 'Report of the Anglo-American Committee of Enquiry', Colonial Secretary, 8 July 1946.

60. CAB 129/11 CP(46)259 'Long Term Policy in Palestine', Colonial Secretary, 8 July 1946.

61. FO 371/52538 E6571/4/31G CP(46)267 'Anglo-U.S. Report — Military Implications', COS, 10 July 1946.

62. CAB 120/659 minute, Ismay to PM, 10 July; CAB 79/50 COS(46)109 meeting, item 2, 12 July; CAB 79/50 COS(46)110 meeting, item 1, 15 July and draft letter annexed, Ismay to PM, 15 July; CO 537/1767 75872/138/22F letter, Ismay to PM, 15 July.

63. PREM 8/627 Part 3 unsigned 'Note for P.M.'s own use', 15 July 1946.

64. FO 371/52547 E7332/4/31G 'Report on CP(46)259 of 8 July 1946', Clayton, undated and minute, Beeley, 6 August 1946; CAB 127/280 'Palestine. Note of Points agreed in conversation with the Foreign Secretary', Brook, 10 July.

65. CAB 127/280, as in note 64. FO 371/52539 E6615/4/31 telegram, Stonehewer-Bird, Baghdad to FO, 13 July 1946 and minute, Baxter, 17 July.

66. FO 371/52539 E6572/4/31G CM(46)67 item 4, 11 July 1946.

67. FO 371/52552 E7940/4/31G telegram, Shone, Beirut to FO, 16 June 1946 and minute, Howe to Sargent, 5 July; FO 371/52552 E7940/4/31G Draft Cabinet Paper 'The Arab proposal for negotiations on Palestine', 3 July.

68. FO 371/52552 E7940/4/31G minutes, Henniker, 8 July 1946, Sargent, 11 July and Howe, 10 July; FO 371/52543 E7065/4/31G minute, Bevin to PM, 21 July; FO 371/52543 E7066/4/31G CM(46)71 item 2, 22 July; FO 371/52543 E7067/4/31G minute, Brook to Howe, 23 July; FRUS 1946 VII, pp 649–50 telegram, Grady, London to S/S, 22 July, p 650 telegram, Byrnes to Grady, 23 July; FO 371/52538 E6523/4/31 telegram, FO to Cairo, Baghdad, Beirut, Jedda, Jerusalem for Amman, 24 July.

69. FRUS 1946 VII, pp 587–8 memorandum of conversation between Bevin, Byrnes and Matthews (Director of the Office of European Affairs), 27 April 1946, pp 601–2 telegram, Byrnes, Paris to Truman, 9 May; FRUS 1945 VIII, p 722 telegram, Byrnes to Pinkerton, Jerusalem, summarizing Truman's remarks of 16 August, 18 August 1945; USNA RG218 JCS Files 1946–7 Box 135 memo, Grantham, aide to Colonel McFarland, 3 May 1946; FRUS 1946 VII, pp 622–3 memorandum, Matthews to Moseley, Secretary of the State–War–Navy Co-ordinating Committee, 7 June, pp 631–3 memorandum, McFarland, Secretary to JCS, to State–War–Navy Co-ordinating Committee, 21 June, p 631n telegram, Byrnes, Paris to Acheson, 26 June, p 638n telegram, Byrnes, Paris to London, 23 June; TL PS Files Box 172 'Matters re. Palestine to be considered before London Conference', undated, with attached covering note labelling these as 'Memorandum of instructions … ', unsigned and undated; FRUS 1946 VII, pp 644–5 'Matters Regarding Palestine … ', approved by President on 9 July.

70. USNA between two separate items 867N.01/6-1864 Box 6756 memorandum 'Considerations bearing upon handling of Palestine Ques-

tion', unsigned, undated, position in file indicating mid-June 1946; FRUS 1946 VII, pp 644–5 'Matters Regarding Palestine to be considered before the London Conference', approved by President on 9 July; TL PS Files Box 172 'Memorandum of the Board of Alternates to the Cabinet Committee on Palestine ... ', unsigned, undated.

71. FO 371/52540 E6728/4/31 record of 7th meeting between Anglo-American official delegations and E6729/4/31 record of 8th meeting, both on 13 July 1946; FO 371/52541 E6794/4/31G note by the British Delegation, 'A Scheme of Provincial Autonomy for Palestine', 13 July.

72. FRUS 1946 VII, pp 646–9 telegrams, Grady, London to S/S, 19 July 1946 and reply, 22 July; CAB 129/11 CP(46)281 'Palestine', Brook, 20 July; FO 371/52543 E7066/4/31G CM(46)71 item 2, 22 July; FRUS 1946 VII, pp 651–2 telegram, Grady, London to S/S, 24 July.

73. FRUS 1946 VII, pp 652–67 telegram, Grady, London to S/S, 24 July 1946; FO 371/52544 E7157/4/31G 'Palestine. Statement of Policy', 26 July.

74. Ganin, p 77; FO 371/52550 E7588/4/31 telegram, Inverchapel, Washington to FO, 5 August 1946; Central Zionist Archives, Z5/385 letter, Mikesell to Glazer, 1 August 1946 in Ganin, p 79; also Wilson, p 92.

75. FO 371/52546 E7331/4/31G CM(46)73 item 2, 25 July 1946; FRUS 1946 VII, p 669 telegram, Attlee to Truman, 25 July; FO 371/52544 E7157/4/31G telegram, FO to Inverchapel, Washington, 25 July; FO 371/52544 E7186/4/31G CM(46)73 item 2, Confidential Annex. 25 July.

76. Frus 1946 VII, pp 669–70 telegrams, Byrnes to Grady, London, 24 July 1946 and reply, 26 July, pp 670–1 record of teletype conference between Washington & London, 26 July; *The Forrestal Diaries*, p 189, entry for 26 July.

77. Nachmani, p 381; AZEC papers, report by McDonald of interview with Truman, 27 July 1946 in Ganin, p 81; FRUS 1946 VII, pp 671–3 telegram, Byrnes, Paris to Truman, 29 July 1946; FO 371/52545 E7258/4/31 telegram, Beeley, Paris to FO, 29 July.

78. Wise papers, AZEC press release, Silver's statement of 25 July 1946 in Ganin, p 80; FRUS 1946 VII, pp 667–8 telegram, Grady, London to S/S, 25 July 1946; Ganin, p 82; Schechtman, pp 166–7; Wallace diary, ed. J. Blum, p 607 in Bullock, *Foreign Secretary*, p 298.

79. Niles papers, letter, Gass, London to Epstein, 28 July 1946 in Sachar, p 39; TL Box 775 Connelly to Truman, 30 July 1946 in Ganin, p 82.

80. FRUS 1946 VII, pp 673–4 memorandum of conversation with Inverchapel by Acting S/S, 30 July 1946; FO 371/52546 E7316/4/31 and E7317/4/31 telegrams, Inverchapel, Washington to FO, 30 July; FRUS 1946 VII, p 674n statement released by White House on 31 July; USNA 867N.01/7-3046 Box 6756 telegram, State Department to Grady, London, 30 July.

81. FO 371/68650 E8350/1078/31G letter, Bromley, Washington to Burrows, FO, 10 July 1948; FRUS 1946 VII, pp 674–5 telegrams, Byrnes, Paris to President, 30 & 31 July 1946; *The Forrestal Diaries* pp 346–7, entry for 3 December 1947.

82. BLPES Dalton Diary Part 1 34 entry for 1 August 1946; FO 371/52546 E7325/4/31 telegram, Inverchapel, Washington to FO, 31 July; FO 371/52546 E7322/4/31G telegram, FO to Paris for PM, 31 July; Hansard vol 426 no 188 cols 974–5 and 990, 31 July; Hansard vol 426 no 189 col 1261 1 August.

83. Schechtman, pp 167–9; FO 371/52551 E7713/4/31 telegram, Inverchapel, Washington to FO, 9 August 1946; FO 371/52551 E7867/4/31G telegram, Truman to Attlee, delivered by US embassy, 8 August and reply, 9 August; FO 371/52552 E8050/4/31G telegram, Truman to Attlee, 13 August and reply, 19 August.

Chapter 4. The London Conference and Truman's Yom Kippur Statement

1. FO 371/52552 E7940/4/31G Draft Cabinet Paper 'The Arab proposal for negotiations on Palestine', 3 July 1946 mentioned above.

2. FO 371/52543 E7066/4/31G CM(46)71 item 2, 22 July 1946; FRUS 1946 VII, pp 649–50 telegram, Harriman, London to S/S, 22 July; FO 371/52543 E7067/4/31G minute, Brook to Howe, 23 July; FRUS 1946 VII, p 691 telegram, Acting S/S to several diplomatic posts, 5 September; FO 371/52559 E9506/4/31 telegram, Inverchapel, Washington to FO, 5 September; FO 371/52556 E8883/4/31 minute, Beeley, 6 September; FO 371/52559 E9506/4/31 memorandum, Beeley to Sargent, 16 September; Snetsinger, pp 6–7; TL Clark Clifford Papers White House press release, 19 January 1949 in Snetsinger, p 135.

3. FO 371/52543 E7066/4/31G CM(46)71 item 2, 22 July 1946; FO 371/52538 E6523/4/31 telegram, FO to Cairo, Baghdad, Beirut, Jedda, Jerusalem for Amman, 24 July; FO 371/52547 E7333/4/31G CP(46)301 'Invitations to Jews and Palestine Arabs', Colonial Secretary, 27 July; FO 371/52547 E7336/4/31G CM(46)74 item 6, 29 July; FO 371E52542 E6900/4/31G minutes, Beeley, 23 & 25 July 1946; Cmd 6873 'Palestine: Statement of Information Relating to Acts of Violence'; FO 371/52542 E6900/4/31G minute, Baxter, 25 July 1946.

4. Minutes of Hadassah, 17 July 1946 p 349 in Ganin, p 85; Minutes of JA, Paris, 3 & 5 August 1946 in Ganin, pp 87, 89.

5. Interview with Godmann, Tel Aviv 1973 in Ganin, p 90; FRUS 1946 VII, pp 679–82 telegram, Acting S/S Acheson to Harriman, London, 12 August 1946, p 682 telegram, Truman to Attlee, 12 August; FO 371/52551 E7750/4/31G telegram, Inverchapel, Washington to FO, 9 August; Minutes of Hadassah, 21 August pp 13–14 in Ganin, p 91; FO 371/52552 E7998/4/31G telegram, Inverchapel, Washington to FO, 14 August.

6. FRUS 1946 VII, pp 684–5 Acting S/S Acheson to Harriman, at Paris, 15 August 1946 giving text to Truman's statement released on 16 August; FO 371/52552 E8005/4/31G telegram, Bevin, Paris to FO, 14 August; FRUS 1946 VII, pp 685–6 telegram, Harriman, London to Acting S/S, 15 August, p 687 telegram, Attlee to Truman, 19 August.

7. Silver papers, telegram, Silver to Ben Gurion, 14 August 1946 in Ganin, p 95; Minutes of JA, Paris, 17 August 1946 p 8 in Ganin, p 95; FO 371/52553 E8203/4/31G telegram, FO to Cairo, Baghdad, Beirut, Jedda, Jerusalem, 19 August 1946; FO 371/52562 E10639/4/31G telegram, Bevin, Paris to FO and FO 800/485 telegrams, PM & Colonial Secretary to Bevin, 30 August.

8. FO 371/52547 E7386/4/31G CP(46)306 'Illegal Immigration into Palestine', Tedder, Montgomery, McGrigor, 29 July 1946; FO 371/52547 E7339/4/31G CM(46)75 Confidential Annex, 30 July 1946; CAB 129/12 CP(46)310 'Illegal Immigration into Palestine', Colonial Secretary, 5 August; CO 537/2346 75872/154/10 'Supplementary Memorandum by the Government of Palestine', submitted to UNSCOP, 17 July 1947; FO 371/52627 E7817/7656/31G minute, Beith, 16 August 1946; also see reports from posts in Eastern Europe and Moscow in FO 371/52544 E7162, FO 371/52627 E7723, FO 371/52629 E8079, E8141 & E8292, and FO 371/52632 E8923, E8947, E9156; FO 371/52631 E8836/7656/31 telegram, Cunningham, Palestine to Colonial Secretary, 24 August 1946; FO 371/52630 E8339/7656/31G telegram, Cavendish Bentinck, Warsaw to FO, 21 August; FO 371/52559 E9467/4/31G telegram, Cunningham, Palestine to Colonial Secretary, 20 September; FO 371/52642 E8915/8035/31 telegram, Bevin, Paris to FO, 5 September.

9. CO 537/2346 75872/154/10 'Supplementary Memorandum by the Government of Palestine', submitted to UNSCOP, 17 July 1947; PREM 8/627 Part V extract from letter, Weizmann to Martin, 16 September 1946; FO 371/52645 E9692/8053/31 telegram, Cunningham, Palestine to Colonial Secretary, 25 September; PREM 8/627 Part V note of interview with Weizmann and minute, Gater to PM, 30 September; FO 371/52645 E9778E8035/31G telegram, Colonial Secretary to Palestine, 27 September; FO 371/52560 E10030/4/31 note of meeting at FO, 1 October; FO 371/52559 E9666/4/31G telegram, Colonial Secretary to Cunningham, Palestine, 25 September; FO 371/52564 E10964/4/31 CM(46)94 item 4, 4 November.

10. FO 371/52560 E9792/4/31G and FO 371/52561 E10262/4/31G telegrams, Cunningham, Palestine to Colonial Secretary, 27 September & 12 October 1946; Montgomery, p 467.

11. FO 371/52550 E7611/4/31G memorandum, Wikeley & Howe to S/S, 6 August 1946.

12. FO 371/52544 E7164/4/31 telegram, Young, Beirut to FO, 26 July 1946 and reply, 7 August; FO 371/52548 E7469/4/31G telegram, Young, Beirut to FO, 3 August; FO 371/52551 E7753/4/31 telegram, Busk, Baghdad to FO, 8 August; FRUS 1946 VII, pp 676–7 telegram, Lyon, Cairo to S/S, 2 August, p 683 telegram, Patterson, Cairo to S/S, 15 August; FO 371/52642 E8783/8035/31 telegram, Young, Beirut to FO, 3 September and E8791/8035/31 telegram, Campbell, Cairo to FO, 3 September.

13. FO 371/52549 E7549/4/31G telegram, Young, Beirut to FO, 5 August 1946; FO 371/52549 E7528/4/31G telegram, Young, Beirut to FO, 5 August, minute, Beith, 8 August and telegram, FO to Beirut, 9 August.

14. FO 371/52551 E7868/4/31G minute, Baker, 15 August 1946; FO 371/52553 E8106/4/31 telegram, Kirkbride, Amman to FO, 16 August and minutes, Wikeley, 21 August and Egyptian Dept, 23 August; FO 371/52554 E8424/4/31 telegram, Campbell, Cairo to FO, 26 August; FO 371/52551 E7868/4/31G minute, Howe, 17 August.

15. FO 371/52555 E8701/4/31 letter, Locker to Bevin, 26 August 1946 and reply, 28 August; FO 371/52555 E8731/4/31G and E8732/4/31G telegrams, Campbell, Cairo to FO, 31 August.

16. FO 371/52555 E8732/4/31G minute, Beeley, 5 September 1946; FO 371/52556 E8873/4/31G telegram, Campbell, Cairo to FO, 2 September; FO 371/52642 E8776E8035/31G telegram, Bevin, Paris to FO, 3 September and minute, Beeley, 5 September.

17. FO 371/52556 E8990/4/31G and FO 371/52643 E8932/8035/31 telegrams, Campbell, Cairo to FO, 8 September 1946; Bullock, *Foreign Secretary*, p 302; CAB 127/280 copy letter, Clayton, Cairo to Smart, 31 August and minute, Brook, 25 September; CO 537/1783 75872/148 Part 2 letter, Cunningham, Palestine to Colonial Secretary, 20 September.

18. FO 371/52556 E8886/4/31G minute, Beeley, 9 September 1946.

19. FO 371/52643 E9119/8035/31 text of PM's speech, 10 September 1946.

20. FO 371/52643 E9121/8035/31 PC(A) (P)1 meeting and E9122/8035/31 PC(A) (P)2 meeting, 10 and 11 September 1946.

21. FO 371/52643 E9123/8035/31 PC(A) (P)3 meeting and E9124/8035/31 PC(A) (P) 4 meeting, 12 September 1946; FO 371/52643 E9125/8035/31 note of interview with Jamali, Beeley, 12 September.

22. FO 371/52644 E9178/8035/31 PC(A) (P)5 meeting, 16 September 1946.

23. FO 371/52644 E9361/8035/31 PC(A) (P) 3 'Joint Statement by the Arab States Delegations', 19 September 1946; FO 371/52644 E9394/8035/31 PC(A) (P)6 meeting, 20 September; FO 371/52644 E9426/8035/31 PC(A) (Committee) 1 meeting and E9472/8035/31 PC(A) (Committee) 2 meeting, 21 & 23 September; FO 371/52645 E9830/8035/31 PC(A) (P)4 'Constitutional Proposals put forward by the Arab Delegations', note by the Secretary, 30 September; FO 371/52645 E9846/8035/31 PC(A) (Committee) 5 meeting, 1 October.

24. FO 371/52645 E9893/8035/31 PC(A) (P) 7 meeting, 2 October 1946.

25. FO 371/52555 E8635/4/31G telegram, Inverchapel, Washington to FO, 30 August 1946 and reply, 3 September; FO 371/52559 E9755/4/31G DO(46)25 meeting, item 3, 19 September.

26. FO 371/52643 E9025/8035/31 minute, Brook, 2 September 1946; FRUS 1946 VII, pp 696–700 telegram, Gallman, London to S/S, 17, 20, 23 September and 2 October, pp 700–1 telegram, Attlee to Truman, 2 October.

27. FRUS 1946 VII, pp 701–3 telegram, Truman to Attlee, 3 October 1946; FO 371/52560 E9938/4/31 telegram, Inverchapel, Washington to FO, 3 October.

28. FRUS 1946 VII, p 691 telegram, Acting S/S, Washington to various posts, 5 September 1946; FO 371/52556 E8871/4/31 telegram, Inverchapel, Washington to FO, 5 September.

29. FO 371/52560 E10160/4/31G despatch, Attlee to Truman, 3 October 1946; FRUS 1946 VII p 704 telegram, Attlee to Truman; PREM 8/627 Part V note, Beards (PM's Private Secretary); FO 371/52560 E10162/4/31G telegram, FO to Paris, Attlee for Bevin; FO 371/52560 E10161/4/31G telegram, FO to Paris; FO 371/52560 E9966/4/31 and E9999/4/31G telegrams, Paris to FO; all 4 October.

30. FO 371/52560 E9987/4/31 telegram, Inverchapel, Washington to FO and FO 371/52561 E10164/4/31G telegrams, FO to Washington, all 4 October 1946.

31. FRUS 1946 VII, pp 693–5 memorandum, Acting S/S Clayton to Truman, 12 September 1946; Niles papers, copy memorandum, Truman to Clayton in Sachar, p 43.

32. TL Democratic National Committee Library Clipping File, HST File, Box 24 advertisement in *New York Herald Tribune*, 30 September 1946; minutes of AZEC, 1 October 1946, pp 2–4 in Ganin, p 102; Niles papers, copy letter, Wise to Rosenblatt, 10 September in Sachar, pp 41–2.

33. Niles papers, copy letter, Wise to Truman, 7 October 1946 in Sachar, p 44; TL copies of documents in Weizmann Archives, Box 1 letter, Epstein to Goldmann, 9 October; Wilson, p 98.

34. Acheson, p 176; M. Truman, p 382; FRUS 1946 VII, p 699 memorandum, Villard to Clayton, giving account of conversation between Truman and Wadsworth, 27 September 1946.

35. FO 371/52560 E9938/4/31 telegram, Inverchapel, Washington to FO, 3 October 1946; USNA 867N.01/10-346 Box 6757 memorandum of conversation, Inverchapel and Acheson, 3 October; Bodleian Library Oxford, dep. Inverchapel 1940s, Box 11 Appointments Diary, 1946; FO 800/485 letter, Inverchapel to Bevin, 20 June; FO 371/52531 E5785/4/31 minute, Beeley, 26 June; BLPES Dalton Diary, Part I 34 entry for 5 October; TL copies of documents in Weizmann Archives, Box 1 letter, Epstein to Goldmann, 9 October.

36. *New York Times*, 7 October 1946, Reston's article in Wilson, p 98; TL copies of documents in Weizmann Archives, Box 1 letter, Epstein to Goldmann, 9 October; minutes of AZEC, pp 1, 4–5, 14 & 21 October in Ganin, pp 106–7; *New York Times*, 30 October in Ganin, p 107; Hartmann, p 26.

37. FRUS 1946 VII, pp 704–5 telegrams, Truman to Attlee and reply, 4 October 1946; PREM 8/627 Part V draft message, Attlee to Truman; Wilson, p 99; FRUS 1946 VII pp 706–8 telegram, Truman to Attlee, 10 October 1946; PREM 8/627 Part V minute, Attlee, 22 October; FO 371/52562 E10692/4/31G memorandum, Dixon to Howe, 25 October.

38. FO 371/52563 E10827/4/31G CM(46)91 item 2, 25 October 1946; PREM 8/627 Part V telegram, Colonial Secretary to Cunningham, Palestine, 10 October and minute, Rowan, 10 October with Attlee's note; FO 371/52561 E10312/4/31 minute, Butler to Howe, 7 October.

39. FO 371/52561 E9670/9632/31 note on talk with Byrnes, Bevin, 26 September 1946; FRUS 1946 VII, pp 710–13 memorandum, Henderson to Acheson, 21 October.

40. FRUS 1946 VII, pp 708–9 letter, Ibn Saud to Truman, transmitted 15 October 1946; Wilson, p 100; FRUS 1946 VII, pp 714–20 telegram, Truman to Ibn Saud, 25 October 1946 and letter, Ibn Saud to Truman, transmitted 2 November; USNA 867N.01/10-846 Box 6757 telegram, Mattison, Damascus to S/S, 8 October.

41. TL Miscellaneous Historical Documents 184 'President's statement of 4 October 1946', memorandum, Merriam to Henderson, 15 October 1946; Wilson, p 100.

Chapter 5. Decision Time: the Winter of 1946–7

1. FO 371/52653 E10044/10044/31G minute, Howe, 3 October and Beckett, 7 October.

2. FO 371/52561 E10358/4/31 despatch, Inverchapel, Washington to FO, 12 October 1946 and minute, Beeley, 21 October; FO 371/52646 E10505/8035/31 minute, Beeley, 21 October; FO 371/52563 E10827/4/31G CM(46)91 item 2, 25 October.

3. FO 371/52562 E10668/4/31G letter, Creech Jones to Foreign Secretary, 18 October and copy despatch, High Commissioner to Colonial Secretary, 20 September.

4. FO 371/52562 E10668/4/31G minute, 'Palestine', Howe to S/S, 23 October 1946.

5. CO 537/1783 75872/148 Part 2 memorandum, 'Palestine Conference, 1946', Harris, 28 October 1946 and minute, Martin to Gater, 29 October; FO 371/52563 E10911/4/31 letter, Martin to Baxter, 4 November.

6. FO 371/52563 E10911/4/31 minute, Beeley, 6 November 1946; CO 537/1783 75872/148 Part 2 memorandum, Harris and minute, Martin, 19 November; *ibid* minute, apparently by Gater, 21 November.

7. CO 537/1783 75872/148 Part 2 minute, Creech Jones, undated, on Harris' memorandum of 19 November 1946.

8. CO 537/1783 75872/148 Part 2 note, 'Meeting with the Secretary of State on November 27th', 1946, unsigned and undated.

9. FO 371/52559 E9509/4/31 minute to Fitzmaurice, 3 October 1946; *ibid* minutes, Fitzmaurice, 7 October and Beeley, 21 September.

10. FO 371/52566 E11785/4/31G PM/NY/46/1 memorandum, Bevin, New York to PM, 26 November 1946; FO 371/52565 E11610/4/31 telegram, Bevin, New York to PM & Cabinet Distribution, 26 November.

11. FO 371/52563 E10827/4/31G CM(46)91 item 2, 25 October 1946; CAB 128/8 CM(46)97 item 4, Confidential Annex, 18 November; FRUS 1946 VII, pp 723–6 memorandum of conversation between Inverchapel and Acting S/S Acheson, 22 November; FO 371/52566 E11785/4/31G PM/NY/46/1 memorandum, Bevin, New York to PM, 26 November; FO 371/52565 E11611/4/31G telegram, Inverchapel, Washington to FO, 26 November; FO 371/52565 E11612/4/31G telegram, Inverchapel, Washington to FO, 26 November.

12. Weizmann Archives, letter, Ben Gurion, Paris to Weizmann, 28 October 1946 in Ganin, pp 112–13; FO 371/52565 E11424/4/31 and

E11549/4/31 record of conversations between Bevin and Silver, 14 & 20 November 1946; FO 371/52565 E11649/4/31 telegram, Bevin, New York to FO for PM, 28 November.

13. PREM 8/627 Part VI minute, Creech Jones to PM appending draft and note, Attlee, 29 November 1946; FO 371/52565 E11649/4/31 telegram, PM to Foreign Secretary, New York, 29 November.

14. FO 371/52566 E11787/4/31G CM(47)101 item 2 and FO 371/52565 E11610/4/31 telegram, PM to Foreign Secretary, New York, 28 November 1946.

15. Montgomery, p 430; FO 371/52565 E11476/4/31G COS(46)169 meeting, item 7, 20 November 1946; CAB 131/1 DO(46)33 meeting, item 1, 20 November.

16. USNA 867N.01/12-3046 Box 6758 telegram, Gallman, London to S/S, 30 December 1946; CO 537/2269 75015/82A report, Wickham, 2 December; FO 371/52567 E12520/4/31G DO(46)145 'Palestine: Use of the Armed Forces', 19 December; *ibid* minute, Beeley, 31 December; CAB 131/5 DO(47)1 meeting, item 1, 1 January 1947.

17. CAB 131/5 DO(47)1 Hurewitz, p 280; BLPES Dalton Diary Part I 34, entry for 20 December 1946.

18. FO 371/52646 E11480/8035/31G CM(46)99 item 3, 21 November 1946; FO 371/52646 E11114/8035/31G telegrams, PM to Foreign Secretary, New York, 14 November 1946 and E11422/8035/31G telegram, Cadogan, New York to FO, 19 November.

19. CAB 127/281 copy letter, Gater to Sargent, 4 December 1946.

20. CAB 127/281 memorandum, 'Note on the Colonial Office letter of 4th December, 1946', unsigned and undated. Physically the memorandum is similar to others in file from Cornwall-Jones to Brook.

21. CAB 127/281 letter, Brook to Beeley and reply, 4 December 1946; CAB 127/281 note, Beeley to Brook, 16 December.

22. FO 371/52567 E12394/4/31G two papers and covering minute 'Palestine' to S/S, 18 December 1946.

23. FO 371/52567 E12395/4/31G memorandum, 'Palestine' and covering minute, Brook to Foreign Secretary, 20 December 1946.

24. FO 371/52567 E12395/4/31G note, E.B. on Brook's minute; E12394/4/31G E.B.'s marginal note on minute, Howe to Sargent, 19 December 1946; FO 371/61761 E74/46/31G minute, Dixon to S/S, 23 December; *ibid* draft note for PM, Beeley, 22 December; *ibid* minute, Creech Jones to Foreign Secretary, 23 December with amended draft.

25. FO 371/61761 E74/46/31G minute, Beeley, 3 January 1947 and note, E.B. on minute from Dixon, 23 December 1946; CAB 127/281 memorandum, C[ornwall-] J[ones] to Brook and memorandum, Brook to PM, 24 December.

26. Ganin, pp 115–17; FO 371/61762 E153/46/31 memorandum, 'Palestine' and covering letter, Creech Jones to Bevin, 31 December 1946.

27. FO 371/61762 E153/46/31 'Palestine. A Comment on the Colonial Secretary's Paper', unsigned and undated and note, Dixon, 1 January 1947.

28. FO 371/61874 E2932/951/31 draft memorandum, Garran, 6 January 1947.

29. FO 371/61858 E140/115/31 minute, Beckett, 6 January 1947; CAB 129/16 CP(47)28 'Palestine: Reference to United Nations', Bevin, 13 January.

30. FO 371/61858 E647/115/31 letter, Howe to S/S, 16 January 1947; FO 371/61858 E877/115/31 minute, Howe to S/S, 21 January; FO 371/61874 E951/951/31 minute, Howe, 22 January & Bevin's minute.

31. CAB 131/5 DO(47)1 meeting, item 1, 1 January 1947; FO 371/61762 E299/46/31G note for S/S's survey of foreign policy at Cabinet on ?3 January, Beeley, undated; DEFE 6/1 JP(47)1(Final) 'Palestine — Strategic Requirements', JPS, 5 January; CAB 131/4 DO(47)3 'Palestine — Strategic Requirements', COS, 6 January.

32. DEFE 4/1 COS(47)9 meeting, Staff Conference, 13 January 1947; Montgomery, p 436.

33. FO 371/61763 E668/46/31G minute, Howe to Sargent, 13 January 1947; CAB 128/11 CM(47)6 item 4, Confidential Annex, 15 January; FO 371/61763 E670/46/31G CP(47)30 'Palestine', Bevin, 14 January.

34. PREM 8/627 Part VI memorandum, 'Palestine', Brook to PM, 14 January 1947.

35. CAB 128/11 CM(47)6 items 3 & 4, Confidential Annex, 15 January 1947.

36. CAB 129/16 CP(47)31 'Palestine: Future Policy', Creech Jones, 16 January 1947; FO 371/61764 E671/46/31G CP(47)32 'Palestine: Future Policy', Creech Jones, 16 January 1947.

37. RH Creech Jones papers, Box 32 File 3 letter, Creech Jones to Callaghan, 30 November 1961; Creech Jones Papers, Box 31 File 3 draft paper 'Palestine: Future Policy', manuscript note 'Colonial Secretary's Partition Plan', undated, listed as January 1947; Ilan in Kedourie & Haim, p 190; Churchill Coll. Cambridge, Attlee papers, ATLE 1/17 draft autobiography, p 8.

38. FRUS 1946 VII, pp 722–3 memorandum of conversation, Goldmann, Henderson, Porter, 6 November 1946, pp 732–5 memorandum, Merriam to Henderson, 27 December, p 732n memorandum, Henderson to Acheson, undated.

39. FO 371/61763 E670/46/31G minute, Howe to Sargent, 16 January 1947; *ibid* 'Notes for a draft telegram to Lord Inverchapel, unsigned and undated and telegram, FO to Inverchapel, Washington, 17 January.

40. FRUS 1947 V, pp 1008–11 memorandum of conversation, Inverchapel, Acheson, 21 January 1947; USNA 501.BB Palestine/1-2147 Box 2181 memorandum, Henderson to Acheson, 21 January.

41. FO 371/61764 E743/46/31G telegram, Inverchapel, Washington to FO, 21 January 1947 and minute, Beeley, 22 January; UN arch. UNSCOP 1947 DAG–13/3.0.0 Box 15 'Palestine. A Study of Partition', CO, April; FO 371/61764 E743/46/31G telegram, FO to Inverchapel, Washington, 27 January.

42. FRUS 1947 V, pp 1014–15 'Written Oral Statement', handed to Inverchapel on 27 January 1947.

43. CAB 127/281 'Palestine', Brook to PM, 21 January 1947; PREM 8/627 Part VI 'Palestine', Brook to PM, 22 January.

44. CAB 128/11 CM(47)11 item 2, Confidential Annex, 22 January 1947.

45. FO 371/61746 E322/2/31 letter, Creech Jones to Bevin, 7 January 1947; FO 371/61747 E981/2/31 letter, Azzam to Campbell, Cairo, 18 January; FRUS 1947 V, pp 1015–17 telegram, Gallman, London to S/S, 28 January.

46. FO 371/61747 E894/2/31 PC(A)(P)8 meeting, 27 January 1947.

47. FO 371/61747 E1075/2/31 minute to Foreign Secretary, 29 January 1947.

48. FO 371/61747 E986/2/31 PC(A)(P)9 meeting, 30 January 1947.

49. FO 371/61747 E1121/2/31 PC(A)(P)10 meeting, 4 February 1947.

50. FRUS 1947 V, pp 1017–21 telegrams, Gallman, London to S/S, 30 January 1947, pp 1025–8 telegrams, Gallman, London to S/S, 4 & 5 February; FO 371/61747 E1061/2/31 telegram, FO to Inverchapel, Washington, 6 February.

51. CAB 125/11 CM(47)11 item 2, Confidential Annex, 22 January 1947; FO 371/61765 E1276/46/31G 'Palestine. Points to be stressed', Bevin for Brook and CP(47)49 'Palestine', Bevin & Creech Jones, 6 February.

52. CAB 128/9 CM(47)18 item 2, 7 February 1948.

53. FO 371/61748 E1231/2/31 PC(A)(P)5 note by British Delegation, 7 February 1947; *ibid* E1328/2/31 PC(A)(P) 6 note by Arab Delegations, 10 February; FRUS 1947 V, pp 1040–2 telegram, Gallman, London to S/S, 11 February; FO 371/61766 E1410/46/31G report on conversation with Shertok, Sir O. Harvey, 10 February; CO 537/2333 75872/152 telegram, Colonial Secretary to Cunningham, Palestine, 13 Febraury 1947.

54. FO 371/61748 E1386/2/31 telegram, Colonial Secretary to Cunning-ham, Palestine, 13 February 1947 summarizing PC(A)(P) 11 meeting, 12 February; FRUS 1947 V, pp 1046–7 telegram, Gallman, London to S/S, 14 February.

55. CAB 129/17 CP(47)59 'Palestine', Bevin & Creech Jones, 13 February 1947.

56. CAB 128/9 CM(47)22 item 2, 14 February 1947; Ben Gurion, 'Memoirs' in 'Jewish Observer and Middle East Review' of 25 December 1964 in Wilson, p 105; for a different view see Ilan in Kedourie & Haim.

57. CAB 128/9 CM(47)22 item 2, 14 February 1947; PREM 8/627 Part VI 'Palestine. (CP(47)59)', Brook to PM, 14 February.

58. PREM 8/627, as in note 57.

59. FO 371/61748 E1435/2/31 PC(A)(P)12 meeting, 14 February 1947.

60. CO 537/2333 75872/152 minute, Martin, PREM 8/627 Part VI 'Palestine. (CP(47)59)', Brook to PM and CAB 128/9 CM(47)22 item 2, all 14 February 1947.

61. CO 537/2334 75872/153 telegram, Cunningham, Palestine to Colonial Secretary, 20 February 1947 and 'Draft of Cabinet Paper. Palestine. Arrangements during the interim period ...', undated.

62. CO 537/2334 75872/153 and note of meeting at CO, 27 February 1947 and minute, Mathieson, 28 February; *ibid* telegram, Cunningham, Palestine to Colonial Secretary, 2 March and note, 'Palestine', Creech Jones after discussion with Bevin, 3 March; FO 371/61802 E1951/48/31 minute, 'Interim policy for Jewish Immigration', 3 March; CO 537/2334 75873/153 minutes, Lloyd, 4 & 18 March and telegram, Cunningham, Palestine to Colonial Secretary, 16 March; CAB 131/5 DO(47)7 meeting, item 1, 12 March; CAB 129/17 CP(47)95 'Situation in Palestine', Creech Jones, 19 March.

63. FO 371/61763 E670/46/31G 'The Present Position', FO paper annexed to CP(47)30 'Palestine', Bevin, 14 January 1947; BLPES Dalton Diary Part 1 35 entries for 17 January, 5 & 24 February; FO 800/514 letter, Dalton to Bevin, 3 March; Hansard vol 433 no 50 col 993 18 February.

64. FO 371/52565 E11526/46/31G memorandum, Sargent to Bevin, 23 November 1946, amended version given to Byrnes 27 November; FO 371/61765 E1276/46/31G 'Palestine. Points to be stressed', Bevin for Brook, 6 February; FRUS 1947 V, p 1032 memorandum of press conference, Marshall, 7 February; FO 371/61748 E1358/2/31 minute, Henniker to Foreign Secretary; FO 371/61765 E1276/46/31G telegram, FO to Washington, Bevin for Marshall, 9 February.

65. USNA 867N.01/2-347 Box 6758 memorandum on conversation with Henderson, McClintock to Ross, 3 February 1947; FRUS 1947 V, pp 1038–9 memorandum, Henderson to Acheson, 10 February; pp 1048–9 memorandum, Acheson to Henderson, 15 February, pp 1051–2 letter, Henderson to Acheson, 17 February, pp 1054–5 telegram, Marshall to Bevin, 21 February.

66. FO 371/61767 E1481/46/31G minutes, Beeley and Howe, 20 February 1947; CAB 128/9 CM(47)27 item 3, 18 February; Hansard vol 433 no 50 cols 992–3 18 February; FO 371/61767 E1481/46/31G telegrams, FO to Inverchapel, Washington, 18 & 21 February; Churchill Coll. Cambridge, Cadogan Diary ACAD 1/18 entry for 26 February; FO 371/61769 E1786/46/31 telegram, Cadogan, New York to FO, 26 February & reply, 3 March; FRUS 1947 V, p 1061 telegram, Acheson, Washington to Austin, New York, 6 March; FO 371/61769 E2041/46/31 minute, Beeley, 11 March; FO 371/61770 E2385/46/31 telegram, FO to Inverchapel, Washington, 20 March; FO 371/61771 E2627/46/31 telegram, Inverchapel, Washington to FO, 25 March & reply, 26 March; FO 371/61771 E2675/46/31 telegram, Inverchapel, Washington to FO, 26 March & reply, 27 March; FO 371/61771 E2764/46/31 and E2861/46/31 telegrams, Cadogan, New York to FO, 29 March and 2 April.

67. FO 371/52571 E11758/14/31 telegram, FO to New York, Creech Jones for Bevin, 30 November 1946; FO 371/52571 E11758/14/31 and E12052/14/31 telegram, FO to Inverchapel, Washington, 7 December & reply, 10 December; FO 371/52571 E12099/14/31 minutes Beeley and Rundall, 16 & 17 December; USNA 867N.01/3-1847 Box 6759 memorandum, Henderson (drafted by Merriam) to Acheson, 18 March 1947.

68. FRUS 1947 V, pp 1056–7 memorandum, McWilliams to S/S, 25 February 1947, pp 1057–8 statement issued by White House, 26 February; Bickerton, pp 90–6.

69. CAB 129/15 CP(46)450 'Withdrawal of British Troops from Egypt', Brook, 9 December 1946 annexing telegram, Bevin to PM, 5 December & memorandum, Secretary of COS Committee to PM, 7 December; CAB 128/6 CM(46)105 item 4, 12 December; CAB 127/281 memorandum 'Palestine', Brook to PM, 21 January 1947; CAB 131/4 DO(47)3 'Palestine — Strategic Requirements', COS, 6 January.

70. DEFE 4/1 COS(47)21 meeting, 6 February 1947; CAB 128/9 CM(47)18 item 2, 7 February; DEFE 4/1 COS(47)24 meeting, item 1, 14 February; CAB 128/9 CM(47)22 item 2, 14 February; PREM 8/627 Part VI 'Palestine. (CP(47)59)', Brook to PM, 14 February.

71. CAB 131/4 DO(47)23 'The Defence of the Commonwealth', COS, 7 March 1947; FO 371/61774 E3452/46/31 telegram, Cadogan, New York to FO, 24 April; BLPES Dalton Diary Part 1 35 manuscript entry for 20 September.

72. BLPES Dalton Diary Part 1 35, entry for 27 January 1947; FO 371/61903 E1721/1585/31 minute, Beeley, 1 March.

Chapter 6. The United Nations Special Committee on Palestine

1. Bullock, *Foreign Secretary*, p 362–3.

2. FO 371/61769 E2019/46/31 telegrams, Cadogan, New York to FO, 6 March 1947 and Sargent to Bevin, Moscow, 13 March.

3. FO 371/61770 E2301/46/31 telegrams, Bevin, Moscow to Sargent, 15 March 1947 and reply, 22 March; FO 371/61771 E2738/46/31 telegram, Bevin, Moscow to Sargent, 30 March, minute, Beeley, 31 March and telegram, Sargent to Bevin, 4 April; FO 371/61772 E3092/46/31 minute, Henniker to S/S, 5 April with E.B.'s marginal note and telegram, Bevin, Moscow to Sargent, 11 April.

4. FO 371/61874 E2490/951/31 minute, Baxter, 24 March 1947; *ibid* E2077/951/31 telegram, Eyres, Damascus to FO, 8 March 1947; *ibid* E2614/951/31 telegram, Campbell, Cairo to FO, 25 March; *ibid* E2616/951/31 telegram, Stonehewer-Bird, Baghdad to FO, 25 March; *ibid* E2638/951/31 telegram, Campbell, Cairo to Baghdad, 25 March.

5. FO 371/61773 E3273/46/31 memorandum, Butler to Sargent, 23 April 1947 and telegram, Sargent to Bevin, Moscow, 24 April; FO 371/61774 E3452/46/31 telegram, Cadogan, New York to FO, 24 April; FO 371/61774 E3458/46/31 extract from House of Lords debates, 23 April and memorandum, Baxter to Sargent, 1 May.

6. FO 371/61774 E3452/46/31 telegram, Cadogan, New York to FO, 24 April 1947; FO 371/61774 E3507/46/31 letter, Stapleton, COS to Garran, FO, 21 April; FO 371/61773 E3368/46/31 telegram, Cadogan, New York to FO, 22 April.

7. CAB 128/9 CM(47)35 item 5, 3 April 1947 and appended letter, Montgomery (CIGS) to Minister of Defence, 9 April; FO 371/61775 E3666/46/31G CM(47)41 item 2, 29 April; PREM 8/859 Part I memorandum by Butler for Sargent for PM, appending Colonial Secretary's view, 27 April; FO 371/61774 E3548/46/31 telegram, Strang, Berlin with Bevin for Sargent, 28 April.

8. FO 371/61774 E3611/46/31 telegram, Cadogan, New York to FO, 30 April 1947 and minutes Beith, 1 May, PM, & Baxter, 2 May; FO 371/61776 E3898/46/31 telegram, Cadogan, New York to FO, 9 May with E.B.'s note and minute, Garran, 12 May.

9. FRUS 1947 V, pp 1068–9 circular telegram from Acting S/S, 4 April 1947, p 1070 note of telegrams, State Dept to US UN delegation, 7 & 9 April; Hadawi (ed.), p vii; Jones, p 123; FO 371/61776 E3726/46/31 telegram, Stokes, Beirut for S/S, 1 May and minute, Beith, 6 May; FO 371/61776 E3722/46/31 telegram, Cadogan, New York to FO, 3 May.

10. FO 371/61772 E3094/46/31 telegrams, Inverchapel, Washington to FO, 11 April 1947, reply, 15 April and Bevin, Moscow to FO, 11 April; FRUS 1947 V, pp 1070–2 memorandum, S/S (prepared by Rusk, Director of Office of Special Political Affairs) for President, 17 April, pp 1072–3 memorandum, Acheson to Henderson, 17 April; FO 371/61773 E3187/46/31 telegrams, Cadogan, New York to FO, 15 April and reply, 26 April; FO 371/61775 E3663/46/31 telegram, Cadogan, New York to FO, 29 April.

11. FO 371/61774 E3486/46/31 draft brief of 18 April 1947 approved by PM, 24 April.

12. FO 371/61773 E3373/46/31 telegrams, Eyres, Ankara to FO, 22 April 1947 and reply, 25 April; FO 371/61875 E3497/951/31 telegram, Campbell, Cairo to FO, 26 April and minute, Garran, 30 April; FO 371/61774 E3608/46/31 letter, Chancery, Washington to FO, 25 April.

13. FO 371/61775 E3699/46/31 telegrams, Cadogan, New York to FO, 3 May 1947 and reply, 7 May; FO 371/61776 E3753/46/31 telegrams, Cadogan, New York to FO, 5 May and FO to Montevideo, 12 May; FO 371/61778 E4169/46/31 and E4392/46/31 telegrams, Montevideo to FO, 16 and 23 May; FO 371/61776 E3874/46/31 and FO 371/61777 E4043/46/31 telegrams, Cadogan, New York to FO, 8 & 14 May; Churchill Coll. Cambridge, Cadogan Diary ACAD 1/18 entry for 13 May.

14. FO 371/61777 E4043/46/31 telegram, Cadogan, New York to FO, 14 May 1947; FO 371/61778 E4170/46/31 and E4264/46/31 telegrams, Hallett, Guatemala to FO, reply and response, 16, 17 and 20 May.

15. FRUS 1947 V, pp 1077–80 editorial note summarizing UN procedures; FO 371/61776 E3828/46/31 and E3874/46/31 telegrams, Cadogan, New York to FO, 7 & 8 May; FO 371/61776 E3899/46/31 and FO 371/61777 E3927/46/31 and E3953/46/31 telegrams, Cadogan, New York to FO, 9, 10 & 12 May; FRUS 1947 V, pp 1083–4 recommendation of First Committee dated 13 May.

16. Churchill Coll. Cambridge, Cadogan Diary ACAD 1/18 entry for 13 May 1947; FO 371/61777 E4115/46/31 memorandum, Garran to Sargent,

23 May; FO 371/61777 E3953/46/31, E4000/46/31 and E4051/46/31 telegrams, Cadogan, New York to FO, 12, 13 and 14 May.

17. FRUS 1947 V, pp 1085–6 memorandum, Marshall to Truman, 16 May 1947; CAB 131/5 DO(47)7 meeting item 1, 12 March; FO 371/61770 E2492/46/31 note of Creech Jones' answer, 19 March; DEFE 4/3 COS(47)50 meeting item 2, 9 April; CAB 128/9 CM(47)30 item 1, 20 March; CO 537/2345 75872/154/6 copy letter, Baxter (for Attlee) to Cadogan, 29 March with appended 'Note on ... illegal immigration'; FO 371/61777 E4051/46/31 telegram, Cadogan, New York to FO, 14 May; FO 371/61780 E5047/46/31 printed 'Report on Special Session ...', Cadogan to Bevin, 13 June.

18. FRUS 1947 V, pp 1084–5 Gromyko's statement, 14 May 1947; FO 371/61777 E4113/46/31 minute, Beith, 19 May; Ganin, p 121.

19. Ganin, p 121.

20. FO 371/61778 E4449/46/31 and FO 371/61779 E4729/46/31 telegrams, Cadogan, New York to FO, 26 May and 2 June 1947; FRUS 1947 V, pp 1103–5 despatch, S/S Marshall to US Representative at UN (Austin), 13 June, pp 1107–12 despatch, Macatee, Jerusalem to S/S, 23 June; Wilson, p 110.

21. FO 371/61781 E5588/46/31 letter, Gurney, Jerusalem to Martin, CO, 17 June 1947; CO 537/2346 75872/54/10 'Supplementary Memorandum ...', 17 July; CO 537/2343 75872/154A 'The Political History of Palestine ...', July; FO 371/61782 E6243/46/31 despatch, MacGillivray, Palestine to Martin, 7 July and minute, Beeley, 17 July; CO 537/2344 75872/154/4 minute, Harris to Martin, 28 March covering memorandum 'Palestine. A Study of Partition' also in UN arch. UNSCOP 1947 DAG-13/3.0.0 Box 15; FO 371/61875 E6515/951/31 minute on meeting in CO, 24 July; FO 371/61785 E7487/46/31 letter, Mathieson, CO to MacGillivray, 15 August; FO 371/61782 E5948/46/31 telegram, Cunningham, Palestine to Colonial Secretary, 5 July and minute, Beeley, 7 July; FO 371/61875 E6515/951/31 letter, Martin to Butler, 18 July.

22. FRUS 1947 V, p 1103 circular telegram from S/S Marshall and pp 1103–5 despatch, Marshall to Austin, both 13 June 1947, pp 1120–3 memorandum, Henderson to S/S, 7 July; USNA Box 2183 no reference, adjacent to 501.BB Palestine/1–548 memorandum, McClintock to Rusk, 21 May; FRUS 1947 V, pp 1101–2 note of White House release of 5 June; *Forrestal Diaries* pp 303–4, TL Box 773 Truman to Wise, 6 August 1947 in Ganin, p 125; UN arch. UNSCOP 1947 DAG–13/3.0.1. Box 10 File R.J.B.'s private correspondence from Geneva, July–August 1947, letter, Bunche to R.F. Power, US UN delegation, New York, 7 August.

23. FRUS 1947 V, p 1102 telegram, Macatee, Jerusalem to S/S, 11 June 1947, pp 1107–12 and pp 1123–8 despatches as above, 23 June and 14 July; Cunningham in Wilson, pp 110–11.

24. FO 371/61767 E1501/46/31 telegram, Cunningham, Palestine to Colonial Secretary, 7 June; FO 371/61875 E5151/951/31 note, Chancery,

Washington to FO, 2 June; FO 371/61875 E7242/951/31 despatch, Pirie-Gordon, Amman to FO, 30 July and minute, Beeley, 9 August; FO 371/61875 E6366/951/31 telegram, Houston-Boswall, Beirut to FO, 16 July; FRUS 1947 V, pp 1128–31 despatch, Macatee, Jerusalem to S/S, 21 July.

25. FRUS 1947 V, pp 1123–8 despatch as above, 14 July; USNA 867N.01/8–447 Box 6760 memorandum, Macatee, Jerusalem to Merriam, 3 August.

26. FRUS 1947 V, pp 1107–12, pp 1117–20 and pp 1123–8 despatches, Macatee, Jerusalem to S/S, 23 June, 7 and 14 July 1947; FO 371/61782 E6085/46/31 telegram, Cunningham, Palestine to Colonial Secretary, 8 July; UN arch. UNSCOP 1947 DAG 13/3.0.1. Box 10 letter, Bunche to Power, US UN delegation, New York, 7 August; *ibid* Box 2 notes on conversation with Begin, 4 August, earlier draft dated 24 June; FRUS 1947 V, pp 1113–16 and pp 1128–31 despatches, Macatee, Jerusalem to S/S, 30 June and 21 July; Wilson, p 110.

27. FO 371/61781 E5468/46/31 telegram, Cadogan, New York to FO, 23 June 1947 and E5455/46/31 telegram, Cunningham, Palestine to Colonial Secretary, 24 June; FRUS 1947 V, pp 1134–5 telegram, Macatee, Jerusalem to S/S, 1 August; Bethell, pp 321–33; FO 371/61876 E6848/951/31 letter, MacGillivray, Jerusalem to Martin, 21 July and letter, Gurney, Jerusalem to Martin, 20 July; UN arch. UNSCOP 1947 DAG 13/3.0.1. Box 10 letter, Bunche to Shore, Division of Trusteeship, 17 July.

28. UN arch. UNSCOP 1947 13/3.0.1., as in note 27. FO 371/61786 E7855/46/31 letter, MacGillivray, Geneva to Martin, 20 August 1947.

29. UN arch. UNSCOP 1947 DAG 13/3.0.1. Box 1 'Memorandum by the Chairman ... ', with manuscript edition in Box 2; FO 371/61877 E7422/951/31 letter, MacGillivray, Geneva to Trafford Smith, 8 August 1947; UN arch. UNSCOP 1947 DAG 13/3.0.1. Box 2 First Informal Meeting, 6 August.

30. UN arch. UNSCOP 1947 DAG 13/3.0.1. Box 2, as in note 29. *ibid* Box 1 'Memorandum by Mr. Rand', date added 12 August 1947 and 'Comments on Mr. Rand's Paper'.

31. UN arch. UNSCOP 1947 DAG 13/3.0.1. Box 2 Fourth Informal Meeting, 8 August 1947; *ibid* Box 1 'Memorandum by Sir Abdur Rahman' and 'Statement by Mr. Simic'.

32. UN arch. UNSCOP 1947 DAG 13/3.0.1. Box 2 'Notes on conversation with Mr. Richard Crossman, M.P.', 13 August 1947; M. J. Cohen, *Great Powers*, pp 19–20; Bullock, *Foreign Secretary*, pp 165–69; UN arch. UNSCOP 1947 DAG 13/3.0.1. Box 2 Seventh and Eighth Informal Meeting, 14 August.

33. UN arch. UNSCOP 1947 DAG 13/3.0.1. Box 1 'The essential factors in a solution of the Palestine Question' (i.e. in Bunche's files).

34. UN arch. UNSCOP 1947 DAG 13/3.0.1. Box 1 'Summary of Views in Informal Discussions'; *ibid* DAG 13/3.0.0. Box 4 'Report of the Informal Working Group on a Federal State Solution', 22 August and 'Working

Group on Constitutional Matters', 26 August; Wilson, p 112.

35. Wilson, pp 111–15; FO 371/61877 E8014, E8015 and E8024/951/31 telegrams, MacGillivray, Geneva to FO, 30 August 1947.

Chapter 7. The Aftermath of the UNSCOP Report

1. FO 371/61877 E7498/951/31 record of meeting in Martin's room at CO, 24 July 1947.

2. FO 371/61927 E4740/4740/31 copy of motions on Palestine tabled at Labour Party Conference, May 1947; FO 371/61780 E4848/46/31 extract from Bevin's speech, 29 May; Bodleian Library, Oxford, Mss Attlee, older chronological series, not foliated, letter, 19 MPs to PM, 23 July; PREM 8/623 minute, 'Palestine', Dalton to PM, 11 August.

3. CAB 126/19 CP(47)161 'Palestine: Financial Situation ...', Colonial Secretary, 18 May 1947; Ovendale, p 101; CAB 128/9 CM(47)42 item 3, 1 May; FO 371/61806 E3791/48/31 PM(47)80 minute, Bevin to PM, 2 May; FO 371/61815 E6218/48/31 and E6277/48/31 telegram, Duff Cooper, Paris to FO and letter, Bevin to Bidault, 12 July; FO 371/61810 E4910/48/31 despatch, Broad, Warsaw to FO, 3 June; FO 371/61784 E7414/46/31 telegram, Cunningham, Palestine to Colonial Secretary, 7 August.

4. FO 800/487 memorandum of conversation on 2 August 1947 between Bevin and Douglas by Dixon, 4 August 1947; *Forrestal Diaries*, p. 303; USNA entered with 867N.01 5-2147 *PM* of 5 June 1947, p 13; USNA 867N.01/5–1547 telegram, Douglas, London to S/S, 15 May, 867N.01/5–2147 memorandum, Meeker, State Dept. to Fahy, Treasury Dept., 21 May and letter, Marshall to Snyder, 17 June, 867N.01/11–2047 memorandum, Henderson to Lovett, 20 November.

5. Hansard vol 441 no 162 cols 2323, 2336, 2342–43, 2355, 2371, 12 August 1947.

6. DEFE 6/3 JP(47)123 (Final) 'Palestine — Report of the UN Committee', JPS, 3 September 1947; CAB 129/21 CP(47)262 'Palestine: Report ... ', Minister of Defence, 18 September with appendix 'Extract from DO(47)3'.

7. FO 371/61878 E8726/951/31 letter, Thomas, CO to Foreign Secretary enclosing memorandum 'Palestine', 16 September 1947; BLPES Dalton Diary Part 1 35, entry for 18 September; CO 537/3885 75872/154/11 minute, Martin to Sir S. Caine, 14 June 1948.

8. FO 371/61878 E8346/951/31 telegram, O.A.G. Palestine to Colonial Secretary, 8 September 1947 and minute, Beeley, 11 September.

9. FO 371/61878 E8725/951/31 minute, PM to Foreign Secretary, 17 September 1947 and draft paper; CAB 129/21 CP(47)259 'Palestine', Foreign Secretary, 18 September.

10. CAB 129/21 CP(47)259, as in note 9. FO 371/61878 E8214/951/31 preliminary draft of Cabinet Paper, Beeley, 3 September 1947 and minute, Garran, 3 September.

11. FO 371/61789 E8913/46/31 JP(47)31(Final) 'Palestine — Implications of Withdrawal', JPS, 19 September 1947 and covering note for Eastern

Department, 20 September; CAB 131/5 DO(47)20 meeting, item 1, 18 September and DO(47)22 meeting, 29 September; DLPES Dalton Diary part 1 35, entry for 20 September.

12. CAB 128/10 CM(47)76 item 6, 20 September 1947.

13. Churchill Coll. Cambridge, Cadogan Diary ACAD 1/18 entries for 23 and 26 September 1947; FO 371/61789 E8916/46/31 and E8917/46/31 telegrams, Cadogan, New York to FO, 25 September; FO 371/61790 E9014/46/31 telegram, Creech Jones, New York to FO for PM and Foreign Secretary, 27 September; FO 371/61879 E9029/951/31 minute, Garran, 1 October; FO 371/61791 E9570/46/31 telegram, Creech Jones, New York to FO for PM and Foreign Secretary, 13 October; FO 371/61791 E9474/46/31 minute, Bevin to PM and reply, 14 October; FO 371/61882 E9666/951/31 telegram, Creech Jones, New York to FO, 16 October.

14. FO 371/61791 E9474/46/31 telegram, Bevin to Creech Jones, New York, 14 October 1947; FO 371/61790 E9247/46/31 Report of Joint Administrative Planning Staff enclosed in JAP/P(47)39 Final, 10 October.

15. FRUS 1947 V, p 1180n; DEFE 4/8 COS(47)130 meeting, item 2, 22 October 1947; FO 371/61885 E10045/951/31 telegram, Peterson, Moscow to FO, 28 October; Krammer; Louis, *British Empire*, pp 460, 467; FO 371/61794 E10434/46/31 telegram, FO to Cadogan, New York, 5 November; CAB 131/5 DO(47)23 meeting, item 1, 7 November; FO 371/61793 E10246/46/31 OCP(47)1, note by Secretary to the Cabinet, 30 October; CAB 131/4 DO(47)83 'Palestine — General Scheme of Withdrawal', OCP, Luke, 5 November.

16. FO 371/61887 E10646/951/31 telegram, New York to FO, 13 November 1947; FO 371/61794 E10536 and E10537/46/31 telegrams, New York to FO, 10 November and E10538/46/31 telegram, FO to Cadogan and Minister of State, New York, 12 November; FO 371/61795 E11176/46/31 telegram, FO to Cadogan, New York, 27 November; Hansard vol 445 no 38 col 1219, 11 December.

17. FO 371/61883 E9727/951/31 letter, Beeley, New York to Garran, FO, 4 October 1947.

18. FRUS 1947 V, pp 1120–3 memoranda, Henderson to Secretary of State, 7 July 1947 and Henderson to Lovett, 27 August; USNA Box 2183 no reference, adjacent to 501.BB Palestine/1–548 memorandum, McClintock to Rusk, 21 May.

19. FRUS 1947 V, pp 1153–8 memorandum, Henderson to S/S, 22 September 1947, p 1151 extract from Marshall's statement, 17 September, pp 1173–4 memorandum of discussion between Marshall, Austin, Johnson, Mrs Roosevelt, Hilldring, Rusk, Bohlen, Fahy, Alling, by Knox, 3 October, p 1180 editorial note of Johnson's statement, 11 October.

20. USNA JCS files RG218 Admiral Leahy files 56 Box 10 memoranda, Leahy to Secretary of Defense, 10 October 1947; FRUS 1947 V, pp 1195–6 memorandum, Henderson to Lovett, 22 October.

21. Niles papers, memorandum, Niles to Truman, 29 July 1947 in Sachar, p 60; Wilson, p 116; Louis, *British Empire*, pp 482–5; FRUS 1947 V, p 1151

extract from Marshall's statement, 17 September.

22. Bickerton, appendix A; FRUS 1947 V, pp 1269–72, telegram, Lovett to US UN delegation and memorandum, McClintock, 19 November 1947; Ganin, pp 139–41.

23. *Forrestal Diaries*, p 309, 322–3; Clifford Papers, memorandum, Clifford to President, 19 November 1947 in Ganin, pp 179–80.

24. USNA 501.BB Palestine/9–1547 Box 2182 memorandum 'Consideration of the UNSCOP Report by the UNGA' with covering note, Babbitt to Henderson, 15 September 1947; FRUS 1947 V, pp 1147–51 excerpts from minutes of 6th meeting of US UN delegation, 15 September; USNA 867N.01/10–1547 Box 6761 telegram, Gallman, London to S/S, 15 October; FRUS 1947 V, pp 1263–4 telegram, Smith, Moscow to S/S, 14 November; FO 371/61794 E10536, E10537 and E10538/46/31 telegrams, New York to FO, 10 November and reply, 12 November; USNA JCS files, RG218 Admiral Leahy files 56 Box 10 memoranda, Leahy to Secretary of Defense, 10 October.

25. Hadawi, pp xvii and 31.

26. FRUS 1947 V, pp 1283–4 memorandum of telephone conversation between Lovett, Johnson, Hilldring and others, 24 November 1947, p 1248 telegram, S/S to Legation in Syria, 10 November; FO 371/61888 E10771/951/31 telegram, Busk, Baghdad to FO, 17 November and E10926/951/31 telegram, Inverchapel, Washington to FO, 20 November with Beith's minute, 21 November; FO 371/61795 E11069/46/31 telegram, Minister of State, New York to FO, 24 November; FO 371/61889 E11040/951/31 telegram, Cadogan, New York to FO, 24 November; M. J. Cohen, *Great Powers*, pp 295–8; Truman *Years of Trial*, p 158; Celler Papers Box 23 letter, Celler to Truman, 3 December in Ganin, p 145; TL OF 204 Box 773 letter, Klein to Truman, 4 December; Goldmann, p 245 and Israel State Archives 2266/15 Comay to Gering both in M. J. Cohen, *Great Powers*; AZEC minutes, p 2, Silver's account on 11 December in Ganin, p 145; FO 371/68528 E416/4/31 memorandum, 'The Palestine Question at the ... General Assembly', Beeley, January 1948.

27. FRUS 1947 V, pp 1281–2 memorandum, Henderson to Lovett, 24 November 1947.

28. M. J. Cohen, *Great Powers*, p 300; FO 371/61795 E11176/46/31 minutes, Wright, 22 November, Beith, 24 November and Burrows, 25 November; Louis, *British Empire*, p 487.

Chapter 8. The End of the Mandate

1. M. J. Cohen, *Great Powers*, p 302, also pp 303–12, 335–44.

2. CAB 129/25 CP(48)71 'The Czechoslovak Crisis' and CP(48)72 'The Threat to Western Civilisation', Foreign Secretary, 3 March 1948.

3. FO 371/61793 E10281/46/31 draft paper 'Withdrawal from Palestine' sent by Burrows to Beeley on 17 October 1947 and by Bevin to Attlee on 22 October; CAB 131/4 DO(47)83 'Palestine — General Scheme of

Withdrawal', OCP, 5 November; CAB 131/5 DO(47)23 meeting, item 1, 7 November; FO 371/61888 E10776/951/31 telegram, FO to New York, 18 November; CAB 131/4 DO(47)91 'Palestine — Plan of Withdrawal', OCP, 25 November; FO 371/61795 E11291/46/31 CM(47)90 meeting, item 2b, 25 November; FO 371/61796 E11573/46/31 CM(47)93 meeting, item 1, 4 December; FO 371/61795 E11176/46/31 telegram, FO to New York, 27 November.

4. FO 371/61888 E10776/951/31 telegram, Cunnigham, Palestine to Colonial Secretary, 19 November 1947; FO 371/61796 E11568/46/31 CP(47)320 'Palestine', Foreign & Colonial Secretaries, 3 December; FO 371/61885 E10152/951/31 note, Clayton, Cairo to FO, 25 October; FO 371/61798 E12028/46/31 telegram, BMEO, Cairo to FO, 17 December; FO 371/68364 Clayton's report, 23 December in M. J. Cohen, *Great Powers*, p 321; FO 371/61796 E11568/46/31 minute, Burrows, 3 December.

5. FO 371/68530 E1091/4/31 telegram, Cadogan, New York to FO, 24 January 1948; Churchill Coll. Cambridge, ACAD 1/19 Cadogan diary, 30 January; FO 371/68531 E1388/4/31 telegram, Cadogan, New York to FO, 31 January and minute, Sargent, 4 February; CO 537/3910 75872/159/15 Part I memorandum, OCP Chairman to Colonial Secretary, 2 February; CAB 128/12 CM(48)12 meeting, item 1, 5 February; Churchill Coll. Cambridge, ACAD 1/19 Cadogan diary, 15 & 19 February; Azcárate, pp 6, 8.

6. FRUS 1948 V, pp 657–8 Austin's statement to Security Council, 25 February 1948; Churchill Coll. Cambridge, ACAD 1/19 Cadogan diary, 5 & 8 March; FO 371/68538 E3628/4/31 telegram, FO to New York, 19 March; CAB 128/12 CM(48)24 meeting, item 6, 22 March; Churchill Coll. Cambridge, ACAD 1/19 Cadogan diary, 1 April; FO 371/68541 E4322/4/31 telegram, New York to FO, 5 April and E4321/4/31 telegram, FO to New York, 7 April; FO 371/68649 E4796/1078/31 draft brief for Foreign Secretary, ?Burrows, 14 April; FO 371/68543 E4756/4/31 telegram, Bevin to Inverchapel, Washington, reporting conversation with US Ambassador, 15 April; FO 371/68551 E6123/4/31 telegram, New York to FO, 11 May; FO 371/68549 E6010/4/31 telegram, FO to New York, 10 May.

7. FRUS 1984 V, pp 852–3 note on Truce Commission, pp 876–7 telegram, Douglas, London to S/S, 29 April 1948; CAB 128/12 CM(48)30 meeting, item 8, 29 April; FRUS 1948 V, pp 891–2 telegram, Lovett, Washington to Douglas, London, 3 May; FO 371/68547 E5673/4/31 telegrams no 1847, 1858, FO to New York, 4 May; FRUS 1948 V, pp 893–4 telegram, Shertok to Rusk, New York, 4 May; FO 371/68548 E5816/4/31 telegram, FO to Damascus, 6 May; FO 371/68549 E5925/4/31 telegram, Broadmead, Damascus to FO, 7 May; FO 371/68550 E6028/4/31 telegram, FO to Jedda, 7 May; FO 371/68549 E6014/4/31 telegram, FO to Jedda repeated to ME posts, 8 May; FO 371/68550 E6015/4/31 telegram, Baghdad to FO, E 6016/4/31 telegram, Beirut to FO and E6017/4/31 telegram, Cairo to FO, all 9 May; FO 371/68550 E6038/4/31 telegram, Amman to FO and E6040/4/31 telegram, Jedda to FO, both 10 May; FO 371/68550

E6030/4/31 telegram, Broadmead, Damascus to FO, 10 May.

21. FO 371/61798 E12028/46/31 telegram, BMEO, Cairo to FO, 17
December 1947 and minute, Burrows, 20 December; DEFE 4/12 COS
Committee Conclusions (48)60 meeting, item 10, 30 April 1948; FO
371/68546 E5595/4/31 and FO 371/68548 E5749/4/31 telegrams, Kirk-
bride, Amman to FO, 2 & 3 May; FO 371/68550 E6023/4/31 telegram,
Houston-Boswall, Beirut to FO, 8 May and record of E.B.'s minute, 10
May.

22. FRUS 1947 V, p 1283 ed. note, memorandum, Royall to Executive
Secretary, NSC sent on 24 November 1947; Forrestal diary, 24 January
1948 in FRUS 1948 V, p 633 ed. note; *Forrestal Diaries*, p 373; FRUS 1948 V,
pp 631–2 draft report by NSC staff, 17 February.

23. USNA RG 59 General Records of State Dept, Office of NE Affairs,
Palestine, Box 1, memorandum, Merriam to Henderson, 11 December
1947.

24. FRUS 1947 V, pp 1313–14 ed. note, report believed to be by PPS, 17
December 1947; FRUS 1948 V, pp 545–54, memorandum, Kennan to S/S,
20 January 1948 covering PPS/19, 19 January.

25. Louis, *British Empire* , p 499–500, see also pp 501–5; FRUS 1948 V, pp
556–62 memorandum, Rusk to Lovett, 26 January 1948, p 573
memorandum, Kennan to Lovett, 29 January, pp 592–5 memorandum,
Wadsworth to Henderson on conversation with President, 4 February, pp
600–3 memorandum, Henderson to Rusk, 6 February.

26. FRUS 1948 V, pp 617–18 memorandum, McClintock, submitted by
Rusk to Lovett, 11 February 1948, pp 619–25 memorandum, Butler to
Lovett covering PPS/21 both of 11 February.

27. *Forrestal Diaries*, p 372; FRUS 1948 V, p 633 memorandum, Marshall to
Lovett, 19 February 1948, pp 648–9 note, memorandum, McClintock to
Lovett, 19 February and memorandum, McClintock to McDermott, 24
February, pp 637–40 message, State Dept to Truman, transmitted 21
February, p 645 message, Truman to S/S, 22 February; TL George M.
Elsey Papers Box 60 cutting from *The Washingtom Post*, by J. and S. Alsop, 27
February.

28. FRUS 1948, V, pp 742–4 extract from Austin's statement in UNSC, 19
March 1948, p 697 telegram, S/S to Austin, 8 March, pp 728–9 telegram,
S/S to Austin, 16 March, pp 729–31 memorandum of telephone
conversation with Rusk by McClintock, 17 March; Louis, *British Empire*, p
507.

29. Ganin, p 157 cites TL Ewing oral history p 276; FRUS 1948 V, pp
690–6 memorandum, Clifford to Truman, 8 March 1948; TL Granoff oral
history (1968), pp 52–5; Ganin, pp 167–8.

30. Truman's calendar entry, 19 March 1948 in M. Truman, p 388; TL
Charles G. Ross papers, Correspondence File Box 6 'Resumed notes' dated
29 March; FRUS 1948 V, pp 749–50 memorandum, Humelsine to S/S, 22
March.

31. FRUS 1948 V, pp 748–9 ed. note Marshall's press conference, 20

March 1948, pp 759–60 telegram, S/S to embassy, Egypt giving text of
Truman's statement, 25 March, p 753 note on Jewish Agency statement, 23
March, p 832 note, telegram, Cairo to S/S, 22 April; *Forrestal Diaries*, p 411;
FRUS 1948 V, p 760 note on Truman's press conference, 25 March and
telegram, Austin to S/S, 25 March with note of Lovett's comment on Rusk's
proposed reply, 29 March, pp 774, 830 Forrestal's diary entries, 29 March
& 18 April, p 833 note on minutes of US UN delegation meeting, 19 April.
32. Ganin, pp 178–89; FRUS 1948 V, pp 807–9 letter, Weizmann to
Truman, 9 April 1948; Louis, *British Empire*, pp 514–15.
33. TL Democratic National Committee Library Clipping File, Box 24 *New
York Times* article by Moscow, 23 March 1948; Ganin, p 181.
34. Niles papers, Niles to Clifford, 6 May 1948 in Sachar, p 90; Ganin, p
183; FRUS 1948 V, pp 972–6 memorandum of conversation at White
House, S/S, 12 May 1948; pp 977–8 Clifford's statement to meeting at
White House, pp 1005–7 memorandum of conversations with Clifford by
Lovett, 17 May, p 992 letter, S/S to Epstein conveying Truman's statement,
14 May; Wilson, pp 146–7.
35. FO 800/487 PA/48/26 record of conversation between PM, S/S and US
Ambassador, 28 April 1948.
36. CAB 134/500 ME(0)(47)21 'Relationship between the UK and the US
in the Middle East', working party of Middle East (Official) Committee, 25
August 1947.

Collections and Works Cited

Collections and documentary classes cited

British Library of Political and Economic Science, London
Hugh Dalton, Diaries and Papers

Bodleian Library, Oxford
Clement Attlee, Papers
Lord Inverchapel, Appointments Diary

The Archive Centre, Churchill College, Cambridge
Clement Attlee, Papers
Sir Alexander Cadogan, Diaries

The Public Record Office, London

AIR 20	Air Ministry Unregistered Papers
CAB 21	Cabinet Registered Files
CAB 65	War Cabinet Conclusions
CAB 66	War Cabinet Papers
CAB 69	Defence Committee (Operations), Meetings and Papers 1945
CAB 79	Chiefs of Staff Committee, Minutes of Meetings 1945–6
CAB 84	Joint Planning Staff, Papers 1945–6
CAB 95	Palestine Committee, 1943–5
CAB 119	Joint Planning Staff, Files 1945–6
CAB 120	Minister of Defence, Secretariat Files 1945–6
CAB 127	Private Collections
CAB 128	Cabinet Conclusions from 1945
CAB 129	Cabinet Papers from 1945
CAB 131	Defence Committee, Meetings and Papers from 1946
CAB 134	Cabinet Committees, General Series from 1945
CO 537	Colonial Office, Supplementary Correspondence
CO 733	Colonial Office, Palestine: Original Correspondence
DEFE 4	Chiefs of Staff Committee, Minutes of Meetings from 1947

DEFE 5   Chiefs of Staff Committee, Papers from 1947
DEFE 6   Joint Planning Staff, Papers from 1947
FO 141   Foreign Office, Embassy: Egypt
FO 371   Foreign Office, General Political Correspondence
FO 800   Foreign Office, Private Office Papers
PREM 8   Prime Minister's Office Records

Rhodes House, Oxford

Arthur Creech Jones, Papers
Fabian Colonial Bureau, Papers

The Middle East Centre, St Antony's College, Oxford

Richard Crossman, Papers
General Sir Alan Cunningham, Papers

Truman Library, Independence, Missouri

Democratic National Committee Library Clipping Files
George M. Elsey Papers
Miscellaneous Historical Documents
PS. President's Secretary's Files
Charles G. Ross Papers
Copies of Documents in the Weizmann Archives, Israel
OF. White House Official Files

United Nations Organization Archives, New York

United Nations Special Committee on Palestine, 1947, Files

United States National Archives, Washington D. C.

501.BB Palestine. State Department files: International conferences etc.
       relating to the Government of Palestine
867N.01 State Department files: Internal Government Affairs of Palestine
Joint Chiefs of Staff files
Office of Strategic Services Research and Analysis Reports
Records of Anglo-American Committee of Inquiry
Records of War Department General and Special Staffs

Published sources cited and referred to

Command Papers

Cmd 5479 Palestine Royal Commission Report, July 1937
Cmd 5854 The Palestine Partition (Woodhead) Report, October 1938
Cmd 5893 Palestine: Statement of Policy by HMG, November 1938
Cmd 5957 Correspondence between Sir Henry McMahon and the Sherif
         Hussein of Mecca, July 1915–March 1916, March 1939
Cmd 6019 Palestine: Statement of Policy by HMG, May 1939

Cmd 6808 The Report of the Anglo-American Committee of Enquiry, May 1946
Cmd 6873 Palestine: Statement of Information Relating to Acts of Violence, July 1946

Foreign Relations of the United States

1945 Volume I
1945 Volume VII
1946 Volume VII
1947 Volume V
1948 Volume V

Hansard: Parliamentary Debates

Volume 413 (1945)
Volume 415 (1945)
Volume 426 (1946)
Volume 433 (1947)
Volume 441 (1947)

Unpublished works cited

I. J. Bickerton. 'President Truman's Recognition of Israel', MA Thesis, Kansas State University 1966 at Truman Library, Independence, Mo.

A. Ilan. 'The Origin and Development of American Intervention in British Palestine Policy 1938–47', Ms D.Phil., Oxford University 1947 at the Bodleian Library, Oxford

A. Nachmani. 'British Policy in Palestine after World War II: The Anglo-American Committee of Inquiry into the problems of European Jewry and Palestine, 1945–46', Ms D.Phil., Oxford University 1980 at the Bodleian Library, Oxford

D. B. Sachar. 'David K. Niles and United States policy toward Palestine', Harvard Senior Honors Thesis, 1959, microfilm copy at Truman Library, Independence, Mo.

Books and articles cited

Published in London unless otherwise stated.

D. Acheson. *Present at the Creation*, New York, 1969.

G. Antonius. *The Arab Awakening*, 1938.

P. de Azcárate. *Mission in Palestine, 1948–52*, Washington, D.C., 1966.

P. J. Baram. *The Department of State in the Middle East*, Philadelphia, 1978.

E. Barker. *Britain in a divided Europe 1945–70*, 1971.

Y. Bauer. *From Diplomacy to Resistance: A History of Jewish Palestine 1939–45*, New York, 1973 (in Hebrew, 1966).

D. Ben Gurion. *In the Struggle*, (Hebrew), Tel Aviv, 1955.

N. & H. Bentwich. *Mandate Memories*, 1965.

N. Bethell. *The Palestine Triangle*, 1979.

A. Bullock. *The Life and Times of Ernest Bevin*. Vol. 2, *Minister of Labour 1940–45*, 1967.

A. Bullock. *Ernest Bevin Foreign Secretary 1945–41*, 1983.

A. Cohen. *Israel and the Arab World*, 1970 (in Hebrew 1964).

M. J. Cohen. *Palestine: Retreat from the Mandate*, 1978.

M. J. Cohen. *Palestine and the Great Powers 1945–48*, Princeton, New Jersey, 1982.

R. Crossman. *Palestine Mission*, 1946.

B. C. Crum. *Behind the Silken Curtain*, 1947.

A. Cunningham. 'The Last Days of the Mandate', in *International Affairs*, 4 October 1948.

L. Dinnerstein. 'America, Britain, and Palestine: The Anglo-American Committee of Inquiry …', in *Diplomatic History*, 1982, pp 283–301.

M. Edelman. *Ben Gurion: A Political Biography*, 1964.

J. Forrestal. *The Forrestal Diaries*, ed. by Walter Millis, New York, 1951.

J. Frankel. *British Foreign Policy 1945–73*, Oxford, 1975.

T. G. Fraser. *The Middle East, 1914–79*, 1980.

Z. Ganin. *Truman, American Jewry, and Israel, 1945–48*, New York, 1979.

M. Gilbert. *Exile and Return*, 1978.

J. B. Glubb. *A Soldier with the Arabs*, 1957.

N. Goldmann. *Sixty Years of Jewish Life*, New York, 1969.

D. Goldsworthy. *Colonial Issues in British Politics, 1945–61*, Oxford, 1971.

J. Gorny. *The British Labour Movement and Zionism 1917–48*, 1983.

P. S. Gupta. *Imperialism and the British Labour Movement, 1914–64*, 1975.

S. Hadawi (ed.). *United Nations Resolutions on Palestine 1947–66*, Beirut, 1967.

S. Halperin. *The Political World of American Zionism*, Detroit, 1961.

S. Halperin & I. Oder. 'The United States in Search of a Policy: Franklin D. Roosevelt and Palestine', in *Review of Politics* 1962, pp 320–40.

S. M. Hartmann. *Truman and the 80th Congress*, Colombia, Missouri, 1971.

D. Horowitz. *State in the Making*, New York, 1953.

J. C. Hurewitz. *The Struggle for Palestine*, New York, 1950.

P. Jones. *Britain and Palestine 1914–48*; archival sources for the history of the British Mandate, Oxford, 1979.

E. Kedourie. *In the Anglo-Arab Labyrinth*, Cambridge, 1976.

E. Kedourie. *Islam in the Modern World*, 1980.

E. Kedourie. *The Chatham House Version*, 1970.

E. Kedourie & S. Haim (eds.). *Zionism and Arabism in Palestine and Israel*, 1982.

G. Kirk. *The Middle East 1945–50*, Oxford, 1954.

A. Krammer. 'Soviet Motives in the Partition of Palestine, 1947–48', in *Journal of Palestine Studies*, 1973.

W. Laqueur. *A History of Zionism*, 1972.

T. E. Lawrence. *Seven Pillars of Wisdom*, 1935.

W. R. Louis. *Imperialism at Bay: 1941–45*, Oxford, 1977.

W. R. Louis. *The British Empire in the Middle East, 1945–51*, Oxford, 1984.

Col. R. Meinertzhagen. *Middle East Diary, 1917–56*, 1969.

E. Monroe. *Britain's Moment in the Middle East, 1914–56*, 1965.

Montgomery. *The Memoirs of Field-Marshal the Viscount Montgomery of Alamein*, 1958.

K. O. Morgan. *Labour in Power 1945–51*, Oxford, 1984.

F. S. Northedge. *Descent from Power: British Foreign Policy 1945–73*, 1974.

R. Ovendale. *The Origins of the Arab-Israeli Wars*, 1984.

W. R. Polk. *The United States and the Arab World*, Cambridge, Mass. 1965.

Sir G. Rendel. *The Sword and the Olive*, 1957.

S. I. Rosenman. *Working with Roosevelt*, New York, 1952.

J. B. Schechtman. *The U.S. and the Jewish State Movement*, New York, 1966.

Z. Sharef. *Three Days*, in translation from Hebrew by J. L. Meltzer, 1962.

A. Shlaim, P. Jones & K. Sainsbury. *British Foreign Secretaries since 1945*, 1977.

A. Sked & C. Cook. *Post-War Britain. A Political History*, 1979.

J. Snetsinger. *Truman, the Jewish Vote and the Creation of Israel*, Stanford, Calif. 1974.

C. Sykes. *Crossroads to Israel*, 1965; Bloomington, Ind. 1973.

H. S. Truman. *Year of Decisions, 1945*, 1955.

H. S. Truman. *Years of Trial and Hope, 1946–53*, 1956.

M. Truman. *Harry S. Truman*, 1973.

M. Vereté. 'The Balfour Declaration and its Makers', in *Middle Eastern Studies*, Vol. 6, No. 1, January 1950.

H. A. Wallace. *The Price of Vision: the Diary of Henry A. Wallace*, ed. by J. Blum, Boston, 1971.

B. Wasserstein. *Britain and the Jews of Europe, 1939–45*, Oxford, 1979.

C. Weizmann. *Trial and Error*, 1949.

F. Williams. *Ernest Bevin: Portrait of a Great Englishman*, 1952.

E. M. Wilson. *Decision on Palestine: How the U.S. Came to Recognize Israel*, Stanford, Calif., 1979.

Index